# THE 30-DAY DIABETES CURE

Russ Canfield, MD, and Jim Healthy

**The Proven Step-by-Step Plan to Reverse Type 2 Diabetes Naturally**
*REVISED AND UPDATED*

**BottomLineBooks**

BottomLineInc.com

# CONTENTS

# FOREWORD

*A hero is no braver than an ordinary man,*
*but he is braver five minutes longer.*

—RALPH WALDO EMERSON, American poet and essayist, 1803–1882

A FEW YEARS AGO, I sat with an elderly friend of mine named Sally who was dying from lung cancer. She'd been a lifelong smoker and now the tumors in her lungs were draining away the little life that remained in her. We both knew her time was very near.

"You know," she said in a faint, raspy voice, "I always meant to quit…but I always thought I had more time."

I recognized a tragic truth in these words—and also how emblematic it is of our human condition. Many, if not most, of us live in a similar state of denial. We are forever promising ourselves that "someday" we will change a bad habit, lose weight, start exercising, return to school, or in some other way change the predictable course in which our lives seem headed.

Sadly, most of us run out of time before "someday" arrives. So strong is our denial and the force of our habits that we are willing to unconsciously trade our health, future happiness, and an extra 10 or 20 years of life—which, once on our deathbeds, we desperately plead and bargain for—in exchange for the "mañana mentality" that is so pervasive in our culture today. This mentality prevents the majority of us from making important interventions in our own lives right now.

Of course, not everyone succumbs to this. We all know people who finally said "Enough." People who made a real commitment to change their lives in order to accomplish something amazing. And who somehow managed to stick with it when the going got tough (as it always does) and eventually made it to the other side. Somehow they found a way to get in touch with their "warrior spirit," to dig deep and activate the willpower to fight the good fight and emerge victorious.

Many of Dr. Canfield's diabetes and prediabetes patients have done precisely this—and it is what we hope this book will help *you* achieve. We are not naïve enough to believe this book will save the world—though that is both our wish and objective. Lots of people have good intentions at the start of a journey, but only a certain number have the grit and determination to reach their destination. We want you to be one of the victorious ones.

Uncontrolled diabetes is a terrible disease that causes people to literally waste away, losing important parts of themselves along the way: their mobility, eyesight, and independence. Their ability to feel anything but pain. Perhaps the greatest loss is the state of comfort most of us take for granted. In his or her final years, a diabetic's life is marked with relentless misery, sorrow, regret, depression, near-constant physical pain, and utter dependence on others for the most basic of human functions.

Now—*right now*—is the time that many people will yearn for when they learn it is "too late" to do anything about their diabetes except live on drugs and watch helplessly as their condition (and body) degenerates. We want you to realize how incredibly precious this present moment is so you can seize this opportunity.

Our hope is that that after reading a little more of this book, you will be inspired to take control of your health and turn your condition around with conviction and daily commitment.

Please don't be like Sally and put it off until later. You may *never* have a better opportunity to sidestep a diagnosis of diabetes—or defeat your diabetes if you have already been diagnosed. In both cases, you will prevent the terrible complications of this dreadful disease.

Awaken your warrior spirit *now*—and fight like hell for your health, your future, and your life. Dr. Canfield and I will be by your side every step of the way, urging you on.

Jim Healthy

July, 2018

# PART 1

## What You Must Know About Diabetes and Today's Treatments

*"If someone is going down the wrong road,
he doesn't need motivation to speed him up.
What he needs is education to turn him around."*

—JIM ROHN, entrepreneur and author, 1930–2009

# THE INCONVENIENT TRUTH ABOUT TYPE 2 DIABETES THAT YOU ARE *NOT* HEARING

*"Listen, are you breathing just a little and calling it a life?"*

—MARY OLIVER, American poet

TYPE 2 DIABETES IS NOW the fastest spreading disease in human history. Its incidence around the world has doubled in the past two decades, prompting the World Health Organization to declare it a global "pandemic." Type 2 diabetes—and the condition that leads to it, insulin-resistance (also called prediabetes)—currently affect close to 30% of the world's adult population.

In 2007, it was estimated that 240 million people worldwide have diabetes. This number was expected to double in just 16 years, but newer studies show this will happen even sooner. Latin Americans, African-Americans, East Indians, and Asians now have dramatically higher rates of diabetes than Caucasians do.[1] Mexico's population has recently become the second most overweight in the world—and Type 2 diabetes is now the leading cause of death there.

In the US, diabetes affects an estimated 30 million adults and teens, with an additional 100 million unsuspecting people walking around with prediabetes. Since Type 2 diabetes is largely a disease without symptoms as it develops, many of these people will not get a diagnosis until it is too late for a full recovery.

We wrote this book because we don't want this to be your fate.

Most people view Type 2 diabetes as another unfortunate, yet quite normal consequence of growing old, like cancer or heart disease. They have been led to believe that having diabetes is "no big deal" because it has become such a common affliction these days—and because so many diabetics seem to be living normal lives thanks to new drugs, glucose monitors and insulin injections.

## Don't You Believe It!

There is nothing normal about Type 2 diabetes. And there is no such thing as living a normal life for people who have it. For instance…

•**Most diabetics constantly worry about what they eat and how it will affect their blood sugar.** Many frequently prick their fingers to monitor blood sugar levels. Those with Type 1 must inject themselves with insulin several times daily in order to stay alive—and go to bed each night fearing their blood sugar might drop so low during sleep that they won't wake up.

• **Having diabetes accelerates the aging process,** causing premature wrinkling of the skin and a hastened destruction of the body's vital organs. People with diabetes often look 15 to 20 years older than their chronological age. That's because biologically they *are* older.

• **People with diabetes suffer more depression…**have higher rates of Alzheimer's disease and dementia… are usually vulnerable to kidney disease…and live under the constant threat of heart attack or stroke, which represents the cause of death for this disease 75% of the time.

• **Diabetes is the fast lane to disability.** More than two dozen studies show that diabetics are between 50% to 80% more likely to suffer from disability compared to non-diabetics their age. Chronically elevated blood sugar levels also damage muscles and nerves, causing muscular instability that can lead to serious falls.

• **Add to this the horrible complications that eventually appear:** Loss of vision and, ultimately, blindness; agonizing nerve pain known as neuropathy; dangerously elevated blood pressure, which often leads to stroke or heart failure; and poor circulation, resulting in oxygen deprivation and the type of gangrene in the extremities that requires limb amputations for many patients.

Tragically, during the years considered "prime" for most adults their age, diabetics will watch helplessly as their bodies and minds waste away, losing their comfort, mobility, mental clarity, independence, and their bodily functions, one by one.

## This Is Not the Description
## Modern Medicine Wants You to Hear

We realize this is a grim picture, unlike the one portrayed in those upbeat TV commercials selling diabetes supplies—or on the glossy covers of diabetes magazines featuring lavish desserts and sweets.

But this is the reality and fate for the average person with Type 2 diabetes. And nothing in your doctor's little black bag or the drug researcher's laboratory is able to change this all-too-typical outcome.

## But It Doesn't Have to Be This Way for You

Type 2 diabetes, which represents 95% of all cases, can be one of the most easily prevented, controlled and *reversed* medical conditions on today's Top 10 Killer Diseases list, often *without* requiring any drugs, vigilant glucose-monitoring or finger-pricking nuisance.

This is proven by numerous scientific studies and by clinicians, including Dr. Canfield, who have gotten patients entirely off their diabetes-related medications…have normalized their blood sugar naturally…have helped repair much of the damage that diabetes had done to their tissues and organs…and have virtually erased their risk of heart attack, blindness, kidney failure, limb amputation, stroke, Alzheimer's, and other serious complications.

This very same approach has also freed Type 1 diabetics from the prospect of these terrible complications, while dramatically reducing their injected insulin by as much as 80%–90%. This book will show you exactly how to achieve these remarkable results for yourself.

## Why Is Type 2 Diabetes So Out of Control Today?

It is no exaggeration to say that diabetes is raging out of control. Every 10 seconds someone is diagnosed, with official estimates pegged at seven million new cases per year. Diabetes contributes to the death of over 230,000 Americans annually.[2]

Not only is diabetes destroying our collective health, it is decimating the world economy at an alarmingly fast rate. Last year, the US spent more than $245 billion on diabetes treatments, while another $58 billion vanished from our economy from lost productivity and sick leave. Even though the world health community spent nearly $500 billion last year fighting the disease, we are hopelessly losing the battle.

The greater tragedy is that Type 2, once called *adult-onset diabetes* because it only affected a small percentage of the elderly, is now a major health problem for children. Consider this sad statistic: about 215,000 children have diabetes (Type 1 or Type 2) and the numbers are growing.[3] Prospects are even grimmer for Hispanic/Latino Americans, African-Americans, Native Americans, and Asians, whose rates of diabetes are 200 to 400% *higher* than those in the general population.

Despite numerous research studies and patient case histories proving that Type 2 diabetes is easily controlled and reversed without drugs, the general public and diabetes patients are not getting the message. Type 2 diabetes continues to grow at alarming rates, which confirms that current medications and medical treatments are failing miserably.

So why do doctors continue to prescribe them to their patients?

## The Short Answer Is "Money"

Type 2 diabetes has become a $500 billion-a-year industry, which is predicted to grow to $1 trillion annually by the end of this decade. This is an enormous, unimaginable sum that has created a medical economy that millions of professionals and workers depend upon. If Type 2 disappeared, this worldwide diabetes industry would vanish with it. There is no financial incentive to conquer diabetes because there is far more money to be made by *treating* it.

This is a bad situation for patients with diabetes because it means that the deck is stacked against you. The diabetes industry does not want to lose you as its customer, so it will never offer you the hope of being free from Type 2. This is why most physicians never counsel their patients about a possible cure—and why the American Diabetes Association adamantly maintains that a cure is simply not possible.

A large and growing body of scientific research contradicts this view. You see, Type 2 is not an infectious disease like malaria that people "catch." Instead, it is a lifestyle condition that can be defeated when patients are properly educated and motivated to stop doing the things that cause and worsen it – and to start adopting the lifestyle practices shown to reverse it. Numerous studies, which we will present throughout this book, have shown that simple improvements in your diet and lifestyle can control Type 2 diabetes far more effectively than current drug treatments—*and can actually reverse it.*

The solution to Type 2 can be just that easy, but the medical community is neither supporting nor publicizing it. On the contrary, this lifestyle approach is being obscured by relentless medical hoopla about new drugs, promising new cures and high-tech monitoring equipment. Snarky propaganda, meanwhile, puts a smiley face on living with this horribly destructive disease that will have a nightmarish outcome for most patients—even when they follow their doctor's orders to the letter.

## The "Conspiracy" to Keep You in the Dark

Powerful forces are at work to keep the public in the dark about just how easily diabetes can be managed and conquered without the need for any drugs or medical interventions. It is scandalous that this utterly reversible condition has been "medicalized" by those who are profiting handsomely from the billions spent on treatments every year—and the trillions more that will be expended over the next decades.

We have no doubt that if the medical community and federal government possessed the will, they could dramatically reduce the incidence of Type 2 diabetes in a single generation—just as they slashed the rates of cigarette smoking and lung cancer two decades ago (1 in 5 Americans smoke cigarettes now compared to over 40% in the 1970s[4]). All that would be needed, in our opinion, is a robust public awareness campaign that educates consumers about the foods and beverages that cause Type 2, coupled with regulations that require companies who make these food products to share the cost of cleaning up the consequences. This is exactly how the US reduced smoking during the Clinton administration and in the years that followed.

But it was a tough battle. Cigarette manufacturers stubbornly denied that the nicotine in their products was addictive—and numerous medical authorities and "experts" upheld this position for decades. We see an eerie parallel in the official denial (despite plenty of scientific evidence to the contrary) that the massive amounts of sugar and refined carbohydrates in the modern diet are responsible for the metabolic disturbances that are spiking today's alarming rates of Type 2 diabetes, obesity, metabolic syndrome, and cardiovascular disease.

Despite plenty of convincing scientific evidence, the medical community prefers to remain "uncertain" and "confused" about the causes of Type 2 diabetes, choosing to blame dietary fat, obesity, genetics, a sedentary lifestyle, and anything *but* the obvious: the enormous and unprecedented levels of sugar, sweeteners and processed carbohydrate food products we are consuming today. You will read more about this obvious connection in the chapters ahead.

It saddens and angers us to witness the ever-increasing rate of Type 2 diabetes in today's world, while knowing that a simple, non-medical solution to the problem already exists. This book is our attempt to turn the tide by helping every person who wants to escape this deadly trap—while they (and this includes *you*) are still able.

## You Can't Afford to Have Diabetes in This—or Any—Economy

Even if you do not have diabetes or have a low likelihood of developing it, chances are that someone very close to you does or one day will. Perhaps it is one or both of your parents. Maybe it will be one of your children or grandchildren. Surely someone in your extended family or circle of friends already has Type 2. The odds are great, so this message is for *you* too.

Today it costs approximately $150,000 a year to care for a chronically ill parent in-home, whether in your home or theirs. Because today's medical treatments are able to prolong the deterioration of diabetic patients, their slow process of wasting away can stretch to over 10 years or longer. That is $1.5 million we are betting you have not stashed away for this purpose.

Diabetes-related drugs, alone, can cost $400 or more a month. Statistics show the average diabetic requires at least $7900 in additional medical care annually compared to non-diabetics (and this is a conservatively low figure).[5] Add to this the intensive physical care a diabetic parent or child requires, not to mention the overwhelming emotional and psychological stress placed on caregivers. Few people today can afford this—especially in these economically challenged times.

Medicalizing diabetes is an expensive strategy that none of us can afford. The US health-care system is already overloaded with medical problems that could easily be prevented—and reversed—with common sense lifestyle modification.

Nearly 47 million Americans do not have health insurance. Medicare is nearly broke. Insurance premiums are skyrocketing along with deductibles. Medical resources are stretched to the breaking point and will undoubtedly soon be rationed, because there simply are not enough resources to go around. At this very moment, we have the power to eradicate diabetes in a single generation with aggressive public awareness programs and patient education.

We earnestly hope and believe that it is just a matter of time before economic restrictions force many of us to resort to a simple, safe and inexpensive diabetes cure. Why wait when you can save yourself the unnecessary expense, suffering and disappointment right now?

The 30-Day Diabetes Cure Plan offers you a proven, effective and inexpensive alternative to costly diabetes drugs and medical treatments so you won't be forced to surrender your life savings to doctors, hospitals and drug companies. This affordable approach can dramatically improve the quality of life—and the ultimate outcome—for the average diabetic, whether Type 1 or Type 2.

# Having Diabetes Is Like Sitting on an Airplane That Just Developed Engine Failure

That is how helpless and out of control a person with diabetes often can feel. It is as though you are plummeting to earth in slow motion, paralyzed by a fear deep in your gut. No matter how you try to distract yourself or deny it, some part of you is always aware that you are falling faster and closer to the ground below with every tick of the clock.

The great tragedy is that 99.9 percent of the four million people who die from diabetes every year never realize they possess a *parachute*—and that if they simply pull the chord, they would float gently down, landing unharmed (and even enjoying the ride!). You and everyone you know who has Type 2 diabetes are wearing just such a parachute right now. We created the 30-Day Diabetes Cure Plan to be a virtual instruction manual that shows you how to locate and pull the release ring to save your own life.

What is this wondrous parachute? Foremost, it is none other than the incomparable ability of the human body to repair and regenerate itself—a truly awesome capacity that modern medicine inexplicably ignores and constantly seeks to circumvent.

Step-by-step and day-by-day, the 30-Day Diabetes Cure Plan shows you how to awaken and strengthen your body's own marvelous self-healing power so you can wrench your destiny from the greedy clutches of the diabetes industry and bring it back home where it rightly belongs.

## Are You Ready to Open Your Parachute Now?

Please have no illusions. You will need more than wishful intentions to succeed on the 30-Day Diabetes Cure Plan. During your journey, you will encounter many of the temptations and seductions that got you sick in the first place. Modern life appeals to the "leisure streak" in all of us. Never before in history has immediate gratification been so possible to achieve at every turn. Living in these times is like being a kid in a candy store who continually stuffs himself and gets sick until he finally learns his lesson.

This plan is no magic bullet. It will take commitment, determination and persistence on your part to turn around this serious condition. But there can be no mistake: This is the best and only viable alternative you have to surrendering your life to diabetes.

And you *can* succeed. Every individual we've advised who has followed and stuck with the 30-Day Diabetes Cure Plan has found improvement. It has yet to fail.

If you have truly had enough and are ready to reclaim your life and health, you have come to the right place. If you are wise enough to understand that the "easy way" almost always turns out to be the most difficult and painful path in the long run, then the 30-Day Diabetes Cure Plan is "just what the doctor ordered."

We urge you to carefully read the following chapters of Part 1 before you begin the actual 30-day plan that starts on page 155. The scientific studies presented in them will convince you of the effectiveness of our approach—as well as the futility of following current conventional medical treatments. This knowledge will help firm up your resolve to defeat this utterly beatable condition once and for all.

More than anything, we hope these recommendations and the real-life case histories of patients who have succeeded on the 30-Day Diabetes Cure Plan will inspire you to trust the miraculous healing power of your own body and mind.

Give it a chance. It will not let you down.

Russ Canfield, MD
and Jim Healthy

# CHAPTER 1

# THE TYPE 2 DIABETES CURE
# RIGHT UNDER YOUR NOSE

*"I've learned that nothing is impossible;
and almost nothing is easy."*

—ANONYMOUS

DESPITE THE BILLIONS of dollars spent every year on medical research, we still have very few cures for the diseases and ills that disable and kill tens of millions of people around the world every year.

Fortunately, this is not true for some of the lifestyle-driven medical conditions, such as heart disease, high blood pressure, Type 2 diabetes, and prediabetes—even though the mainstream medical community refuses to acknowledge this.

If you were attracted by the word "cure" in the title of our book—and it aroused hope in you—let us assure you that Type 2 diabetes does not have to be a life sentence. There is a proven way to beat and defeat it.

In the chapters that follow, you will be introduced to a number of individuals who have completely freed themselves from the symptoms and dangers of diabetes, as well as all the drugs they used to take to control them. Today, they are, for all practical purposes, "ex-diabetics." This means they have no signs or symptoms of diabetes. In fact, if they were examined by a new doctor, he would not be able to detect that they ever had the condition.

## Does this Represent a "Cure?"

So have they been *cured*? This is a question that elicits raging controversy among doctors and diabetics alike. Conventional doctors maintain there is no cure for Type 2 diabetes. The best you can hope for, they say, is to successfully manage diabetic symptoms with a robust program of diet and lifestyle improvements. But this cannot be called a cure in their eyes because if you return to the foods and beverages that caused your diabetes in the first place, your blood sugar problems would immediately return. Therefore, they prefer to use the term "reversed" or "put into remission" instead of "cure."

We feel this is splitting hairs. In our judgment, we believe it is fair to say that a person who has been diagnosed with either Type 2 diabetes or prediabetes can be considered "cured" if he or she:

•**Is able to consistently maintain blood glucose in the normal, healthy range;**
•**Requires no medication to achieve this state;**

- •**No longer experiences or displays the typical symptoms of Type 2 or prediabetes; and**
- •**Has a pancreas that is producing sufficient amount of insulin on its own.**

Isn't this what really matters if you or a loved one has been diagnosed?

Some people say these criteria do not represent a real cure because they do not allow patients to go back to eating and drinking the junk that gave them diabetes in the first place. To this we respond: "Why in the world would you *want* to?"

Every day, over 5,000 Americans are diagnosed with Type 2 diabetes and prediabetes because their bodies can no longer tolerate the excessive levels of sugar and simple carbohydrates in their diet that have wrecked their blood sugar.[6] Why should being "cured" of diabetes exempt them from the same consequences? Having this type of carbohydrate immunity would not constitute a cure; it would be a miracle. No cure lasts if the patient returns to the behavior that originally caused the problem.

Interestingly enough, the American Medical Association does admit that the "complete remission of Type 2 diabetes" is possible. It defines this as "glucose normalization without medication" and attributes what it calls "continuous, and sustained remission" to lifestyle interventions,[7] such as those you will read about in this book.

## There Is No Medical Cure for Type 2 on the Horizon

This controversy parallels the "diabetes cure" that surgeons claim for bariatric surgery.[8] With the approval of the American Diabetes Association, these surgeons advertise that gastric bypass surgery puts Type 2 in remission by restoring the body's sensitivity to insulin and reviving the depleted pancreatic cells that produce the hormone. It is never made clear whether the surgery itself produces this cure, or if it is a result of the extremely low-calorie diet that patients must follow for the rest of their lives. Indeed, it seems to be the diet that produces the results—because when patients stray from it, they regain all of their lost weight (plus much more) and their diabetes returns. Nevertheless, this does not deter physicians and surgeons from making "cure" claims and avoiding criticism or controversy.

Webster defines "cure" as "recovery or relief from a disease"…"to restore to health, soundness, or normality"…"to bring about recovery from a disease"…and "to be free from something objectionable or harmful."[9] None of the medical approaches administered today by physicians and surgeons can offer you this.

## The Only Possibility of a Cure—At Least for Now

Currently, the only possibility of becoming completely free—or cured—of Type 2 diabetes and prediabetes lies in improving your diet and lifestyle along the lines of the approach we describe in the 30-Day Diabetes Cure Plan in Part 2 of this book. This is not to say that our Plan is the only way to reverse Type 2. It certainly is not. There are many diabetes-reversing plans available today that produce admirable benefits. The most successful ones have one thing in common: They encourage you to avoid consuming the foods and beverages that raise your blood sugar and insulin levels so high that Type 2 diabetes results.

That said, there is a lot of confusion today regarding these diabetes-reversing diets and plans. Some say you must become vegetarian. Others claim the key is losing weight. Still others blame dietary fats and tell Type 2 diabetics to restrict them. And then there are the exercise gurus who maintain that frequent, high-intensity exercise is the only way to bring your blood sugar back into balance.

## How Our Plan Is Different

All these ideas can certainly get confusing—that's why we created The 30-Day Diabetes Cure Plan. In creating our Plan, we examined all the scientific research and clinical studies about what really works for reversing Type 2 diabetes and prediabetes. Then, we placed the most effective remedies at the beginning of our Plan, so people would experience significant improvements right away. This, we feel, would prove how effective our approach can be—and encourage them to stick with it until they reach their goal of reversing the condition and normalizing their health. "Nothing succeeds like success," as the old saying goes.

We cannot judge whether or not our Plan is the best one available—but it is certainly the easiest to follow. Every day, you simply make one small adjustment to your diet, your thinking, or your behavior. By the end of 30 days, you find yourself living what we call a diabetes-healing lifestyle. You may not be completely cured after 30 days—although many people *are* diabetes-free by then—but you will be well on your way.

How fast and how well you succeed in reversing your diabetes or prediabetes depends entirely on your commitment and your daily efforts. We have provided a roadmap that is proven to lead you to your destination. But you must navigate and travel this path every single day for the rest of your life. This is the only "catch" to this cure.

## The Road Will Get Easier, But It Will Never End

Reversing Type 2 diabetes requires that you turn your back on the foods and old habits that caused the condition in the first place, in favor of a healthier lifestyle. Becoming diabetes-free is just one of the many benefits you will enjoy as a result. For example, you surely will lose weight without dieting or even "trying." Your risks of heart attack, stroke, kidney failure, and Alzheimer's will plummet. Your energy level, enthusiasm, moods, and sex life will perk up dramatically. And you will be tacking on extra vibrant years to your lifespan. We think that is an excellent trade-off.

Of course, it will be up to you to maintain your "cured" status. Returning to your old ways and dietary habits certainly will invite your diabetes back. Your situation is a bit like the ex-alcoholic who remains cured of his acute alcoholism as long as he refrains from drinking. Every day that he refuses to drink, his body heals a little more—and every healthful activity he engages in (whether eating a good diet, taking nutritional supplements, getting regular physical activity, or improving his emotional well-being) will accelerate the healing process. The moment he slips up and takes a drink, he runs the risk of lapsing back into alcoholism.

So it is with ex-diabetics, too. A return to sweets or soda can reawaken your addiction to them (yes, sugar is very addictive!)—and before you know it, your blood sugar and insulin will be out of control again.

## Is It Worth It to Go Back to Damaging Habits?

We surely don't think so. Your health and future are far more important than the temporary, fleeting pleasure of nibbling something sweet. Our advice is: Get cured and *stayed* cured! The 30-Day Diabetes Cure Plan will show you how.

# Dr. Canfield's Story: Why I Became an Integrative Family Physician

Early in my life before medical school, I observed how many physicians were quite knowledgeable in anatomy, physiology and drug pharmacology, but weren't as versed in safe, natural therapies. I observed doctors making limited eye contact when interacting with patients and focusing exclusively on the latest lab test numbers or MRI scan reports, which defined the physical illness—and it felt to me like something was missing in the clinical encounter.

Somehow, there was much less appreciation for, and emphasis on, how a patient's thoughts, fears, attitudes, relationships and lifestyle habits play a vital role in the cause and cure of illness. I became convinced that the healing partnership between patient and physician, in which we acknowledge and prioritize the patient's goals and concerns, was just as important as the doctor's knowledge base in anatomy, physiology and disease pathology.

I strive to see the big picture and chose Family Practice because I was interested in learning about all aspects of medicine; and I couldn't see myself focusing only on one organ system or part of the body as a specialist. In my Family Medicine residency training at the University of New Mexico, I learned and identified with the "Biopsychosocial Model," which recognizes not just the biological and physical side of health and disease, but also the psychological, social, and environmental aspects of health. I enjoyed shadowing family doctors who got to know their patients more deeply and were able to facilitate longer-term transformational changes in how people live their lives.

As you read *The 30-Day Diabetes Cure*, it is important to examine how you are currently living and to identify patterns in your daily routines that aren't working for you. Our goal in this book is to teach you critically important health-promotion concepts and to empower you to feel and be your best.

We hope you will learn to enjoy healthy high-fat and protein-rich foods, while eliminating starchy and sugary foods that stress your metabolism. We also encourage you to incorporate regular physical activity that you enjoy and that fits into your routine. In addition, we hope you will seek help from natural therapies that can further support a healthy metabolism. We recognize that each person's way of implementing these changes is very much individual and should depend on his or her particular interests and life situation.

Most people don't realize that much of a physician's continuing medical education is funded by the pharmaceutical industry. My professional path has been quite different. After my years of formal training (and as I practiced medicine), I continued to study independently around natural therapies in more depth than we were taught in our overly drug-centered schooling. Through formal post-graduate training from organizations such as the American Holistic Medical Association, the Institute for Functional Medicine and the Association for the Advancement of Restorative Medicine I have refined my understanding of how genetics, environment and lifestyle interact as a total system.

As a result, I now diagnose and treat illnesses based on patterns of imbalance and dysfunction, rather than treating the symptoms of the illness specifically. Functional Medicine goes beyond the quick fix of masking symptoms with medication; rather, it treats the unique individual who has the disease.

After 20 years of experience in working with patients of all ages, and specializing in this integral, 360° approach to health and well-being, I tend to recommend a foundation of naturopathic therapies and, when indicated, complement them with powerful conventional medical treatments.

I maintain board certification from the American Board of Family Medicine and have sought further training in mindfulness meditation and in transpersonal studies from Naropa University because I recognize the critical importance that maintaining a calm presence can bring to the healing process.

My interest and expertise in insulin resistance and Type 2 diabetes treatment deepened during a phase of my career when I worked for the US Public Health Service in rural New Mexico with a Native American population devastated by diabetes complications. In service to my patients, I became a Certified Diabetes Educator and volunteered my time after hours, teaching this native population ways to change lifestyle in order to the prevent heart, kidney and blood vessel complications of this disease.

I have always been deeply committed to educating my patients, which is why my nurses and I take the time to teach our patients in our Santa Fe, New Mexico private practice. I have also been a clinical assistant professor at the University of New Mexico School of Medicine, teaching holistic primary care to medical students and residents. I have written for and have been quoted in newspapers and magazines.

As an integrative family physician, I concern myself with the physical and biological elements that influence health such as diet, exercise, and nutritional supplements, as well as the internal, felt dimensions of mental, emotional and spiritual health and wellbeing. Both dimensions exist for all of us on the individual level, but also on the collective levels of our family and community.

Our physical environment is becoming increasingly polluted and toxic and our culture increasingly divisive and stressful. In my current practice, we strive to artfully combine therapies for powerful synergy and balanced overall effects. During an office visit, we discuss your health concerns and goals on multiple levels and from different perspectives. Some treatments may serve to immediately control the troubling medical symptoms while other deeper strategies serve to balance both body and mind in a detoxifying and replenishing way.

Many of the patients in our medical practice have benefitted greatly from the self-help concepts outlined in *The 30-Day Diabetes Cure*. I hope you read the book with enthusiasm and optimism, as you realize how easily you can improve your health and your life by making simple changes in your diet and lifestyle habits day by day. If you are on diabetes or blood pressure medications, it is very possible that your doses will need to be adjusted as your metabolism changes. It is ideal to work with a medical provider who can follow your care periodically through this transformational process. We hope that you incorporate these proven recommendations into your daily life and enjoy a transformational change in your health that impresses you and your doctors.

Take Good Care,
Russ Canfield, MD

# CHAPTER 2

# WHAT IS DIABETES, ANYWAY?

*"Perhaps everything terrible is in its being
something that needs our love."*

—RAINER MARIA RILKE, poet and novelist, 1875–1926

CHANCES ARE you have purchased this book for one of three reasons. Either...
- **You have a diagnosis of Type 2 diabetes or prediabetes;**
- **You have a friend or loved one with this diagnosis whom you want to help;**
- **You have Type 2 diabetes in your family**—and you want to make sure you don't get it.

In any of these instances, we have these words of urgent advice for you:

## "Please Take Action Now!"

Far too many people *do not*—and, as a result, Type 2 diabetes is a leading cause of death and disability in the developed world. For decades, heart attack, stroke and cancer have shared the top three positions on the global list of top 10 causes of death. But it is only recently that health researchers have begun to recognize the important role that diabetes plays in the development of cardiovascular diseases and cancer, as well as many other chronic and crippling conditions.

Please do not take a diagnosis of Type 2 diabetes or prediabetes lightly—either for yourself or a loved one. Since these conditions produce no noticeable symptoms during their development, it can take 15 to 20 years before most people begin to notice that there is "something wrong." During this time, diabetes can wreak substantial damage on your body and brain—damage that sometimes cannot be undone.

## The World's Number One Health Problem

"Type 2 diabetes is the single biggest global health epidemic of our time,"[10] writes Mark Hyman, MD, in his book *The Blood Sugar Solution*. Not only is it growing faster than any other medical condition[11] but it is one of the leading causes of heart disease, cancer, dementia, and premature death in the world. Yet, as you will read in this book, it is almost 100% preventable and curable.[12]

Here's what is likely to happen if you don't take action:

- **You will probably suffer a heart attack or stroke.** People with diabetes and prediabetes are four times more likely to die from heart disease—or become disabled by a stroke.[13]

- **You will likely come down with dementia such as Alzheimer's disease.** There is a four-fold increased risk of dementia in diabetics.[14]

- **There is a high probability you will develop some form of cancer.** The cancer link is well documented and is driven by insulin-resistance.[15]

- **You probably already have high blood pressure—or soon will.** Some 75% of people with diabetes also suffer from hypertension.[16]

- **Chances are good that you will develop fatty liver disease and, ultimately, liver failure.** The rate of liver disease for people with diabetes is triple the rate of the general population.[17]

- **You will likely suffer from depression—if you don't already.** Type 2 diabetes is a significant cause of depression and mood disorders.[18]

- **You will lose the sensation in your hands and feet,** which frequently leads to injury… which can lead to amputations.[19]

- **Your eyesight will begin to fail.** Diabetes is the leading cause of blindness among people between the ages of 20 and 74.[20]

- **Your kidneys will stop working properly,** requiring you to need kidney dialysis three times a week. Diabetes accounts for nearly half of all new cases of kidney failure every year.[21]

- **You will age faster and die earlier than non-diabetics your age.**[22] On average, a person diagnosed with diabetes at age 50 dies eight years earlier than someone without diabetes.[23]

- **You will eventually have to inject yourself with insulin several times a day,** which can increase your weight significantly.

## Are We Scaring You?

We hope so. We want you to be so frightened by the consequences of diabetes that you will decide: "This will not happen to me!" You see, these and other disabilities aren't what *could* happen to you if you fail to turn your diabetes around; these events will surely occur. It is just a matter of time. (You will read a more detailed description of the complications of uncontrolled diabetes in Chapter 4)

If you have received a diagnosis of either Type 2 diabetes or prediabetes from your doctor, no doubt you have been advised to begin taking some type of medication to control your blood sugar. In addition, it has probably been suggested you also take a cholesterol-lowering drug called a statin, as well as one or more drugs to reduce your blood pressure and thereby protect your kidneys from permanent damage.

Doctors like to tell their diabetes patients that they can enjoy a long and relatively normal life if they take these drugs. But studies of these drugs and of patients who take them tell a different story. As you will read in Chapter 6, these drugs will *not* sufficiently protect you against the serious complications of diabetes, including heart disease, heart attack and stroke, kidney failure, dementia, and the other medical conditions we listed above.

Furthermore, the drugs your doctor is recommending for you will *never* give you the opportunity to be free of diabetes. They are meant to treat and manage your symptoms, not cure them. If you decide to go down the drug path, you will very likely find your health getting worse year-by-year. You will find yourself needing more and stronger medications to keep your diabetic complications at bay. You will see your daily schedule becoming consumed by testing your blood sugar…injecting yourself with insulin…remembering to take your many medications…visiting yet more doctors, specialists, and testing laboratories… making sudden visits to the emergency room…and filling out endless paperwork for insurance.

Perhaps worst of all, you will helplessly witness diabetes destroying your body over time, part by part—until you have become completely dependent upon others for your most basic needs. Type 2 diabetes is called a "wasting disease" because your body and mind slowly waste away, even though you may be following your doctor's orders perfectly.

## The Truth You Are Not Hearing

This does not have to be your fate. Instead, your life can be free of Type 2 diabetes and prediabetes—and you can begin to reverse them *the very same day* you quit doing and eating the things that are causing them. This is exactly what *The 30-Day Diabetes Cure* will show you how to do. But no one can make this decision for you. It is entirely up to you. And it is a decision you must recommit to every single day of your life.

How will you accomplish this? With *knowledge*. You see, the ultimate cause of diabetes and so many other "lifestyle-created" health problems is ignorance—ignorance about how the human body works…how health is created and destroyed…how foods affect our health, happiness, and longevity.

And it is not just the consuming public that is ignorant about these things. Far too many physicians and healthcare professionals are mistaken and ill-informed about the lifestyle connection to today's leading killer and crippling diseases. Despite their many years of education and clinical experience, their eyes have been blinded and distorted by official medical dogma which has been overly influenced by the drug and food industries and by medical politics.

We believe that once you understand how your diet, your lifestyle activities, and your daily decisions affect your health, you will be motivated to make smarter choices. So here is a brief education:

## How Your Body Makes Energy

Your body converts the food you eat into energy. Specifically, it uses or converts the naturally-occurring sugars in your foods into *glucose* (sometimes called blood sugar), which is a source of instant energy that allows your muscles to move and your brain to function. When combined with oxygen, glucose is burned (usually referred to as "metabolized") in your cells to produce energy, akin to how oxygen and gasoline are ignited in your automobiles engine to produce movement.

Food is divided into three categories: protein, fat, and carbohydrates—with carbohydrates containing the greatest amount of these sugars. There are two types of carbohydrates: complex and simple.

Complex carbohydrates include fruits, vegetables, and cereal grains in their natural state. This means they contain the natural oils (fats) and fiber (also called roughage), as well as the naturally occurring sugars. Simple carbohydrates are the result of refining and processing complex carbohydrates. In this processing, much of the fiber and oil content is removed and the sugar content is more concentrated. For example, sugarcane is a complex carbohydrate, while table sugar is a simple carbohydrate. An orange is a complex carbohydrate, while orange juice is a simple carbohydrate. Oats are a complex carbohydrate, while Cheerios are a simple carbohydrate. See the difference?

The important difference is that when consumed, a complex carbohydrate takes longer to digest—meaning that its sugar content is not readily broken down into glucose in the blood. This is because your body must first digest the roughage and oils before the sugars become available. But with simple carbohydrates, processing has already removed the fiber and oils so that the sugars are rapidly transformed into glucose. When you consume a simple carbohydrate, such as drinking a glass of orange juice or eating a bowl of Cheerios with a couple of teaspoons of sugar sprinkled on top, they immediately break down into glucose and raise the level of glucose in your bloodstream.

## The Role of Insulin in Your Metabolism

It may surprise you to learn that your body contains about one gallon of blood—and in this gallon there is only one teaspoon of glucose. If this amount dropped lower, you would feel weak and faint, and quite possibly pass out because your brain was not getting enough glucose to power it and keep you conscious. If your glucose level rose to one tablespoon in that gallon, you would run the risk of developing hyperglycemia (high blood glucose), and even dying.

Your body knows that too much glucose in your bloodstream is harmful to it. For instance, excess glucose irritates the delicate tissue that lines the inside of your blood vessels, thereby causing inflammation. Too much glucose also thickens your blood and "gums up" its circulation, with the result being that the oxygen and nutrients that your blood carries cannot flow into the tiny capillaries of your eyes and distant limbs, such as fingers and toes.

For these and other reasons, your body is programmed to keep your glucose level steady, within a range of approximately 60 to 100 mg/dl (or 3.3 to 6.4 mmol/L, according to the European system*) all the time. A glucose level that is consistently above100 mg/dl is considered

---

*Mg/dl, or *milligrams per deciliter,* is the unit of measurement commonly used in the US. The rest of the world uses the International System where the units are noted as mmol/L, which means millimoles per liter. To get mmol/L, you divide mg/dl by 18. Therefore, 200 mg/dl equals 11.1 mmol/L.

to be "prediabetes," while a level above 126 mg/dl indicates Type 2 diabetes. But as we will discuss in Chapter 3, these levels and diagnoses are more or less arbitrary. The spectrum of health risks caused by chronically elevated glucose and insulin levels—including heart disease, cancer, dementia, stroke, kidney disease, and nerve damage—actually starts at much lower numbers. Numbers that almost all doctors consider "normal."[24] More about this later as well.

Your body works very hard to maintain this "one teaspoon" level of glucose in your bloodstream at all times. It accomplishes this with the help of the hormone insulin, which is produced by your pancreas. Consuming a meal, beverage, or snack that is high in sugar or simple carbohydrates produces a rapid rise in blood glucose. To compensate for this, your pancreas releases insulin into your bloodstream to lower your blood glucose level so you will not die.

Glucose cannot enter your muscle and brain cells by itself. It needs insulin as an "escort" to unlock the tiny doors on these cells, called *insulin receptors*. Insulin's main job is to keep the glucose in your bloodstream within a healthful range. So when you consume a carbohydrate-rich food or drink that raises your blood glucose level, insulin is called upon to escort the glucose into your fuel-burning cells so energy can be created or stored in your muscles and liver as *glycogen*.[25] In this role, insulin acts as a kind of gatekeeper that rings the doorbell to open the insulin receptor "doors" on your muscle and brain cells so glucose can enter and be utilized.

## How Insulin-Resistance Occurs

When your muscles are active, they are able to use the glucose "fuel" efficiently—or store it as glycogen for future use—so that your levels of blood glucose and insulin remain in the normal ranges. Everything is working as nature intended.

But when you are *not* physically active and continue to consume simple carbohydrate foods and beverages (such as soda pop, sweets, pastries and baked goods, chip, snacks, and processed foods), glucose levels are continually rising and remaining high. This in turn triggers more insulin output from your pancreas. And this is where real trouble begins.

After years of chronically high insulin levels, your muscle cells begin to ignore insulin's urging to "open up." It is as if insulin was constantly ringing the doorbell and banging on the doors of your muscle cells—but the person inside, knowing that the cell is already full of glucose and glycogen, simply ignores insulin. This state is called *insulin-resistance* (also known as prediabetes) and is the early stage of Type 2 diabetes.

Now your bloodstream is flooded with both glucose and insulin, a doubly inflammatory combination. Together, they literally "burn" tissues and organs in a process called *glycation*, crusting them with a layer of oxidized sugar called *advanced glycation end products* (AGEs). Elevated levels of AGEs accelerate the aging process, which is why people with diabetes have prematurely wrinkled skin and organs that are 15 to 20 years older *biologically* than their chronological age. This explains why diabetics tend to age faster and die much earlier than non-diabetics. (More about this in Chapter 4.)

## How Insulin Makes (And Keeps) You Fat

Insulin's job is to keep blood glucose levels within a safe, healthy range. But when the insulin receptors on your muscle cells refuse to cooperate because of insulin-resistance—and when glycogen storage has reached capacity—insulin is forced to switch to a secondary strategy: It escorts the glucose to the liver where it is converted into fats called *triglycerides* and stored there. Chronic fatty buildup in the liver is not a good thing. It can lead to non-alcoholic fatty liver disease (NAFLD), which is rapidly becoming a common medical condition these days—especially among people with Type 2 diabetes (we discuss this in more detail in Chapter 4).

Storage capacity in the liver is very limited and when it is reached, triglycerides are transferred to your fat cells (usually around your belly) for storage. Insulin is the body's fat storage hormone—so the more of it you are producing, the fatter and more apple-shaped you will become. And what produces insulin the most? *Over-consuming simple carbohydrates.*

Insulin not only makes you fat, but it also *keeps* you fat. You see, as long as insulin is present in the bloodstream, it will not allow the triglyceride fats stored in your fat cells to be released. Normally, this would occur between meals and during sleep. These triglycerides would escape your fat cells and break down into essential fatty acids, which would actually feed and nourish your body. (This is how prolonged fasting works. By not eating, insulin is absent from the bloodstream—which allows stored fats to be released. The body is literally fed and nourished from its stored fat reserves.)

## The Vicious Cycle of Insulin

Consuming the typical Western diet composed of simple carbohydrates creates a vicious cycle of weight gain and insulin-resistance. For instance, gulping down a 20-ounce soda or a huge sticky bun will trigger a big spike in blood glucose, followed by a massive release of insulin. The insulin then clears your bloodstream of the glucose, which creates a "crash" as your blood sugar plummets.

This crash can make you feel sleepy and tired, anxious and irritable, confused, and in a fog. It will also make you hungry again as your glucose-deprived brain demands energy. Desperate, you are likely to grab anything that will give you a quick pick-me-up, such as a candy bar or another soda and then—bingo!—your body gets another hit of insulin. Result? This new load of glucose gets converted into still more body fat—and before you know it, you are hungry yet again. This is the vicious cycle of "carbohydrate craving"—and it is the underlying cause of weight gain, obesity, and insulin resistance that very few doctors and health experts are recognizing.

Repeat this carbohydrate-insulin cycle often enough and your cells become so resistant to insulin that your blood glucose remains high and your poor pancreas cannot keep up with the demand. This is when you cross the line from prediabetes to full-blown Type 2.

# The Real Problem Is Too Much Insulin— *Not* Too Much Blood Sugar

The big mistake that many doctors are making with insulin-resistance and Type 2 diabetes is that they are treating them as a problem caused by high glucose levels. But, as we have just explained, the real problem is having too much *insulin* in your bloodstream. This is a very important distinction, although it may not be readily apparent to you. Understanding this difference will completely alter your understanding of Type 2 diabetes and the best way to correct it.

In the simplest of terms, doctors view the problem of too much blood glucose as not having *enough* insulin. Since the body regulates glucose levels by increasing insulin, doctors believe they should mimic this strategy by administering drugs the lower blood glucose. It is mind-boggling that they rarely consider addressing the *cause* of elevated blood glucose, which is the consumption of too many simple carbohydrates. Of course, the reason for this becomes apparent when you realize that the Diabetes Industry cannot possibly profit from this strategy.

Instead, we have numerous drugs that reduce blood glucose by increasing insulin levels—either by stimulating the pancreas to crank out more of the hormone or by adding synthetic insulin. Yes, both approaches *do* succeed at temporarily lowering glucose, but with unfortunate consequences. Increasing your insulin levels also makes insulin-resistance (the underlying problem) worse. High blood levels of insulin are also inflammatory and increase your risk of inflammation-driven medical conditions such as heart disease, kidney disease, and Alzheimer's. Finally, as we have previously explained, insulin makes—and keeps—you fat.

Indeed, this is how insulin "works" for lowering glucose levels. Your liver transforms glucose into glycogen and stores it there and in your muscle cells to be used as energy during physical activity. When storage capacity is reached in the liver and muscles, the liver releases fatty triglycerides into the bloodstream, and insulin stores them in fat cells around your belly. (Remember, insulin is your body's fat storage hormone.) As long as insulin is present in the bloodstream—either your body's own or from a drug—that stored fat will stay put, no matter how steadfastly you diet or exercise. As long as these drugs keep your insulin levels high, you will never lose weight, and you will continue to gain. And remember: any extra weight gain further decreases the insulin sensitivity of your cells,[26] thus worsening your condition so that your body requires even more insulin to get your blood glucose levels down. This is a vicious cycle that you can never escape as long as you take medications and consume foods and beverages that raise your insulin levels. (We will address other problems associated with diabetes drugs in more detail in Chapter 6.)

## Too Much Insulin Is a Killer

The more insulin you have in your bloodstream due to insulin resistance, the higher your risk of artery disease, heart attack, and stroke will be. This is why heart disease is the most common complication of diabetes—and why 75% of all people who have diabetes will die from it. The inflammation caused by excess insulin damages arteries and initiates plaque-formation, which is directly responsible for heart attack and stroke. (We explain this in more detail in Chapter 4.)

It is not a stretch to say that insulin resistance is responsible for the lion's share of chronic medical conditions in the industrialized world. They are so common that researchers have given them the CHAOS Complex, which stands for Coronary disease, Hypertension, Adult-onset diabetes, Obesity, and Stroke.[27] These are not separate conditions, but actually develop on a continuum, with insulin resistance as the common causative factor. As we previously mentioned, high levels of insulin increase the amount of triglycerides in your bloodstream—and high triglycerides increase your risk of heart disease far more than high cholesterol does. In addition, too much insulin lowers your amount of protective HDL cholesterol, while raising your blood pressure (both of which are serious risk factors for heart attack or stroke).

Too much insulin causes high blood pressure in two ways. First, it constricts your arteries, thus making them narrower. This forces your heart to work harder to pump blood through them. Second, insulin forces your kidneys to hold on to salt (sodium), which results in increased water retention as the kidneys try to dilute the sodium. This extra water increases the volume of your blood and increases your blood pressure and the workload on your heart. This explains why more than 70% of people with high blood pressure also have insulin resistance.[28] And the greater your insulin resistance, the more your risk of high blood pressure rises.[29]

The good news is that reducing your insulin resistance can lower your blood pressure and therefore help you prevent a heart attack or stroke.[30] The best way to reduce blood levels of insulin is to reverse insulin resistance—which can only be accomplished by ditching the foods and beverages that spike your glucose levels, and getting more physical activity to increase your body's insulin sensitivity. Sorry, drugs cannot help you here.

## The Top 10 Signs of Insulin-Resistance (Prediabetes)

Insulin-resistance creeps up on you sneakily and does serious damage to your pancreas, blood vessels, kidneys and heart long before you suspect trouble is brewing. It is often called "prediabetes" because it leads directly to full-blown Type 2 diabetes, in which the insulin-producing beta cells in your pancreas die from exhaustion.

Not getting your insulin levels under control at this early stage virtually ensures you will become a Type 2 diabetic before long. If you have any of the symptoms below, see a doctor to get the tests we recommend later in this chapter. If a diagnosis of insulin resistance is confirmed, your doctor may want to start you on medications immediately. This is usually *not* necessary however. The official treatment protocol is to put a patient with prediabetes on a program of diet and lifestyle modifications first. Unfortunately, many doctors do not do this because they are unfamiliar with what really works—and they have almost no time to supervise and motivate your compliance.

Rest assured that prediabetes can usually be reversed with the simple, inexpensive and highly effective step-by-step lifestyle modifications you will read about in The 30-Day Diabetes Cure Plan. Here are the telltale signs of insulin-resistance…

**1. Belly fat.** A large abdomen or "potbelly" is an early sign of insulin-resistance in men. In females, it appears as belly fat combined with prominent buttocks. Men with waists that measure 40 inches or more and women whose waists are 35 inches or more are likely candidates for insulin resistance.

**2. Depression.** Depressed individuals are often insulin-resistant because the stress associated with depression actually causes the liver to flood the body with high levels of *cortisol* (the so-called "worry hormone"), which elevates blood sugar. When depression or stress is chronic, the extra insulin produced by the pancreas can damage arteries, cells and the kidneys. If you tend to feel depressed, sad or "blue," be sure to see your doctor and request the tests listed below instead of just taking antidepressant drugs.

**3. Low blood sugar.** If you feel agitated, jittery and moody, and experience an almost immediate relief once food is eaten, you might be hypoglycemic (a state of low blood sugar). If this is accompanied by any of the other symptoms listed here, especially physical and mental fatigue, you might be experiencing insulin-resistance.

**4. Fatigue.** Insulin-resistance wears people out. If you feel tired without an apparent reason, such as exertion or lack of sleep, it might indicate how hard you body is working to metabolize excess blood glucose.

**5. Brain fogginess.** The fatigue caused by insulin-resistance often expresses itself as a mental tiredness. Inability to focus, poor memory, loss of creativity, poor grades in school often accompany insulin-resistance, as do various forms of learning disabilities.

**6. Intestinal bloating.** People who consume simple carbohydrates—especially sodas and sweets – suffer from lots of gas. This may be a tipoff that your metabolism is not functioning properly because of insulin-resistance.

**7. Too much or too little sleep.** A recent study by the American Academy of Sleep Medicine found that people who sleep too little (six hours or less) or too much (10 hours or more) each night are much more likely to develop chronic conditions, such as diabetes, obesity, and coronary heart disease.*

**8. Dental problems.** Because of blood vessel changes that occur with insulin resistance, the flow of nutrients and removal of wastes from body tissues can become less effective. This impaired blood flow can weaken the gums and bone, making them more susceptible to infection.[31]

**9. Frequent infections and slow-healing wounds.** A bloodstream overrun by sugar blocks the action of cells that fight infection, causing vaginal and bladder infections and making skin sores slow to heal. Also, people with prediabetes often have reduced circulation, leaving tissues starved for the oxygen-rich blood that promotes healing.

---

*http://www.sciencedaily.com/releases/2013/10/131001105059.htm

**10. Sexual difficulties.** Between 35% and 50% of men with prediabetes and Type 2 diabetes experience erectile dysfunction and sexual problems. Excess insulin in the bloodstream created by insulin resistance damages the endothelium, the layer on the inside of blood vessels that instructs the vessel to contract or relax. Making matters worse, the anger and frustration this usually causes can be stressful and depressing, thus triggering cortisol release. Some women with blood sugar problems can experience vaginal inflammation or urinary tract infections.

## Standard Prediabetes Screening

If you are experiencing one or more of these symptoms, we encourage you to investigate the possibility that your metabolism is in the state of insulin-resistance by requesting the diagnostic tests below from your physician:

**1. Blood glucose.** A blood glucose test measures the amount of glucose in a sample of your blood. The test is typically done in one of two ways: after you have not eaten anything for at least 8 hours (fasting) or at any time of the day (random).

**2. Hemoglobin A1C.** This is a standard screening test for prediabetes. It measures how much glucose has attached to the hemoglobin in your blood. If your score is 5.7%, you are at risk for diabetes and cardiovascular disease.

**3. Triglycerides.** High triglycerides in the blood are often found in overweight persons and those on the brink of diabetes. But even those who are not overweight may have stores of fat in their arteries as a result of insulin-resistance. These triglycerides are the direct result of excessive consumption of sugar and sweets, sodas, alcoholic beverages, and fatty foods—in addition to simple carbohydrate foods. These create a glucose overload, which results in extra insulin being required to convert it into body fat.

**4. Hypertension (high blood pressure).** There is a direct relationship between the level of insulin and blood pressure. Excess levels of insulin constricts and narrows arteries, which increases blood pressure and to forces the heart to work harder. In addition, high levels of insulin raises blood pressure by making the kidneys retain sodium and extra fluid. This is why high blood pressure is a telltale sign of insulin-resistance.

## The Leptin Connection

There is another hormone at work that triggers insulin-resistance that you rarely hear about. Called *leptin,* its job is to send the "I'm full" signal (called *satiety*) to your brain after you have consumed enough calories for basic nourishment. Under normal circumstances, leptin also triggers the release of your body's stored fat so it can be burned for energy.

Unfortunately, the leptin signal gets shut down by overeating, eating rapidly, and by high fructose corn syrup (HFCS)—a nasty sweetener widely used in soft drinks, fruit drinks, baked goods and most commercial food products. In these instances, *leptin-resistance* can develop and your brain never hears the "Enough, already!" signal.

■ A recent study confirms that consuming large amounts of fructose-containing beverages and food products causes leptin resistance and elevated triglycerides in laboratory animals.

Those fed a high-fructose diet ate more and gained more weight than animals fed a high-fat, high-calorie diet.[32]

■ Research done in early 2010 at Princeton University showed rats who ate high-fructose corn syrup gained a lot more weight—and an extra helping of belly fat—than rats who ate table sugar, despite taking in an equal number of calories.[33] The reason for this disparity is that consuming HFCS blocks the leptin signal and therefore leads to overeating.

Leptin-resistance also seems to be the underlying reason many dieters cannot lose weight even when they follow a severely calorie-restricted regimen. Those extra pounds do not budge because the brain never receives leptin's message to burn up stored fat, and wants you to eat again instead.

Worse, when the brain does not hear leptin's message, the pancreas keeps producing insulin to deal with all the extra glucose in your bloodstream. The result is excess insulin in your bloodstream. If you are not prediabetic yet, you could actually become hypoglycemic (low blood sugar) from all that insulin. In reality, leptin-resistance is a step toward insulin-resistance and diabetes—although most doctors are completely unaware of the connection.

## Central Obesity = Belly Fat

Whether you call it a beer gut or a potbelly, having a large waist circumference seems to be quite common among Americans in mid-life (and even early ages). Despite all those ads for six-pack abs, no amount of exercise can turn this type of belly into a flat, ripped midsection if you have a damaged metabolism.

Belly fat is excess weight around the waist, usually carried by people with normal-sized arms and legs (and not much muscle mass). This condition is often called "apple-shaped obesity," distinguishing it from "pear-shaped," in which extra body fat is carried in the hips, buttocks, thighs, and legs. A well-informed doctor knows that when a patient's waist is larger than the hips (the waist-to-hip ratio is greater than 1), it is a dead giveaway of impending cardiovascular problems caused by elevated levels of blood glucose and insulin. (Keep this in mind as you assess your own symptoms.)

As we explained earlier, chronically high insulin levels that are caused by the "carbohydrate craving cycle" is what makes—and keeps—you fat. This is why drugs that raise your insulin levels are counterproductive because they never solve the underlying problem. Instead, they make your condition *worse* by increasing your body fat and weight. Remember: high blood levels of insulin create the accumulation of abdominal fat around your belly.

You probably have heard that belly fat is bad for your health, but you may not know why. Here's the story: Fat cells (called *adipocytes)* secrete highly inflammatory substances called *cytokines*.[34] And inflammation is the driving force behind almost all chronic diseases, including heart disease, cancer, dementia and, depression, and of course, Type 2 diabetes. (We will explain more about this in Chapter 4, when we discuss the nasty complications of diabetes.) These inflammatory cytokines produced by visceral fat cells also shut down your body's production of leptin, the hormone that signals "I'm full" when you've had enough to eat. Leptin-resistance is a major cause of overeating and, of course, still more body fat accumulation.

## Inflammation: The Root of the Problem

Out-of-control inflammation causes your muscle cells and liver to be less responsive to insulin. This is the real culprit behind insulin resistance. When your body is resistant to insulin, your pancreas must produce greater quantities of insulin to metabolize blood glucose. But remember, high levels of insulin will make your body accumulate more body fat. This means even more inflammation, which increases your insulin resistance. This is a deadly cycle which you must break—or else your pancreas will eventually burn out and quit producing insulin. When this occurs, you will have insulin-dependent diabetes (also called Type 1 diabetes). This will require you to inject yourself with insulin several times a day to avoid going into a diabetic coma and dying.

## How Abdominal Fat Causes Cancer

Abdominal fat is also dangerous because these fats cells are tiny estrogen-producing factories. Estrogen is the hormone that fuels the development of breasts and wider hips on females beginning at puberty. Until menopause, the female body contains high levels of estrogen—but surplus estrogen produced by abdominal fat can trigger the development of estrogen-driven cancers, such as breast and uterine cancer.[35] In fact, studies show that female abdominal fat is linked to a fourfold increased risk for breast cancer.[36]

Males are especially sensitive to any increase in estrogen. Since estrogen stimulates the growth of breast tissue, it often causes man to develop larger breasts, or "man boobs" (called *gynecomastia*).[37]

High levels of blood glucose also fuel cancer development. In 1924, German scientist Otto Warburg was awarded the Nobel Prize for discovering that cancer cells use glucose as their primary fuel. Subsequent research shows that when cancer gets a toehold in the body, blood glucose that should be used for normal functions gets hijacked by cancer cells. This generates excess lactic acid, causing overwhelming fatigue in patients and a welcoming environment in which cancer cells multiply and form tumors. When you have cancer, 95% of your glucose gets diverted to it, instead of your healthy cells. This deprives the body of the nutrition, and so cancer patients die from malnutrition.

## The Simple Solution to Central Obesity

The solution to central obesity is simple: By replacing your consumption of simple carbohydrate foods and beverages with fiber-rich complex carbohydrates (also referred to as "slow carbs" and explained and described on Day 7 of the 30-Day Diabetes Cure Plan), you will be targeting this belly fat without requiring daily jogging or countless sit-ups and crunches. Slow carbs are true "flat-belly foods." We promise you will come to love your tape measure, because your shrinking waistline will be the most visible evidence of your progress on our plan. The inches you lose will correspond directly to your body's reversing insulin resistance.

Remember, the 30-Day Diabetes Cure Plan is not a vanity diet. This is about your health. Your belly is a barometer of your body's resistance to insulin. Do not fall into the trap set by many so-called experts who claim that losing weight will reverse prediabetes and Type 2. This is a counterproductive strategy because it takes your focus off the real goal. Weight-loss diets are tough to stick with and are self-defeating. In fact, studies show that they fail 95% of the time over the long haul. And for those who are lucky enough to succeed at losing weight, most eventually gain it all back—and then some—within three years or less.

Yes, we do want you to get your belly under control because it is a symptom of prediabetes and quite possibly *metabolic syndrome*, described below. But healing your metabolism through the 30-Day Diabetes Cure Plan will naturally result in weight loss—without even trying to lose an ounce. This is a lifestyle overhaul that you can stick with for life.

## Metabolic Syndrome

The next stage in the development of full-blown diabetes is the condition known as metabolic syndrome. It is estimated that one-quarter of all Americans, or more than 80 million, are unknowingly walking around with it. It is a more aggravated stage of insulin-resistance directly related to central obesity, just explained above.[38] But metabolic syndrome also includes a combination of other conditions—including hypertension, elevated triglycerides, abdominal fat, and low HDL ("good") cholesterol—which make it extremely dangerous.

## Lifestyle Modifications Can Reverse This

Amazingly, you can reverse metabolic syndrome by making two simple lifestyle changes. First, a multi-year study at Duke Medical Center called STRRIDE (Studies of a Targeted Risk Reduction Intervention through Defined Exercise) examined the effects of increased physical activity on middle-aged, overweight men and women.[39] The results showed that a person can lower risk the of metabolic syndrome by 50% merely by walking 30 minutes a day, six days per week—even if you don't make any dietary changes. Duke cardiologist William Kraus, MD said, "Some exercise is better than none; more exercise is generally better than less, and no exercise can be disastrous."[40]

Second, poor diet plays a major role in metabolic syndrome.[41] The Dietary Intake and the Development of the Metabolic Syndrome study compared the risk of metabolic syndrome between the "typical Western diet" consisting of refined grains, processed meats, fried foods, poor-quality red meat and soda pop, and the "prudent diet," heavy on cruciferous vegetables such as broccoli and cabbage, carotenoid vegetables (carrots, pumpkins), fruit, fish and other seafood, poultry, whole grains, and low-fat dairy (otherwise known as the Mediterranean diet).

The results were impressive. Individuals with the highest scores from the "typical Western diet" had an 18% higher risk of developing metabolic syndrome, compared with those who followed the Mediterranean diet.[42] Individuals with the highest consumption of low-quality, fatty red meats (hamburgers, hot dogs, and processed meats such as cold cuts, bacon and sausages) had a 26% greater risk, compared with those who ate the least. On the other hand, consuming dairy products seems to be protective, producing a 13% lower risk of developing metabolic syndrome. (Don't miss the fascinating discussion on healthy saturated fats on Day 10 of the 30-Day Diabetes Cure Plan. Consumption of fried foods, fast foods, sodas and diet sodas were also associated with metabolic syndrome.)

By following the 30-Day Diabetes Cure Plan, you will be making the important lifestyle modifications that have been shown by rigorous scientific research to protect you from metabolic syndrome and diabetes.

## Type 2 Diabetes

When insulin-resistance and metabolic syndrome are not checked by making improvements in your diet and lifestyle, your condition can quickly turn into Type 2, the most prevalent form of diabetes, encompassing 95% of all cases. In Type 2, the pancreas continues to produce insulin (too much, in fact), but it is no longer effective in ushering glucose into cells. This leaves large amounts of glucose circulating in your bloodstream, along with loads of ineffective insulin—both of which are highly inflammatory. This combination causes cardiovascular damage and other serious health problems.

As we previously mentioned, when insulin is rebuffed by fuel-burning cells, it converts glucose into fatty triglycerides and stores the end product as body fat. This does not occur immediately, though, so in addition to a bloodstream flush with highly-inflammatory glucose and insulin, it also becomes loaded with fat, which can get deposited as plaque on artery walls. Cardiologists love to blame cholesterol for heart disease, but it is really too many triglycerides—triggered by excess insulin caused by the consumption of simple carbohydrates—which are a far more dangerous risk factor for heart attack (the cause of death in 75% of all diabetic-related deaths).

The prime areas for this fat storage are around your waist, bottom and thighs (otherwise known as central obesity.) Under normal circumstances, the leptin response will command the body to use this stored energy for fuel. But overeating, being overweight, and the resulting inflammation all interrupt the normal functioning of leptin, so its signal never reaches the brain, which leads to the further accumulation of body fat. That is the real reason that diabetes and obesity are intimately linked. You can clearly see that being overweight does not cause diabetes—*it happens the other way around*. (You can also now understand why sugar and refined carbs are the true underlying cause of heart disease, instead of meat consumption, saturated fat, and elevated cholesterol, as current medical thinking suggests.)

# The Top 18 Signs of Type 2 Diabetes

The risk factors for Type 2 follow the 10 symptoms of insulin resistance and prediabetes previously listed. Having one or more of these factors places you at greater risk for developing diabetes:

1. **Belly fat**
2. **Depression**
3. **Low blood sugar**
4. **Fatigue**
5. **Brain fogginess**
6. **Intestinal bloating**
7. **Sleep habits: too much or too little**
8. **Dental problems**
9. **Infections**
10. **Sexual Problems**

To these 10 signs of insulin resistance, let us add:

11. **Diagnosed insulin resistance**
12. **Diagnosed metabolic syndrome**
13. **Frequent urination, plus increased thirst.** These effects are caused by your astonishingly smart kidneys trying to dilute all the extra glucose in your bloodstream by signaling the thirst center in your brain to "drink more." Naturally, this increases the frequency of urination.
14. **Dizziness, plus sweating.** As your kidneys try to flush glucose from your system, the loss of fluids can prompt a drop in blood pressure, triggering dizziness and a sweaty feeling. As your sugar levels increase, so too does the thickness of your blood. And the thicker it gets, the more difficulty it has flowing through the tiniest capillaries. This often causes increased perspiration.
15. **Numbness, plus tingling in feet or hands.** High levels of glucose in the blood damage the tiny nerve endings that spider out into your legs, feet, and hands. *Neuropathy* is the medical term for nerve damage, which triggers these sensations.
16. **Age.** Those age 45 and older are at greater risk. Over time your body—and especially your pancreas—accumulates damage from environmental toxins, nutrient-poor foods, accumulated stress, plus a lack of antioxidants in your diet (which counter the oxidative damage done by free radical molecules).
17. **Low or inactive thyroid.** When your thyroid is underperforming, you feel sluggish and lack the energy for basic tasks. Your metabolism slows and your insulin rises. Chronic stress and poor nutrition can also burn out your thyroid, causing inflammation, weight gain, high insulin, and high blood sugar. (See also page 42.)

**18. Polycystic ovary syndrome (PCOS).** This condition is a women's hormonal imbalance that causes weight gain, irregular periods, ovaries with multiple cysts, infertility, fatigue, acne, and excess facial or body hair. Many women who have PCOS are overweight or obese, have Type 2 diabetes, and/or are insulin-resistant. Scientists have uncovered an undeniable link between insulin resistance and PCOS, offering women with this array of symptoms a real chance to turn it around. If you have PCOS symptoms, see your doctor—and then begin our 30-day plan.

## Who Should Get Tested?

If you display any of the symptoms above, we recommend you get tested right away. We also suggest you have your blood glucose levels tested periodically even if you are not displaying any of these symptoms and signs. This is because glucose levels directly reflect how much inflammation is happening in your body—and inflammation, as we have explained, is the driving force behind the majority of today's health problems. Chapter 3 will explain which tests to request and what your results indicate.

## New Forms of Diabetes

Although the following types of diabetes do not have universal definitions and treatments, it is fascinating to note that this disease keeps evolving in different patterns and influencing different parts of the body.

**Type 1.5 diabetes.** Relatively new, this condition is diagnosed in adults who do not immediately require insulin for treatment and have little or no resistance to insulin. When special lab tests are done, patients are found to have antibodies that attack their beta cells. It is sometimes called Slow-Onset Type 1 or Latent Autoimmune Diabetes in Adults (LADA).

About 10% of people diagnosed with diabetes have Type 1.5.[43] They are often diagnosed as Type 2 because they initially respond to diabetes medications and have adequate insulin production. The first line of treatment is diet and exercise. If that is ineffective, standard Type 2 medications are given and many Type 1.5 patients usually end up on insulin injections. Curiously, many individuals who have Type 1.5 are often slender and physically fit and do not exhibit typical signs of Type 2 diabetes, such as the metabolic syndrome cluster of high triglycerides, low HDL or high blood pressure. In addition, their insulin sensitivity is normal. Luckily, when their blood sugars are controlled, people with Type 1.5 have less risk for heart problems found in Type 2 diabetics with high cholesterol and blood pressure.

**Type 3 diabetes.** This is a newly identified category of diabetes that is "brain-specific." A study conducted in part by the Rhode Island Hospital identified a link between insulin problems, Type 2 diabetes and Alzheimer's disease.[44] In fact, some researchers refer to Alzheimer's disease as "diabetes of the brain." They believe elevated blood glucose levels create tangles in the brain matter called plaques, which block neurotransmitters from communicating with each other, thus causing memory loss and other cognitive dysfunction. Researchers discovered that an earlier onset of Type 2 diabetes—usually before age 65—is a risk factor for dementia, including Alzheimer's.

All stages and types of diabetes are very serious, requiring your immediate and continuing care. Numerous studies show that diet and lifestyle modification is the most effective way to halt and reverse all diabetes-related health problems (with the exception of Type 1, although here too they are very helpful). The 30-Day Diabetes Cure Plan makes it easy for you to adopt a diabetes healing lifestyle on a step-by-step, day-by-day basis.

## Patient Case Study: Caroline

My name is Caroline and I have had prediabetes for about six months now. Because of my family history of diabetes—my brother and my father have it—I was eager to get treatment early.

After working with *The 30-Day Diabetes Cure*, I'm feeling much better. With the monitoring of my blood sugar, I am now in the normal range for blood sugar. I am no longer prediabetic. Of course, we're still watching the diabetes to make sure it doesn't progress.

I am so thankful for this program. I was very concerned about developing the problems associated with diabetes, such as heart attack, stroke and kidney failure. I now know that this won't happen to me. *The 30-Day Diabetes Cure* has been a lifesaver.

# CHAPTER 3

# WHAT YOUR TEST RESULTS MEAN

*"Though no one can go back and make a brand-new start,*
*anyone can start from now and make a brand-new ending."*

—CARL BARD, author, Scottish theologian

NEXT TO YOUR BLOOD PRESSURE READINGS, your blood glucose levels are the most important indicators of your health and your chances of serious illness. This is why we recommend that everyone keep close track of these two important factors after age 40—regardless of whether you have Type 2 diabetes and/or high blood pressure or not. Of course, regularly monitoring these two factors is absolutely essential if you have a diagnosis of either condition. (We explain the why's and how's of monitoring your blood pressure in our book, *The 30-Day Blood Pressure Cure*; the comments here will focus on keeping track of your blood glucose levels.)

As we noted in the previous chapter, inflammation is the driving force behind today's most dangerous killer conditions, including heart attack, stroke, cancer, dementia, and Alzheimer's, kidney failure, and others. But inflammation is also a major cause of chronic conditions that cause pain and generally make life miserable, including arthritis, allergies, anemia, fibromyalgia, gum disease (gingivitis), pancreatitis, and psoriasis, to name just a few. Finally, the amount of inflammation you have determines the rate at which your body and brain age.

In a nutshell, greater inflammation means faster aging, more disease, and a shorter lifespan. Why are we telling you this in a book about diabetes? Because nothing creates more inflammation in your body than high levels of glucose and insulin in your bloodstream. Together, they "burn" the delicate lining of your arteries and organs, while creating a smoldering "fire" throughout your entire body that "cooks" you from the inside. (We will describe this destructive process in more detail in Chapter 4.)

## Excess Glucose: The Silent Killer

The point we want to make is that *you* determine your degree of inflammation by what you eat and drink. Consuming sugar, sweets and sweeteners, plus simple carbohydrates jack up your blood levels of glucose and insulin, which initiates destructive inflammation.

Glucose is like gasoline. It provides the fuel that powers our body and our physical movement. But when it is not properly utilized, excess glucose builds up in our bloodstream—which, like spilled gasoline, create a highly-combustible environment that can ignite a raging blaze of inflammation. The question is: How much blood glucose is too much?

"Much less than doctors currently believe," seems to be the disturbing answer.

## Doctors Are Wrong About "Healthy" Glucose Levels

Currently, a person officially has Type 2 diabetes when his/her fasting glucose level is 126 mg/dL. The diagnosis is prediabetes when the fasting glucose level is above100 mg/dL. These are the official guidelines distributed to all doctors by the American Diabetes Association (ADA). But, as Mark Hyman, MD points out, these definitions are "arbitrary"—and we believe dangerous. Why? Because these cutoff levels ignore the risk and damage done to the body (including artery disease, cancer formation, dementia development, stroke, plus kidney and nerve damage[45]), which begins at much lower levels of blood glucose. And, tragically, these levels are currently considered "normal" by the ADA and almost all doctors.

More than a decade ago, the DECODE study of 22,000 people examined the continuum of cardiovascular risk measured by a glucose tolerance test (the body's blood glucose level after a big sugar drink) instead of the fasting glucose level. The study found there was a significant risk of heart disease and complications starting at glucose levels considered perfectly "normal" (95 mg/dl), well below the official cutoff for prediabetes and Type 2 diabetes.[46] Another important study found that the risk of heart attack increases with any increase in average blood sugar, even for those who do not have diabetes.[47] The most recent research shows that glucose begins to damage the body at levels above 85 mg/dL[48]— and that the risk of cardiovascular disease increases significantly from this point.[49]

## Why Prediabetes Is a "Lie"

When patients receive a diagnosis of prediabetes, many believe it is no big deal. Unfortunately, too many doctors agree and offer these patients little advice or help; opting to wait until they cross the line to Type 2 diabetes, when official treatment guidelines can be employed. This is a mistake that can have tragic consequences, because great harm may have already been done.

Here is a surprising fact: Many people with prediabetes never get Type 2—yet they are at serious risk for cardiovascular disease, life-threatening health problems and death, just the same. A study performed at Crittenton Hospital Medical Center in Detroit showed that 36% of people with prediabetes already had coronary artery disease, similar to the 42% with Type 2 diabetes. In addition, most people with prediabetes already show signs of retinopathy (eye damage), nephropathy (kidney damage) and neuropathy (nerve damage), all of which are common complications of diabetes.[50] This risk is confirmed by another study that found that nearly two-thirds of all patients admitted to the emergency room with heart attacks had prediabetes or undiagnosed diabetes.[51]

Popular diabetes blogger Riva Greenberg put it succinctly in her article *Prediabetes Is A Lie*, which appeared in the Huffington Post: "Prediabetes doesn't exist. And the lie we tell that it does, does incredible harm. It stops the nearly 80 million Americans who have it from making the lifestyle changes necessary to prevent advanced Type 2 diabetes. Prediabetes is, in truth, Stage 1 diabetes."[52]

# Don't Let Your Test Results Fool You

To be forewarned is to be forearmed. We want you to realize this most serious mistake doctors are making about diabetes and heart disease. While they continue to determine your risk for a heart attack or stroke based on your cholesterol level, a more reliable gauge is your blood glucose level.

Please do not relax your guard if your physician or health care provider assures you that your glucose level is "perfectly normal" or that you have prediabetes. Unless your levels are consistently below 85 mg/dL, you should be vigilant and proactive by strictly limiting (or completely avoiding) the consumption of sugar, sweets and sweeteners, simple carbohydrates—and by following The 30-Day Diabetes Cure Plan. Having said this, let us examine the various diagnostic tests for determining Type 2 diabetes and prediabetes.

# Diabetes Testing Made Simple

If you display any of the symptoms described in Chapter 2—or if you have a family history of diabetes, heart disease or kidney disease—we urge you to have yourself tested. The following tests can be obtained through your doctor, or at most hospitals and walk-in diagnostic labs.

The following diagnostic tests are recommended to determine Type 2 diabetes or prediabetes:

**Glycated hemoglobin (A1C) if test.** This blood test indicates your average blood glucose level over the past 90 days. It works by measuring the percentage of glucose attached to the oxygen-carrying protein in your red blood cells, called hemoglobin. The higher your glucose levels, the more hemoglobin you will have with glucose molecules attached. An A1C level above 5.5% is considered prediabetes—and the patient has a threefold chance of developing diabetes in the next six years. A level of 6.5% or higher on two separate tests indicates you have Type 2 diabetes. (Certain conditions can make the A1C test inaccurate—such as if you are pregnant or have an uncommon form of hemoglobin, known as a hemoglobin variant.)

**Fasting blood glucose test.** A blood sample is taken after you fast for at least eight hours or overnight. With this test, a blood glucose level lower than 100 mg/dL (5.6 mmol/L) is considered normal. A blood glucose level from 100 to 125 mg/dL (5.6 to 6.9 mmol/L) is considered prediabetes. A level of 126 mg/dL (7.0 mmol/L) or higher indicates Type 2 diabetes.

**Oral glucose tolerance test.** A blood sample will be taken after you fast for at least eight hours or overnight. Before the test, you will drink a sugary solution. Two hours later, your blood sugar level will be measured again. This test determines how well your body metabolizes sugar and indicates how well your insulin is functioning. A blood sugar level less than 140 mg/dL (7.8 mmol/L) is considered normal. A blood sugar level from 140 to 199 mg/dL (7.8 to 11.0 mmol/L) is prediabetes. A blood sugar level of 200 mg/dL (11.1 mmol/L) indicates diabetes. (If you have already been diagnosed with diabetes, you don't need to do the 2-hour glucose-load test.)

This is the gold standard of diabetes testing—and it is the most important indicator of the presence and severity of diabetes. It measures both glucose and insulin—and is therefore the most accurate. This is because insulin resistance may not display an increase in blood glucose levels for some time, making it difficult to detect by other tests. (Your glucose level can be normal, even though your insulin can be elevated and your body insulin resistant.) Unfortunately, this test is rarely performed by most doctors. As a result, diabetes is not correctly diagnosed in 90% of the people who actually have it.[53]

# Insulin Tests

When you are diagnosed with diabetes, all you know is that your sugars are too high. But this does not tell you whether your pancreas is producing enough insulin, or whether your level of insulin resistance is too high. Your insulin productivity can be checked in two ways:

**C-peptide test.** Connecting peptide (C-peptide, for short) is found in amounts equal to insulin because insulin and C-peptide are linked when they are produced by the pancreas. The level of C-peptide in the blood can show how much insulin is being made by the pancreas. C-peptide does not affect the blood sugar level in the body. This test is usually administered to determine whether a person has Type 1 or Type 2 diabetes. If your pancreas is not making any insulin (Type 1 diabetes), you will have a low level of C-peptide. With Type 2, the test will display a normal or high level of C-peptide.

C-peptide is reported in nanograms per milliliter (ng/ml). Normal is 0.5–3 ng/ml. A lower level shows that little insulin is being produced by your pancreas.

The C-peptide test can also determine the cause of low blood sugar (hypoglycemia), such as excessive use of medicine to treat diabetes or a non-cancerous growth (tumor) in the pancreas (insulinoma). Since synthetic insulin does not have C-peptide, a person whose low blood sugar is caused by taking too much insulin will have a low C-peptide level. An *insulinoma* is a tumor in the pancreas that causes the pancreas to produce too much insulin, which causes blood glucose levels to drop, resulting in hypoglycemia. A person with an insulinoma will have a high level of C-peptide in the blood.

Before having this blood test, you may be asked to stop eating and drinking for eight hours. Insulin and some oral medicines used to treat Type 2 diabetes can change the test results. Your doctor may ask you to stop these medicines before your blood test.

**Fasting blood insulin test.** A simple glucose test will check your fasting glucose level, however it will not tell how much insulin is in your bloodstream. (It is possible to have low fasting glucose, yet have significantly elevated insulin levels. If this is the case, it means that you are essentially prediabetic and need to take steps to improve your insulin sensitivity.)

To find out your insulin levels, ask your physician for a fasting blood insulin test. It is one of the least expensive tests, yet one of the most reliable tests available to help you take back control of your health. A normal fasting blood insulin level is below 5 units / milliliter of blood (u/ml), but ideally you will want to be below 3. A lower level indicates you are not producing enough insulin; a higher level means you are making too much. High levels indicate that your body is aging rapidly and is experiencing insulin resistance and possibly Type 2 diabetes.

Insulin and/or c-peptide tests will probably only need to be done once, to make sure you are producing insulin. Then, by getting good control of your diabetes, you can ensure that insulin production will not drop much further, although there is a small natural drop-off with age.

## Important Tests You Also Should Request

Since heart disease is the most serious complication of insulin resistance and diabetes, it is the medical condition you most want to avoid and prevent. The following diagnostic tests will reveal the current health of your cardiovascular system.

**NMR LipoProfile.** The standard cholesterol test (standard lipid profile) that the majority of doctors are still ordering for their patients is outdated and obsolete. Your total cholesterol – and your levels of LDL and HDL—are basically useless when it comes to predicting your risk of a heart attack or stroke. A far more reliable determinant is the *particle size* of your cholesterol. If your doctor recommends that you get the "standard lipid profile" test, ask him or her to order one of these newer tests instead.

The only LDL cholesterol you should be concerned about is the portion that consists of smaller particles called "Pattern B." These small, dense LDL particles are the ones that damage your arteries and cause plaque. The larger size LDL particles (called "Pattern A") are benign and may even be slightly beneficial. This means that you can have a high LDL level, but if most of your particles are Pattern A, your risk is low.

HDL, the so-called "good" cholesterol, also falls into these two subtypes. Large HDL particles are especially protective against heart disease because they reduce inflammation. Smaller HDL particles, on the other hand, are not very protective—and can even be harmful. This means you can have a high level of HDL that does not provide very much protection, if the majority of your particles are small.

This new understanding of particle size subtypes explains why some people can have the ideal cholesterol profile (low LDL with high HDL), yet still suffer a heart attack or stroke. In fact a recent study revealed that of all patients admitted to the hospital for heart disease, nearly half of them had LDL levels under 100mg/dl—which is the new target level that doctors have been pushing for the past few years because they believed it was "safe."

The NMR LipoProfile test determines the size and number of your LDL and HDL particles. Small, dense particles are dangerous and an indicator of diabetes, even if your overall cholesterol is normal (with or without medication). You should have fewer than 1,000 total LDL particles and fewer than 500 small, Pattern B LDL particles (the dangerous subtype). This test is performed by LipoScience (*www.liposcience.com*) and can be ordered by your health-care provider—or directly through LabCorp (*www.labcorp.com*), which offers a "find a lab in your town" locator on its website.

Other tests that reveal particle size include the Lipoprint from Quantriximet (*www.quanti metrix.com/lipoprint)*, the Lipid Subfractionation from Berkeley HeartLab (owned by Quest Diagnostics), the VAP (Vertical Auto Profile), and the LPP (Lipoprotein Particle Profile). Any of these newer tests can be ordered through your doctor or healthcare provider.

**Triglycerides.** Most, if not all, of the advanced lipid tests mentioned above will also provide your level of triglycerides. Having elevated triglycerides is a serious risk for heart disease, though many doctors still place more importance on cholesterol levels. Triglycerides are bundles of fats found in the bloodstream that the body manufactures from the carbohydrates and fatty foods we consume. Some doctors refer to triglycerides as "ugly fat" because it is associated with arterial plaque buildup and heart disease.

High triglyceride levels (above 150 mg/dl) in the blood tend to coexist with low levels of HDL ("good") cholesterol, contributing to a condition called *diabetic dyslipidemia*. This relationship of triglycerides and HDL is a far more accurate way to predict your risk of heart disease than your cholesterol levels, according to Stephen Sinatra, MD, in his excellent book, *The Great Cholesterol Myth*.

"If, for example your triglycerides are 150 mg/dl in your HDL is 50 mg/dl, you have a ratio of three (150:50). If your triglycerides are 100 mg/dl and your HDL is 50 mg/dl, you have a ratio of two (100:50)," he explains. Anything higher than a ratio of three should be cause for concern—and action.

An elevated triglyceride level also indicates the likelihood that you have the small, dense, undesirable (Pattern B) type of LDL cholesterol—even if your LDL cholesterol level is in the normal range. The combination of high triglycerides, low HDL and central obesity are the hallmarks of metabolic syndrome, which occurs in 80% of people with Type 2 diabetes. This combination of risk factors greatly increases the likelihood of premature death from heart disease.

Common causes of high triglycerides include insulin resistance, obesity, excessive consumption of simple carbohydrates and fatty foods, excess alcohol intake, liver and or kidney disease, and certain drugs such as birth control pills, steroids and some blood pressure medications.

## Other Valuable Blood Tests for Your Heart Health

**High-sensitivity C-reactive protein (hs-CRP).** C-reactive protein (CRP) is a marker of inflammation in your body that reflects your cardiovascular health. You will recall that inflammation is the driving force behind insulin resistance and many of the serious complications of diabetes, so knowing your levels can motivate you to reduce them. Be sure to ask your doctor for the high-sensitivity version of this test, known as hs-CRP. A normal level of CRP is less than 0.8 mg/dl.

**Lipoprotein (a).** Commonly referred to as Lp(a), this lipoprotein is like a glue gun that uses cholesterol to repair damaged blood vessels. Problems arise when damage is widespread throughout the arterial system. This causes the body to produce high levels of LP(a), which is highly inflammatory and contributes to plaque formation and buildup.

A high level of Lp(a) is a very serious risk factor for heart attack, which some cardiologists call the "widow maker" blood factor. It is also one of the most difficult to treat – and there are no medications that lower it. In fact, some statin drugs actually raise its levels.

Lp(a) levels are generally determined by genetics and do not readily respond to lifestyle modifications. Having a high level should inspire you to work diligently to improve your cardiovascular health by upgrading your diet and lifestyle. Dr. Sinatra recommends an Lp(a)-lowering supplement regimen that includes 1–2 grams of high-quality fish oil, 500-2,500 mg niacin (*not* the slow-released type), and 200 mg of *lumbrokinase* (also known as Boluoke), which is a natural extract that thins the blood and helps prevent clots by breaking down fibrinogen.

**Fibrinogen.** This is a protein that makes the blood thick and sticky by causing platelets to clump together—resulting in thicker, slower-moving blood flow (*hyperviscosity*). Fibrinogen helps in the normal clotting process, but excess levels can lead to the formation of dangerous clots. Normally, levels should be in the 200-400 mg/dl range, although any type of inflammation can elevate them. Most doctors do not usually test fibrinogen levels in their patients, so you will have to request this. The test is especially important if you have a family history of heart disease.

If your levels test high, a supplement of nattokinase (commonly referred to as natto) can be helpful. Natto is extracted from a traditional Japanese fermented soy food and has been shown to be a natural blood-thinner. Lumbrokinase, described above, is another natural blood-thinner and clot-buster that you can take on a daily basis. A high-quality fish oil is also recommended.

**Coronary calcium scan (CCS).** This is the Cadillac of all tests for coronary artery disease. It was developed by famed cardiologist, Arthur Agatston, MD, creator of the South Beach Diet. The CCS, also known as the Agatston Score, measures the amount of calcification in the coronary arteries. The more calcium present, the greater the risk of heart attack.

Studies show that individuals with Agatston Scores above 400 have an increased occurrence of heart attacks and deaths, in addition to having more coronary procedures such as bypass surgery, stenting and angioplasty. Those with scores over 1,000 have a 20% chance of heart attack or cardiac death within one year.[54]

The CCS test is performed using a non-invasive CT scan of the body. The scan takes one second and many diagnostic centers now offer it for $99. If you experience shortness of breath or chest pain upon exertion, consult your cardiologist about having this scan as soon as possible. It is the most reliable test available that shows if you have coronary artery disease or not. This test is a lifesaver.

**Toxins.** Heavy metal toxins can be a significant factor affecting your diabetes. These heavy metals are directly toxic to the beta cells of the pancreas. They also affect all your hormonal organs, especially the adrenals and thyroid. A simple urine test will show if you have heavy metal toxicities—and to which metals. Dr. Canfield strongly believes that the clearing of those toxins will help reverse Type 2 diabetes. Discuss this test with your doctor.

**Hormones.** Type 2 diabetes is a hormonal disorder. Your pancreas is an organ that produces a hormone called insulin. However, the pancreas is regulated by the other five key hormones of the body. It helps to think of these hormones as a "family," with a mother, father, and three children.

**Cortisol.** The "father hormone" is cortisol, the most important hormone in the body. Without oxygen we die in four minutes and without cortisol we die in four hours. Few doctors ever check their patients' cortisol levels. Even when they do, the blood levels are given as "normal" across a very wide range, which can hide deficiencies. The key is to know that the optimal level is in the top 10% of the range. For example, if the normal range is 4–19, optimal would be 17–19. (Note that too high is not good either.)

Hormones work best in a very narrow range of optimal conditions and levels. Like the three bears story, "not too high, not too low, just right" is the ideal. Saliva is the best way to measure your cortisol levels. Four samples are taken throughout the day to get an idea of the person's circadian rhythm. This is the normal pattern throughout the day, where cortisol peaks between 6 am and noon and slowly declines after that. Dr. Canfield believes that having a normal cortisol level is key to reversing Type 2 diabetes. This is because your pancreas depends on cortisol to regulate its metabolism. Discuss this test with your doctor.

**Thyroid.** The "mother hormone" is thyroid. Many diabetic patients display low-level thyroid function. Most doctors do not catch this because they usually only check the TSH level. (TSH is a hormone that stimulates the thyroid gland to produce more hormones.) However, your thyroid produces mostly T4, which is not the active form of thyroid hormone (T3 is the active form that is converted in the cells). Discuss with your doctor checking free T3, free T4, and TSH to get an accurate picture of total thyroid function. This is another important—but unrealized—reason why most diabetics are overweight.

**Other hormones.** The "child hormones" are estrogen, progesterone, and testosterone. These hormones represent what makes you a man or woman. They must be in balance for your pancreas to work correctly. They also represent the stored reserve for your cortisol. The saliva test will show your levels, so please have them properly checked.

## Kidney Function Tests

Your kidneys are vital organs because they filter toxins out of your blood and dispatch them in your urine. Without properly functioning kidneys, you would quickly die. Kidneys are easily damaged by diabetes and high blood pressure. That is why many people with Type 2 wind up on dialysis. To guard against this, you should monitor your kidney function regularly—perhaps once a year until your diabetes is fully reversed. Kidney damage can be totally prevented by keeping your blood glucose and blood pressure in the normal ranges. The ideal way to accomplish this is with a good diet, regular physical activity, relaxation, and stress reduction—

although medications sometimes help at the beginning, if your condition is serious. The three main kidney (or "renal function") tests are:

**BUN (Blood Urea Nitrogen).** This is a waste product formed when dietary protein is digested. Normally, healthy kidneys will readily dispose of it. The normal range for BUN is generally 6-20 mg/dL. If yours is higher, diabetes may be damaging your kidneys—or something else may be going on (which you will want to have checked). Some drugs and illnesses—or too much protein in your diet—can raise BUN. A high BUN reading should be checked out immediately. You should never take chances with the health of your kidneys.

**Creatinine.** This is a waste product produced by the normal breakdown of muscle tissue. As creatinine is produced, it is filtered through the kidneys and excreted in your urine. The kidneys' ability to handle creatinine is called the creatinine clearance rate, which measures how well your kidneys are filtering your blood (or the glomerular filtration rate, GFR). As renal function declines, creatinine clearance also goes down, indicating poor renal function.

While the filtering ability of your kidneys declines with age, a normal GFR is 0.7 to 1.3 mg/dL for men and 0.6 to 1.1 mg/dL for women. A high creatinine level is often due to kidney damage from diabetes or some other disease, but high creatinine can also result from dehydration or weight loss.

**Microalbumin.** This is a test to see if protein is "leaking" in the urine since, ordinarily, there should be no protein in urine. In diabetes, one of the first indicators of a kidney problem is microalbumin in the urine. The microalbumin level can be measured on a "spot" urine sample (that is, a sample taken any time of day), or can be measured in a 24-hour urine sample.

## Tests for Fatty Liver Disease

Fatty liver, formally known as non-alcoholic fatty liver disease (NALFD), is usually found in people with Type 2 diabetes and prediabetes because of all the sugar and simple carbohydrates they consume. As you will learn in Chapter 4, glucose is converted to fat in the liver and stored there. Having a fatty liver increases inflammation, insulin resistance, high blood pressure, and significantly raises your risk of heart attack and cancer. Fatty liver disease can become the more severe form of fatty liver known as non-alcoholic steato-hepatitis (NASH), which may progress to cirrhosis and, ultimately, liver failure. Here are the tests that will show if you have fatty liver disease:

**Total bilirubin.** This test measures the amount of bile pigment in the blood. Bilirubin is responsible for the yellow color of bruises and the straw-yellow color of urine. If blood levels of bilirubin become very elevated, the patient may have a yellow color to the skin and eyes; this is known as jaundice. Elevated levels of bilirubin may indicate certain diseases, including fatty liver. The normal range for this test is 0.174 to 1.04 mg/dL.

**Blood protein.** These proteins are manufactured by the liver and are measured in the blood test for liver function. Their normal ranges are as below:

Total protein: Normal range is 60 to 80g/L.

Serum albumin: Serum albumin is a reliable guide to the severity of fatty liver disease. A healthy liver manufactures abundant levels of albumin, so declining levels of blood albumin indicate deteriorating liver function. Normal range is 38 to 55g/L.

Globulin protein: Elevated levels of globulin proteins in the blood usually mean excessive inflammation in the liver and/or immune system. Blood levels of globulin may be abnormal in fatty liver disease. Very high levels may be seen in some types of cancers. Normal range is 20 to 32g/L.

**Liver enzymes.** These tests, formerly called liver function tests (LFTs), are a group of blood tests that detect inflammation and liver damage. They can also check how well the liver is working. When liver cells are damaged or destroyed, the enzymes in the cells leak out into the blood, where they can be measured by blood tests. Therefore, measuring liver enzymes is only able to detect liver damage, although it does not measure liver function in a highly sensitive way. Liver tests check the blood for these enzymes:

AST (aspartate aminotransferase) can also be elevated in heart and muscle diseases and is not liver specific. The normal range of AST is 0 to 50 U/L (units per liter of serum, the liquid part of the blood).

ALT (alanine aminotransferase) is more specific for liver damage. The normal range of ALT is 7 to 56 U/L.

ALP (alkaline phosphatase) is elevated in many types of liver disease, but also in non-liver related diseases. The normal range of ALP is 30 to 120 U/L.

GGT (gamma glutamyl transpeptidase) is often elevated in those who use alcohol or other liver-toxic substances to excess. The normal range of GGT is 0–45 U/L.

**Understanding your test results.** Your doctor probably will look first at the GGT result. Normally, the level of GGT is not greater than 45. If your GGT is greater than 100, the doctor will inspect the levels of the other liver enzymes for possible causes of liver damage. Here are some possible combinations of abnormally high enzyme levels and what that might mean:

**Medications that can raise liver enzymes.** A wide variety of medications can cause abnormal liver enzymes levels in some individuals. Some common medications with potential liver toxicity include:

- **Acetaminophen (Tylenol)**

- **Antibiotics**

- **Cholesterol-lowering drugs (statins)**

- **Cardiovascular drugs, such as amiodarone**

- **Niacin**

- **Antidepressant drugs (the tricyclics)**

# Imaging Techniques to Visualize the Liver

**Ultrasound scans.** These can be very useful to detect fatty accumulations in the liver. They are inexpensive, quite reliable, and do not expose you to any radiation. If fatty changes are found in more than 30% of liver lobes, a diagnosis of fatty liver is made.

**MRI and CAT scans.** Non-enhanced CAT scans and MRIs are almost equal in their ability to determine the degree of fat accumulation in the liver (hepatic steatosis). For detecting mild grades of fatty liver, MRI scans are better than unenhanced CAT scans. (CAT scans expose you to significant radiation, whereas MRI scans do not.)

**Magnetic Resonance Elastography (MRE).** Mayo Clinic researchers have invented an extremely accurate imaging technology that can detect very early stages of liver disease. The MRE measures the elasticity of the liver and can detect abnormal hardening or stiffness of liver tissue. Healthy liver tissue is elastic and soft, whereas scar tissue (cirrhosis) is fibrous and hard. The MRE can easily detect this difference with 99% accuracy.[55]

Many thanks to Sandra Cabot, MD, for this important information. Dr. Cabot is an Australian physician specializing in liver health. She has written several popular health books, including her most famous, *Liver Cleansing Diet*, which was awarded The Australian People's Choice Award.

**Additional tests.** Other relevant lab tests for people with Type 2 diabetes may include a testosterone level test and an antibody test to make sure your body is not attacking its own pancreas and destroying insulin production.

Lab tests can help you know if and—more importantly, why—your glucose levels are up. They also can help you monitor your progress as you begin to reverse your insulin resistance and diabetes by following the 30-Day Diabetes Cure Plan.

## Keep Good Records of Your Test Results

Be sure to keep records of all your lab tests. This will keep you motivated by reminding you of your steady improvement. It will also be important to show your doctor so he can lower your medication doses—or withdraw them completely. You can get most of the important information from glucose self-testing and by paying attention to how your body feels. As you start to recover, your numbers will improve along with your energy level and symptoms.

## If Your Test Results Are Abnormal

In most cases (other than in immediate medical emergencies), making some key upgrades to your diet and lifestyle—such as those described in the 30-Day Diabetes Cure Plan in Part 2 of this book—will produce significant improvements in your metabolic and cardiovascular health.

Research has shown repeatedly that you can reverse your body's resistance to insulin by minimizing your intake of certain foods and beverages. Quitting processed carbohydrate foods, such as sweetened drinks, breakfast cereals, and white flour products—while replacing them with whole, fiber-rich natural foods—can correct and repair your damaged metabolism.

Decreasing your intake of sugar, sweets and simple carbs will result in better insulin activity—and insulin resistance will clear up as a result, without the need for drugs or medical interventions. Add a little extra physical activity and your cells will become more sensitive to insulin, so that your body needs less of the hormone. A lovely by-product of this process is natural weight loss, without dieting or extreme exercise.

This improvement kicks in as soon as you begin the 30-Day Diabetes Cure Plan. In a matter of a few days, you will notice your desire for sweets, sodas and processed foods will weaken—because you will be breaking the vicious cycle of "carbohydrate craving." Your blood chemistry will begin to balance itself naturally and you will reduce overall cholesterol and triglycerides. As you improve your nutrition and activity level, your body will repair the damage done to it. And your risk of heart disease and other serious diabetic complications will lessen. This is the perfect recipe for reversing diabetes and improving your overall health.[56]

## Patient Case Study: David

David Aquino's success is typical of individuals who faithfully followed *The 30-Day Diabetes Cure* program.

"I followed the directions given in the book to the letter and my diabetes is gone!" he says with pride and enthusiasm.

"I used to suffer from painful neuropathy in my feet, but no longer. My blood sugar is now in the normal range—and my A1C, which used be 7.0, is currently a healthful 5.7."

Weight loss is also typical of the program's results. And in David's case, there was a lot of it: *more than 50 pounds!*

"I went from 230 to 180," he says. "I cut out sugar and read food labels carefully when shopping. It worked like a charm."

David isn't the only one who is delighted by his results. "My doctor is very pleased with my progress," he says. "She has encouraged me to continue to live this new lifestyle."

# CHAPTER 4

# THE TERRIBLE COMPLICATIONS
# OF TYPE 2 DIABETES

*"Looking back, we see with great clarity, and what once appeared
as difficulties now reveal themselves as blessings."*

—DAN MILLMAN, award-winning athlete and inspirational author

IF YOU HAVE TYPE 2 diabetes or prediabetes, you have higher than normal blood sugars most of the time. But, so what? Besides making you feel tired all the time and sapping your energy, what harm does chronically elevated blood sugar do?

Unfortunately, plenty. Too much sugar in your blood corrodes your blood vessels and your nerves. This eventually can cause a host of severe complications that could disable or even kill you.

## Diabetic Complications Occur on a Continuum

The complications of diabetes are not separate or unrelated medical conditions, even though doctors treat them as such. The truth is, diabetes develops on a continuum, much like a train traveling across a large continent. At the beginning of this trip, things are pretty normal. Because there are no symptoms associated with high blood sugar, you may never recognize there is a problem until you have traveled quite a ways. The first complication may be weight gain, which is easy to accept as no big deal, because there is so much of it all around you these days. More time passes before you encounter a health problem such as high blood pressure. Before you realize it, the speed at which these complications develop gathers momentum—as does their severity. Soon these health concerns multiply and worsen until they reach a point much like a runaway freight train—they will be unstoppable.

The pattern that these complications follow is very predictable. If you experience one complication, your chances of experiencing others are great. Like a locomotive gathering speed, one health problem triggers another, and so on. Over time, this pattern will surely lead to the severe complications, which we discuss in this chapter.

The reality is that Type 2 diabetes, itself, is never fatal. Rather, its complications are what kills the diabetic. And we are going to be very frank here: These complications are not pretty. Type 2 is called a "wasting disease" because it steadily depletes the body of oxygen and nutrients that are necessary for health and life. This deprivation accelerates the aging process, making a person look and feel much older than one's chronological age. In fact, it is quite common for diabetics to appear 15 to 20 years older than they actually are. We will explain why this is so, a little later in this chapter.

## Killing You Slowly

As the disease advances, the diabetic loses his freedom and independence, as he becomes more dependent on medications and doctors. Next to go is the diabetic's mobility, as painful neuropathy makes mere walking a misery. Then, the diabetic's eyesight goes, as the tiny capillaries that nourish the eyes become clogged and blocked by blood thickened by excessive glucose. By this time, the diabetic is highly susceptible to a sudden heart attack or stroke, due to the damage that elevated insulin and blood glucose have done to his arteries and circulatory system. (Cardiovascular disease, which includes heart attack, stroke and heart failure, is the leading cause of death for 75% of all diabetics.) Next, will come cognitive dysfunction, memory loss, early dementia, and finally, Alzheimer's disease. The diabetic literally watches himself fall apart piece by piece during his golden years when others are enjoying their grandchildren, retirement, travel, and hobbies.

We realize it is not pleasant to read about all these dire consequences or to imagine what will likely happen to you if you fail to take action to reverse your diabetes. But, it is important that you know what lies ahead. If you currently are experiencing any of these problems, we encourage you to treat them as the warning signs that your condition is advancing. Hopefully, you are not at the point of experiencing severe symptoms yet—and that becoming aware of these complications will motivate you to change course now.

## High Blood Pressure (Hypertension)

High blood pressure almost always accompanies Type 2 diabetes and prediabetes. This is because elevated insulin levels cause the kidneys to retain sodium. Sensing this mineral imbalance, the kidneys retain water, which increases the volume of fluid being pumped through your blood vessels. This added volume increases the pressure in your blood vessels and forces your heart to work harder. Over time, this extra labor fatigues the heart to the point at which it simply fails (congestive heart failure).

Blood coursing through your vessels at this higher pressure can also create weak areas in your arteries, especially where they turn and bend. To patch these weakened areas, your immune system lays down fats and calcium as *plaque* to protect them from bursting. However, over time, this process calcifies or "hardens" arteries, making them less flexible and therefore increasing blood pressure even more. Should one of these plaques break off under the increased pressure, the plaque particle or a blood clot (called an embolism) can block one of the smaller capillaries feeding the heart or brain, depriving either organ of oxygen. The result is a heart attack or stroke, respectively. This is why high blood pressure is the leading cause of both conditions, which are fatal in 50% of all occurrences.

High blood pressure damages the kidneys, as well. The kidneys' job is to purify the blood of toxins and waste products, clearing the body by way of urine. The kidneys contain tiny filters called *nephrons*, which cease to function efficiently when hypertension is prolonged. When this occurs, the body can be poisoned by its own wastes.

# Kidney Failure

According to the National Kidney Foundation, 10 to 40%[57] of people with Type 2 diabetes eventually will suffer from kidney failure. It takes years to develop, and has no symptoms until very late stages. At this point, symptoms may include swelling in the feet and ankles (due to fluid retention), chronic itching, fatigue, and pale skin color. Once a person reaches the stage of failure, they will need life-long dialysis or a kidney transplant to survive.

With this condition, tiny filters in the kidney become damaged and leak protein into the urine. Over time, this can lead to kidney failure. Urine tests showing *microalbuminuria* (small amounts of protein in the urine) are telltale signs of kidney damage.

# Fatty Liver Disease

One of the liver's many responsibilities is to help regulate the body's blood sugar. It does this by converting the glucose it absorbs from the blood into fatty acids called triglycerides. These are then stored in the liver and the body's fat cells. In certain circumstances, producing and storing the fat can cause the liver itself to retain large amounts of fat—known as fatty liver disease. When fat builds up there, it becomes more difficult for the liver to control fasting glucose levels. This stored fat also makes the body more resistant to insulin, which, in turn, strains the pancreas and speeds up the development of Type 2 diabetes.

Because the liver is responsible for so many of the body's vital processes (chief among them, removing toxins), a fatty liver can lead to a host of complications, including cardiovascular disease (CVD) and Type 2 diabetes. Though commonly associated with alcoholism, fatty liver disease also affects people who have diabetes, are obese, or both. Nonalcoholic fatty liver disease (NAFLD) is, in fact, the most widespread liver disease in the United States, affecting perhaps 30% of the adult population.[58]

# Metabolic Syndrome

Metabolic syndrome is a condition that often goes hand in hand with diabetes and fatty liver disease. It includes a cluster of other complications—including hypertension, elevated triglycerides, and low HDL cholesterol, and excess belly fat—which make it extremely dangerous.

The American Heart Association and the National Heart, Lung, and Blood Institute note that metabolic syndrome is present if you have three or more of the symptoms mentioned below. Also, if you meet three of these five risk factors for metabolic syndrome, you are at serious risk for developing cardiovascular disease and Type 2 diabetes—in addition to having a sudden heart attack or stroke. Symptoms of metabolic syndrome include:

**1. Large waist circumference** (measured as length around the waist): Men with waists that measure 40 inches or more and women whose are 35 inches or more are likely to have metabolic syndrome.

**2. Elevated triglycerides.** Blood fats called triglycerides are often present in overweight individuals. But, even those who are not overweight, may have stores of fat in their arteries as a result of insulin resistance. These triglycerides are the direct result of consuming too many sugary foods and beverages, plus refined carbohydrates. Triglyceride levels equal to or higher than 150 mg/dL suggest metabolic syndrome.

**3. Hypertension.** It has been shown that most people with high blood pressure also tend to be insulin resistant. This is because there is a direct relationship between the insulin levels and blood pressure (as insulin levels elevate, so does blood pressure). Blood pressure equal to, or higher than, 130/85 mmHg, in the presence of these other symptoms, indicates metabolic syndrome.

**4. Cholesterol.** Insulin resistance lowers protective HDL cholesterol and raises LDL levels. Low HDL cholesterol (men under 40 mg/dL and women under 50 mg/dL), in conjunction with other symptoms, suggests the presence of metabolic syndrome.

**5. Hemoglobin A1C.** This is a standard screening test for Type 2 and prediabetes. It measures how much glucose has attached itself to the hemoglobin in your blood. Glucose levels higher than 6.5% of total blood volume indicates Type 2 diabetes.

**6. Fasting blood sugar (FBS).** This simple test measures your blood glucose level after you have been fasting for at least eight hours. Levels equal to or higher than 100 mg/dL suggest metabolic syndrome.

What can you do if you display the symptoms of metabolic syndrome? Amazingly, even if your tests show that you have these risk factors, you can reverse this condition with two simple lifestyle changes. First, a multi-year study at Duke Medical Center called STRRIDE (Studies of a Targeted Risk Reduction Intervention through Defined Exercise) examined the effects of increased physical activity on middle-aged, overweight men and women. The results showed that a person can lower the risk of metabolic syndrome by about 25% merely by walking 30 minutes a day, six days per week—even if you do not make any dietary changes.[59] Duke cardiologist William Kraus, MD, said: "Some exercise is better than none; more exercise is generally better than less, and no exercise can be disastrous."

Second, poor diet plays a major role in metabolic syndrome.[60] The Dietary Intake and the Development of the Metabolic Syndrome Study compared the risk of metabolic syndrome resulting from the "typical Western diet" (consisting of refined grains, processed meats, fried foods, poor quality red meat, and soda), and a diet heavy on cruciferous vegetables (such as broccoli and cabbage), carotenoid vegetables (carrots, pumpkins), fresh fruit, fish and seafood, poultry, whole grains, and low-fat dairy. This eating plan is commonly known as the Mediterranean diet.

The results were impressive. Individuals with the highest scores in the "typical Western diet" had an 18% higher risk of developing metabolic syndrome, compared with those with the Mediterranean diet. Individuals with the highest consumption of fatty red meat (hamburgers, hot dogs and processed meats) had a 26% greater risk, compared with those who ate the least of these foods. On the other hand, consuming dairy products seems to be protective, producing a 13% lower risk of developing metabolic syndrome. (Read the fascinating discussion on healthy saturated fats on Day 10 of the 30-Day Diabetes Cure Plan.) Consumption of fried foods, fast foods and diet soda were also associated with metabolic syndrome, while coffee and nuts were not.

By following the 30-Day Diabetes Cure Plan, you will be making the lifestyle modifications that have been shown by rigorous scientific research to protect you against metabolic syndrome and Type 2 diabetes.

## Heart Disease

The symptoms of metabolic syndrome all point to the strong correlation between diabetes and heart disease. When insulin is rebuffed by fuel-burning cells, it converts glucose into fatty triglycerides and stores the end product as body fat. This does not occur immediately, though. So, in addition to a bloodstream flush with glucose and insulin, it also becomes loaded with fat, which becomes oxidized and deposits itself as plaque on artery walls. Cardiologists love to blame cholesterol for heart disease, but too many triglycerides—triggered by excess insulin—are a far more dangerous risk factor for heart attack. Cholesterol is harmless unless it has been oxidized, at which time it triggers inflammation in the arteries.

Diabetes also speeds the progression of atherosclerosis (hardening of the arteries), which can lead to coronary artery disease, heart attack or stroke. Nerve complications we describe below can also produce heart abnormalities. This is why people with diabetes are far more prone to have heart complications—and to die from them—than non-diabetics. Heart attacks and strokes account for the vast majority of deaths in patients with diabetes. This is the number one complication that you must guard against.

## Amputations, Foot Infections and Nerve Complications

Peripheral neuropathy (PN) is the most common complication that people with diabetes experience. Diabetics can develop symptoms such as sharp pains and cramps, tingling or numbness (loss of feeling) in the hands, arms, feet, and legs.[61] Loss of pain sensation is a particularly serious problem for diabetics and frequently leads to lower limb amputations.[62] According to statistics, the most common cause of non-traumatic lower-extremity amputations in the US and Europe is diabetes.[63]

Poor leg and foot circulation can lead to foot infections which are resistant to healing and eventually lead to loss of part of the limb, if not full amputation.

Charcot foot, a condition that causes weakening of the bones in the foot, is another complication to be aware of. It can affect people who have experienced significant nerve damage and can make it impossible to bear any weight.

Gastroparesis (GP) is caused by damage to the vagus nerve, which keeps the muscles of the stomach and intestine from functioning properly. In effect, the stomach is paralyzed. Food is not moved and absorbed through the intestines. This can lead to indigestion, constipation, decreased appetite and chronic vomiting.

# Cancer

If you have chronically elevated blood glucose, your arteries, tissues and nerves are in a near-constant state of inflammation. Massive amounts of free radical molecules are generated by all this inflammation, which destroy healthy tissue (including beta cells in the pancreas). When free radical populations reach a critical mass, they overwhelm the antioxidant defense system that protects the body's DNA. Once the body's genetic blueprint has been breached and damaged, cancer begins to develop. It is especially important to note here that glucose is cancer's preferred fuel, feeding tumors just like fertilizer feeds a plant's growth. Continuing to consume sugary carbs when you have diabetes or insulin resistance is inviting a diagnosis of cancer.

# Alzheimer's Disease

**The link between diabetes and Alzheimer's is stronger than ever.** In fact, people with diabetes are more than twice as likely to develop Alzheimer's disease. Diabetics also have an increased risk of developing early dementia.[64] It is not only "senior citizens" who are affected, either. Problems in attention and memory can affect people under 55 who have had diabetes for a number of years.

Insulin resistance causes damage throughout the body—and cells in the brain are no different. When brain cells (called neurons) become insulin-resistant, tiny "tangles" in the brain, called amyloid plaques, develop. These plaques block neurotransmitters from communicating with each other, which causes memory loss and cognitive impairment. Symptoms include muddled thoughts and mental confusion. Personality changes are also common.

A study from Northwestern University found a link between insulin problems, Type 2 and Alzheimer's disease, with excess blood sugar being the cause. Studies like this one have led researchers to classify Alzheimer's as Type 3 diabetes.[65] This newly identified category of diabetes specifically affects the brain.

# Accelerated Aging

When you have diabetes, your bloodstream is flooded with glucose and insulin. Together, they literally "burn" tissues and organs (a process called *glycation)*, crusting them with a layer of oxidized sugar called *advanced glycation end products* (AGEs). These harden the arteries (atherosclerosis), cloud the lenses of the eyes (cataracts), and gunk up the neuron connections in the brain (dementia). While these conditions are common in older people, AGEs are the true cause. Elevated levels of AGEs also accelerate the aging process, which is why people with diabetes have prematurely wrinkled skin and organs that are 15 to 20 years older *biologically* than their chronological age. This also helps to explain why diabetics tend to die as much as two decades earlier on average than non-diabetics.

## Sexual Dysfunction

Optimal sexual function requires good blood flow and proper nerve function in the genitals. Diabetes can interfere with both. A recent study found that one third of women with diabetes may experience sexual dysfunction; that number is as high as 40% with men.[66]

Sexual complications as a result of diabetes include erectile dysfunction (ED) and loss of desire in men…vaginal dryness in women…painful intercourse…plus loss of pleasure and low desire. The correlation between ED and high blood sugars is strong,[67] but the good news is that men frequently recover full sexual function when they get their sugars in the normal range. Unfortunately, few studies have been done with women.

## Vision Loss and Other Eye Complications

According to National Institutes of Health, uncontrolled diabetes is the leading cause of vision loss and blindness among adults. People with diabetes are also at higher risk for developing cataracts and some forms of glaucoma. These complications are triggered by a disease known as *diabetic retinopathy*, which is caused by changes in the blood vessels of the retina—the light-sensitive tissue in the rear of the eye. When this happens, weakened vessels leak blood into the center of the eye, resulting in blurred vision. This is *proliferative retinopathy* and is the most advanced stage of the disease. Ultimately, severe hemorrhage or retinal detachment can result, causing significant loss of vision or blindness.

Fluid also can leak into the center of the *macula*, the part of the eye where sharp, straight-ahead vision occurs. The fluid makes the macula swell, so that vision becomes blurred. This condition is called *macular edema*. It can occur at any stage of diabetic retinopathy, although it is more likely to occur as the disease progresses. About half of the people with proliferative retinopathy also have macular edema.

## Skin Problems and Gum Disease

Diabetic skin complications include thickening of the skin…rashes, bumps, blisters…white, brown or reddish discoloration…plus, frequent bacterial and fungal infections. Others problems are hair loss, shiny or patchy skin, nail thickening due to poor circulation, and literally dozens of others with long Latin names. Most of these conditions are not serious, but can have a major effect on your appearance. Along with lowering your blood glucose levels, proper skin care can reduce your risk of skin problems.

Gum disease makes diabetes worse, and diabetes makes gum disease far more likely. High glucose levels encourage bacteria to grow, which promotes chronic gum infections. The infections increase insulin resistance, raise blood sugar levels and can lead to loss of teeth. There is a high correlation between gum disease (gingivitis) and heart disease. The ideal treatment is to keep glucose under control, plus sound dental hygiene, including regular brushing, flossing, the use of antiseptic mouthwash, and regular professional care.

## A Few Final Words About These Complications

We warned you that this review of diabetic complications would not be pretty. It is our hope that by knowing what to look for, you will be better prepared to avoid these health problems entirely. If you embrace a more healthful diet and lifestyle, there is no reason you should develop or succumb to these complications. If you have already experienced the onset of one or more of these complications, you should consult a doctor immediately.

All of these complications are mainly the result of high blood glucose and insulin. We suggest that you make a solemn pledge to yourself to clean up your diet and lifestyle so you can put an end to the damaging glucose-insulin cycle, before it ends you. Following The 30-Day Diabetes Cure Plan, which begins on page 155, can help you reclaim your health and longevity before it is too late.

# CHAPTER 5

# WHAT YOUR DOCTOR
# ISN'T TELLING YOU

*"The doctor of the future will give no medicine,
but will interest his patients in the care of the human frame,
in diet, and in the cause and prevention of disease."*

—THOMAS EDISON, American inventor, 1847–1931

YOU ALREADY KNOW that Type 2 diabetes is a big business. It is not a stretch to say it will be a trillion-dollar "industry" by the end of this decade.

Despite overwhelming evidence about the power of lifestyle interventions, the medical industry—including the AMA and ADA—remains "unconvinced" that diet and physical activity can reverse both prediabetes and Type 2 diabetes. Of those doctors who do recognize the power of diet and other lifestyle improvements, most believe that the necessary modifications involved are too strict for the average patient to follow long enough to make a difference. As a result, the vast majority of patients never hear about them. Often a doctor will say something like: "Lose some weight and come back in six weeks"—and when the patient does return unchanged (or worse), he will be placed on drug treatment.

But the truth is, these lifestyle improvements are *not* that difficult to make. And most patients would be willing to make them if the doctor provided them with a specific plan. Indeed, Dr. Canfield has never met a diabetes or prediabetes patient who did not want to get better—and to get off these drugs. What is lacking, in physicians and their patients, is the knowledge of what really works and the motivation to go for it.

An overwhelming number of clinical studies on actual patients with Type 2 and prediabetes (which you will read about in the next chapter) clearly demonstrate that with a few simple improvements in your diet and lifestyle, it is completely possible to reverse these conditions and reduce or even eliminate the need for all glucose-lowering medications—as is true of a host of other diabetes-related drugs, including those for high blood pressure, high cholesterol, depression, and kidney protection (to name just a few).

## Your Doctor May Not Be
## Guiding You in This Direction

So what is really stopping the conventional medical community from going all out to promote this easy, inexpensive and effective approach? We believe the underlying motivations behind the medical community's resistance to a non-drug diabetes protocol have more to do with politics and economics than with science-based results.

Our healthcare system in the US and many other industrialized societies focuses on acute care—emergencies requiring immediate and often dramatic attention. Doctors in the Western world excel at these heroic surgeries and interventions. From removing a ready-to-burst appendix to unimaginably intricate brain surgery, we receive top-notch care in this arena from modern allopathic physicians.

But these doctors are far less effective in the face of chronic medical conditions. And they fail miserably at preventing them. This is tragic in several ways, but perhaps most of all because multiple studies show that up to 90% of all chronic medical conditions could be prevented or alleviated with proper patient *education*.

## "The System"—Not the Doctor—Is to Blame

The truth is, doctors do not get paid for educating their patients about healthful diet and lifestyle habits. In our profit-based healthcare system, insurance companies will not reimburse for such education, so there is little incentive for doctors to teach their patients how to manage and heal their conditions without drugs. That is just one of the ways our healthcare system works against you in your attempt to heal yourself of diabetes naturally. Here are some others…

**Fewer physicians specialize in diabetes treatment.** Since reimbursement for assessing, educating and treating diabetes patients is not very profitable, there is minimal appeal for young doctors to specialize in diabetes. In fact, 85% of diabetes patients are treated by general practitioners who have little training in proper diabetes management.

**Most doctors do not know much about nutrition.** MDs receive very little nutrition education in medical school—and zero hours on herbal remedies, supplements, lifestyle counseling, and alternative medicine. But, they do know about prescription drugs, and that information comes not only from drug reps and salespeople who wine and dine physicians into prescribing their products, but also from the very medical schools at which our future doctors are trained. A study published in the prestigious *Journal of the American Medical Association* reported that almost two-thirds of academic department heads surveyed at US teaching hospitals and medical schools have financial ties to the drug industry. Drug companies "are involved in every aspect of medical care," according to the lead author.[68]

**Today's physician is time-crunched.** Doctors spend an average of 8 to 12 minutes with each of their patients—barely sufficient for diagnosing the underlying cause of the problem, let alone providing adequate health education for preventing and reversing it. Even if your doctor is aware of the nutrition and lifestyle changes that could reverse your diabetes, there is simply not enough time in his or her busy schedule to educate you and keep you motivated. Physicians do not even have the time to listen to their patients. A study found that a doctor interrupts his or her patient a mere 23 seconds after the start of their conversation.[69] Check your watch at your next office visit to see if this is true for you.

To be fair, this is not your doctor's fault, either. It is common knowledge that most people have a hard time committing to changing their diet in order to reverse or successfully manage a disease. Likewise, after an initial burst of good intentions, gym memberships often go unused. Because of this, many (if not most) doctors simply do not believe patients like you will stick with a diet or exercise program, even though it could save you thousands of dollars a year—and even save your life.

But the real reason many patients do not stick with a diet and exercise plan is because their doctors do not provide enough specific information in the first place—or any ongoing support so patients are inspired to continue. There just is not enough time or money allowed for it, given the way our profit-driven healthcare system is set up. Most doctors are bright, caring, idealistic individuals who enter the profession with the goal of helping others. But The System has morphed the practice of medicine into the *business* of medicine. The pressure on doctors to use drugs as their primary treatment is overwhelming.

**Your doctor could lose his or her license.** Doctors are scrutinized very closely by licensing boards. By recommending an "unofficial" treatment (even if it's simple diet and lifestyle improvements), physicians run the risk of lawsuits and losing their medical license if a patient complains or is somehow injured. It is much safer to "go by the book" and follow the Standard of Treatment protocols, which almost always involve prescribing drugs. The patient may not get any better, but at least the doctor will not wind up in court.

**Investors—and doctors—stand to make a bundle.** Health industry "insiders" are counting on the Diabetes Boom to generate loads of new revenue and profits. The US already spends $245 billion every year on diabetes care alone, and that number will multiply as diabetes continues to spread like wildfire. Doctors have kids in college and mortgages to pay, too.

Big Pharma exerts a powerful influence over doctors. Billions of dollars are raked in every year from diabetes drugs alone. And that means the pharmaceutical industry has plenty of money to spend on encouraging physicians to prescribe their products[70] (more about this in Chapter 6). The global insulin market is projected to grow by 8% over the forecast period of 2015 and 2020, according to MarketsandMarkets.com. Make no mistake, this is big money. Anything that might reduce these sales (such as widespread adoption of lifestyle modifications) is a threat to Big Pharma's bottom line and will be discouraged and discredited whenever possible.

## What They Are Not Telling You

Here are a few important revelations that you probably will not hear from your doctor or healthcare provider:

**Type 2 diabetes is not a blood sugar disease.** Instead, it is a metabolic disorder caused by too much insulin in your system. Prolonged, excess insulin causes your body to become resistant to its effect. This is why your blood glucose shoots up and why your body keeps producing more. But the more insulin it produces, the less effective it becomes. This downward spiral leads to the complete failure of the hormone—and the pancreas, the organ that produces it. When this occurs, you need to stay alive for the rest of your life on insulin injections.

**Lowering insulin, not blood glucose, is the only real solution.** Increasing your body's insulin levels with drugs just makes the problem worse. The way to halt and reverse Type 2 and prediabetes is to keep insulin levels low. This naturally reduces your blood glucose, while lowering your risk of diabetic complications—including heart attack, stroke, hypertension, kidney disease, and Alzheimer's. The only known way to lower your insulin levels is to stop consuming the foods and beverages that trigger the hormone's release.

**Too much insulin, not overeating, makes us fat.** It isn't *how much* we eat that packs on the pounds; rather, it is the *type* of foods we consume. Simple carbs, sugar, sweeteners, and processed foods hit your bloodstream immediately as blood glucose and trigger a surge of insulin. Insulin turns that glucose into fat (triglycerides) and stores it in your fat cells. Limiting the foods that trigger insulin will solve your weight problem without dieting or exercise.

**Obesity does not cause diabetes.** It is the other way around. When your bloodstream is always flooded with insulin, your cells become resistant to it—so even *more* of the hormone is required to move glucose out of your bloodstream. More insulin means more weight gain. Cut the insulin and your body will start burning its fat reserves for fuel.

**Losing weight is a misguided goal.** Shedding pounds is healthy—but this is like taking the long way home if you are doing it to reverse diabetes. The direct route to reversing Type 2 diabetes is to quit eating insulin-provoking foods. This will begin to repair your metabolism instantly. The pounds will fall off automatically as a result. Make "healthy eating" your goal, not weight loss. That is a goal you can live with for life.

**Exercise is a poor way to lose weight.** Changing your diet is far more effective. *Example:* It takes an hour to walk off 100 calories. Eliminating one soda pop subtracts 150 calories. Which has greater impact? Which is easier?

**Drugs will not save you.** Some diabetes drugs stimulate insulin production, which actually increases your weight. Drugs won't save you from diabetic complications, either (and these complications are what's killing people with diabetes). Your greatest, best hope is to lower your insulin response by rejecting the foods that spike your blood sugar. This way, your doctor can lower your medication dose—or completely withdraw your drugs.

**Reversing Type 2 diabetes and prediabetes is simple.** You don't need a weight-loss diet or a gym membership. You won't have to go on a weird diet or swallow expensive supplements. The 30-Day Diabetes Cure Plan in Part 2 of this book guides you day by day in making small changes that will pay you big rewards at the end of 30 days.

## Try Modification Before Medication

You *can* return to a normal, drug-free life and have a "second chance." Plenty of people already have. Now it is your turn!

If you want to avoid becoming another victim of the current diabetes epidemic, you must take matters into your own hands. You already have taken the first step by purchasing this book. Now, you must follow through by educating yourself—and then steadfastly committing to reversing your condition and reclaiming your health. Nothing less than saving your own life —or that of a loved one—depends upon your action now.

Please do not count on mainstream medicine to solve the problem for you or find a cure. You could die waiting. You can significantly improve your current condition *right now* without medications, finger-sticking, bariatric surgery, weight-loss dieting, slavish exercise, or a strict food regimen. On the 30-Day Diabetes Cure Plan, you will eat delicious food…shed pounds without trying…and nurture your body back to health. This represents a simple, natural, inexpensive and proven way out of today's distressing diabetes conundrum. We hope you will heed it.

## Patient Case Study: Shirley

One of the benefits you can expect by following *The 30-Day Diabetes Cure* program is a reduction in number and/or the amount of medications you'll have to take.

That's what happened for Shirley Griffin Anderson. Before starting the program, she was taking four different drugs daily. But once her doctor saw her progress, he reduced the number and dosages.

And that was just the beginning of the good news. Shirley's triglycerides (unhealthy fats in the blood linked to heart disease) plummeted from 291 to 146. In addition, her VLDL (the most dangerous type of cholesterol) fell from 58 to 29, while her HDL (the "good" cholesterol that protects against heart disease) rose 48 to 50. Overall, her total cholesterol went from 247 to 204.

But perhaps the benefit that pleases Shirley the most is the 16 pounds that she lost on the program—*all without dieting!*

# CHAPTER 6

# WHY DRUGS ARE NOT A SOLUTION

*"It's never too late to be what you might have been."*

—GEORGE ELIOT, English author, 1819–1880

DRUGS HAVE THE ABILITY to lower your blood sugar numbers. This will make your doctor very happy, but your pancreas may not be as pleased. Since some of these glucose-lowering drugs stimulate your pancreas to work harder, this small organ will wear itself out under the heavy load. Eventually, the insulin-producing beta cells will become exhausted and die off. When this occurs, you will need to provide your body with insulin by injecting it several times a day. The vast majority of people with Type 2 diabetes can avoid this fate by improving their eating and lifestyle patterns—and by taking steps to heal the damage that inflammation and glycation have already caused to their tissues and organs. This is what The 30-Day Diabetes Cure Plan will help you achieve.

It is important to note that everyone loses beta cells as a natural part of the aging process, and for most people this loss is not critical. However, it is a different story for a person with Type 2 diabetes or insulin resistance. High levels of glucose in the blood caused by insulin resistance is the primary killer of beta cells (known as *glucotoxicity*). The more beta cells your pancreas loses, the sooner you will develop insulin-dependent diabetes and the serious diabetic complications described in Chapter 4.

## The Big Problem With Medications

If you are diagnosed with insulin resistance or prediabetes, your doctor might want to put you on blood sugar lowering medication such as Glucophage (metformin) as the first line of "defense" against developing Type 2. We urge you not to go down this slippery slope right away. Official medical protocol for the treatment of prediabetes and Type 2 asks physicians to try diet and lifestyle modification *before* drugs (except in emergency situations).

Lowering blood glucose with drugs that force your pancreas to churn out more insulin—or that add more insulin to your body—is not a good solution. Since excess insulin is the underlying problem, your body does not need more of it. Instead, your cells need to become more *insulin sensitive*, which means they should be better trained to use the insulin your body is already producing more effectively. Drugs cannot possibly accomplish this. Only a combination of reducing your consumption of sugar, sweets and other simple carbohydrate foods (which convert quickly into blood glucose) can achieve this. Increasing your physical activity (which lowers the amount of insulin your body requires) serves to compound this effect. That is exactly what the 30-Day Diabetes Cure Plan helps you achieve.

This is the *only* way to lower your blood glucose without raising your insulin levels. This will protect your blood vessels from the inflammatory damage caused by *glucotoxicity* and reduce your risk of cataracts and blindness, high blood pressure, nerve damage, and kidney damage. In addition, you will be much better protected against heart attacks, stroke and artery disease and dementia.

Glucose-lowering medications will not accomplish this—and taking them can give you a false sense of security that you are being protected. These drugs have great appeal because they present the illusion that you can eat anything you want, just as long as you take them. Tragically, most patients do not realize this until great physical damage has been done, and it is too late to turn back.

Fortunately, there is plenty of proof that diet and lifestyle modifications are the most effective way to battle and defeat Type 2 diabetes and prediabetes.

In 2001, the Diabetes Prevention Program (DPP), which was the largest head-to-head study ever conducted, and compared diet and lifestyle improvements against diabetes drugs, found that the lifestyle modifications were significantly more effective than the leading drug, metformin (Glucophage), in preventing prediabetes from turning into full-blown Type 2, especially in individuals 60 or older.[71]

As you will read in Chapter 7, many other studies confirm the superiority of diet and lifestyle improvements over diabetes medications for managing blood glucose and insulin levels. More importantly, diet and physical activity offer you the best chance of reversing insulin resistance and Type 2, while protecting you from the onset of diabetes' deadly complications.

In this chapter, we discuss the effects of the most commonly prescribed diabetes drugs, so you and your doctor can make an informed decision about the treatment that is best for you.

## The "Secret" Dangers of Diabetes Drugs and Aggressive Glucose Lowering

If you have Type 2 diabetes, your doctor probably has told you to regularly monitor your blood glucose levels—and has prescribed one or more medications to help you lower it. Doctors have long believed that lower glucose levels help prevent diabetic complications—such as vision loss, kidney failure, heart attack, stroke, and other complications.

While this is true, studies dating back five years or more show that using drugs to lower your blood glucose to normal levels actually increases your risk of serious complications and death. Here are a few examples:

•**In 2008, a large study sponsored by the National Institutes of Health, which was called ACCORD** (Action to Control Cardiovascular Risk in Diabetes)[72] was conducted to see if this was true. As reported in the February 2008 issue of the *New England Journal of Medicine* (NEJM), patients who had their blood sugar lowered (using drugs) the most, actually experienced the *highest* incidence of heart attack, stroke and death. These results were so shocking, that the study was abruptly stopped two years early to protect the surviving patients in the trial.[73]

•**A similar result was seen in a meta-analysis of thirteen studies in the UK,** which was reported in the *British Medical Journal*. Researchers found that aggressive glucose control with drugs in patients with Type 2 diabetes did not significantly reduce all-cause mortality or cardiovascular death. On the contrary, drug treatment caused more than a twofold increase in the risk of severe hypoglycemia and resulted in a 47% higher risk of congestive heart failure.

Mind you, this finding was drawn from thirteen studies and was spelled out in the finding's conclusion: "The overall results of this meta-analysis do not show a benefit of intensive glucose lowering treatment on all-cause mortality or cardiovascular death. A 19% increase in all-cause mortality and a 43% increase in cardiovascular mortality cannot be excluded."[74]

•**A large-scale study at Duke University School of Medicine,** published in the *New England Journal of Medicine*, showed that despite serious risks and dangerous side effects, diabetes drugs offer few benefits and simply do not live up to their claims. Duke researchers found that the drugs failed to reduce risk of heart attack *at all*. Lead researcher, Robert Califf, MD, of the Duke study said, "This is a sobering confirmation of the need to continue to focus on lifestyle improvements."[75]

## Diabetes Drugs Will Not Protect You from Heart Disease and Death

Type 2 diabetes rarely kills people (except when blood glucose drops too low). Instead, people with diabetes usually die from its complications—most commonly, from heart attack, stroke and kidney failure. (We discussed these complications in detail in Chapter 4) It is clear from the abundance of research that glucose-lowering drugs do not provide protection from these endpoints.

This is why doctors also usually add a cholesterol-lowering drug to protect against heart disease—and anti-hypertensive medication(s) to guard against kidney damage and high blood pressure. But as you will see, these drugs are equally ineffective at saving patients' lives. For instance…

In another aspect of the aforementioned ACCORD study, researchers examined the effectiveness of cholesterol-lowering drugs called *statins* to protect diabetics from heart disease, stroke and heart attack, the most common and most serious of all diabetic complications. In this portion of ACCORD, doctors added a drug that lowers triglycerides and a cholesterol drug called a *fibrate* to their patients' cocktail of pharmaceuticals, in addition to a statin drug. The results showed that combining the fibrate and the statin drug for diabetic patients did not reduce the risk of cardiovascular disease or death, compared to simply taking only one drug or the other. The study also showed that using drugs to lower blood pressure to "normal" levels did not reduce the incidence of cardiovascular disease or death.[76]

# A Few Words About Statin Drugs

Interestingly, an analysis of multiple studies published in 2010 and involving 91,000 patients found that statin drugs actually *increased* the risk of developing diabetes, with higher doses contributing to higher risks. Yes, you read correctly: statin drugs can cause diabetes. A review of five major clinical trials on statins published in the *Journal of the American Medical Association* found that 8.4% of the patients developed diabetes as a result of the drug. Those on the highest doses of the more potent statins (such as Zocor, which more and more doctors are pushing these days) were at the greatest risk for developing diabetes.[77]

Doctors prescribe statin drugs to protect diabetes patients from its most serious complications: heart attack and stroke. This is based on the assumption (and we emphasize the word "assumption") that heart disease is caused by high cholesterol levels. In fact, several large clinical trials published in the *New England Journal of Medicine* indicate just the *opposite*: that these drugs fail to prevent heart attacks and death (with the mild exception of second heart attacks).[78, 79, 80]

Newer research confirms that statins are useless for primary prevention of heart disease (first-time heart attacks), even though over 75% of prescriptions are handed out for this purpose. (These drugs do seem to work for the prevention of a second heart attack, but only modestly.) The Cochrane Collaboration, a highly regarded independent research group, performed a comprehensive review of 14 major studies (involving 34,000 patients at low risk for a heart attack) which used statins to prevent heart disease. The group found that the drugs produced little or no benefit.[81] Unless you have already had a heart attack, these drugs will not help you prevent one, despite what the TV ads and many doctors claim.

In addition to being ineffective, statin drugs produce significant adverse side effects. They routinely cause muscle weakness and damage, chronic aches and cramps, plus exercise intolerance,[82] sexual dysfunction, liver and nerve damage, in addition to other problems.

# The Dark Side of Diabetes Drugs

Many diabetes drugs are accompanied by significant health risks. Here is a look at the concerns and dangers that health experts have about several diabetes medications:

**Heart problems.** No drug has proven to be more dangerous than Avandia (rosiglitazone), manufactured by the pharmaceutical giant GlaxoSmithKline. Approved by the FDA in 1999, Avandia reduces the amount of glucose in the blood. A once-commonly prescribed drug, it contributed to the deaths of 47,000 people from heart disease in the first 11 years of its use.[83] In a subsequent criminal investigation and trial, it was revealed that Glaxo knew of the dangers that Avandia posed, yet hid them from the public and the FDA. As a result of the scandal, Glaxo was fined $3 billion, the largest penalty ever assessed to a pharmaceutical company. Nonetheless, even though Avandia is banned in Europe, it remains on the US market and is still being prescribed to treat Type 2 diabetes patients. Incredibly, the FDA lifted many restrictions on the drug in late 2013—which means the drug could become widely available again very soon. The labels for both Avandia and Actos (pioglitazone—a medication in the same class as Avandia) contain warnings that the drugs may cause or exacerbate congestive heart failure in certain patients.

**Cancer.** In 2009, four large-scale studies from Sweden, Germany, Scotland, and the UK, and published by the journal Diabetologia, raised questions about a possible link between the diabetes medication Lantus (insulin glargine) and an increased risk of cancer.[84] Lantus, is a long-acting basal insulin analogue, given once daily to help control blood sugar. Type 2 diabetics who used insulin glargine reportedly experienced a nearly three-fold greater incidence of cancer. The American Diabetes Association responded to the report, describing it as "conflicting and confusing" and "inconclusive." They advised patients against discontinuing insulin glargine and warned against "over-reaction."[85] In August of 2013 the FDA posted a report stating that so far the agency has not found conclusive proof that Lantus causes cancer, however its study of the drug is ongoing.*

**Vision risks.** Diabetes medications in a class of drugs called thiazolidinediones (also known as glitazones)—which include Avandia and Actos—appear to produce a higher risk for macular edema.[86] The labels for Avandia and Actos warn that anyone taking these medications who experiences vision problems should promptly see an ophthalmologist.

**Fractures.** Both Avandia and Actos are reported to double the risk of bone fractures in women (but not in men), according to a review published in the *Canadian Medical Association Journal*.[87] The research examined ten clinical trials involving more than 13,000 diabetics who were taking Avandia and/or Actos, or neither medication. The medications seem to reduce bone density in the hips and spine of the women taking them. The labels for Actos and Avandia both contain warnings about increased fracture risk in women.

**Liver toxicity.** The consumer group Public Citizen reports that it has identified 14 (including 12 deaths) cases of liver failure directly linked to Avandia between 1997 and 2006. Many of the patients, according to Public Citizen, had gotten liver-function tests not long after starting Avandia, and the results were either normal or mildly elevated. The patients took Avandia for anywhere from half a week to more than four years. (Liver toxicity has been observed in laboratory animals that were given Avandia, according to Public Citizen.)[88]

## Why Diabetes Drugs Do Not Work

Type 2 diabetes has become the drug industry's fastest growing market. There are at least eight categories of diabetes medications—and new drugs appear frequently, each one being put forth as a "breakthrough" for people with diabetes.

While all these drugs can bring down glucose numbers, the effect is never permanent or sufficient. Damage to nerves, blood vessels, pancreas, and other organs continues. Serious complications, such as heart attack and stroke, are not prevented. All these drugs have adverse

---

*http://www.fda.gov/Drugs/DrugSafety/DrugSafetyPodcasts/ucm240508.htm

side effects and dangers that persist, while their glucose-lowering benefits usually wear off after a few years. Here's what studies tell us:

**No reduced risk of heart disease.** Even when blood glucose numbers do come down with drugs, some large studies show that risks of heart attack, stroke and early death do not improve. A study of 1,700 veterans published in 2009, found that subjects with near-normal A1C (glucose) values of less than 6.9% had no less cardiac or stroke risk than those with high A1C level over 8.4%.[89]

**No cardiovascular benefit.** Two major studies of heart and blood vessel complications compared "tight blood sugar control" (with drugs) with less strict control (also with drugs). These trials, called ACCORD (mentioned previously) and ADVANCE, found no cardiovascular benefit to the lower blood sugars. As you will recall, the ACCORD trial was stopped early because so many more people in the "tight control" group were dying.

## The Right and Wrong Way
## to Lower Blood Glucose

You might ask, "How could this be?" We know that chronically elevated blood glucose is the major cause of diabetes complications. So how could it be that lowering them fails to help?

The answer lies in *how* blood sugars are lowered. Lowering them through diet, regular physical activity and stress reduction has powerful benefits and actually can reverse the disease completely for many people. But lowering them with drugs does not have the same benefits.

There are three reasons for this surprising situation. One has to do with insulin. Three classes of diabetes drugs—insulins, sulfonylureas, and meglitinides (all discussed below)—lower blood glucose by raising insulin levels. Unfortunately, as we have discussed, having more insulin in your body leads to more insulin resistance, which is the major cause of Type 2 diabetes, high blood pressure and obesity in the first place. Increasing insulin only makes things worse.

Diabetes specialists are now saying that high blood pressure and "bad" (LDL) cholesterol are at least as important as blood sugars when it comes to complications.[90] According to diabetes expert Richard Bernstein, MD, insulin resistance raises risk of other conditions, such as high blood pressure and unhealthy cholesterol levels. So by increasing insulin levels, and thus insulin resistance, we might also be increasing the risk of heart disease and stroke.

Second, drugs themselves can cause complications that then get blamed on the diabetes. For example, a widely used category of diabetes drugs called the TZDs (or glitazones) do reduce blood glucose and insulin resistance, but cause liver failure, heart failure, and heart attacks.[91]

Finally, too many people use drugs as a reason not to make changes in their eating, activity levels, or stressful lives. They believe the drugs will keep them safe. In this way, drugs get in the way of the life changes needed to prevent complications and reverse their diabetes.

# Drugs That Increase Insulin

Drugs do have a place in diabetes care—especially in emergency situations. But, generally speaking, we believe they should be seen as a temporary rescue measure to reduce dangerously high glucose levels, while you apply the real cure, which includes healthy lifestyle changes. "Temporary" could mean weeks—or it could mean months or years—but your ultimate goal should be to use these drugs as little as possible until you get better, instead of relying on them for life.

We also believe that you should know how these diabetes drugs function, so you can choose to use them or not. The section below describes diabetes drugs that increase insulin, how they work, and the problems they may cause.

**Sulfonylureas.** The original oral diabetes drugs are called sulfonylureas, which stimulate the pancreas over several weeks to produce more insulin in order to lower blood glucose levels. However, by raising insulin, they further increase insulin resistance. As they overtax the pancreas, they destroy what natural insulin function you have left, potentially leading to hypoglycemia. They also promote weight gain.

For these reasons, the blood glucose benefits typically wear off over a span of five to ten years. Because insulin is stimulated whether or not it is needed (such as when you skip a meal), sulfonylureas have a high risk of causing low blood glucose (hypoglycemia—a dangerous consequence.

There are approximately 20 sulfonylurea drugs in use today. Some of the oldest and best known are *tolbutamide* (brand name Orinase,) and *chlorpropamide* (Diabinese). Others include Glipizide, Gliquidone and Tolazamide. Keep in mind that there is nothing that sulfonylureas will do for you that a healthy diet cannot do better. We recommend avoiding them.

**Meglitinides** improve on sulfonylureas because they are short-acting. They stimulate insulin, but only for one or two hours. If you take them right before eating, you have less risk of hypoglycemia. The medicine will "cover" the carbohydrates eaten at the meal and be out of your system by the time the food is gone.

The downside is that they are not especially effective. Studies show A1C reductions of around 0.5–1.5%.[92] And they simply have not been around long enough to evaluate the effects on complications. There is still some risk of hypoglycemia with meglitinides, and weight gain is highly likely.

The main drugs in this class are *repaglinide* (Prandin) and *nateglinide* (Starlix). Since they basically cover the starches you eat at a meal, you can get the same effect by eating less starchy foods.

**Insulin** is the most direct way to get sugar out of your blood and into your muscle, liver, and fat cells. If you are far out of control, injecting insulin is better than walking around with sky-high glucose levels corroding your blood vessels and nerves.

Because insulin is the most effective way to bring glucose levels down, doctors are starting people with Type 2 on insulin earlier and earlier. However, some clinicians and researchers question this strategy. Since more insulin leads to greater insulin resistance, this approach may not be preventing the major complications of diabetes.

Should you decide to go on insulin, it will change your life. You will have to check your glucose levels regularly, give yourself shots, plus buy equipment and supplies. You will also have to be vigilant about your glucose going too low (hypoglycemia) and passing out, having a car accident or other difficulties. On insulin, you will certainly gain weight.

In considering insulin use, be aware that it comes in many forms. Different types come on at different speeds and last different lengths of time. For instance…

•**Rapid-acting** insulins work for 15–90 minutes. You inject them before meals to handle the carbs you are eating.

•**Short-acting and intermediate-acting** insulins work for 30 minutes to 18 hours, depending on which product you inject. Because these intervals are not very exact, it is difficult to control sugars precisely with these insulins. There also is a danger of highs after meals and lows between meals and at night.

•**Long-acting** or basal insulins last a full day and can keep your sugars from rising during the night. However, they are not strong enough to cover meals. Long-time diabetics whose pancreases produce no insulin at all might benefit from a basal insulin—at least until their pancreases recover.

If you have Type 2, you should avoid rapid-acting, short-acting and intermediate insulin if possible. But if you need it, you should see it as a temporary measure. As you adopt a healthier diet, your need for insulin will decrease and probably cease. Make sure to let your doctor know when you are doing this, so you do not take more of an insulin dose than you need (otherwise your blood sugar could drop too low).

For some people with long-term diabetes, basal insulin can be a good idea; even that should be temporary, however.

You can read more about the different kinds of insulin at the Joslin Diabetes Center's site: *www.joslin.org* (search Types of Insulin).

## Drugs That Do Not Increase Insulin

So far, we have discussed the drugs that lower blood glucose by raising insulin levels. Those drugs are basically ineffective at preventing most diabetic complications because they do nothing to reduce the problem of insulin resistance—and actually make it worse. However, there are other diabetes drugs that work differently. They include…

**Metformin.** Usually, the first medicine given to new Type 2 patients is metformin. The most common brand name is Glucophage, but generic metformin is effective and affordable. Metformin is called a *biguanide* drug because it works by telling the liver not to produce unneeded glucose. The liver's overproduction of glucose is a huge part of diabetes for many Type

2s. Insulin is supposed to stop the liver from churning out glucose, but in Type 2 diabetes, the liver ignores insulin's action because it has become insulin-resistant. Fortunately, many insulin-resistant livers will "listen" to metformin.

Unlike insulins and sulfonylureas, metformin actually *does* reduce the likelihood of diabetic complications. It does not cause weight gain and even helps some people lose weight. Even so, studies show metformin is much less effective than lifestyle change for preventing diabetes and probably its complications.[93]

The main side effects of metformin are diarrhea and stomach pain, which occur in 30% of patients. Usually, these symptoms are manageable by changing your diet or the times you take the drug. However, sometimes symptoms are severe and force people off the drug. You should not take metformin if you have kidney or liver disease.

**Incretin drugs.** Your body produces natural hormones called *incretins*, whose job it is to signal the pancreas to produce insulin when needed and tell the liver to store glucose instead of releasing it. They decrease appetite and promote weight loss. People with Type 2 do not make enough incretins.

A new class of diabetes drugs called "incretin mimetics" are designed to mimic this action. These are injected drugs that can lower blood glucose levels without the danger of lows, or the weight gain that comes with insulin or sulfonylureas. Because incretin mimetics are so new, their long-term effect on complications is not known. Nor do we know the long-term risks, dangers or adverse side effects. Another downside is the expense, which can be $300 to $400 a month—and many insurance plans do not pay for these drugs.

The drugs in this class are *exenatide* (Byetta and the long-acting version, Bydureon) and *liraglutide* (Victoza). The side effects that are known include nausea and diarrhea. The most dangerous reaction so far has been pancreatitis, a serious illness that requires hospitalization.[94]

**Oral incretin drugs.** There are some new oral medications that also improve incretin function. They are called DPP-4 inhibitors. (DPP-4 is short for dipeptidyl peptidase 4, a protein that destroys incretins.) By inhibiting DPP-4, these drugs help natural incretins stay in the blood longer. DPP-4 inhibitors include Januvia (*sitagliptin*), Onglyza (*saxagliptin*) and Tradjenta (*linagliptin*.)

By increasing incretin levels, these drugs lower glucose levels and reduce appetite. Common side effects include nasopharyngitis (the common cold), headache, nausea, and urinary tract infections. Like the incretin mimetics, DPP-4 inhibitors have been associated with increased risk of pancreatitis. They are very expensive for a pill, costing about the same as the injectable incretin drugs.[95]

**Amylin.** Another injectable drug is *pramlintide* (brand name Symlin), a synthetic version of the hormone *amylin*, which plays a role in glycemic regulation by slowing gastric emptying and promoting satiety. This prevents post-prandial (after-meal) spikes in blood glucose levels. (Natural amylin tends to be deficient or absent in people with diabetes.) Symlin acts like insulin's helper, especially in the liver, keeping glucose stored. It also slows the rate at which glucose gets into the blood after a meal, while decreasing appetite.

Symlin is usually given along with insulin. Side effects include low blood sugar (hypoglycemia,) headache, cough, nausea, and vomiting. It costs $200 to $300 per month, depending on your insurance.

**Thiazolidinediones (TZDS).** The oral TZD drugs work by reducing insulin resistance in the muscles, liver and fat cells. This action helps your natural insulin work better to reduce glucose levels. This sounds like a big benefit and, indeed, TZDs were greeted with great excitement when they came out. They made tighter glucose control possible, without the risk of hypoglycemia or weight gain.

Unfortunately, these drugs turned out to have major negative effects. *Rosiglitazone* (Avandia) has been found to increase heart attacks[96] and liver disease. *Pioglitazone* (Actos) is strongly associated with heart failure[97] and bone fracture. *Troglitazone* (Rezulin)[98] was associated with over 100 deaths from liver failure; it is now off the market.

These drugs were "fast-tracked" through the approval process because they were promoted as "breakthroughs" in diabetes control. The FDA failed to investigate the harm they might cause. Modern medicine typically gets excited about new drugs and their potential benefits, and downplays or ignores potential harm. So, we as customers have to be cautious. It is often better to wait a few years before jumping on a new drug bandwagon.

**Alpha-glucosidase inhibitors.** *Alpha-glucosidase* is a naturally-occurring enzyme that our intestines use to break down starches into simple sugars. Then the sugars are absorbed into the blood, where they raise glucose levels. Alpha-glucosidase inhibitor drugs mimic this effect by slowing down the transformation of starches into glucose, so it enters your bloodstream more slowly and does not raise your blood glucose as high.

The theory sounds good, but the actual effect is modest. These drugs have been shown to cause "no improvement in mortality, morbidity (sickness) or quality of life."[99]

The main side effects are intestinal gas and diarrhea. The main drugs in this category are Glyset and Acarbose. Since all they do is slow the rate of starch breakdown, you can get the same benefit and more by reducing the amount of starch you eat.

**SGLT 2 inhibitors.** On March 29, 2013, the FDA approved the Johnson & Johnson drug, Invokana (generic name *canagliflozin*), for use in adults with Type 2 diabetes. This is the first drug in a new class of medicines known as sodium glucose cotransporter 2 (SGLT2) inhibitors.

SGLT 2 inhibitors work in the kidneys. Healthy kidneys do not excrete glucose in the urine. Instead, they reabsorb glucose and put it back in the bloodstream. However, people with diabetes typically have too much glucose in their blood already.

Scientists wondered, "Wouldn't it be nice if the kidneys just excreted the extra glucose?" And that is exactly what SGLT 2 inhibitors do. By blocking SGLT 2, the kidneys are prevented from reabsorbing glucose.

Invokana seems to help people lose weight and lower blood pressure. The major side effects are dehydration and yeast infections. It sounds pretty good, but this drug is extremely new—so we know very little about it. Already, regulators have concerns about heart, liver and cholesterol problems related to SGLT 2 inhibitors.[100]

In recently released FDA documents, studies showed that canagliflozin raised levels of LDL (bad cholesterol), and slightly increased risk of heart attack, stroke or death, compared to two other types of diabetes medications.[101]

Data from nine large patient studies also showed the pill increased risks of urinary tract infections and fungal infections in the genital area. This is because canagliflozin works by boosting blood sugar excretion *via* urine; and germs thrive on that sugar.[102]

## Should You Use Medications?

With the possible exception of metformin, all these drugs have problems or potential problems and risks that outweigh their limited effectiveness for most people. If you are recently diagnosed, and your doctor wants to start you on one of these drugs, you might wish to ask for a month or two to control your diabetes with lifestyle changes first.

If your glucose numbers are too high, or you are already on medications, you might benefit from a drug like basal insulin, metformin or an incretin drug—but ask your doctor what it will take to get off them as soon as possible. Inquire if there is a glucose number or an A1C reading that would cause him or her to reduce or stop your medication. If he or she says you will never get off them, you might want to start looking for another doctor.

Upgrading your diet and lifestyle will accomplish what drugs can—only better. If your pancreas does not produce enough insulin, try eating a low-carb, low-sugar diet. This will allow the insulin-producing cells in your pancreas to recover. Your insulin resistance will tend to fade away when the cells no longer need to protect themselves from too much starch and sugar. Although a minority of people with diabetes (about 20%) seem to have other problems that may require ongoing metformin, basal insulin or nutritional supplements, most people can usually reduce and eliminate diabetes drugs.

We advise that you view any drug as a temporary crutch that can provide assistance until you do not need it anymore. This may take more time or less, depending on how long you have had diabetes, how severe it has been, and how diligent and committed you are in adopting a healthier lifestyle.

We designed The 30-Day Diabetes Cure Plan to make it as easy as possible for you to make these important improvements in the shortest time possible. We suggest you begin the Plan as soon as you finish reading Part 1 of this book.

## Patient Case Study: Jeff

My name is Jeff and I'm 69 years old. I live in Florida. I've had Type 2 diabetes for about fifteen years now.

When I was first diagnosed, they told me that I could try and find a diet, but most people couldn't do that; and of course that challenged me a little bit and I decided that I would do it by diet. But as time went on and I was fully diagnosed with diabetes, the diet wasn't always working. I began following *The 30-Day Diabetes Cure*.

I've discovered that as I do it my blood sugar stays down—I have it under control at last. If I deviate from the plan—like when I go on trips and things like that—my sugar goes back up over 100 and I don't feel as good. I'm seeing a definite connection between organic foods, proper exercise, and the low sugar testing. I've never taken any medicine; and I believe in taking a number of supplements. I am so pleased with *The 30-Day Diabetes Cure*.

# CHAPTER 7

# TYPE 2 DIABETES CAN BE REVERSED: THE MEDICAL PROOF

*"Your mind is like a parachute —
it only works when it is open."*

—ANTHONY J. D'ANGELO, founder, Collegiate Empowerment

WHICH OF THE FOLLOWING statements about diabetes do you believe is correct?

■ Prediabetes (insulin-resistance) is a common blood sugar abnormality you can live with "normally" as long as you monitor your glucose levels and keep them controlled with medications.

■ Type 2 diabetes is progressive, incurable, and irreversible (unless you have bariatric weight-loss surgery), but researchers are closing in on a cure.

■ Type 1 diabetes is a purely genetic misfortune. There is nothing you can do about it except take insulin injections and hope for a pancreas transplant—or a new research break-through.

■ Diabetes is no big deal these days. By closely monitoring your blood sugar and follow-ing your doctor's orders, you can enjoy a normal life and escape the horrific complications of diabetes, including nerve damage, going blind and losing limbs through amputation—not to mention heart attack, stroke and Alzheimer's disease.

## Surprise: They Are All False!

Every one of these popular beliefs about diabetes is dead wrong—and in this chapter, we will show you clinical research that disputes each of them. Not only are all of these statements false, they are extremely *dangerous* if you have Type 2 diabetes or are on your way to devel-oping it. We realize you have probably heard each of these pronouncements from numerous respected sources: your doctor…your diabetes educator or dietician…the American Diabetes Association…the pharmaceutical industry…and the mainstream media.

Here is the critical thing to remember: The medical establishment has failed to contain the current diabetes epidemic. This is a serious failure of The System and *de facto* evidence that something is very, very wrong with the current "official" approach to diabetes. In *The 30-Day Diabetes Cure*, we will give you a positive, renewed sense of hope for your condition and your future health.

Can you trust that a simple lifestyle approach to such a serious health problem will work? *Absolutely.* While you probably are not hearing this from your doctor, plenty of scientific research proves that both prediabetes and Type 2 can be reversed with a few simple diet and lifestyle modifications, just like those presented in The 30-Day Diabetes Cure Plan. In addition to the personal testimonies of ex-diabetics in this book, we are including some of the most impressive research studies and historical anecdotes in this chapter. It is our hope that this scientific validation will give you confidence to embrace this approach.

## Lifestyle Modifications: From Past to Present

■ As far back as 1797—long before Type 2 was recognized as an official "disease"— Scottish physician John Rollo created the first dietary treatment that successfully managed his patients' symptoms. His prescription was an "animal food" diet that left no room for sugar, bread, or carbohydrates.[103]

■ In 1871, French physician Apollinaire Bouchardat noticed the disappearance of *glycosuria* (sugar in the urine) in his diabetes patients during the rationing of sugar, flour and bread during the Siege of Paris in the Franco-Prussian War. Noting his patients' improvement, he formulated a dietary approach that successfully treated this condition by withholding these foods from their diet.[104]

■ In 1982, nutritional researcher Kerin O'Dea restored a group of severely diabetic Australian aboriginal men to good health simply by getting them off the typical Western diet of refined carbohydrates and its accompanying sedentary lifestyle (the two major causes of Type 2). Not a drop of medication or insulin was required.[105]

The men were badly overweight and insulin-resistant, with seriously elevated cholesterol, triglycerides and high blood pressure (all major risk factors for heart attack and stroke). They were headed for a shortened lifespan with miserable complications – including blindness, heart failure, various cancers, and amputations of digits and limbs caused by nerve damage and gangrene. After just seven weeks on her plan, O'Dea drew blood samples and discovered these dramatic changes…

•**Triglycerides, glucose and cholesterol levels had plummeted into the healthy range.**

•**Blood pressure had dropped significantly and normalized.**

•**The men had lost an average of nearly 20 pounds each.**

In O'Dea's own words, "All of the metabolic abnormalities of Type 2 diabetes were either greatly improved or completely normalized." The markers for diabetes and heart disease were completely gone!

Her discovery, in our view, was as significant as some of the most famous in medical history. O'Dea's discovery could have prevented untold suffering and saved millions of lives had it been heeded and adopted in mainstream practice.

# Other Positive Clinical Studies

Other research has confirmed O'Dea's findings regarding the prevention and reversal of Type 2 and prediabetes, notably...

■ In 1984, the journal *Diabetes* reported on a clinical study done at the University of Vermont College of Medicine proving that increased physical activity boosts cell sensitivity to insulin – thus reversing the insulin resistance that is the precursor to (and underlying cause of) Type 2 diabetes.[106]

■ The findings of the Vermont study were confirmed by a 2003 research trial published in *Diabetes Care*, demonstrating that sedentary adults who simply added walking to their daily routine cut their risk of developing insulin resistance (prediabetes), *even if they didn't lose any weight.*[107]

■ Researchers at the UCLA School of Medicine found that 50% of Type 2 patients were able to reverse their diabetes in just three weeks by making small changes in their diet and adding moderate exercise. "The study shows, contrary to common belief, that Type 2 diabetes and metabolic syndrome can be reversed solely through lifestyle changes," according to lead researcher Dr. Christian K. Roberts.[108]

■ In 2001, the *New England Journal of Medicine* published research showing that even the simplest dietary changes can reduce the risk of developing Type 2 diabetes by nearly 60%. Subsequent studies (which included switching to many of the delicious, healthful foods you will discover in The 30-Day Diabetes Cure Plan) improved this reduction in diabetes to greater than 95%.[109]

■ Also in 2001, the largest study ever conducted to test the ability of diet and exercise to prevent prediabetes from turning into full-blown Type 2 proved to be a smashing success. Doctors at 27 medical centers around the country enrolled 3,234 people and assigned them to receive the drug metformin (Glucophage), a placebo, or a lifestyle program involving classes and coaches who kept track of their progress. After three years, the lifestyle program cut the participants' risk of developing diabetes by more than 50%—a much better result than metformin provided. "I do not see this as out of reach for the 10 million people who are at high risk for diabetes," said David Nathan, MD, of Massachusetts General Hospital. (That figure is closer to 80 million Americans today.)[110]

■ A study published in the medical journal *Nutrition & Metabolism* found that increasing the protein content in the diet of people with Type 2 diabetes, while reducing the amount of carbohydrates (similar to the diet modifications you will be making on The 30-Day Diabetes Cure Plan), produces the same glucose-lowering effect as the leading diabetes medications.[111]

This simple dietary swap allowed patients to reduce and eliminate their pharmaceutical medications.

■ A 2005 study conducted by researchers at Duke University Medical School found that diabetic patients who reduced their consumption of high-GI carbs were able to significantly reduce their medication or discontinue it altogether.[112]

■ Another Duke University study in 2007 found that Type 2 diabetics who reduced their consumption of carbohydrates achieved better blood sugar control and more effective weight loss than those who went on a typical calorie-restricted diet. After just six months, the low-carb group had lower A1C results and lost more weight, with 95% being able to reduce or even completely eliminate their diabetes medications. Plus, as little as a 5% weight loss—about 10 pounds for most people in the study—reduced the risk of diabetes by 58%. That is truly remarkable.

"It is simple," says Eric Westman, MD, director of Duke's Lifestyle Medicine Program and lead author of the study. "If you cut out the carbohydrates, your blood sugar goes down, and you lose weight, which lowers your blood sugar even further. It is a one-two punch."[113]

■ An extraordinary study in 2011 in the UK demonstrated that even people with advanced Type 2 diabetes—when the pancreas is exhausted and its insulin-producing beta-cells are damaged—can become diabetes-free quite quickly by making dietary changes.

In the study, patients with advanced Type 2 diabetes were put on a very low-glycemic, low-calorie, plant-based diet. After just one week, their blood sugars normalized, triglyceride levels fell and the pancreas recovered (as measured by MRI) to the point where they were taken off their medication.[114]

According to Mark Hyman, MD: "This remarkable result showed unequivocally that even people with advanced Type 2 diabetes, when the pancreas has pooped-out and the insulin-producing beta cells are damaged, can recover and diabetes can be reversed rather quickly (*one week!*) through dramatic changes in diet (a very low-glycemic, low-calorie, plant-based diet)."[115]

This study adds to the mounting body of evidence indicating that Type 2 is not a progressive, incurable condition—and that diet, alone, can be more therapeutic than medication.

"To have people free of diabetes after years with the condition is remarkable," said Dr. Roy Taylor, professor of medicine and metabolism at Newcastle University in the UK, commenting on the impressive results.

■ A 2012 study sponsored by the Centers for Disease Control and Prevention (CDC) and published in the *Journal of the American Medical Association*[116] demonstrates that complete remission of Type 2 diabetes (defined as "glucose normalization without medication") can be achieved by lifestyle interventions, alone. Participants in the study who succeeded were able to eliminate medications by implementing simple diet and lifestyle improvements.

■ The Look AHEAD Study is a 13-year ongoing study of 5,000 people funded by the National Institutes of Health. It is comparing the effects of group lifestyle modifications and educational programs for diabetes prevention to regular medical care, consisting of individual visits to a diabetic educator, nutritionist and physician. To date, the lifestyle program has proven remarkably more effective at lowering blood sugar, heart disease risk factors, blood pressure, and weight than conventional medical care.[117] When this study is completed, it may radically alter the way Type 2 and other lifestyle health problems will be treated in the future.

## Yes, You Can Reverse Type 2 Diabetes

Do not let anyone tell you that Type 2 diabetes has no cure. As the aforementioned and other studies show, this is simply not true. Type 2 diabetes is not a life sentence (unless you choose to go on drugs)—you do not have to live with it forever. Nearly 100% of all Type 2 diabetics can successfully eliminate their symptoms of diabetes and reduce the high risk of developing disabling and deadly complications. All you need to do is implement the lifestyle changes described in *The 30-Day Diabetes Cure*. These same improvements will also drastically reduce your risk of developing Type 2 in the first place.

### Patient Case Study: Michelle

Hello, my name is Michelle and I live in New Mexico. I was diagnosed with diabetes 17 years ago. For years I took prescription medications—first one, then two, then three. I gained weight. I felt tired. I was depressed. I ate right and exercised but year after year my diabetes just got worse. Then I heard of the *30-Day Diabetes Cure*.

I was determined to follow it and have been able to do so now for over a year. I now have so much more energy, and I weigh less too. I no longer take prescription medications, my blood sugar is under control, and now feel great.

# CHAPTER 8

# 12 COMMON DIABETES MYTHS
# THAT KEEP YOU SICK

*"The great enemy of the truth is very often not the lie,
deliberate, contrived and dishonest,
but the myth, persistent, persuasive and unrealistic."*

—JOHN F. KENNEDY, 35th U.S. president, 1917–1963

IN THE LAST CHAPTER, we made you aware of some of the most important facts that you are not hearing about lifestyle treatments for Type 2 diabetes and prediabetes. Now we want to debunk some of the most prevalent myths and misconceptions that you are hearing from doctors, drug companies, the mainstream media, and the government. In our opinion, these myths are very dangerous because they keep you dependent on doctors and drugs for your well-being. Even worse, they deprive you of the hope of ever being free from diabetes.

Of course, the greatest myth people are hearing from their doctors and the media is that Type 2 diabetes is not reversible or curable. We hope that we have convinced you of the utter falsehood of this claim in Chapter 1. So now, let us examine some of the other equally egregious misconceptions and misunderstandings about diabetes, so that you and your loved ones will know the truth.

## Myth 1: "Type 2 Diabetes Is Genetic"

While it is true that Type 1 diabetes (sometimes referred to as insulin-dependent diabetes or juvenile diabetes) is genetic in origin, Type 2 is not. Some people with Type 2 are convinced that it is hereditary because they have a family history of it. They may have diabetic grandparents, aunts or uncles, even parents and siblings and believe "I got it because it's in my family." But that's not quite how it works.

The human genome is like a collection of switches that get turned off or on by how and where you live your life. Even if there were specific genes for Type 2—and scientist are still searching for them[118]—they could only be switched on (expressed) by diet, lifestyle and environmental factors that cause diabetes. The same is true for cancer and many other health problems. A European study in 2000 determined that 90% of our health risks are due to environmental triggers, not genetics.[119] This includes the inflammation in our bodies, our levels of insulin and glucose, the biological consequences of stress, the amounts of free radicals in us, and the beneficial or pathological bacteria in our gastrointestinal tract. Our environment affects our genes, as well. Factors such as the quality of our food, air and water also affect gene expression.

It is not scientifically accurate to say that Type 2 diabetes is a genetically predetermined condition that will happen to you no matter what. Even if the genes you may have inherited from your parents or grandparents could put you at greater risk, this does not mean you are destined to develop it. Your diet and lifestyle determines whether these genes get turned on or not. So, in the end it is up to you. You are more powerful than your genetics.[120]

## Myth 2: "Eating Fatty Foods Causes Diabetes"

You probably have heard this one before from mainstream health experts, doctors and passionate vegetarians and vegans. But they are wrong. Type 2 diabetes and prediabetes are caused by chronically high insulin levels, which lead to insulin resistance, abdominal fat accumulation, death of pancreatic beta cells, insulin-dependent diabetes, and all of the other serious complications that occur with diabetes and metabolic syndrome.

Since dietary fat does not trigger insulin release, it cannot be responsible for insulin resistance and Type 2 diabetes. Only carbohydrates—and especially simple carbohydrates such as sugar and refined grains—can do this.

Humans evolved on a diet of fatty animal foods over millions of years. Diabetes was virtually unknown in the Paleolithic and Neolithic Ages, when humans were hunter-gatherers and existed on a diet of predominately animal protein and saturated fat. This is confirmed by archaeological observations of modern hunter-gatherer societies.[121, 122]

Entire populations and tribes of certain cultures have existed almost exclusively on fat-rich animal foods (some still do) without any sign of diabetes or its complications. These include the Masai tribe and Samburu nomads of Africa, the Inuit Eskimos of Greenland and Alaska, Australian Aborigines, and Native Americans of the Great Plains, to name a few. The Inuit diet, for example, consists almost entirely of fatty fish (most notably whale blubber) and wild game. They ate fat and protein almost exclusively—and only about 3% carbohydrates, consisting of scarcely available plant foods and seaweed. Prior to the introduction of the Western-style diet of processed foods, sugar and refined carbohydrates, the Greenland Eskimos had the lowest incidence of heart disease and diabetes on Earth.

The emergence of adult-onset diabetes coincided with the introduction of agriculture, by which grains and refined carbohydrates entered the human diet. In the beginning and through the ages, diabetes was limited to corpulent royalty and the idle rich, who feasted nightly on banquets featuring breads, sweet puddings, beer and ale, and lavish desserts. It was not until the last half of the nineteenth century and into the twentieth century, when the consumption of table sugar (sucrose) increased across all classes of society, that diabetes became more widespread.[123] The result was bulging bellies of abdominal fat, obesity, prediabetes and diabetes, and heart disease on a scale never before seen. The refined carbohydrate, not dietary fat, was —and still is—the cause.

In fact, long before the discovery of synthetic insulin by the Canadian physician, Frederick Banting (who won the Nobel Prize for this in 1923), the standard treatment for diabetes was the substitution of animal protein and fat in place of carbohydrates in the diet, and a strict limitation of carbohydrates to 10 grams per day.[124]

■ In 1862, the great British surgeon, Dr. William Harvey, after attending a lecture on diabetes given by the French physician, Claude Bernard, formulated a dietary regimen based on Bernard's revelations. He prescribed a diet consisting exclusively of meat and dairy foods (both containing high levels of fat) to halt the secretion of sugar in the urine of diabetics, while having patients completely abstain from sugars and starches. Harvey's diet proved successful.[125]

■ Apollinaire Bouchardat, a nineteenth-century French physician, observed that sugar in the urine of his diabetes patients diminished during the 1871 siege of Paris by the Prussian army, during which food—especially bread—was in short supply. When the siege was over, he astutely duplicated this result by having his patients abstain from bread, baked goods and other starchy carbohydrate foods, and to fast intermittently.[126]

■ In 1892, Dr. William Osler, one of the four founders of the Johns Hopkins Hospital, authored one of the iconic medical texts of the modern age, *Principles and Practice of Medicine*. In it, he advised treating diabetics with a diet consisting of 2% carbohydrates.[127]

■ Before the discovery of insulin, the leading treatment for diabetes was a high-fat, low-carb diet. Dr. Elliott Proctor Joslin, MD, a Harvard- and Yale-educated physician, relied on it more than a century ago to successfully sustain dozens of diabetic patients—including his own mother. His treatment? A diet made of 70% fat and just 10% carbohydrates.[128]

This dietary approach is still proving successful today. For instance, Jeff Volek, PhD, RD, of the University of Connecticut, and his research team, have repeatedly demonstrated in both humans and animals that a high-fat, low-carbohydrate diet reverses insulin resistance and diminishes abdominal fat. The diet he used was composed of 63% fat, 28% protein, and 9% carbohydrate.[129, 130]

Dr. Volek's high-fat diet is referred to as "ketogenic," meaning that insulin levels drop so low that the body enters a state called ketosis. In ketosis, the muscles and tissues are able to burn stored body fat for energy in the form of essential fatty acids. This is possible because insulin, which keeps body fat imprisoned, is not present. (This is normally what happens between meals, during sleep and when fasting.) Instead of glucose, the brain utilizes fat molecules called ketones, which have been transformed from fatty acids by the liver. In essence, with insulin absent, your body is able to live off your reserves of stored body fat. And without needing to regulate blood glucose, your insulin-producing beta cells and pancreas are allowed to rest and repair themselves.*

---

*Ketosis is often confused with diabetic *ketoacidosis*, a serious and often fatal state that develops when the body is unable to produce enough insulin. Ketoacidosis occurs when the body is producing large quantities of ketone bodies via the metabolism of fatty acids (ketosis), but insufficient insulin to slow this production. The excess ketone bodies can significantly acidify the blood. In healthy individuals or Type 2 diabetics still producing sufficient insulin, this normally does not occur because insulin is still being produced in response to rising ketone/blood glucose concentration. Ketoacidosis can be smelled on a person's breath as sour fruit or nail polish remover due to acetone, a direct by-product of the spontaneous decomposition of acetoacetic acid.

Ketosis is a normal physiologic state that evolved in the human body over millions of years of feast and famine. It is an elegant backup system that allows the body and brain to function from stored body fat when food calories are not available. Some researchers report that the heart and brain run 25% more efficiently on ketones than blood glucose.[131]

Certainly one of the most impressive displays of the power of the ketogenic diet over Type 2 diabetes was conducted by Duke University's Eric Westman, MD, which we briefly mentioned in Chapter 3. In this study, obese Type 2 diabetics were allowed unlimited amounts of animal foods (i.e., meat, chicken, turkey, other fowl, fish, shellfish) and eggs; limited amounts of hard cheese (e.g., cheddar or Swiss, four ounces per day), fresh cheese (e.g., cottage or ricotta, two ounces per day), salad vegetables (two cupfuls per day), and non-starchy vegetables (one cupful per day)—but almost no grains or refined carbohydrates, including wheat products and baked goods, sugars, rice, potatoes, or fruit (carb intake was limited to 20 grams per day). The composition of this diet was very similar to that used by Drs. Osler and Banting prior to the discovery of insulin.

The results of Dr. Westman's diet were nothing short of spectacular. After six months, participants lost, on average, 25 pounds and five inches from their waistlines (representative of reductions in dangerous abdominal fat)…and triglycerides were reduced by 70 mg/dl. More importantly, A1C was reduced from 8.8% to 7.3%. And 95% of participants were able to reduce their diabetes medications—with 25% being able to completely eliminate them, including insulin.[132]

Indeed, the effects were most impressive in the patients taking insulin. Those taking from 40 to 90 units of insulin before the study were able to completely eliminate their insulin use, while also improving their blood glucose levels.*

This means that 25% of the diabetics adopting Dr. Westman's ketogenic diet for just six months became "ex-diabetics" who no longer needed medication. The remainder, while still diabetic, enjoyed better blood glucose control and reduced need for insulin and other medications. Lifestyle modification using low-carbohydrate diet interventions are effective for improving obesity and Type 2 diabetes, and may play an important role in reversing the current epidemic of "diabesity" (the term used for the comorbidities of Type 2 diabetes and obesity).

So, we reiterate the question we posed in Chapter 1 "Is this a cure?" We certainly think so.

And so does William Davis, MD, physician and author of *Wheat Belly*, the *New York Times* bestseller that encourages everyone—especially diabetics—to abandon wheat products to get control of their blood sugar levels, to avoid serious medical conditions such as heart disease, cancer, and Alzheimer's, and to improve their general health. Here is what he writes about these remarkable new research findings regarding reversing Type 2 diabetes:

---

*Because this effect occurs immediately upon implementing the dietary changes, individuals with Type 2 diabetes who are unable to adjust their own medication or self-monitor their blood glucose should not make these dietary changes unless under close medical supervision. Dr. Westman reports that Type 2 diabetics taking insulin need to reduce their dose by 50% *the first day* they engage in such a diet to avoid excessively low blood sugars (hypoglycemia).

"The studies to date have achieved proof of concept: Reduction of carbohydrates improves blood sugar behavior, reducing the diabetic tendency. If taken to extremes, it is possible to *eliminate* diabetes medications in as little as six months. In some instances, I believe it is safe to call that a *cure* (emphasis ours), provided excess carbohydrates don't make their way back into the diet. Let me say that again: If sufficient pancreatic beta cells remain and have not yet been utterly decimated by long-standing glucotoxicity, lipotoxicity, and inflammation, it is entirely possible for some, if not most, prediabetics and diabetics to be cured of their condition, something that virtually never happens with conventional low-fat diets such as that advocated by the American Diabetes Association."[133]

## Myth 3: "Your Body Needs Carbohydrates"

This will come as a shock—but your body does not need carbs.

No doubt you have been hearing since high school biology how vital these big three macronutrients – protein, fat, and carbohydrate—are to your health and very life. But the truth is, only two of these are actually *essential* in this respect.

"Essential" means that your body is not able to produce or synthesize these and must rely on dietary sources. While there are many different types of fats, your body cannot live without the essential fatty acids (EFAs). These are the omega-3 and omega-6 fatty acids. Protein, too, is essential because it is made up of amino acids—the building blocks of muscle and tissue and a prime source of energy for your brain. Your body cannot manufacture all the different amino acids it needs and therefore must obtain its essential amino acids from your diet.

But carbohydrates are a different story. There is no such thing as an "essential carbohydrate." While it is true that carbohydrates break down into glucose and glucose is the prime energy source for the muscles in your brain, carbohydrates are not essential for this glucose. As you have just read, your body is perfectly capable of converting your stored body fat (in the absence of insulin and carbohydrates) into ketones that will fuel your muscles, organs, tissues, and brain. In a similar fashion, your body is also able to convert protein into glucose through a process called *gluconeogenesis*. If you never ate another carbohydrate again, you would not die.[134] So please do not believe anyone who tries to tell you: "You must eat enough carbohydrates every day to provide your body with energy in the form of glucose in the blood."

Instead, you should prioritize the macronutrients in your diet according to their importance to your body. This means healthy fats first, high-quality protein second, and finally vitamin-rich complex carbohydrates loaded with fiber. We suggest a balance of 50% healthy fat, 30% clean protein, and 20% (or less) complex carbs (50:30:20). The complex carbohydrates should be vegetables and fruits in their whole, natural form to provide your body with the vitamins, minerals, fiber, and phytonutrients necessary for optimum health.

It is certainly possible to achieve this ratio without animal products. Vegetables contain protein and fat as well as carbohydrates, after all. Nuts and seeds are good sources of protein and fat. And almost all foods have some carbohydrate content, even meat and eggs (only fat is completely entirely carbohydrate-free). But in going the vegetarian and vegan routes, you must be careful not to consume too many carbohydrates—even if they are complex carbs—at the expense of your fat and protein intake. Whole grains and starchy vegetables such as beans, for instance, can be a problem for some people with insulin resistance because they will elevate blood glucose and insulin levels. (Vegetable oils, such as corn oil and canola oil, should be avoided because they oxidize rapidly in the body and have been linked to inflammation, cancer, and other serious health problems.) The only way to tell is to test your glucose level one to two hours after eating, to monitor the effect these foods have on your metabolism. (We call this "smart monitoring," which you will learn on Day 1 of The 30-Day Diabetes Cure Plan.) Achieving a 50:30:20 ratio of healthy fat/protein/complex carb on a plant-based diet will require knowledge and planning on your part.

Consuming vegetables, fruits, whole grains, beans, legumes, and other starches—features of a vegetarian diet—can improve blood glucose control and make your body more responsive to insulin. This can result in taking less medication and lowering your risk of diabetes-related complications. But even a vegetarian diet can have the opposite effect on blood glucose if it is rich in simple carbohydrates—especially starches such as sugar, flour, bread, cereal, pasta, potatoes, and rice. These simple carbohydrates trigger insulin, which can store the calories you eat into fat. The more protein you eat, the more the fat-burning hormone glucagon is released. The more carbohydrates you eat, the more insulin will be released. This is why we have included animal products in The 30-Day Diabetes Cure Plan.

Reducing the carbohydrate content in this equation further, while increasing the fat and protein, will give you even better control of your blood glucose and insulin levels. For example, a study compared the glucose-lowering effect of three diets: a very low-fat diet (VLF), a high unsaturated fat diet (HUF) and a very low carbohydrate diet (VLCARB) over an eight-week period. Here is the composition of each diet:

- **VLF: 10% fat, 20% protein, 70% carb**
- **HUF: 30% fat, 20% protein, 50% carb**
- **VLCARB: 61% fat, 35% protein, 4% carb**

The results were very revealing. Those on the VLCARB diet lowered their fasting insulin by 33%, compared to a 19% reduction on the HUF diet, and no change on the VLF. The VLCARB meals also resulted in significantly lower glucose and insulin readings after the meal, compared to the VLF and HUF meals. All three diets decreased fasting glucose, blood pressure and CRP (a measure of inflammation). The authors concluded that the VLCARB diet was more effective in improving triglyceride levels, increasing HDL cholesterol, and improving fasting and post-meal glucose and insulin concentrations. They noted that VLCARB diets may be useful in the short-term management of insulin resistance and high blood triglycerides.[135] Clearly, the lower carbohydrate diet produced the more desirable responses in blood glucose and insulin.

# Myth 4: "You Should Eat a Low-Fat Diet"

The diet that the American Diabetes Association (ADA) generally recommends for people with Type 2 and prediabetes is the official low-fat diet that has been foisted on the public since the 1980s. This is because the medical community ardently believes that dietary fat—and saturated fat, in particular—is a leading cause of heart disease, despite copious research that prove this is simply not so. Since heart disease is the leading complication and cause of death among diabetics, the ADA embraces and encourages this low-fat obsession, too.

Here is the "essential diabetes diet" advice that people are receiving from mainstream doctors, diabetes educators, dieticians, and the popular press: "People with diabetes should make sure their diet is balanced and healthy, which means including:

- **Plenty of fruits and vegetables;**
- **Lean, skinless meats, like chicken and turkey, and fish;**
- **Fiber-rich foods, such as peas and beans;**
- **Whole grains, such as whole wheat bread, brown rice, and whole wheat pasta;**
- **Low-fat or fat-free dairy products;**
- **Limited intake of fat and salt."**[136]

Perhaps you have heard this advice before? Well, it might surprise you to learn that the ADA recommends that diabetics consume between 45–60g of carbohydrates at each meal. According to the ADA, more than half of your plate at every meal should contain carbohydrate foods, such as brown rice, whole wheat pasta, and whole wheat bread[137]—even though all of these foods will spike your blood glucose and insulin levels, because they are referred to as "high-glycemic-index carbohydrates."

The Glycemic Index (GI) is a rating system that ranks how much and how rapidly a food raises your blood glucose. The lower a food's GI number, the less it affects your blood sugar and insulin levels. For example, a small handful of peanuts has a low GI rank of 7, so it will cause your blood glucose to barely budge. On the other hand, a slice of whole wheat bread has a GI rating of 71. By way of comparison, white sugar has a GI rating of 60. Yes, whole wheat bread spikes your blood sugar higher and faster than eating table sugar! (For the GI ratings of over 100 common foods, see Appendix B, beginning on page 370.)

As you will recall from Chapter 2, foods and beverages that spike your blood glucose trigger a surge of insulin within minutes. The resulting rush of insulin stores the glucose away as glycogen and fat. A few hours later, your blood sugar drops lower than it was before you ate. Your body has run out of fuel, but your blood insulin level is still high enough to prevent you from burning your own fat. The result is hunger and a craving for more carbohydrates. This is a vicious cycle that increases your weight and worsens your insulin resistance.

So why would the ADA, the world's leading advocate for diabetic health, recommend a diet that is high in foods that raise blood glucose and insulin?

# Triglycerides and Heart Disease

There is plenty of research that proves the correlation between triglycerides and heart disease...

•In 1956, research by John W. Gofman, MD, PhD, called "The Father of Clinical Lipidology," discovered that the majority of people with heart disease have elevated triglycerides and depressed HDL—not "high cholesterol." Gofman blamed heart disease on consuming too many *carbohydrates (carbohydrate-induced lipemia)*. "Restricting carbohydrates would lower this risk," he wrote.[138]

•Gofman's findings were confirmed in 1961 by E.H. "Peter" Ahrens Jr., MD, of Rockefeller University and Margaret Albrink, MD, of Yale, who reported that elevated triglycerides were associated with increased risk of heart disease and that low-fat, high-carbohydrate diets elevated triglycerides and increased the risk of heart disease.[139]

•In 1967, Peter Kuo, MD, of the University of Pennsylvania published a research paper in the *Journal of the American Medical Association* reporting that 90% of his heart patients displayed elevated triglycerides, with normal cholesterol levels.[140]

•Three years later, researchers Albrink, Kuo, Lars Carlson, and Joseph Goldstein announced that elevated triglycerides are more common in heart disease patients than high cholesterol. They confirmed that the majority of people with heart disease have what Gofman's study called *carbohydrate-induced lipemia*.[141]

•In 1976, the FDA approved hydrogenated oil (later identified as trans fats), even though biochemist, Mary Enig, PhD, warned that these fats interfere with insulin receptors on cell membranes, thus increasing the risk of Type 2 diabetes. More than 30 years later, the FDA lumps them together with saturated fat and weakly warns Americans against consumption of these "bad fats."[142]

•In the early 70s, the National Institutes of Health spent $115 million on a huge, decade-long clinical trial to test its stubbornly held belief that eating less saturated fat would curb heart disease. The clinical trial, known as the Multiple Risk Factor Intervention Trial (commonly referred to as MRFIT, or "Mr. Fit"), was a colossal failure. It could not show that a single heart attack had been prevented. When the disappointing results were published in 1982, *The Wall Street Journal* headline announced: "Heart Attacks: A Test Collapses."[143]

•In 1988, Gerald Reaven, MD, of the University of California announced his discovery of "Syndrome X" after 20 years of research in carbohydrate metabolism. Now referred to as metabolic syndrome (or diabetes-related heart disease), it is a cluster of metabolic abnormalities that include high blood glucose, elevated insulin levels, high triglycerides, and low levels of protective HDL cholesterol. In his book *Syndrome X*, Dr. Reaven states that the real culprit in heart disease is excess sugar and excess simple carbohydrates, which elevate triglycerides—not dietary fat or red meat.[144]

We wonder, too, because low-fat, high-carb diets do not improve insulin resistance—nor do they decrease your risk of heart disease, heart attack, or stroke. On the contrary, low-fat, high-carb diets make these conditions *worse* because they elevate triglycerides in the blood, a more dangerous risk factor for heart disease, insulin resistance, and obesity than cholesterol or dietary fat.

The fats that cause heart disease are not dietary fats. Rather, they are triglyceride fats, which are converted in the liver from excess blood glucose into a lipoprotein molecule called VLDL (short for very low density lipoprotein), a dangerous form of LDL cholesterol that inflames and damages artery walls, which, in turn, initiates the plaque-formation process there. In addition, excess levels of triglyceride fats destroy beta cells in the pancreas (lipotoxicity) and impair insulin production.

So, yes—fat *is* a cause agent in Type 2 diabetes and cardiovascular disease. But, with the exception of hydrogenated trans fat and refined polyunsaturated vegetable oils, the fat that causes all this trouble is not dietary fat or saturated fat. Instead, it is triglyceride fats manufactured in the liver and caused by the overconsumption of sugar, sweets, and simple carbohydrates.

More than a dozen peer-reviewed studies published since 2003 show that a *low-carb, high-fat diet* is more effective at reducing overall heart-disease risk than the ADA's low-fat, high-carb guidelines.

"Many people are essentially cured of their [Type 2] diabetes by low-carbohydrate diets, but that message is not getting out," says Richard Feinman, PhD of the SUNY Downstate Medical Center in Brooklyn, New York.

Dr. Nuttall's studies at the Minneapolis V.A. Medical Center, which were published in the medical journal *Diabetes*, found that Type 2s significantly improved their blood glucose levels simply by switching from the ADA's low-fat diet to a low-carb diet (50% fat, 30% protein, and 20% carbs).

"We were shocked," said Dr. Nuttall. "We thought they'd be improved, but we didn't think it would be improved as much as it was. The results were better than you get when you put patients on oral agents (drugs)."

Two months later, Dr. Nuttall released another cutting-edge study in *Nutrition and Metabolism*, which also found that diabetics can manage and control their disease simply by eating ample protein and fats, and restricting carbs—without needing to lose weight or taking insulin medications. These are the same results being achieved by Type 2s (now "ex-Type 2s") who have followed The 30-Day Diabetes Cure Plan.

It's not the latest discovery. This proof has been around since the turn of the 20th century. The cure for diabetes is what you eat—not the pills you take.

# Myth 5: "The ADA Acts in Your Best Interests"

Why would the ADA promote a diet that is dominated by carbohydrates which are known to raise blood glucose? And why are ADA treatment guidelines not more aggressive in discouraging carbohydrate consumption in favor of more healthy fats and protein, which actually reduce triglyceride levels in the blood?

The answer can be found in its official three-pronged approach to the treatment of diabetes: "For most people with Type 2 diabetes, blood glucose levels can be managed through diet, exercise, and oral diabetes medications." But when you look at how modern medicine "manages" Type 2, all you see is the third prong: medications. The vast majority of doctors emphasize the need for their diabetic patients to "normalize" their blood glucose, but recommend that this be accomplished with oral drugs or insulin therapy, rather than restricting carbohydrate consumption.

Most people believe the ADA is a group of dedicated researchers and doctors, tirelessly searching for a diabetes cure. But probe deeper and some troubling conflicts of interest become apparent. The lion's share of the ADA's funds comes from drug manufacturers, pharmacy chains, food companies, and the makers of products that benefit from the diabetes explosion. As of October 2012, its annual revenue was reported in excess of $200 million.[145]

The lion's share of the ADA's funds comes from drug manufacturers, pharmacy chains, food companies, and the makers of products that benefit from the diabetes explosion. Its 2009 annual report cites a 12-month budget to be a whopping $205 million—more than 60% of which came from "donations and special events."

The ADA's corporate sponsors include Walgreens, Rite-Aid Pharmacies, Roche Laboratories, Catherine's Plus Sizes, Boehringer Ingelheim Pharmaceuticals, Bristol-Myers Squibb, and many other pharmaceutical companies. In fact, the list of ADA donors is a who's who of Big Pharma, with the major drug companies kicking in millions in 2008 alone[146]—including $2.8 million from Takeda Pharmaceuticals, the maker of the ADA-approved diabetes drug, Actos.

And the ADA is not shy about where it's true allegiance lies. Its 2008–2011 *Strategic Plan* stated that the organization's internal goal is to "maximize corporate, pharmaceutical and foundation contributions"…in order to achieve "an annual compound growth rate of 9.1%." The ADA's 2012–2015 Plan is focused on community strategy and recognition of diabetes as a global epidemic, but it states that one of the organization's primary goals is to "Execute a comprehensive, coordinated constituent engagement strategy to increase loyalty and lifetime value of donors and event participants" (see *http://main.diabetes.org/dorg/PDFs/American_Diabetes_Association-2012-2015-Strategic-Plan.pdf*). Do they hope to achieve this by helping to generate more sales for their pharmaceutical "partners?"

More than half of the ADA's massive $200+ million budget goes for "information, advocacy, and public awareness"—but it seems to be "advocating and informing" the public more about drug treatment than refraining from carbohydrate consumption. When you visit their website (*www.diabetes.org*), you will see that the ADA's primary "Stop Diabetes" educational strategy is to vigorously encourage diabetics to test their blood sugar regularly and to take their drugs faithfully. But it is hard to imagine how this approach will halt the spread of diabetes, which is already a global epidemic (now 400 million people worldwide and counting).

Given its close ties to the drug industry, it is hard for us to believe that the ADA is objective and impartial in its treatment and public education recommendations. Drug companies are expected to sell $20 billion worth of diabetes drugs in the US this year—and the ADA is the lynchpin of their marketing strategy. A revealing article in the *New York Times* explains how these drug companies continually advertise to doctors in ADA journals and announce new medicines at ADA conventions, where a coming-out party for a new drug can drive a stock price higher.[147]

Food companies are in on the action, too. SnackWell's Sugar-Free Lemon Créme cookies have sported the ADA logo, despite the fact that these cookies contain almost as many calories as ordinary sweets; so have Sugar-Freedom Eskimo Pie and Frosted Shredded Wheat. Kraft Foods' deal with the ADA allowed it to paste the ADA logo on Post Raisin Bran, Cream of Wheat, Sugar-Free Jell-O, and Cool Whip Lite.

"Of particular concern," the *Times* article notes, "is a three-year, $1.5 million sponsorship deal with Cadbury-Schweppes, the world's largest confectioner. Under the deal, which meets the new guidelines, Cadbury is promoted as an ADA sponsor in several settings, and has permission to use the ADA logo on its Diet-Rite sodas, Snapple unsweetened tea, and Mott's Apple Sauce, among other products. Critics say the ADA affiliation has helped Cadbury pose as a concerned corporate citizen, even as it supplies grocery stores with sugary and fattening foods like Dr Pepper and the Cadbury Creme Egg."

Those deals have expired and the ADA has tightened up its requirements for selling its seal of approval for $400,000 per year. However, the ADA's Continuing Education Courses for registered dieticians are being taught by the Coca-Cola Company's Beverage Institute.[148] Current food-related sponsors include Domino sugar, Equal and Splenda artificial sweetener, Cary's sugar-free syrup, Boar's Head lunch meats, and the weight loss program Nutrisystem.[149]

The ADA diet continues to be carb-centric, with carbohydrates comprising up to 60% of what its doctors say diabetics should be consuming, including (remember?) whole wheat bread, brown rice, and whole wheat pasta. Many of these carbohydrate foods spike blood glucose almost as soon as they are eaten.

"They're contradicting themselves," says Richard Feinman, PhD, of the SUNY Downstate Medical Center. "They want diabetics to take medication to lower their blood sugar, but recommend a diet that has the opposite effect."[150]

According to Walter Willett, MD, DrPH, of Harvard School of Public Health: "Overconsumption of sugar and other rapidly-absorbed carbohydrates can cause excessive demand for insulin and ultimately lead to failure of the pancreas to secrete adequate amounts of insulin."[151]

Dr. Willett cites three major, long-term studies confirming this: The Nurses' Health Study I (127,000 participants), the Health Professionals Follow-Up Study (52,000 participants), and The Nurses' Health Study II (116,000 participants).[152]

"All three studies showed that people with a higher intake of refined starches and sugars had approximately twice of risk of diabetes compared to those with a low intake," he concludes.[153]

We should not forget that the ADA sets treatment guidelines for diabetes—and its primary emphasis is on drugs, not diet. Our biggest concern is that this emphasis on medications over modifications sends a dangerous message to patients: "Do not worry too much about what you eat. Your meds will keep your blood glucose in check and you will be okay."[154]

As you have already seen, patients who rely on diabetes drugs will certainly *not* be okay.

## Myth 6: "You Must Test Your Glucose Levels"

This is a little tricky. Glucose monitoring is necessary and useful for Type 1 patients who take insulin—and occasionally for some Type 2 patients prone to low blood sugar (hypoglycemia), particularly those on insulin or sulfonylurea drugs. But in general, Type 2 diabetes can be managed quite effectively with the simple diet and exercise you will discover in the 30-Day Diabetes Cure Plan. Vigilant, glucose self-monitoring several times a day is a nuisance and has been shown to be ineffective for most Type 2 and prediabetes patients (except those on insulin).

The only time we recommend glucose monitoring is when you perform what we call "smart monitoring," which you will learn on Day 1 of the 30-Day Diabetes Cure Plan, beginning on page 165. We call it "smart" monitoring because you will be observing how certain foods and situations directly affect your blood glucose levels. Instead of taking our word that fruit juice or whole wheat bread or a bran muffin will spike your numbers, you will see the proof with your own eyes. You will also be able to see how emotional stress kicks up your glucose—and how meditation, yoga, and relaxation lower it. And you will be able to tell which types of exercise are best for reducing your glucose levels. This is the smart way to use your glucose monitor because it can educate you about what works to improve your health—and what does not. Testing your blood with this purpose will also call your attention to the nutritional supplements that help keep your numbers in the healthy range. Having this direct feedback is like a compass that can lead you on a direct course home.

Other than for this purpose, we see little value in monitoring your glucose levels. Clinical studies conclusively show that glucose monitoring does little-to-nothing for preventing or improving diabetic complications. Furthermore, self-monitoring of blood glucose may encourage some patients to continue the same bad diet and poor lifestyle habits that allowed the disease to get a foothold in the first place. For example, you could eat a high-carb meal and "cover it" with a dose of medication. The result might be that your glucose level appears to be normal. As a result, you might conclude that you can eat whatever you like and remain safe from complications. But you would be making a big mistake. Two studies published in the *British Medical Journal* confirm this:

■ The first, known as the ESMON Study (O'Kane, 2008), split a group of newly diagnosed Type 2 patients into equal self-monitoring and no-monitoring groups. After 12 months, the diabetes (as measured by hemoglobin A1C testing) was no better in the self-monitoring group than in the group that did not monitor.[155]

■ The second study (Gulliford, 2008), divided a separate population of Type 2 patients into three groups: No monitoring, moderate monitoring, and intense monitoring. Not only did self-monitoring fail to improve control over diabetes, it also cost more. More importantly, monitoring actually decreased the patients' quality of life.[156]

The conclusions of the ESMON study and the famous DiGEM Trial (Diabetes Glycemic Education and Monitoring)[157] are summed up by a report in the medical journal *Endocrine Today*, which states, "High costs and reports of decreased quality of life make self-monitoring more of a hindrance than a help." (A polite way of saying "worthless.")

Nonetheless, monitoring blood sugar levels continues to be a standard practice recommended by almost all physicians.

## The Case Against Self-Monitoring

There have been many other studies that confirm the ineffectiveness of self-monitoring in Type 2 patients not taking insulin. Because these findings are so alien to the accepted practice of self-monitoring in the conventional treatment of Type 2 diabetes, we are going to cite the most significant of these in hopes of convincing you:

•Self-monitoring of blood glucose failed to show any significant improvements in HbA1c, hypoglycemic events, or quality of life in patients not taking insulin in two different meta-analyses.[158]

•Twelve randomized, controlled trials involving more than 3,000 patients with Type 2 diabetes, who were not using insulin, did not find any significant improvements for self-monitoring. The outcomes they were looking for included improved HbA1c, health-related quality of life, well-being and patient satisfaction, reduced fasting plasma glucose levels, hypoglycemic events, morbidity, adverse effects, and costs.[159]

•The aforementioned results are consistent with those from another meta-analysis published in 2010 that studied 10 trials comparing self-monitoring with no self-monitoring. That analysis showed no effect on patient satisfaction, general well-being, or general health-related quality of life.[160]

# Myth 7: "Prediabetes Is No Big Deal"

A blood glucose level from 100 to 125 mg/dL is officially considered "prediabetes." As you learned in Chapter 2, a diagnosis of prediabetes is definitely something to be concerned about—and to act upon immediately. Your doctor may treat your prediabetes casually because he neither has the time nor the training to guide you in reversing prediabetes by improving your diet and lifestyle. In most cases, doctors wait until patients cross the line to Type 2 diabetes (a blood sugar level of 126 mg/dL or 7.0 mmol/L or higher), when official treatment guidelines—meaning drugs—can be employed. Allowing blood glucose to linger at these levels, however, can cause great harm to your cardiovascular system and your general health.

One study found that two out of three patients admitted to the emergency room with heart attacks already had prediabetes or undiagnosed diabetes.[161] Another study discovered that the risk of heart attack worsens with *any* increase in average blood glucose, even for those who do not have diabetes.[162] Please remember that many people with prediabetes never get Type 2—yet they are at serious risk of cardiovascular disease, life-threatening health problems, and death, just the same. Most people with prediabetes already show signs of retinopathy (eye damage), nephropathy (kidney damage), and neuropathy (nerve damage), all of which are common complications of diabetes (which we discussed in Chapter 4).

Elevated blood glucose and triglyceride levels are not the only factors causing this damage. Studies show that high insulin levels also cause artery disease and make it worse—and this can happen in people who do not have diabetes.[163] This was demonstrated in the late 1960s by Dr. Robert Stout of Queen's University in Belfast, who reported that insulin facilitates the transport of cholesterol particles and fats into artery walls, thus initiating plaque buildup.[164] It is therefore easy to understand why any diabetes drug that increases insulin in the body is actually *accelerating* the process of heart disease.

High levels of blood glucose in prediabetes also can harm your brain, causing memory loss, cognitive impairment, and "pre-dementia" or early Alzheimer's disease. Researchers have discovered that diabetics have a fourfold increased risk of developing Alzheimer's[165] As we've stated, many researchers are now referring to Alzheimer's disease as "Type 3 diabetes."[166] You need not have diabetes to suffer brain cell damage from chronically elevated glucose and insulin levels. Prediabetes also can cause this.

So please do not hesitate or procrastinate if your doctor says you have prediabetes. What he is really telling you is that you have Stage 1 diabetes and your body is already being damaged by it. Remember, prediabetes can kill you with a heart attack, stroke or cancer before it ever becomes Type 2 diabetes.[167]

# Myth 8: "You Must Lose Weight in Order to Reverse Type 2 Diabetes"

There is a lot of confusion and controversy about this idea today—even among doctors and researchers. So let us make it perfectly clear: *You do not have to lose weight to reverse Type 2 or prediabetes.*

Insulin resistance is the true cause of overeating, weight gain, obesity, and Type 2 diabetes. Because they exist together (co-morbidities), doctors mistakenly believe that Type 2 is caused by weight gain. This is because they have witnessed the reversal of insulin resistance and diabetes in people who have lost weight. That is why they admonish their overweight, diabetic patients to simply "eat less and exercise more." But if you have ever tried this approach, you are well aware of how frustrating and futile it is.

For one reason, hunger is such a strong biological urge, that it is almost impossible to resist. Few people can muster the iron willpower to overcome it. Exercising your excess pounds away is even more difficult. That is because the larger your body, the less energetic you feel. This fact is even more exaggerated if you are dieting at the same time. The last thing you feel like doing is hitting the gym or the jogging trail.

But suppose you force yourself to exercise? Do you realize that 30 minutes on a stair-stepper—or a brisk one-hour walk—only burns about 100 calories, the equivalent of a single slice of white bread! It is certainly no exaggeration to say that current weight loss advice is trapped in the last century. Simply eating less food is not the answer. *How much* you eat is not nearly as important as what you eat. This is why we encourage you to build your diet around the diabetes-healing superfoods you will discover in Chapter 10.

Before we leave the topic of losing weight, we would like to say a word or two about exercise as the main causal agent: "It is pretty useless." This is not just our opinion, but it is the conclusion of Eric Ravussin, PhD, head of the Department of Diabetes and Metabolism at Louisiana State University who was quoted in a *Time* magazine cover story entitled, "The Myth about Exercise."

In his study, Dr. Ravussin randomly assigned overweight women to four groups. Women in three of the groups were asked to work out with a personal trainer for 72 minutes, 136 minutes, or 194 minutes every week for six months. Women in the fourth group (the control) were told to maintain their usual physical activity routines. All the women were asked not to change their eating habits one bit.

The findings were surprising, to say the least. All the women lost weight, but those who sweated it out with a trainer several days a week lost no more than the non-exercising control group did. Surprisingly, many of the exercising women actually *gained* weight—with some adding 10 pounds or more![168]

This certainly is not the first research study to show that focusing on exercise alone is an ineffective way to lose weight. In fact, exercise has never been proven to do so. But just like

# How Your Body Gains Weight

Weight gain does not cause insulin resistance and diabetes. It is actually the other way around: Insulin resistance is the underlying reason why we gain weight and abdominal fat. We touched upon this in Chapter 2, but it bears elaboration here so that you really understand the connection between what you eat and how much you weigh. So let us review how your body actually gains weight in 10 simple steps:

**1.** Consuming simple carbs, such as sugar, sweets, bread and baked goods, spike your blood glucose, which triggers the release of the hormone insulin.

**2.** Normally, this glucose is burned by your muscles to power physical activity. But if you are not particularly active, the glucose is transformed into fat (triglycerides) in your liver and stored in your body's fat cells (especially around your waist as abdominal fat) and liver for use later.

**3.** Because insulin has cleared your bloodstream of the glucose, your blood sugar dips and your brain feels foggy, irritable, and unable to think clearly. Deprived of glucose, your brain also thinks you are starving, so it begins to conserve energy by making you feel sleepy.

**4.** This drop in your glucose level also makes you feel hungry. So hungry, in fact, that you reach for anything that will pump up your blood sugar again. Usually, this is a sugary, caffeinated beverage, a bag of chips or a candy bar—or all three.

**5.** What happens next? More insulin is released and clears your bloodstream of the new glucose by creating more triglycerides and storing them in your fat cells and liver.

**6.** When this happens often enough, your cells begin to ignore the insulin (insulin resistance)—which leads to your pancreas pumping out even more of the hormone.

**7.** Insulin's main job is to keep excess glucose out of your bloodstream, anyway it can. So, as long as the hormone is present in your blood, it will not allow your stored belly fat to exit your fat cells and enter your bloodstream so it can be burned as energy. (This is what normally happens between meals, during sleep, and when you are fasting or starving. Your body literally feeds off of your stored body fat.)

**8.** The more sodas and simple carbs you consume, the higher your insulin levels rise. Insulin is the "fat storage hormone," so the more of it you have in your blood, the fatter you become—and the hungrier you feel. In fact, insulin is compelling you to crave carbohydrates for most of your waking hours—and even while you sleep. (Some people experience such strong blood glucose dips during sleep that they get out of bed for a 3 a.m. snack.)

**9.** More insulin means greater insulin resistance. Eventually, your cells do not respond to insulin at all. The result is that your bloodstream remains flooded with glucose and insulin all the time. This is Type 2 diabetes and the direct path to a heart attack or stroke.

**10.** No matter how hard you try, dieting and willpower cannot defeat this process because your hunger is driven by your out-of-whack hormones. If you have ever been on a diet, you know this is true.

the "eating fat makes you fat" dogma that the general public has come to believe, the idea that "calories in must equal calories out" has taken up residency right next door in our psyches. Both beliefs are wrong.

Hopefully, we have convinced you that consuming dietary fat—as long as it is a healthy fat—will not add to your weight because it does not trigger your body's insulin response. Now let us examine the "energy balance" notion: the idea that we get fat because we consume too many calories and expend too few.

At its heart, as noted science author Gary Taubes points out in his *Time* cover story, is the rationale that if we consumed fewer calories and increased our level of physical activity to burn off what we took in, we would never gain weight. This advice appears everywhere: in the official government guidelines, medical commentary and mainstream health advice. "The same amount of energy *in* and energy *out* over time (equals your) weight staying the same," the NIH website counsels Americans, while the CDC site announces: "Overweight and obesity result from an energy imbalance."

But this idea is simply not scientifically valid, because it ignores insulin's role in weight gain. All calories are certainly *not* created equal. Carbohydrate calories—especially those from sugar, soda pop, refined carbs, and processed foods—have a much different effect on fat accumulation and weight gain than do calories from protein and fats. The solution then is not eating less, but rather eating *better*. Losing weight and controlling our appetite is not a matter of willpower—it is about consuming foods that will keep insulin out of our bloodstream in a meaningful way. That way we cease craving refined carbohydrates, so our body can stop manufacturing and hoarding fat.

But please, don't take this as an excuse to NOT exercise! Physical activity is an integral part of the 30-Day Diabetes Cure Plan (see chapter 11 and Day 6 of the Plan in Part 2, page 208). It lowers your glucose levels naturally, controls blood pressure, and decreases your risk of heart attack. Exercise—all kinds, from running to cycling to swimming—will help you maintain strength, balance and agility…and it will boost your mood. There are so many reasons to get your heart pumping and remain active…but weight loss is not one of them.

Here is a crazy fact: Do you realize that a three-mile run only burns up the amount of calories in a small candy bar? And when the run is over, most people will probably be hungry enough to eat more calories than you extinguished in the run. That is exactly why there are so many overweight people who exercise regularly.[169] We bet you have a few friends like this.

# 11 Tips for *Really* Losing Weight

If you really want to trim down, here is our advice: Losing weight is 80% diet and 20% physical activity. Why would anyone walk for an hour, only to negate the calories burned by eating a sandwich or a plate of pasta? Losing weight or reversing Type 2 diabetes follows this same game plan:

**1. Never make "losing weight" your goal.** While it is often true that losing significant weight can reverse Type 2, most people attempt weight loss in very unproductive ways (diets, calorie-restriction, exercise, etc.). They try, they fail, they get frustrated, and they give up. Instead of trying to lose a certain amount of weight, make it your goal to have "a healthy lifestyle." This is something you can stick with for life.

**2. Keep your insulin levels low.** The best way to do this is to go "cold turkey" on sugar, sweets, sodas, beer, and desserts, plus anything made with white flour or refined corn. This includes baked goods, chips and commercial snacks. In addition, because they have a high Glycemic Index rating (meaning they convert to blood glucose very quickly), you should also avoid pasta and white rice. Pass on fruit juices, too, because of their high sugar content and lack of fiber.

**3. Only eat real food.** In general, if a food comes in bag or a box, leave it on the shelf. Pick foods as close to their natural state as possible. (Frozen vegetables and canned and frozen beans are okay.) Following this strategy will ensure that the foods you're eating contain maximum fiber and nutrients to control your blood sugar and sugar craving.

**4. Consume protein with every meal.** Protein and fat quash your hunger—and satisfy you longer. Choose eggs for breakfast (a vegetable omelet is ideal). Alternate with steel-cut Irish oats (not instant or quick-cook oatmeal) topped with full-fat, unsweetened yogurt, fresh berries and a sprinkling of bran or flax meal. Try a protein smoothie with protein powder or spirulina, plus hemp milk, berries, and flax meal. Eat chicken or tuna salad for lunch. And enjoy some high-quality fish or meat for dinner. If you're trying to lose weight, don't eat anything after 8 p.m.

**5. Have three meals and only healthful snacks.** Eating regularly—whether you're hungry or not—will keep blood sugar and cravings under control. You do not have to eat a lot, but train yourself to get in the habit of regular meals. Studies show that people who skip meals actually eat much more at the next meal.

**6. Pack your meals and snacks with you.** This is a great survival tactic in today's carb-crazy culture. Make sure your snacks include some protein, fat, and complex carbohydrate. Good examples are nuts, cheese, hard-boiled eggs, natural meat jerky, crunchy vegetable slices, and nut butters. There is more detail on healthful snacking on Day 13 of the 30-Day Diabetes Cure Plan.

**7. Tote healthy beverages with you, too.** Always carry your own water. For a change of pace, flavor it with a slice of lemon, lime or orange. Chilled green tea or herbal tea is perfect, too. Hot tea and coffee are perfectly acceptable. Avoid diet sodas and artificial sweeteners. These actually increase your hunger and sugar cravings. If you need your beverage sweetened while you work down your sweet tooth, use a tiny bit of stevia, which will not spike your blood sugar.

**8. Be patient.** If you have a strong sweet tooth, the first three days may be uncomfortable. But I encourage you to be strong and stick it out. The longer you abstain from sugar, the weaker your cravings will become. Break yourself from the habit of having dessert after every meal. (Have fresh fruit instead, if you simply must have something sweet.) During the day, if cravings get too intense, suck on an ice cube or a frozen grape. Some people find that chewing gum helps—or a timely tooth-brushing.

**9. Accentuate the positive.** Behavioral scientists have found that the best way to break a bad habit is to substitute a good one. Instead of focusing on giving up sugar, think about "eating more healthfully"—plus all the good benefits that will be yours as a result.

**10. Begin the 30-Day Diabetes Cure Plan right away.** All of the preceding tips are built into the Plan, so all you have to do is follow each daily step. This is like being guided by your car's GPS navigation system. We made it this simple so that your success would be easy and assured.

**11. Create a satisfying new lifestyle for yourself.** This is the most important step, but one you will not be able to accomplish right away. Getting well is just the first step in getting better. Ultimately, you want to create a lifestyle for yourself that is vibrant, creative, challenging, healthy, and so satisfying that it makes you happy every day. Self-improvement never ends. Always endeavor to "keep getting better" and life will reward you a thousand-fold.

When you follow the 30-Day Diabetes Cure Plan, the pounds will fall off you easily and effortlessly—and you will never have to diet or feel hungry ever again. This simple step-by-step system has worked for thousands of people who have lost significant amounts of weight. As she reported on our Facebook page, Alison Chastain's brother-in-law lost 40 pounds and is now off all his diabetes drugs. As of this writing, her sister was on Day 17 of the Plan and already had lost 15 pounds and cut her medication dose in half. And her husband was so impressed that he started the Plan five days ago and had already dropped 3 pounds.

Doug N., one of our top success stories (read his inspiring story on page 350 in Day 28 of *The 30-Day Diabetes Cure*) lost an amazing 120 pounds (he went from weighing 306 to 186) in less than two years—while getting completely off insulin and his other drugs.

We suggest you make your first goal to get off diabetes medications (if you are currently on them) by following the 30-Day Diabetes Cure Plan. Next, create a routine, an eating plan and a lifestyle that really supports your desire to get—and stay—healthy. Finally, imagine a career or hobby that really makes you happy…and go for it!

## Drew Carey's Extreme Weight Loss Regimen

In 2010, Drew Carey, comedian and host of the popular TV show "The Price Is Right," made the news by reversing his Type 2 diabetes and claiming he is now "a new man."

"I'm not diabetic anymore. No medication needed," Carey announced.

Carey is living proof that the solution to today's diabetes epidemic is right under our nose. Literally. But we do not recommend you follow Drew Carey's example. Here is why:

In order to reverse his diabetes, the 55-year-old comic lost 80 pounds, going from a size 44 waist to a 34 in about seven months. His secret? "Lots of cardio," he said. "At least 45 minutes, six days a week." He also worked with a personal trainer who watched over him, providing regular advice and motivation.

Then there was his diet: He cut out carbohydrates and ate lots of egg whites, skinless chicken breasts, fruit, and Greek yogurt. His sole beverage was water. He also relied on a "custom-made appetite suppressant administered by a Hollywood nutritionist."

Hats off to Carey for sticking with such a Draconian regimen for so long. But Man does not live by egg whites and water alone. Had he followed The 30-Day Diabetes Cure Plan, Drew could have reversed his diabetes and lost all that weight without starving and exercising like crazy.

We congratulate Drew on his success, but hope you do not follow his extreme example. As you will soon see, reversing Type 2 and losing a lot of weight can be much, much easier than the path he took.

A very important part of your recovery from diabetes will be determined by your commitment to taking control of your life and your future. We say this, because more than anything, Type 2 diabetes is a consequence of following what the so-called "experts"—and by this we mean the doctors, the food companies, the drug industry, and the media—say we should be consuming and how we should be living our lives. We receive this indoctrination at a very early age (mostly from TV) and few of us question it in adulthood. We trust what our government, our medical authorities, our sports heroes, and our celebrities encourage us to eat and drink, despite the fact that they are being paid huge sums of money to influence our habits, desires, cravings, and "brand loyalties."

The vast majority of overweight people with diabetes are not that way because they are lazy and lack willpower. The real culprit is the bad information they are receiving from doctors, health gurus and the media. Clearly, conventional wisdom has failed them. It is time to rethink this failed approach if we hope to reverse the twin epidemics of diabetes and obesity. Just do not wait for the "experts" to come to their senses. You could be waiting a long time.

# Myth 9: "Diabetes Is Your Own Fault"

Health experts love to "blame the victim" for today's lifestyle-driven medical conditions. Though they rarely come right out and accuse you, the attitude that "you did it to yourself" prevails among doctors, lawmakers, and social scientists. But there is much more to the story than this simplistic explanation. The truth is, powerful forces are at work behind the scenes to promote the overconsumption of sugar, sweets, sodas, and refined carbohydrate food products—factors that have nothing to do with willpower (or the lack of it).

For instance, the main sweetener in commercial foods, high fructose corn syrup (HFCS), inhibits leptin, the hormone that signals your brain to stop when you have eaten enough. This is a big reason why people overeat—and food industry scientists are well aware of it. Leptin resistance (see pages 27–28) is widely-recognized as the precursor to insulin resistance, diabetes, and obesity. When leptin is blocked, the only signal you get to stop eating is when the box, bottle, or bag is empty. Another problem: HFCS is converted into fat and accumulates in liver cells where it becomes resistant to the action of insulin. As a consequence, more insulin is secreted. This results in elevated levels of insulin, the hallmark of Type 2 diabetes.[170]

A greater problem is that our entire food system is dominated by sugar and processed foods that are made from refined carbohydrates. These carbs represent the cheapest calories in our food supply (thanks to generous government subsidies)—and the most attractive (because of massive ad campaigns). They are also the biggest profit items for food companies, which can afford to pay today's sports heroes to endorse them and pay Washington lobbyists to make sure the food industry receives favorable legislation. These processed foods represent a $1 trillion dollar industry in the US alone—and is the largest manufacturing sector of our economy (a frightening fact, indeed).[171] We will discuss the sugar problem in a moment. But first we'll explain why there has been such a proliferation of refined carbohydrates in the world's food supply since the 1980s.

Carbohydrates dominate our current food supply for one reason: They are cheap to grow and extremely profitable when marketed as processed foods and beverages. Governments, including our own, are enticed into supporting "carbohydrate agriculture" because they fear they cannot feed their populations any other way. Farmers can get about eight times as many calories from an acre of corn as they can from the flesh of cattle or pigs fed on this same crop.[172]

The big mistake here, of course, is that governments and food manufacturers remain unconcerned about the *quality* of the calories they feed us. Nor are they held accountable for the health consequences and medical costs generated by our carbohydrate-dominated food system. But this (conveniently) provides a steady stream of new customers for the medical and drug industries. One could say that Big Food is raking in a fortune from foods that make us sick—while Big Medicine and Big Pharma make a killing by treating those ills, until they do us in. Such is "the System" in which millions of people in the developed world (and now, developing nations, too) find themselves trapped. And since this System is not about to reform itself anytime soon, your only hope of escape is to reclaim your health before it is lost forever.

Economics drives food manufacturers to generate significant profits each year—and most of this growth comes from new food products. There is just one problem. The human capacity for food is limited. But the food industry has come up with a way to stretch this capacity: by packing more calories into a serving of food, usually by adding sugar and sweeteners to make the food product "hyper-palatable." This is a polite food industry term meaning *addictive*, as in the famous Lay's Potato Chip ad campaign, "Bet you can't eat just one."

If you doubt that food companies intentionally design their foods to be addictive, we strongly encourage you to read *Salt, Sugar, Fat: How the Food Giants Hooked Us* by Pulitzer prize-winning author Michael Moss. The book exposes how food chemists are paid big bucks to develop new foods and beverages that are so addictive that consumers are practically powerless to say no to them. Once the product is developed, food companies use behavioral psychologists to create marketing and advertising campaigns that exploit consumers' weaknesses to habitually purchase and consume these products—even though they know they are bad for their health and weight. The average consumer does not stand a chance.

This is especially true when a food product contains sugar or sweeteners, because sugar is addictive. Sugar and sweeteners stimulate the very same "reward center" of our brains (technically, the striatum) as do nicotine, cocaine, sex, caffeine, and alcohol. Sweets stimulate the release of the mood-elevating brain chemical called *dopamine* which creates feelings of pleasure and euphoria. This is why sweets and refined carbohydrates are often referred to as "comfort foods" (think of Ben & Jerry's or Mac-and-Cheese). This soon becomes a problem if sweets and refined carbs are the main sources of pleasure in your life.

It is natural to want to feel good, but if we continually rely on food (or alcohol, drugs, or nicotine) for these feelings, we can fall into a trap. Like all addictive substances, the more we use them, the more we want them. But frequent consumption of them drains the brain of its dopamine reserves, while simultaneously building up a tolerance to our drug of choice. Result? We need a stronger and more frequent dose to get the same effect.

Running low on dopamine causes us to feel sad, depressed, irritable, angry, and negative—the typical symptoms of withdrawal. To perk ourselves up, we reach for another "fix," in this case a bag, or bowl, or bottle of sugary carbohydrates. This is a perfect example of the roller coaster of addiction. This yo-yo rhythm of highs and lows is what makes so many people crave sweets, sodas, and carbs. In effect, they are self-medicating their unpleasant feelings —but with devastating effects on their metabolism, their bodies, and their health.

And this is where things really get serious. A steady diet of sugar increases body weight and health problems, which further lowers self-esteem and represses positive emotions (such as hope, confidence, and the courage to change). Relieving this stress and discomfort with still more sugar turns the situation into a downward spiral that usually ends in Type 2 diabetes and its nasty complications.

Sugar addiction is a double-whammy because your body gets into the act, too. As you already have read, consuming sweets and carbs triggers a gush of insulin into your bloodstream which causes your blood glucose to drop. This creates a strong craving for more carbohydrate foods, especially sweets. All this insulin eventually causes insulin resistance and Type 2 diabetes. And remember: As long as insulin is present in your blood, your fat cells never get a chance to empty out, which leads to weight gain and obesity.

Now you can begin to understand why we have a global epidemic of Type 2 diabetes and obesity on our hands. The international food industry has created a world of "sugar junkies" who are rapidly becoming obese diabetics. It is shocking to realize that the average American consumed 150 pounds of sugar and sweeteners last year—along with 53 gallons of sodas and soft drinks. This is the equivalent of 22 teaspoons of sugar every day (and 32 teaspoons for the average child)!

It is difficult to comprehend why mainstream doctors are not connecting the dots. When you track the rise of sugar consumption in the US since 1900 alongside the increase of Type 2 diabetes, heart disease, and obesity, the two paths are practically identical. According to science writer Gary Taubes: "In 1980, roughly one in seven Americans was obese, and almost six million were diabetic, and obesity rates, at least, hadn't changed significantly in the 20 years previously. By the early 2000s, when sugar consumption peaked, one in every three Americans was obese, and 14 million were diabetic."[173] During this same period, US consumption of red meat, dairy products, and saturated fat actually *declined*. This means that animal products and saturated fat cannot possibly be responsible for the increased rates in Type 2 diabetes, heart disease, and obesity during that period. Yet, the ADA, AHA, and AMA continue to claim that they are.

Why are we telling you all this? We do not want you to feel shame or guilt about your diabetes (or your weight). We want you to realize just how the deck is stacked against you. From the time you were a toddler, you have been bombarded with TV commercials for fast food, candy, sodas, and snack foods. Super-slick advertising convinced you and your parents that these products were "fun"—and even good for you. Celebrities and sports heroes promised you would be cool and "in" if you consumed the same foods and beverages they did.

And guess what? Before long, you made those products your "favorites." You came to love and relish the flavors. You imagined how good a Big Mac with fries and a Coke would taste at lunchtime. You dreamed of how good a Pizza Hut pizza and a cold beer would go with Monday night football. Skittles, Hershey Kisses and M&Ms became your traveling companions. And when you were thirsty, you yearned for a Pepsi, 7-Up or Diet Dr. Pepper to quench it. Without you even realizing it, your brain and blood sugar became addicted—exactly the way the brand managers planned it.

Then, when the doctor announced that you have diabetes, the various food associations and the medical community made you feel like it was *your* fault. They said you ate too much. They claimed you should have known the dangers. They insinuated that you have no willpower. They made it sound like it was all your fault. But do you know what? *It was not your fault.* Doctors, health officials, and lawmakers should have been there to warn you, to educate you, and to protect you from these addictive foods and beverages. They were not there for you because they had been bought off by the food industry. Fast food and soda lobbyists spent $33

## Why You Are Surrounded by Fattening Foods

Do not blame yourself if you have Type 2 diabetes, prediabetes, or you are overweight. Powerful forces are at work to coerce you to consume the foods and beverages that are directly responsible for these health problems. For example:

**1. Farm subsidies** (your tax dollars) give corporate farmers and food companies an unfair advantage. Billions of dollars are awarded to the largest growers and manufactures every year, which decreases their products' price tags and makes them more economically attractive to consumers. Organic farmers and vegetable growers, on the other hand, receive far fewer subsidies, which in part contributes to the higher prices of their products.

**2. Enormous advertising budgets** are available to giant food manufactures, allowing them to bombard us and our kids with thousands of commercials every day. Most consumers do not have a chance against this barrage.

**3. Ingredients such as sweeteners,** fat, and salt have been shown to be just as addictive as opiates, affecting the same brain pathways. There's a reason you feel better after downing a pint of Ben and Jerry's or a Big Mac with fries: These foods and beverages have a powerful medicating effect on one's mental and emotional state. And given the never-ending stress facing us these days, it is no wonder we are over-consuming these so-called carbohydrate "comfort foods" in record quantities.

**4. Profit trumps health and nutrition.** The USDA encourages food producers to maximize production. (The biggest producers receive the largest subsidy payments.) So growers have transformed traditional farming and ranching practices into unnatural, inhuman "food factories" that emphasize quantity over quality. Current practices include: Injecting cows with growth hormones…fattening cattle by feeding steers blood, excrement and dead carcasses…creating genetically-modified crops and fish…even "growing" flesh-like protein matter in factory labs—it is all permitted and FDA-approved. *Ugh*.

**5. The food industry does not have to clean up its messes.** They don't share in the medical expenses that their products create. Nor do they pay for the environmental clean-up of feedlot refuse…agricultural chemical run-off…soil erosion…or air and water pollution. That cost is left to us *via* state and federal programs funded by our tax dollars.

million in 2015 to hide the truth about how harmful their products are to the public's health and to kill any bills that might restrict them. (Visit *www.opensecrets.org/lobby/indusclient. php?id=N01&year=2015* to see how much each company actually spent to get lawmakers to close their eyes and turn their backs on your health and well-being.)

This is how the "game" works, dear reader. And now that you know what you are up against, you can no longer pretend to be innocent. Getting diabetes was not your fault, but now that you have it, *it is your responsibility*. How you decide to deal with your condition will determine whether you trade your dependency on Big Food for reliance on Big Pharma— or declare your independence from both of them.

Ultimately, your decision will be about how "free" you want to be. As we see it, real freedom starts with your personal health. It is difficult to be truly free if you are hobbled by a medical condition that keeps you weak and dependent upon doctors and drugs. If your freedom is precious to you, then now is the time to fight for it. This is your opportunity to cast off those old addictions. It's time to say "I'll pass" to a life sentence of medications, doctor visits, hospital stays, and endless health problems caused by the complications of diabetes.

This is your chance to take a stand—and we are here to help you every step of the way.

## Myth 10: "Bariatric Surgery Cures Diabetes"

"The relationship between diabetes and obesity should be screamed from the rooftops," says Christine Ren Fielding, MD, FACS, an associate professor of surgery at the New York University Program for Surgical Weight Loss. "Many people don't understand just how closely diabetes and obesity are related," she says.

While this is true, we must remember that being "related" does not mean they are the "same." Obvious proof of this is found by comparing the incidence of Type 2 and obesity. According to official statistics, two-thirds of the US population is estimated to be either overweight or obese. At the same time, only about 10% of the population has been diagnosed with Type 2 diabetes. Even if the actual number of people with Type 2 diabetes is higher, it is safe to say that there are more obese people walking around who do not have diabetes than who do. (Just as there are plenty of normal-weight people who have Type 2.) If being obese were the cause of diabetes, every obese person in the country would have the disease. And this is clearly not the case.

We must remember that co-existence is not causality. Just because firefighters are at the scene of the blaze does not mean they were responsible for it. But lumping diabetes and obesity together, bariatric surgeons are able to claim that gastric bypass surgery is the new solution to the Type 2 epidemic.

That is the new promise made by two 2012 studies published in the *New England Journal of Medicine*.[174] The research reported that gastric bypass surgery is "more effective than the standard drug treatment" in obese and overweight diabetics. As a result, surgeons everywhere are hailing the procedure as "the new surgical cure for Type 2." This is more than a small exaggeration, given how ineffective diabetes drugs actually are—and bariatric surgeons are not shy about letting you know this.

"Traditional treatments for diabetes do not work," bluntly declared Neil E. Hutcher, MD. "Even people with good medical control still go on dialysis, lose limbs and have significant heart attacks, drug reactions and other complications."

By "good medical control," he means Type 2 patients who follow their doctor's orders to a "T"—including testing their blood several times a day, plus taking a battery of drugs to control their blood sugar, cholesterol, blood pressure, and other risk factors for diabetic complications. Dr. Hutcher is reinforcing what we have been saying throughout this book: that the protection you get from diabetes drugs is a mirage.

One reason Dr. Hutcher isn't shy about bashing diabetes drugs is because he's a bariatric surgeon—and the past president of the American Society for Metabolic and Bariatric Surgery (ASMBS). As one of his industry's chief "salesmen," he touted the gastric bypass as the new diabetes cure in front of millions on TV's *60 Minutes* (which should get these surgeons loads of new business). Joining the push was Francesco Rubino, MD, one of the study's leaders, who claimed the procedure is such an excellent treatment that it should be called "diabetes surgery." These surgeons want the operation offered much earlier to people with Type 2—not just as a last resort. Obviously, there is a pile of money to be made. They even have the insurance industry on board, because this is an attractive money saver for providers over the life of a patient.

The researchers claim that the surgery immediately normalizes blood glucose levels and reduces or eliminates the need for medications. Some patients were able to stop taking insulin as early as three days after their surgery because their bodies started producing more of the hormone. Insulin resistance was also reduced, so that the body's insulin is no longer ignored by the cells.

In one of the studies, most surgery patients were able to stop all diabetes drugs immediately after their procedure—although the researchers admit they do not understand why this occurs. Some theorized that re-directing food to the lower intestine stimulates a substance called glucagon-like peptide 1, which can increase insulin production. Another explanation suggests that hormones that trigger hunger may be dulled by rearranging the anatomy, resulting in fewer cravings for sugar and carbs, which means better blood sugar levels.

But both of these "explanations" ignore the obvious. What the surgeons are failing to mention is that post-surgical patients are put on a very strict low-calorie, low-carb diet that forbids sugar… fat…fried or breaded food…soda pop…sweetened drinks…syrups…candy…and any meat, other than the leanest pork and chicken. As you already know, this type of diet has the power to reverse insulin resistance and Type 2 diabetes almost immediately, all by itself.

You will recall the remarkable UK study from Chapter 7 in which people with Type 2 diabetes were placed on a drastically low-carb and reduced-calorie diet, just like the one that bariatric surgery patients are placed on. This rather extreme diet allowed many of these diabetics to completely eliminate their medications in the first week. By the end of eight weeks, all signs of Type 2 had completely disappeared—and pancreatic function was restored to normal. This reversal lasted for as long as the study participants remained on the diet—which is exactly what happens with the post-surgery patients![175]

Gastric bypass is grossly misunderstood by most lay people. They fail to realize that you still have to eat right and exercise regularly to manage your weight and your diabetes. If you don't, your weight and your diabetes will return, which they do in a large number of patients.[176]

The main benefit of bariatric surgery is that compliance is not voluntary. If patients binge on any of the forbidden foods, they can become violently ill with vomiting and diarrhea. This is why, far from becoming the first line treatment for Type 2 (as the surgery lobby is suggesting), we believe bariatric surgery should be reserved for morbidly obese patients who have failed repeatedly at diet and lifestyle modification. For these Type 2s who cannot stop consuming the high-carb foods and beverages that trigger insulin (and thus drive fat storage), surgery may be a lifesaving option. But we feel that every effort must first be made to educate these patients about the foods and beverages that lead directly to obesity and insulin resistance. Unfortunately, doctors and surgeons do not seem to be doing this. Nor are the downside and dangers of the bariatric surgery being thoroughly explained to candidates.

There are other risks, too—including hospital-bred infections, internal bleeding, anesthesia complications, deep vein thrombosis, ulcers, pulmonary problems, and the possible removal of the spleen. After the surgery, many bariatric patients have great difficulty obtaining adequate nutrition from the small portion of food they are permitted to eat. It is also common for post-surgical patients to develop vitamin deficiencies and/or anemia because the surgery left the patients unable to absorb certain vitamins and nutrients.

While many *do* lose weight, they must be vigilant in not regaining their lost pounds. According to the Mayo Clinic, "Gastric bypass surgery can provide long-term, consistent weight loss *if* (emphasis ours) you exercise and eat a healthy diet." So gastric bypass is no shortcut—you still have to eat right and exercise regularly to manage your weight and your diabetes.

Here is the big surprise: Long-term success is rare. While the two-year success rate that researchers cite appears impressive, studies show that long-term diabetes-reversal and weight-loss results are pretty dismal. In reality, a majority of patients eventually revert to their old eating habits, thus regaining the weight and their Type 2.

A 2010 study published in *Eating Disorders Review* stated that "significant deterioration of diabetes control and hypertension became evident over time." Using weight loss of 25% of the patient's pre-surgery body weight to define treatment success, the Dutch researchers found that about 80% of the patients retained their weight loss during the first three years. After this, there was a steady decline to 64% of patients at five years, and only 20% at 10 years. Similarly, control of diabetes, hypertension and gastro-esophageal reflux (GERD) all deteriorated significantly over time. Besides regaining their weight and their Type 2, many patients experienced medical complications, some of which required multiple surgeries to correct the damage.[177]

The real takeaway from these new studies and the push for gastric bypass surgery (at least for us), is that they prove how current drug treatments are *failing* people with Type 2 diabetes. They also illustrate how unwilling Big Medicine is to get behind the most effective solution we have for insulin resistance, Type 2, and their very serious health complications: that is, a low-carbohydrate diet and an active lifestyle.

## Myth 11: "There Is No Getting Off Insulin Once You Start It"

The new trend in Type 2 treatment is to start patients on insulin early. This is because doctors feel they can achieve greater reductions in blood glucose this way.[178] (It should be noted that this research was funded by drug companies who manufacture and market insulin.)* But, as Mark Hyman, MD notes: "Insulin treatment in diabetes is a slippery slope, because increased insulin dosage often leads to increased weight gain, higher blood pressure, and elevated cholesterol."[179] This is because, as you will recall, insulin is your body's fat storage hormone. It also increases your appetite and feeds the fires of inflammation. Yes, insulin treatment will drive down your glucose numbers, but it will not protect you against heart attack and stroke, the most serious complications of diabetes.

We agree with Dr. Hyman that insulin should be the last resort—not the first option. If it is absolutely necessary, you should be on the lowest possible dose—but, we feel you and your doctor should hold off until you first give diet and lifestyle improvements, such as the 30-Day Diabetes Cure Plan, a vigorous trial. You may find that you do not need to go on insulin at all.

Some patients fear that once they start insulin, they will have to take it for life. This is a possibility because elevated insulin and high blood glucose cause and worsen inflammation in the body. Insulin also increases body fat accumulation—and these fats cells secrete cytokines which add to the body's inflammatory load. In addition, levels of *adiponectin* (a primary anti-inflammatory hormone) begin to fall. Chronically elevated inflammation worsens insulin resistance and destroys the beta cells that produce natural insulin. So the sooner you and your doctor can halt insulin therapy, the better it will be for your pancreas.

If you are currently on insulin therapy, it is very important that you take the diet and lifestyle interventions laid out in the 30-Day Diabetes Cure Plan very seriously. Studies show that reversing Type 2 diabetes in halting insulin treatments can be successfully accomplished.[180]By following our Plan, Doug N., was able to completely eliminate his insulin treatments—which were as high as from 280 units a day. (Read his story on page 350 in Day 28.) Since he began taking insulin, his weight ballooned dangerously. But by following The 30-Day Diabetes Cure Plan, he was able to lose an amazing amount of weight, going from a high of 306 pounds down to 181. You can view a brief video of his inspiring transformation on YouTube at *http://www.youtube.com/watch?v=Pmo_NCCj34k.*

---

*The publication of this finding was made possible in part by unrestricted educational grants from Eli Lilly, Ethicon Endo-Surgery, Generex Biotechnology, Hoffmann-La Roche, Johnson & Johnson, LifeScan, Medtronic, MSD, Novo Nordisk, Pfizer, Sanofi-Aventis, and WorldWIDE.

# Myth 12: "Insulin-Producing Beta Cells Do Not Regenerate"

Type 1 diabetes is a chronic, autoimmune disease that affects children, adolescents and adults, a disease whereby the immune system attacks and destroys the beta cells in the pancreas that produce insulin. (Insulin is the hormone that enables the body to convert food into energy.) People with Type 1 are dependent on insulin injections for the rest of their lives. In Type 2 diabetes, beta cells die off from being overworked and from being poisoned by chronically elevated levels of glucose (glucotoxicity). It is widely believed that once beta cells die, they are gone for good. When this occurs in patients with Type 2, they become "insulin-dependent diabetics" and must inject themselves with the synthetic form of the hormone for the rest of their lives, in order to stay alive.

But fascinating new research is questioning this belief. For one thing, Type 1 diabetes is rapidly rising right along with Type 2. Data from large epidemiologic studies worldwide indicate that the incidence of Type 1 diabetes has been increasing by 2% to 5% worldwide and that the prevalence of Type 1 diabetes is approximately 1 in 300 in the United States by 18 years of age.

How can this be true if genetics are responsible? Human genes do not change that rapidly, but our lifestyle and environment certainly have. One emerging theory is that Type 1 is not an autoimmune malfunction at all, but rather the immune system disposing of beta cells that have been damaged in some way—by a virus, environmental toxins or food chemicals, including alloxan in white flour and bread. You will read more about this beta-cell killer on Day 7 of *The 30-Day Diabetes Cure.*

Research is also disproving the "once they are gone, they are gone" theory about beta cells. Preliminary studies show that certain foods and supplements may indeed regenerate beta cells in the pancreas so they can produce insulin again. Other nutrients have been found to strengthen the remaining beta cells in Type 2 diabetics so that they can once again produce insulin naturally. This is certainly good news for Type 2s.

Finally, simple lifestyle modifications described in *The 30-Day Diabetes Cure* can increase the body's insulin sensitivity, allowing Type 1 patients to dramatically reduce their insulin dosage. One of the 30-Day Diabetes Cure Type 1 diabetes patients, a young man named Jon J., is a good example. He was able to cut his insulin dose by 80% when he began following our Plan. Insulin reductions like these allow patients to avoid diabetic complications later in life, while helping them to control their weight during treatment.

This may sound cynical, but we are not seeing very much mainstream curiosity about reviving the strength of beta-cells—or about how Type 1 patients can lower their doses of insulin (even though this would greatly improve their outcomes). The global insulin market is currently worth $21 billion. Need we say more?

A Type 1 diabetic must monitor blood sugar and take insulin to stay alive. But there is much more you can—and must—do. Every step in the 30-Day Diabetes Cure Plan works together to heal the damage done by diabetes and to prevent complications from developing.

Most doctors believe it is not possible to repair a damaged pancreas, but we are not so sure they are right. They said that about brain cells and heart cells, only to have those beliefs overturned by recent discoveries. We never think it is wise to underestimate the human body's remarkable ability to heal itself. Besides, there has been some promising new research indicating that the pancreas may, in fact, be able to be repaired, thus reversing diabetes naturally...

■ Beta cells were able to be regenerated in laboratory animals, according to research published in 2004 in the journal *Nature* involving Harvard scientists. Although similar studies have yet to be performed on humans, this is an exciting development.[181]

■ Several human studies already have shown that both weight loss and exercise can reduce insulin-resistance by increasing cell sensitivity to insulin.[182] This means that less natural insulin is required for glucose management, thereby de-stressing your beta cells and boosting their potential productivity and longevity.

■ In 2008, the journal *Obesity* published a study examining the effect of exercise on a group of obese young women. After just four months of regular exercise, their insulin sensitivity improved markedly.[183] Losing weight and being active not only significantly lowered their odds of developing Type 2 diabetes, these lifestyle improvements also increased the participants' insulin sensitivity and improved beta cell function.

In *The 30-Day Diabetes Cure*, you will also discover supplements that have been shown in preliminary research to enhance the function of your remaining beta cells—and perhaps even regenerate new ones. To learn more, be sure to read the Special Report that accompanied your purchase of this book, entitled *How to Heal Your Pancreas*.

# CHAPTER 9

# START REVERSING YOUR DIABETES NOW

*"Start by doing what's necessary; then do what's possible; and suddenly you are doing the impossible."*

—Francis of Assisi, 1182–1226

THE GOOD NEWS ABOUT TYPE 2 DIABETES is that in most cases you don't have to use drugs to treat it. In fact, the only way you can reverse it is through diet and lifestyle changes—not drugs. As you will learn more about in *The 30-Day Diabetes Cure*, changing what you eat will have biggest impact on healing yourself. The best part? It will have the quickest impact, too.

The very first step you must take to normalize your blood glucose is twofold: Increase your intake of the diabetes-healing foods we describe in Chapter 10 and cease consuming the foods and beverages that worsen prediabetes and Type 2 diabetes. These foods either spike your blood sugar to dangerously high levels or they add to the inflammation load in your body. Often these foods and beverages do both.

## The Foods to Avoid

Your consumption of the following foods, food products and beverages should be reduced or eliminated as soon as possible. Make sure you read food labels carefully to be sure you aren't unknowingly consuming these detrimental substances. For a full list of the foods to avoid—and which ones to replace them with—see Appendix A, page 367.

**Sweeteners,** including sugar, high fructose corn syrup (HFCS), agave syrup, brown sugar, honey, molasses, fruit juice, corn syrup, artificial sweeteners (Splenda, NutraSweet, Sweet 'N Low), and all sugar alcohols (such as sorbitol, malitol and erythritol).

**Soft drinks,** both regular and "diet" sodas, fruit juices, sports drinks, energy drinks, and sweetened teas.

**Sweets,** including candy, energy bars, granola bars, puddings, ice cream or sorbet of any kind, and any other type of sweetened dessert. Be particularly vigilant about eliminating all foods and beverages containing high fructose corn syrup (HFCS).

**Sweetened dairy products and flavored yogurts.**

**Bread and baked goods.** Eliminate any foods containing refined wheat, including white flour, white rice flour or soy flour. These include muffins, bagels, rolls, pastries, cookies, do-nuts, waffles and pancakes prepared with these refined ingredients.

**Refined grain products,** including prepared breakfast cereals, sweetened granola, chips, crackers, pasta, and all processed snack foods.

**Fast food,** including burgers, hot dogs, French fries, fried chicken and the other usual fare.

**All deep-fried foods.**

**Starchy, high-glycemic,** cooked vegetables, such as white potatoes, corn and white rice.

**Margarine and foods containing hydrogenated or partially-hydrogenated oils.** This includes most snack foods and processed cheeses (such as Velveeta or American slices). It also includes margarines touted as heart-healthy, such as Smart Balance and Benecol.

**Refined vegetable oils,** including corn, safflower, sunflower, soybean, peanut, and canola.

**All highly-processed meats,** cold cuts, sausages, and jerky containing nitrates and chemical preservatives.

**Ketchup,** sweet condiments, creamy salad dressings and relishes (because they usually contain HFCS or sugar).

**Avoid all beers and ales** (they contain barley malt and dextrose). If you must drink alcohol, limit yourself to one glass per day of wine or spirits. Avoid cocktails made with soda or juice mixers.

## Four Important Shopping Tips and Reminders

1. Beware of food products labeled "fat-free," "lite," "diet," and "Great for Low-Carb Diets." These often contain sweeteners, sodium and other chemicals that are harmful to your body.

2. Avoid prepared deli foods containing hidden sugars and starches (for example, potato salad, coleslaw and baked beans).

3. Check labels of liquid medications, cough syrups, cough drops, and other over-the-counter medications that may contain sugar or other sweeteners.

4. Check salad dressings carefully. Many contain sweeteners, such as HFCS and sugar.

## "Gosh! This doesn't leave me much to eat."

At first glance, you may be thinking that these healthy guidelines may seem like harsh dietary restrictions. However, if you look a little closer, you will see that many of the "foods" we are encouraging you to avoid aren't really foods at all, but rather factory- and lab-created food-like substances.

Will choosing diabetes-healing superfoods require some changes for you? Probably. But the long-term benefits are wonderfully worth the short-term effort it takes to choose to be healthy. Especially when you consider the very serious health dangers and complications you're facing with Type 2 diabetes—or the nasty side effects you will have to endure on drug therapy.

Besides, you really do have a wide selection of delicious, healthful foods and beverages that can improve or reverse your diabetes, as you will see in Chapter Ten.

Your diet is the single most important factor that determines your health, for better or worse. Indeed, poor diet is one of the main causes of Type 2 diabetes in the first place. Time and again, we've seen dramatic improvements in peoples' blood sugar levels when they restrict or reduce their consumption of those highly-processed and artificial foods and beverages.

But why do people crave and over-consume those harmful "foods" in the first place?

## The Evolution of Human Eating

It may surprise you to learn that our primitive, reptilian brains are genetically and biologically programmed to "seek and eat" high-calorie, fatty foods. You see, the brain's urge to binge on sweet, fatty, calorie-rich foods stems from the days when our ancestors were hunter-gatherers. Eating as many calories as possible, whenever possible, enabled our ancestors to store excess calories as fat so they could survive lean times. Consuming high-fat food whenever it was available was a survival strategy that worked well for the human race for 2.4 million years.

Today, that same strategy is killing people. Fat and sugary calories are cheap and abundant today, so our genetic programming is backfiring by making us sick and overweight. We are operating in a modern world with ancient appetites.

This is because our brains have not evolved fast enough to keep pace with our food environment. Prior to about 10,000 years ago, when agriculture developed, the human diet was restricted to the animals we could hunt or find and the wild plants we could gather. This is very different from today when we are literally surrounded by tens of thousands of food products and cheap calories.[184]

All that hunting and gathering was also hard work. Our ancestors expended a tremendous number of calories acquiring their food. So, when they were successful in locating a food supply, they gorged on it. Food preservation and storage was not an option.

Foods that were calorie dense, such as carbohydrates and fats, were the most prized—and animal protein (red meat, fowl and fish) was the most common and important food that hunter-gatherers ate. They also consumed wild fruit and berries, roots, grasses, seeds and nuts. This was the diet that sustained the human race since its appearance on the planet.

This is how our preference for sweets and fats developed. Hunter-gatherers came to recognize that foods with the highest concentrations of calories either tasted "sweet," as did wild berries and fruit; or were "fatty," like the organs of animals, which were usually consumed on the spot at a kill. Over time, our ancestors came to attach feelings of pleasure to these foods as they stimulated the reward center in the brain. This is why eating a scoop of ice cream, a hunk of chocolate or a slice of cheesecake feels so delightful today. They contain both sensations of sweet and fat.

## Why It Feels So Good to Be Lazy

Another important component of our brain's programming is the conservation of energy. Just as sweets and fatty foods taste good to us today, it generally feels good to relax on the couch and do nothing. This stimulates the same reward centers—and has its primal origins in a time when conserving energy was also an important survival mechanism. Early human life was arduous, and those hunter-gatherers who were well-rested were usually the ones who could outrun a hungry predator, defeat an attacking enemy, or keep hunting until they found game. This is why relaxation feels so pleasurable to us in modern times, even if we have a 9-to-5 desk job.

With the advent of agriculture about 10,000 years ago—and the era of industrialization which followed it—the human diet and lifestyle changed dramatically. Carbohydrates, in the form of bread and grains (and later sugar) became the predominant source of calories. For the first time in human history, we could relax and even sleep undisturbed because our food supply was assured.

Today, 60% of our calories come from refined carbohydrates— foods that our ancestors never ate, including cereal grains, sugary drinks, baked goods, chips, snacks, and processed foods.[185] Yet, the primitive brain is still driven to gorge on these abundant and easily obtained calories, even though our modern bodies and metabolism suffer from this excessive consumption and inadequate physical activity. Lifestyle-related diseases such as hypertension, obesity, Type 2 diabetes, heart disease, stroke, and various cancers are sickening us and striking us down in record numbers.

## Chronically Elevated Blood Sugar and Insulin Are Killing Us

As you will recall from Chapter 2, when you consume sugar and refined carbohydrates, they break down almost instantly into simple sugar (glucose) and quickly enter the bloodstream. Immediately, blood sugar levels rise. To control this rise in glucose, the body releases the hormone insulin, which opens cells so the sugar can enter and be metabolized as fuel. As sugar exits the bloodstream, healthy levels are restored and insulin retreats.

But when sugar and simple carbohydrate foods are continuously consumed, the body must produce and release increasing amounts of insulin. Over time, the cells become resistant to insulin and still greater amounts are required. This is the condition known as insulin resistance, the precursor to Type 2 diabetes.

Insulin resistance causes the body to accumulate belly fat, raises blood pressure, produces blood fats called triglycerides, increases cholesterol levels, triggers widespread inflammation throughout the body, damages brain cells, causes depression and fatigue, blunts the sex drive, impairs circulation (especially to the eyes and limbs), and feeds tumor growth.

Left unchecked, the result can be heart attack or stroke, cancer, Alzheimer's disease, kidney failure, and death. These are the very "plagues" of modern civilization that kill and cripple millions every year.

It would seem ironic, if it weren't so tragic: The same consumption impulses and programming that led to our survival through millions of years of evolution, now threaten our decline and demise.

## We Must Break With Our Genetic Programming

These twin impulses, to gorge on calories and conserve energy, remain strongly programmed in our brains. Yet, if we are to escape their unfortunate consequences, individually and collectively, we have some important choices to make—choices that our environment always made for us in the past. It was difficult to over-consume in ancient times because calories were too scarce. In addition, we couldn't take it easy as we do today because there was just too much to do in order to survive.

We must confront and defy our ancient programming if we are to enjoy good health and a long life. If we don't change our behaviors, our genetically driven impulses will be our undoing.

In truth, the killer diseases of our time are *behavioral* problems, not true medical conditions. As such, we must address and correct them with behavioral changes, instead of relying on pharmaceutical solutions to save us. This is why, with regard to Type 2 diabetes, changes in your diet and lifestyle can be the best "medicine" at your disposal.

## Three Easy Steps to Success:

You can—with awareness, determination, and practice—learn to control those primitive parts of your brain, effectively "rewiring" your brain by making better food and lifestyle choices. Making the decision to eliminate the harmful foods listed on pages 108–9 from your diet is an important first step. In the next chapter, you will learn how to replace them with diabetes-healing superfoods. For now, here are the three most important changes you can make today that can help you make a quick transition to a healing lifestyle:

**1. Eliminate sodas, soft drinks, fruit drinks, and artificial sweeteners.** Soda pop is the leading source of empty calories in the modern diet.[186] This one action will produce a dramatic improvement on your blood sugar, your blood pressure and your weight. Sodas are full of HFCS, which damages your liver.

Here's a quick snapshot of just a few ways drinking sodas wrecks havoc on your body:

•**Sodas lead to diabetes.** Sugary soda leads directly to weight gain, high blood sugar and insulin resistance.[187] It also suppresses your immune system and reduces chromium in your body, which raises your diabetes risk. Sugar can also lead to inflammation which damages your retinas and harms your nerve endings.

•**Soda harms your heart.** Sugary soda raises LDL (bad) cholesterol and triglycerides, while lowering HDL (good) cholesterol, which increases your risk for heart disease. A 2012 Harvard study found that men who drank one sugar-sweetened beverage daily had a 20% higher risk of coronary heart disease than men who drank none.[188] This finding mirrored a similar study of women conducted in 2009.

•**Soda can cause Alzheimer's disease.** Ongoing research indicates that diabetes and Alzheimer's have similar origins.[189] Your brain needs insulin for healthy blood vessels and neuron function. When your brain cells become insulin resistant due to overconsumption of sweets, you suffer memory loss, disorientation and personality loss.

Fruit juices aren't much better for you because they are loaded with sugar, too, and will also spike blood glucose. And diet sodas and beverages containing artificial sweeteners may be the worst of the lot. There's extensive evidence linking artificial sweeteners such as aspartame to health problems ranging from brain tumors to fatty liver disease. In fact, scientists have discovered that those who drink *diet soda* are fatter than those who consume regular sodas.[190] This is because diet drinks fool your body into thinking it is ingesting sugar, which creates the same insulin spike and cravings as regular sugar.

What does all this mean to you? Stick with water, coffee and green tea. Tea contains plant compounds, such as polyphenols and flavonoids, that are good for your health.

**2. Eat a high-quality breakfast.** Why are you always hearing that breakfast is the most important meal of the day? *Because it is.* Breakfast jump starts your metabolism and gets your energy going—provided you eat protein for breakfast. But breakfasts consisting of fast carbs such as breakfast cereal, a bagel and OJ will immediately break down into glucose and spike your blood sugar and insulin. Then, once your bloodstream is cleared, your body and brain start screaming for more glucose. How? By making you feel drowsy, unable to focus and hungry again (otherwise known as the "mid-morning slump").

This will not happen when you build your breakfast around protein (such as eggs, Greek yogurt, nitrate–free bacon or steel-cut oats), healthy fat (as in eggs, avocado, butter and full-fat yogurt) and slow carbs (such as berries, black beans, or the veggies in an omelet). A protein-based breakfast will perk you up mentally without spiking your blood sugar and insulin levels. This way, glucose will be slowly released into your bloodstream for a steady energy supply. The fat in your morning meal will keep your hunger satisfied until lunchtime. Best of all, your carb cravings will diminish or vanish; and you will lose weight without trying, because insulin, the body's fat storage hormone, will remain in the shadows.

**3. Take a 30-minute walk every day.** The great thing about physical activity is that it is the spark that gets your body's metabolism going. This isn't about exercise or trying to lose weight. Instead, it's realizing that your body and brain just work better when you're physically active. Blood glucose gets burned off, your cells use insulin more efficiently (so you need less of it), more oxygen gets into your bloodstream and to your organs, and your mood and self-confidence perk up.

Physical activity is another trait we share with our hunter-gatherer ancestors. They were constantly in motion and therefore in peak physical condition. Scientists tell us that after periods of physical activity, brain chemicals called endorphins kick in to create a sense of euphoria and well-being.

These three simple practices—eliminating sugary drinks, eating a protein-rich breakfast and walking at least 30 minutes a day—are the foundation upon which you can build your entire diabetes-reversing lifestyle.

## Use Your Willpower to Rein In Your DNA

Psychologists have found that it generally takes at least 21–28 days to replace a bad habit with a good one. This is why most drug and alcohol recovery programs last at least one month. This also is why we designed The 30-Day Diabetes Cure Plan for you, which follows in Part 2 of this book.

While you will need to exert some effort to maintain a regular practice in the beginning, these efforts will become natural after a short time. They will become ingrained habits that you will find yourself performing automatically and unconsciously. In short, you will be rewiring your brain to create healthy blood sugar and good health for yourself.

Imagine: No longer must you cave in to the urges that seduce your primitive reptilian brain. Instead, you will exert conscious control over your caveman (or cavewoman) cravings—and actually start *enjoying* the state of healthfulness. In the process, instead of being a slave to your impulses, you will be cultivating real personal power and the freedom to make choices that truly matter.

In this way, healing your diabetes can actually heal your entire life. It will heal our world, too. Because as your family, friends and co-workers notice your marvelous transformation, they'll be inspired to heal and improve their lives, too.

You see, you really *can* change the world.

Remember: Nothing succeeds like success. Once you begin to experience the fruits of your labors (more energy, positive moods, appreciation for your life, more meaningful relationships—in addition to your slimmer waistline and better glucose levels), you will just naturally want to keep getting better.

## Patient Case Study: Helene

Hello, my name is Helene and I have been a Type 2 diabetic for four years. I live in Santa Fe, New Mexico and I work with the government. It is very stressful. My hemoglobin A1C was 8.4 (normal is less than 6) and my blood sugar averaged 192 (normal is less than 100). I was started on two diabetes prescription drugs. I was very upset by the side effects. I felt tired all the time. I gained weight. And my blood sugar got worse and worse. I had to do something. I was desperate.

I heard about the *30-Day Diabetes Cure*. I consulted with my doctor and he suggested I follow it immediately. Literally within a week I felt so much better, stronger, and happier. My blood sugar tests improved after 30 days back to normal. I am now off all prescription medications and am thrilled.

# CHAPTER 10

# THE DIABETES-HEALING SUPERFOODS

*"One cannot think well, love well, sleep well,
if one has not dined well."*

—VIRGINIA WOOLF, English writer, 1882–1941

AS TERRIFYING AS A DIABETES diagnosis can be, you don't have to be scared. Far from it. There are safe, effective ways to avoid or reverse diabetes and prevent its complications—ways that do not include medication. It can be as simple as eating your next meal, especially if each meal contains some of the diabetes-healing superfoods you will read about in this chapter.

The best diabetes-healing superfoods have a low Glycemic Index (see below)...are rich in fiber, vitamins and minerals...and include plenty of healthy fats and clean protein. By eating a diet rich in these foods, you can gain control over your blood glucose levels and begin to normalize your natural insulin-producing function. Furthermore, study after study shows that they are directly associated with reducing the risk of heart disease and they will help you lose excess weight, which is linked with the risk of diabetes and its complications.

If you eat too much sugar or carbohydrates, the medical solution is to just put more insulin in your system. Yet, studies show that changing what you eat can improve your insulin sensitivity, protect against heart, kidney and nerve damage and actually reverse Type 2 diabetes. This approach also can help Type 1 diabetics reduce the amount of insulin they must inject every day.

## Get to Know the Glycemic Index

Knowing how individual foods and beverages affect your blood glucose is an important piece of this healing puzzle. If the body becomes unable to produce enough insulin to metabolize glucose as it comes into your bloodstream, elevated glucose levels turn into a slow-acting but steady poison, wreaking havoc throughout your entire body, including your blood vessels and your organs. In Type 1 diabetes, there is no natural insulin production taking place in the body, so it must be injected in exactly the right amounts to avoid problems; too much is as dangerous as too little. In Type 2, if excess blood glucose goes unchecked long enough, the disease can potentially develop into Type 1, with the prospect of a life-long dependence on an external source of insulin.

So how do you know what to eat? In order to determine how fast carbohydrates covert to blood glucose, researchers developed the Glycemic Index (GI). Glycemic refers to glucose; the index refers to the amount of glucose in your bloodstream after you eat. A high GI number would indicate a food that produces high blood glucose, and a low GI means a food that does not significantly raise your blood glucose.

Scientists learned some unexpected things about food as a result of analyzing their GIs. For instance, nutritionists used to believe that all simple carbs like sweet desserts caused a rapid rise in blood glucose, and complex carbs like grains and starchy vegetables, which digest more slowly, would not cause such a rise. By measuring actual levels of blood glucose after specific carbohydrates were eaten, scientists discovered some interesting facts:

- While sweet and sugary foods do have high GIs, some starchy foods such as potatoes and white bread scored higher than honey or table sugar.

- Meats and seafood are mostly protein and fat, so they have extremely low GIs.

- Some high GI foods can be lowered by eating them in combination with low GI foods.

Diabetes-friendly foods ideally have a GI of under 50. Because GIs can be surprising, using this measurement is a helpful guide for choosing what to eat. To find out the GIs of specific foods and products, go to *www.glycemicindex.com*. We've also included a list of the GIs of a variety of popular foods, including those mentioned above, in Appendix B on page 370.

Unfortunately, there are two problems with relying on the Glycemic Index when choosing your foods. One is that true GIs can only be determined by testing, and there are very few places that conduct these tests. That means the number of foods with proven GIs is limited. The second problem is that manufacturers are producing food combinations faster than they can be evaluated.

Also, your body's glycemic response depends on two factors: not only the type of carbohydrate you eat but also the amount consumed. It turns out that even if a food has a high GI, if you eat just a little of it, it won't throw your blood glucose out of whack. Thus, a new guideline was developed, the Glycemic Load (GL). In order to get a more accurate measure of food's impact on blood glucose, Walter Willett, MD, PhD, and colleagues at the Harvard School of Public Health developed this formula:

GL = GI/100 x Net Carbs

(Net Carbs are the Total Carbohydrates minus Dietary Fiber)

Low Glycemic Load foods, just like low Glycemic Index foods, help keep your blood glucose at healthy levels. So now you can control your glycemic response by consuming low-GI foods and/or by restricting the quantity of high GL carbohydrates. If you are diabetic, you can consume about 80 GL points a day, split evenly between meals and snacks. This offers much greater variety in food choice—but watch those portions! You can find a great resource for nutrition information at NutritionData.com.

# The 12 Top Diabetes Superfoods

Our diabetes-reversing eating plan is not a fad diet based on eating one kind of food or none of another. This is a long-term plan to improve your lifestyle by adding a superfood to each of your meals and snacks.

We have identified a dozen superfoods that work wonders in healing diabetes and preventing its complications. These foods are naturally abundant in nutrients such as antioxidants, essential fatty acids (EFAs), and vitamins and minerals that improve insulin sensitivity, protect against blood glucose spikes and quell the systemic inflammation that leads to serious illness. Not only are these superfoods delicious and easy to incorporate into your daily diet, they offer multiple healing benefits that keep blood glucose in a healthy range and also help you lose weight. All of these foods have an extremely low GL, too.

In this chapter, we will introduce you to these diabetes-healing superfoods and discuss the excellent nutritional benefits they offer, as well as the clinical studies that have proven just how powerful they really are.

| The Top 12 Diabetes-Healing Superfoods | | |
|---|---|---|
| **Food** | **Serving Size** | **GL** |
| 1.  **Beans** | ½ cup | 7 |
| 2.  **Lean meat** | 1 ounce | 0 |
| 3.  **Salmon & omega-3 rich fish** | 1 ounce | 0 |
| 4.  **Yogurt (plain low-fat)** | ¾ cup | 8 |
| 5.  **Nuts** | 1 ounce | 0–5 |
| 6.  **Whole grains** | 1 slice multigrain bread | 5 |
| 7.  **Broccoli & other crucifers** | 1 cup | 3 |
| 8.  **Romaine lettuce** | 1 cup | 1 |
| 9.  **Onions** | 1 cup | 5 |
| 10.  **Grapefruit** | 1 cup | 7 |
| 11.  **Olive oil** | 1 teaspoon | 0 |
| 12.  **Curry** | 1 teaspoon | 0 |

# #1: Beans and Legumes

Beans and legumes are our favorite diabetes superfood because of how well they regulate blood glucose. Since they break down into glucose slowly, they do not overwhelm the body's insulin response, and their high protein and low calorie content make them a valuable helper for losing or preventing the excess weight that is so dangerous for people with diabetes.

Beans rank low on the Glycemic Index (under 50 for most varieties) which means they break down into glucose slowly in the bloodstream, as opposed to high GI foods like white bread or soda pop. A slow entry into the bloodstream gives the body's natural insulin response adequate time to escort that glucose along at its appropriate pace, rather than being overwhelmed by a rush of sugars, which creates insulin resistance and eventually results in diabetes. In a five-year study of 64,000 women, reported by the *American Journal of Clinical Nutrition*, eating beans regularly resulted in a 38% reduction in risk for Type 2 diabetes.[191]

**Beans keep glucose levels steady.** Not only do beans and legumes have a low GI, they actively control blood glucose. The same pigments that give nutrient-dense berries their color are also present in beans, and those pigments are actually an antioxidant polyphenol called anthocyanin. Anthocyanins help control blood glucose and limit the damage diabetes causes to blood and arteries. Adding just three cups of beans per week to your diet—that is about one cup of lentils or black beans, one serving of bean soup, and one serving of three bean salad— can significantly improve your blood glucose and reduce your risk of developing diabetes, especially if you substitute beans for high GI refined carbohydrates like noodles, bread and white rice.

**Beans reduce dependence on meds.** For people who already have diabetes, beans can reduce your need for insulin medications. James Anderson, MD of the Human Nutrition Research Center of the USDA was one of the early research pioneers on the health benefits of fiber, and he found that people with Type 1 diabetes were able to reduce their need for insulin by 38% just by eating beans. And for those with Type 2 diabetes, eating beans not only reduced their need for insulin and other diabetic medications, but in some cases all but eliminated the need for supplemental insulin.[192]

**Slim your midsection.** People with diabetes often struggle with weight, especially with dangerous belly fat. Beans are high in protein and low in calories, making them an ideal ally in the weight-loss efforts of people with diabetes. Eating beans instead of meat at several meals a week can lower your calorie intake, thus helping you drop excess pounds (and helping you manage your budget, as well). Because of this slow transition of bean's carbohydrates into sugars in your bloodstream, beans assist your body's insulin response to glucose and help you burn fat faster.

**Beans boost fiber intake.** Beans are high in soluble fiber, which binds to carbohydrates and slows their digestion into the bloodstream, preventing wild swings in blood glucose levels. They also contain generous amounts of resistant starch, which means that beans are less digestible than other carbs in the small intestine, so they move into the large intestine faster. Once there, they limit the sharp rise of glucose levels and insulin that can follow a meal.

**Beans open insulin doorways.** Beans are loaded with pectin and other fibers that help sensitize your cells to insulin and aid in its uptake by producing extra insulin receptors on the cells. These insulin receptors function as doorways that make it easier for insulin to do its two-fold job of removing glucose from the blood and ushering it into the cells where it's used as the body's essential fuel.

**The choice is yours.** There are literally dozens of beans to choose from. Beans are part of the legume family, which includes lentils, split peas, string beans, as well as all the dry beans like pinto and red beans—offering a cornucopia of colors, textures and recipe possibilities. Black beans and red kidney beans top the list for total dietary fiber and resistant starch. Lentils and chickpeas rate very low on the Glycemic Index, making them the stars of the legume family in terms of stabilizing blood glucose. Whether it's a three-bean salad, boiled beans, refried beans, bean soup, or bean dip—beans cook up in endless ways. All these bean dishes are packed with healthy fiber, which will help you control and stabilize your blood glucose levels and keep your weight down.

## #2: Lean, Clean Protein

Diabetics need to build strength, keep blood glucose balanced, and have sustained energy throughout the day. That is why each meal and snack should include a protein source—lean meats, eggs, beans, dairy products, and nuts are smart options.

**Grass-fed—not grain-fed.** One of the best lean meats you can choose is grass-fed beef, which has a number of benefits to recommend its use, from its high content of healthful fats to its low calorie count. Grass-fed beef is also high in a number of nutrients, including beta-carotene and vitamin E, and is considerably less likely than factory-farmed, grain-fed beef to transmit infectious bacteria such as *E. Coli*. In addition, grass-fed cattle are easier on the environment.

Grass-fed beef is high in omega-3s, an essential fatty acid that is vital for all the body's functions, including cardiovascular health, proper blood glucose balance (essential for treating diabetes or avoiding it altogether), and reducing inflammation—which is the cornerstone of most debilitating diseases.

Grass-fed cattle are two to four times higher in omega-3, in fact, than grain-fed beef, which makes grass-fed beef a superior choice for animal protein in the diet. Sixty percent of the fatty acids in grass are omega-3s, which accounts for the high level in grass-fed beef. When cattle are taken from the pasture to the feedlot to eat corn and other grains, which are low in omega-3, their omega-3 content plummets. The longer they stay in the feedlot, the lower their omega-3 drops.

Grass-fed beef is also superior for its super-low ratio of omega-6 to omega-3 essential fatty acids—a very desirable 2:1. This figure is important because a high ratio has been correlated with an increased risk for cancer, cardiovascular disease, allergies, depression, obesity and autoimmune disorders. Grain-fed beef has a ratio of 14:1. The lack of healthful omega-3 foods in the average diet—such as grass-fed beef—to balance out the essential amount of omega-6 necessary in the diet, means a population at much greater risk for a number of diseases.

**Leaner, greener, and cleaner.** Grass-fed beef is also much leaner than grain-fed beef, which is specifically raised to have a high fat level, even though more and more consumers, as well as medical professionals, shun the high saturated fat content of the beef-centric American diet as a danger to heart health. Add in a 2:1 omega ratio for grass-fed instead of 14:1, and you can see why the culprit in our diet is not beef, but rather the low-quality, factory feedlot beef that wreaks havoc with our nutritional balance.

The meat from grass-fed cattle is four times higher in the powerful antioxidant vitamin E than grain-fed beef; it's even higher than the vitamin E in feedlot cattle given vitamin E supplements. Vitamin E is highly protective against free radicals and the damage caused by oxidation, which makes it a powerful ally against heart disease, cancer and other diseases. It is also involved in immune function and normal cell activity, and according to studies, appears to be most effective when taken as part of a whole food rather than isolated as a supplement, making grass-fed beef and dairy products an ideal option.

**Easier weight loss.** Grass-fed cattle produce meat and dairy products that contain three to five times more conjugated linoleic acid (CLA) than animals on grain diets. CLA is a naturally-occurring polyunsaturated fatty acid that has been linked to a higher metabolic rate (so the body burns calories faster) and the lower incidence of many cancers. French cheese actually has among the highest amounts of CLA to be found, which is not so surprising when you consider the French reliance on traditional grass-fed cattle—and might also be one reason why the French have such low incidences of cancer even though their diet is high in fat. Soft French cheeses that are slightly aged have CLA levels between 5.3 and 15.8 mg/g, whereas most American-made cheese from grain-fed cattle ranges from 2.9 to 7.1. But you do not have to travel to France, of course, for this benefit: You can buy American grass-fed beef and dairy products, which are amply available at farmers markets, health food stores and online, and immediately reap the benefits of this superior protein source.

## #3: Wild-Caught Fish

Wild salmon, rainbow trout, mackerel, halibut, shellfish, and sardines are some of the healthiest foods on the planet, thanks to their high levels of nutritious fats. These omega-3 essential fatty acids have well-known health benefits for diabetes. They…

- Improve insulin sensitivity
- Lower triglycerides
- Reduce abnormal heart rhythms
- Lower inflammation
- Reduce blood pressure
- Improve blood clotting regulation

Most of the benefits of omega-3 seafood are also important indicators of heart health. As we've said previously, diabetics have a high risk of developing—and dying from—heart disease.

**Lessons from the North.** Scientists have learned a great deal about the impact of a diet high in fatty fish by studying Alaskan and Greenland Inuit. These native people tradition-ally had a diet high in cold-water seafood as well as very low incidence of cardiovascular disease or diabetes. The Japanese, who also consume large amounts of fish, also have much lower rates of heart disease and diabetes than Americans. Conversely, since these popula-tions began eating like modern Americans (namely, a diet high in processed foods, refined carbohydrates and damaging trans fats) and exercised less, their rates of obesity and diabe-tes have soared.[193]

To examine the connection between American-style eating habits, heart disease, and dia-betes, Sven Ebbesson, PhD of the University of Virginia studied 44 contemporary Inuit who had early signs of diabetes—impaired glucose tolerance and excess weight. For the study, they ate more traditional foods, especially fish and other marine animals. After four years, not a single person had advanced to Type 2 diabetes.[194]

**Resolvins fight inflammation.** Much of the diabetes-healing impact of wild salmon has to do with inflammation. Researchers at the University of California, San Diego and Switzerland's University of Fribourg discovered a connection between inflammation and diabetes.[195] Their research showed that inflammation provoked by certain immune cells called macrophages can lead to insulin resistance and then to Type 2 diabetes. Omega-3s found in the fat of cold-water fish help your body produce anti-inflammatory resolvins from eicosapentaenoic acid (EPA) and docosahexaenoic acid (DHA), which also help lower blood glucose levels.

**Omega-3 helps your heart.** If you have diabetes, you have four to five times the risk for getting heart disease than non-diabetics, so anything you can do to protect your heart is im-portant. Part of the reason omega-3s in salmon lower heart attack rates is because they lower a fat in the bloodstream called triglycerides. High triglycerides contribute to metabolic syn-drome, a combination of conditions that increase the risk for diabetes, stroke and cardiovas-cular disease. In a 6-month study of overweight adults published in the *Journal of Nutrition*, those who ate fish high in omega-3s were able to drop their triglyceride levels by almost 7%.[196] In another large study of more than 11,000 people with heart disease, the daily consumption of about one gram of fish oil (equivalent to a 3-ounce serving of salmon) reduced heart attacks by an amazing 45%.[197]

**Say no to weight gain.** Excess weight is also directly linked to insulin resistance, because it is a very visual indication that your cells have not been metabolizing glucose properly for some time. When your glucose-overloaded cells start to resist insulin's ability to metabolize blood glucose, some of it just circulates around in your bloodstream, damaging your blood vessels and other organs; large amounts are also shuttled over to your fat cells as triglycerides. This insulin resistance, combined with excess weight, puts you on the fast track to developing full-blown diabetes.

So the first line of defense is to learn how to manage your appetite—with the help of omega-3—so you don't start packing on the pounds in the first place. The EPA in omega-3s stimulates the secretion of the hormone leptin that tells the brain when the stomach feels full. Without that signal—which is often chemically circumvented when you eat processed foods—it is easy to overeat. Chronic overeating leads, of course, to weight gain and obesity.

Trevor Mori, PhD at the University of Western Australia recently showed that people on a weight-loss diet that included daily consumption of omega-3 fish, like salmon, improved glucose and insulin metabolism.[198] People on the same diet without fish had no such improvements. Also, both groups lost the same amount of weight, but blood pressure reduction was greater among the fish eaters than the non-fish eaters. Lowering blood pressure reduces the ever-present risk of heart problems for diabetics.

**Avoid toxic, unhealthful seafood.** Eating salmon and other omega-3 fish has huge diabetes-healing benefits, but not all omega-3 fish are healthful. Despite being rich in this diabetes-healing fat, most commercial seafood is loaded with contaminants. Larger ocean varieties tend to be contaminated with mercury residue generated by acid rain (created primarily by coal emissions). Since high levels of mercury have been linked to brain disorders, government officials advise that pregnant women, nursing mothers, young children and women who might become pregnant avoid swordfish, shark and king mackerel, and limit their consumption of other large fish, including albacore tuna, salmon and herring.

The best fish you can eat, which is both toxin-free and has a high content of omega-3s, is wild Alaskan salmon. Regrettably, overfishing has created a shortage of this healthful, wild-caught fish, but don't be lured into choosing farmed fish instead. In fact, you should avoid farmed fish of any kind. They may have high levels of PCBs and chemicals from plastics, and farmed fish often contains lower amounts of healing omega-3s compared to truly wild-caught fish.

Farmed fish also have unhealthy levels of pro-inflammatory omega-6 fatty acids—an essential fat that is only useful when it is in the proper ratio to omega-3. Farmed salmon are fed excessive amounts of soy pellets instead of their natural food source; processed soy increases the ratio of omega-6 and promotes chronic inflammation in humans. Remember, inflammation is associated with insulin resistance and Type 2 diabetes.

Farmed salmon also are fed large amounts of antibiotics to control diseases caused by the crowded, unnatural conditions in which they are raised. Those antibiotics get into those of us who eat the fish and impair our bodies' natural resistance to illness. Instead, choose truly wild Alaskan salmon known as Chinook (also called King), Sockeye, Coho, chum, and pink (most of which is canned or frozen).

**Fish oil supplements.** If you find it difficult to eat a lot of fish every week, consider fish oil supplements. They'll deliver the perfect amount of balanced essential fatty acids. But do fish oil capsules contain mercury and PCBs? The watchdog researchers at Consumer Labs evaluated 20 different brands and found no detectable mercury levels.[199] Almost all fish oil companies thoroughly filter their products to remove mercury residues, but check the labels to be sure, and purchase only the fish oil supplements labeled as having undergone a process called molecular distillation, which eliminates toxins. And be certain the product you pick contains a combined minimum of 500mg EPA and DHA, vital components of omega 3 fatty acids.

# #4: "Super Yogurt"

Yogurt is known for its good bacteria that help digestion, but the important news for diabetics is that yogurt improves glucose metabolism, insulin sensitivity, high blood pressure, and cholesterol. The beneficial bacteria are probiotics, which means "for life," and yogurt truly is a diabetic's life-healer.

**It's alive!** One reason yogurt is such a dynamic healer is because it's a living food, the result of adding beneficial bacteria to milk and keeping it warm until the lactose, or milk sugar, turns to lactic acid and ferments. This provides the perfect breeding ground for good bacteria so they can multiply. So, eating live yogurt regularly is like sending in the cavalry to reinforce the beneficial bacteria in your GI tract. These beneficial bugs represent one way in which nature keeps the bad gut bacteria (such as e. coli, salmonella, listeria, campylobacter, and clostridium perfringens, which cause food poisoning and other health problems) from overwhelming your body and challenging your immune system. For the best diabetes-healing power, make sure your yogurt has *Lactobacillus* and *Bifidobacterium*, which give yogurt its characteristic lemony taste.

**Pro-bacteria.** Yogurt's bacteria help in the first line of defense for diabetics: good digestion. Insulin resistance prevents nutrients from passing across cell membranes, so diabetics' cells are actually being starved of nutrition. Probiotic bacteria in yogurt along with lactose, protein, calcium, magnesium, and potassium slow the digestion of food sugars so they don't assault the blood stream.

**Lower your blood pressure.** Diabetics have another reason to add probiotic yogurt to their daily diet. High blood glucose causes plaque buildup in arteries, increasing the risk for high blood pressure (hypertension), heart attack and stroke. In several large studies, including one that involved 12,550 adults, the development of Type 2 diabetes was 2.5 times more likely in those with hypertension. And it's a double whammy because once you have Type 2 diabetes, you're twice as likely to also have hypertension. This affects 30% of Type 1 diabetes patients, too. The good news is that a study conducted by the American Heart Association showed that people who ate yogurt long-term (the study lasted 15 years) had a lower systolic blood pressure as well a decreased risk of developing high blood pressure.[200]

**Go Greek.** Yogurt is one of the few probiotic foods that Americans regularly eat. But not all yogurts are equal. Many store-bought products can be loaded with sugar, artificial flavors and additives that are not good for you. Check the package to make sure you are getting the benefits of active diabetes-healing probiotics: Lactobacillus and Bifidobacterium.

The very best yogurt for diabetics is Greek yogurt because the whey has been removed to create a thicker consistency. Whey is mostly lactose and it can spike insulin levels in people with Type 2 diabetes as well as in healthy people, according to a research report in *The American Journal of Clinical Nutrition.** Insulin spikes make us hungry, which may make us gain weight—which increases the risk of diabetes. Greek yogurt is higher in protein, which digests more slowly than typical fat-free and low-fat yogurts.

# #5: Seeds and Nuts

Seeds and nuts are a smart choice for people with diabetes, thanks to their abundant healthy fats, vitamins and minerals that help keep the disease under control.

We usually think of seeds and nuts as being too high in fat and calories for a weight-loss diet. Surprisingly, nuts help you lose weight. Weight loss is ultimately about eating the right amount and kind of fats. Seeds and nuts are the perfect snack food, too. Try a handful or two for a midday snack, and stick to raw or lightly roasted nuts without added salt, sugar, oils, or extra seasonings. Almond butter on whole grain toast or flax seeds sprinkled on steel-cut oats both make a satisfying high-protein breakfast; add grapefruit for extra fiber and extra diabetes protection—and enjoy a smart start to your day.

Avoid the bulk bins for nuts unless you are sure they are emptied and cleaned frequently, and stick to organic, raw or dry roasted, and lightly salted or salt-free nuts.

Here are a few best nut choices:

**Almonds** are particularly beneficial because they're both high in protein and low on the Glycemic Index. Twenty different flavonoids in almond skin, including catechin (found in green tea) and naringenin (found in grapefruit) join up with vitamin E in the meat of the almond to double the antioxidant power. Antioxidants scavenge free radicals and help prevent the oxidative damage they do to blood vessels, which leads to inflammation, metabolic syndrome and diabetes. Plus, a quarter cup of almonds contains almost 45% of your daily nutritional value for vitamin E.

Almonds are also high in magnesium, which helps the blood flow more easily; a deficiency in magnesium can lead to free radical damage to the heart. A quarter cup of almonds contains almost 25% of your daily nutritional value for magnesium. Almonds are also high in manganese, which helps protect against the oxidation of LDL cholesterol, preventing the buildup of plaque in the arteries, which can lead to atherosclerosis, cardiovascular disease and stroke. A quarter cup of almonds provides 45% of your daily nutritional value for manganese.

**Walnuts** keep your heart healthy, and that's critical for diabetics who often suffer from heart complications. Walnuts, pecans and chestnuts are exceptionally high in antioxidants, which can lower the risk for coronary heart disease that often results from having diabetes.

**Peanuts** are technically a legume—rather than a nut—but they are rich in diabetes-healing fats, like most nuts are. They contain oleic acid, the same healthy fat found in olive oil. They are also high in vitamin E and other powerful antioxidants. Peanuts are also high in the

---

**http://ajcn.nutrition.org/content/82/1/69.full*

flavonoid, resveratrol, an antioxidant also found in red grapes and red wine. Be careful how you store peanuts because they are susceptible to mold and fungus, including one that is a known carcinogen.

## #6: Whole Grains

Whole grains can be an excellent superfood for managing and healing your diabetes. Here are their best attributes:

**Reduce blood glucose levels.** Whole grains prevent blood glucose surges. Refined carbohydrates such as white flour products, processed foods, soft drinks, and sugar, all spike your blood glucose in minutes and require more insulin, a hormone secreted by the pancreas, to digest it. Whole grains are complex carbohydrates, which still have their beneficial fiber and nutrients intact. Because they digest slowly, releasing blood glucose into the bloodstream at a steady pace, whole grains prevent rapid swings in blood glucose.

You will see that whole grains generally rank very low on the Glycemic Index. This is especially important for people with diabetes. Eating foods with a high GI, such as most refined carbs, causes blood glucose to spike and requires extra insulin to digest it. Generally speaking, white foods such as white bread, white pasta, white rice, and white potatoes, have high GI scores. Foods with low GI scores, such as oat bran and barley, are also high in fiber and cause only a slight rise in blood glucose. That makes them ideal foods for glucose control. It's safe to assume that the least-processed foods, which appear closest to their natural state, have lower GI scores than processed ones.

**Counter insulin resistance.** Whole grains such as wheat, oats, barley, rye, wild rice, and brown rice also help cells overcome insulin resistance. Insulin resistance, a precursor to full-blown diabetes, occurs when your body no longer responds to the insulin being secreted by the pancreas. Greater amounts of insulin are then required to manage the glucose in your bloodstream. The more responsive your cells are to insulin, the better they are able to metabolize glucose, and the less likely you will be to develop diabetes. Whole grains require less insulin to digest, which helps prevent the toxic buildup of excess glucose in the bloodstream.

**Rich in fiber.** Whole grains are loaded with fiber, making them a strong ally in the fight against weight gain and obesity, which are serious risk factors for developing diabetes or complications from diabetes. How quickly a carbohydrate is broken down into glucose depends on its overall fiber content. Since fiber slows the absorption of glucose into the bloodstream, eating foods rich in fiber helps control and stabilize glucose levels. Whole grains are high in insoluble fiber, the no-calorie roughage that fills you up and helps move waste out of your system. That's important for people with diabetes because these foods aid in weight loss, which lowers insulin resistance and allows your natural insulin to do its job.

Soluble fiber is the fiber found in oatmeal, oat bran, seeds, and beans. When digested, soluble fiber turns into a sticky gel that slows the digestion of sugars and starches, controls blood glucose spikes and traps cholesterol and other fats clogging your bloodstream.

**A healthful "comfort food."** Whole grains are healing comfort foods that are most beneficial when eaten moderately and consistently. Rather than packing in a big load of carbs one day and skipping them the next day, which puts your blood glucose on a wild ride, it's best to eat roughly the same amount of complex carbs every day. Portions are important too. Because of their roughage content, whole grains help you feel full much faster than refined or processed carbohydrates, so you will not need large platefuls to satisfy your hunger. Bite for bite, vegetables and whole grains provide more nutrients and fiber, with fewer calories, than any other food group. They are your best allies when it comes to controlling your weight and your glucose levels simultaneously.

**Options.** Below are a handful of common whole grains to consider. Bear in mind that some—such as spelt, barley and rye—contain gluten; if you have gluten allergies, these three whole grains should be avoided.

- Oats are especially high in fiber and loaded with vitamins and minerals. They also contain saponin, which helps the pancreas regulate insulin production.

- Brown rice is another diabetes buster and is high in manganese, a critical component in antioxidant enzymes, which protect the body from damaging free radicals.

- Buckwheat helps stabilize glucose levels in the blood.

- Spelt, an ancient form of wheat, that some people with gluten allergies can still tolerate, is higher in protein than wheat and is also high in fiber.

- Rye, another high protein grain, also triggers a slower release of glucose into the bloodstream and is a good source of magnesium, a mineral that aids the body in metabolizing glucose.

- Barley, which many diabetics consider the perfect grain, is high in soluble fiber and boasts the lowest GI of all the grains.

**A word of caution.** Some diabetics find that whole grains actually raise their blood glucose levels. We suggest using the smart monitoring technique you will discover on Day 1 of The 30-Day Diabetes Cure Plan on page 165 to see how whole grains affect your levels before committing to them.

## #7: Queen Broccoli

Broccoli is one of the most powerful diabetes-healing foods on earth, thanks to its plentiful array of vitamins, minerals, fiber, and especially antioxidants that help prevent damage from free radicals. Broccoli boosts your immune system and helps you avoid diabetes and all its complications, especially cardiovascular disease.

**Solid heart protection.** The key healing compound in broccoli is *sulforaphane*, which plays a major role in protecting damaged blood vessels. Too much glucose in the bloodstream eventually damages and constricts the blood vessels, which is also why people with diabetes suffer from circulation problems in their feet, lower legs and hands. But sulforaphane encourages the production of enzymes that reduce the blood vessel damage triggered by high blood glucose levels, thus helping to minimize the devastating effects of diabetes.

All of broccoli's cruciferous cousins contain sulforaphane—including kale, cabbage, collards, bok choy, mustard greens, kohlrabi, turnips, cauliflower, arugula, and watercress. If you don't like broccoli or its cousins, try broccoli sprouts, which have the very highest concentrations of sulforaphane.

**More vitamin C than orange juice.** Broccoli has additional diabetes-healing power with its high levels of vitamin C, even more than oranges. Because the body can't manufacture vitamin C, we must get it from the food we eat. One cup of broccoli delivers about 116 milligrams of this powerful antioxidant, almost twice the minimum recommended daily amount for adults.

**Re-sensitize your insulin receptors.** Broccoli is a great source of the trace mineral chromium, used to manufacture glucose tolerance factor, or GTF, which helps break down blood glucose. According to the Linus Pauling Institute, the chromium in broccoli helps lower your blood glucose, cholesterol and triglycerides, which greatly reduces your risk of diabetes and cardiovascular disease.[201] Chromium aids in the metabolism of glucose by re-sensitizing the insulin receptors on the surface of every cell. Many Americans are chromium-deficient because a diet heavy in refined carbohydrates such as white sugar and white flour is not only low in chromium, it also depletes chromium from your body.

**Fight diabetes with fiber.** Dietary fiber is the roughage that makes you feel full without gaining weight, and broccoli is loaded with it. Foods that are high in fiber help slow the metabolism of glucose and control blood glucose levels, thus reducing your risk of developing diabetes or cardiovascular disease. High-fiber foods such as broccoli also support weight loss, which helps to lower insulin resistance. The less cells resist insulin, the more insulin can usher glucose into your body's cells.

**Broccoli for better eyesight.** One of the complications of diabetes is retinopathy, which causes a slow loss of vision. Broccoli is rich in beta-carotene, which your body uses to make vitamin A, another powerful antioxidant that is necessary for healthy eyes. When selecting broccoli, choose those stalks with the darkest color, because that means it has the most beta-carotene. Eat it raw or lightly cooked and don't forget to eat the stems and leaves, too. The stems are not only sweet and mild-flavored, they're much higher in fiber than the broccoli florets, and the leaves are the richest source of beta-carotene.

# #8: Romaine Lettuce

Not all lettuce is created equal. Romaine lettuce is far superior to its popular rival, iceberg lettuce, when it comes to vitamins, minerals, phytonutrients, and dietary fiber—all necessary for people with diabetes. Romaine lettuce—and similar nutrient-rich lettuces like red leaf and green leaf—helps metabolize glucose and stabilize blood glucose levels, combats the damaging oxidation done by free radicals and helps prevent heart disease.

**Romaine breaks downs blood glucose.** Romaine lettuce and other leafy greens are rich in chromium, an essential mineral your body uses to manufacture the glucose tolerance factor (GTF) in order to break down blood glucose and keep it from accumulating in your bloodstream. As explained above, chromium works by re-sensitizing the insulin receptors on the surface of every cell.[202] Chromium not only helps lower your blood glucose, it lowers cholesterol and triglycerides as well, which helps reduce your risk of developing metabolic syndrome, the precursor to diabetes. Refined carbohydrates such as white sugar and white flour are not only low in chromium, they deplete it from your body. No wonder many Americans are chromium-deficient. Two cups of romaine lettuce contains 13% of your daily nutritional value (DNV) of chromium.

**Promotes insulin sensitivity.** Low-calorie romaine lettuce is packed with dietary fiber. Remember that eating unprocessed, high-fiber foods is essential for people with diabetes because they help slow the metabolism of glucose, increase insulin sensitivity and stabilize blood glucose levels. Dietary fiber-rich foods such as romaine lettuce also help your body eliminate toxins, lower high cholesterol, and lose weight. Four low-cal veggie wraps made with four big leaves of crunchy romaine will give you up to 8% of your DNV for dietary fiber.

**A bundle of vitamins and minerals.** Here is the special diabetes-healing power you will get with a salad made with two cups of romaine:

**Manganese.** One serving of romaine (one cup) delivers 35% of your DNV for manganese. Manganese is a mineral that aids in the metabolism of fats and carbohydrates, and romaine is full of it. Manganese is a component of manganese superoxide dismutase (Mn-SOD), an antioxidant that scavenges for free radicals and repairs the damage they cause. Manganese also helps protect against the oxidation of LDL (bad) cholesterol, preventing the buildup of plaques in the arteries, which can lead to atherosclerosis, cardiovascular disease and stroke.

According to a recent study conducted by the University of Maryland, as many as 37% of Americans are manganese-deficient.[203] Why? Because refined foods are deficient in this essential mineral. Interestingly, some research has found that people with diabetes have much lower levels of manganese than normal, but it is unknown whether this is a cause or an effect of diabetes. Add some summer squash, green beans, mushrooms, and brown rice to your romaine lettuce and you will have almost all the manganese you need.

**Vitamin A.** You will also get 60% of your DNV for vitamin A. Romaine lettuce is extremely high in the pro-vitamin A carotenoid, beta-carotene. Beta-carotene helps stop LDL (bad) cholesterol from forming into artery-blocking plaques. Add a quarter cup of grated carrots to your salad and you will top 100%.

**Vitamin "see."** Need more reasons? Romaine lettuce and other leafy greens like spinach are an excellent source of the antioxidant lutein, another carotenoid, which the body coverts into zeaxanthin. Lutein not only neutralizes oxidative damage done by free radicals and helps prevent atherosclerosis, but it also helps improve eye health. This is important for people with diabetes, who are at much greater risk for developing retinopathy, cataracts and macular degeneration.

**Antioxidants for cardiovascular health.** Romaine also delivers 45% of your DNV for vitamin C. Romaine's antioxidant vitamin C scavenges for free radicals and prevents the damage they do to blood vessels. The team of vitamin K, vitamin C, plus beta-carotene helps prevent cholesterol from becoming oxidized and sticky, which makes it build up in your arteries to form damaging plaques.

**Artery benefits.** Your body will also receive a whopping 140% of your DNV for vitamin K, which helps prevent arterial plaque and may also improve insulin resistance.

**Better blood pressure.** Finally, one serving of romaine contains 38% of your DNV for folate. Romaine lettuce and other leafy greens are high in folic acid, a B vitamin, which helps lower high blood pressure and prevent damage to blood vessels, thereby reducing the risk of heart attack and stroke.

**Keep it local.** Local produce is always more nutritious. Industrially grown lettuce, even if it's touted as organic, is often transported over long distances, sometimes halfway around the world. It's washed with chlorine and often treated with other chemicals to prolong its shelf life. While these practices may benefit the big industrial grower and vendor, they do not do much for your health. Instead, consider supporting the growers at your local farmer's market; they make every effort to differentiate their growing practices from those of big agribusiness. And the lettuce and greens you buy locally will taste better and be healthier for you because they will be much fresher. You can take even more control of your health by growing lettuce yourself.

# #9: Onions

Onions and their close cousins—garlic, chives, scallions, shallots, and leeks—are valuable allies in the fight against diabetes because they help lower blood glucose levels, increase sensitivity to insulin, and prevent diabetic complication such as heart disease and stroke. Packed with phytonutrients, they are a good source of beneficial vitamin C, contain no fat and are loaded with dietary fiber.

**Onion's amazing antioxidant powers.** Onions and garlic have positive cardiovascular effects because they are a rich source of dietary flavonoids, a class of plant compounds known for their antioxidant activity. (Antioxidants play an important role by inhibiting free radicals from damaging the body's cells, tissue, organs, and eventually, entire systems.) Researchers at Cornell University found that flavonoids such as those found in onions are associated with a reduced risk for cancer, heart disease and diabetes.[204]

Onions contain the potent antioxidant flavonoid called quercetin, which helps protect against the eye problems associated with diabetes, especially retinopathy. The amount of quercetin your body absorbs from onions is more than 300% greater than that from apples and twice what you get from tea. A report published by the New Mexico State University estimates that onions contain between 22mg and 52mg of quercetin per medium-sized onion, and that the daily consumption of onions increases the accumulation of quercetin in the blood.*

---

*http://onion.nmsu.edu/healthy-facts.html*

**Onions metabolize glucose.** Onions are also very high in chromium, a trace mineral essential for metabolizing glucose and helping promote insulin sensitivity. Some studies show that eating foods rich in chromium, such as onions, helps decrease fasting blood glucose levels, improve glucose tolerance and decrease total cholesterol and triglycerides.

According to biophysiologist and nutritionist, Kurt D. Grange, PhD, chromium levels naturally decrease with age. However, chromium deficiency may already be a widespread problem in the US, since the body's reserves of chromium are depleted by consuming refined sugar and white flour and by insufficient exercise. Chromium deficiency can lead to glucose intolerance, obesity and Type 2 diabetes. Only one cup of onions supplies 20% of your daily chromium needs.

**Pungency equals potency.** In general, the milder the onion's flavor, the less potent it is as a healing food for diabetes. Researchers at both the University of Wisconsin and Cornell University found that the more pungent the onion, the more health benefits you will receive in terms of anti- platelet activity, which keeps blood cells less sticky, so they don't clump together and form clots (which can cause a heart attack or stroke).[205] So chop up those onions (raw or cooked) and weep with joy at the diabetes-healing power you are about to put in your meal.

## #10: The Great Grapefruit

Grapefruit is a great fruit in the diabetes-healing diet because of its low GL and abundant store of antioxidants like vitamin C and lycopene, which boost immunity and prevent cell damage. Grapefruit is also rich in pectin, an enzyme that helps control blood glucose.

**A treasure chest of antioxidants.** Grapefruit is packed with antioxidants, which combat the damage free radicals cause to cells and organs. One grapefruit supplies over 78% of the recommended daily amount of the powerful antioxidant vitamin C. Pink grapefruits are also loaded with another powerful antioxidant, lycopene, which accounts for its rosy color.

Both vitamin C and lycopene boost immunity and prevent free radical damage that can trigger aging, high cholesterol, diabetes and diabetic complications such as cardiovascular disease. Researchers from Hebrew University's Hadassah Medical School, who performed studies on the health benefits of grapefruit, found that eating just one red grapefruit a day helped reduce heart-damaging cholesterol and triglycerides by 17% (white grapefruit came in at 15%).

**Plenty of pectin.** Grapefruits (and other citrus fruits) are also rich in pectin, an enzyme that helps moderate wild swings in glucose levels by binding to carbohydrates and slowing their digestion in the bloodstream. Pectin also helps sensitize your cells to insulin and aids in its uptake by producing insulin receptors on the cells. These insulin receptors function as a kind of doorway that makes it easier for insulin to do its two-fold job: removing glucose from the blood and ushering it into the cells where it is needed for the body's essential fuel.

The pectin in grapefruit also helps prevent blood vessels from clogging up with cholesterol, putting a person with diabetes at risk for cardiovascular disease, as well as poor circulation, loss of feeling and a reduced ability to heal from wounds, which can lead to gangrene and amputation.

**Fabulous flavonoids.** Grapefruit and other citrus fruits are rich in flavonoids that help the liver burn up surplus fats instead of allowing them to accumulate in the body. This is great news for people with diabetes, who must be careful about weight gain. Eating grapefruit reduces levels of insulin and glucose, because the enzymes in grapefruit change how the body metabolizes fat.

**Potential interaction with prescription medications.** Be aware that grapefruit can interfere with certain prescription medications. If you are taking prescription medications, be sure to consult your doctor before adding grapefruit (and other citrus fruits) to your diet.

## #11: Extra Virgin Olive Oil

A diet rich in olive oil has enhanced the health of Mediterranean peoples for thousands of years, making it a time-tested—as well as highly researched—ally for people with diabetes. Olive oil is one of the monounsaturated fats that are especially important for people with diabetes. These fats help stabilize glucose levels and prevent complications such as stroke and heart disease. Many nutritionists believe that diabetics should eat a low-fat/low-carb diet—low in fat to help prevent heart damage and fewer carbohydrates to avoid severe swings in blood glucose levels. But new research finds that a diet rich in monounsaturated fats such as olive oil is even more effective in controlling diabetes.[206]

**Olive oil = good cholesterol.** Olive oil also helps lower cholesterol. Researchers have also found that the monounsaturated fats present in olive oil help lower LDL (bad) cholesterol, keep triglyceride levels in check, and increase HDL (good) cholesterol.[207] This is important information for people with diabetes, because cardiovascular disease is one of its most serious complications. Doctors often prescribe medication to balance cholesterol and lower triglycerides, so eating olive oil regularly can be an effective way to reduce your need for so many pills.

**The weight-loss "fat."** Surprisingly, olive oil helps you lose weight. Researchers in Spain concluded that a calorie-controlled diet high in monounsaturated fat such as olive oil did not cause weight gain among people with diabetes, an important consideration, because excess weight exacerbates the disease.[208] They also found that including olive oil was more realistic (and pleasing) than eating a strict low-fat diet.

Eating the highest quality olive oil you can afford is important in order to obtain all its diabetes-healing nutrients. Extra virgin olive oil has the most benefits because it's from the first pressing of the olives. Best when unfiltered, olive oil should have a deep golden yellow to dark green color and come in a dark bottle or be stored in a dark pantry. Choose cold-pressed, which means it was not processed with heat or chemicals (both of which can destroy this delicate oil's nutritional value).

## #12: The Diabetes-Healing Spices

Curry, a mainstay of Asian cuisine, is a diabetes-fighting powerhouse. Several spices that make up traditional curries—including turmeric, cinnamon, fenugreek, cilantro, chili, and ginger—help combat diabetes because they help reduce inflammation and insulin resistance, repair and prevent the damage done by free radicals, and slow the metabolism of glucose in the bloodstream. Whether you use a curry spice or the individual spices listed below, you will reap diabetes-healing benefits.

**Turmeric gets the gold star when it comes to helping heal many diseases, especially diabetes.** The key ingredient in turmeric that accounts for curry's characteristic golden glow is curcumin (not to be confused with cumin). Researchers at Columbia University have found that curcumin is a powerful anti-inflammatory.[209] As you remember, chronic inflammation

### How Curcumin Heals

- It eases insulin resistance, which in turn lowers excess glucose levels in the bloodstream.
- It is a powerful antioxidant, important for combating the damage free radicals cause to blood vessels over time.
- It helps prevent cholesterol from being oxidized in the body, which is important because oxidized cholesterol damages blood vessels, builds up plaque and leads to diabetic complications such as heart disease and stroke.
- It helps heal wounds, which can be difficult to heal in people with diabetes.

plays a big role in developing metabolic syndrome, the precursor to Type 2 diabetes.

**Cinnamon** in curry powder helps insulin response by lowering glucose levels and improving your body's ability to take in insulin. Scientists at the Human Nutrition Research Center under the USDA found that a compound in cinnamon makes cells more sensitive and responsive to insulin, by promoting one enzyme that helps this process and by curbing another that blocks it.[210]

**Fenugreek,** another curry ingredient, helps control and lower glucose levels by curbing insulin resistance. Fenugreek helps increase the number of insulin receptors in red blood cells, thus helping cells absorb glucose from the bloodstream. Fenugreek is also a rich source of dietary fiber, which helps delay the absorption of glucose. This slightly mucilaginous fiber helps reduce fat absorption, which helps protect against obesity and metabolic syndrome.

Fenugreek contains many antioxidant and anti-inflammatory compounds that help reduce the clumping of platelets, which can lead to heart disease and stroke.

**Cilantro,** also known as coriander or Chinese parsley, is a potent curry spice that's beneficial for people with diabetes. Cilantro helps reduce blood glucose levels by promoting the release of insulin needed to usher glucose into the cells. Both the fresh leaves and seeds of cilantro are high in phytonutrients, flavonoids and polyphenols, including quercetin, which protects against cardiovascular disease and the eye problems associated with diabetes, especially retinopathy.

Cilantro contains powerful antioxidants that combat free radicals and help reverse the damage they do over time to blood vessels. Chlorogenic acid (also present in coffee, red wine and chocolate) helps slow the release of glucose after eating. Beta-carotene helps stop LDL (bad) cholesterol from forming into arterial plaques which can lead to diabetic complications like cardiovascular disease and stroke. Cilantro does even more: Indian research has found that cilantro helps reduce cholesterol and triglycerides. According to USDA scientists, cilantro also eases digestion.

Diabetes compromises your ability to naturally detoxify, so cilantro's cleansing properties are especially useful. Japanese research has found that cilantro helps clear up infections, a risk for people with diabetes. Cilantro is also an excellent (and inexpensive) plant remedy for removing (or "chelating") heavy metals such as mercury from the body.

**Chili pepper** lowers blood glucose and protects the heart. The main active compound in all chili peppers, from cayenne to jalapeño, is capsaicin, which also gives curry its heat. The antioxidants in capsaicin help combat free radicals and fight inflammation, too.

Chilis are high in vitamin C and carotenoids both of which improve insulin regulation. Two teaspoons of chili peppers provide 6% of your daily value for vitamin C and 10% of vitamin A, both of which help boost immunity (often compromised by diabetes). Chilis also help you lose weight, because the heat you feel after eating them takes energy to produce and that means calories burned.

**Ginger** is a spicy curry flavor, and it's also anti-inflammatory because of compounds called gingerols. Ginger also boosts the immune system and helps soothe the digestive system. This is important for people with diabetes because elevated blood glucose tends to impair digestion and lead to gastrointestinal complications.

**Be adventurous with curry.** Prepared curry dishes are common in natural food stores, either frozen or refrigerated. But you can also try your hand at cooking with curry. Start by adding typical curry spices into your daily menus. Ginger is a perfect healing companion to baked squash, or grated into hot water and lemon juice for a soothing tea. Chili powder can be added to everything from egg salad to brown rice, and cilantro adds a lively kick to salads and lightly steamed greens. Once you're familiar with the individual spices and flavors, browse through some Indian cookbooks in particular, set aside an afternoon, and try your hand at a simple curry for maximum healing benefits.

As well, try adding the individual spices to a wide array of common meals for some extra healing power. For instance, cinnamon easily tops off yogurt and fresh fruit. Season steamed vegetables with turmeric and add fenugreek to roast chicken or other meats.

## Start Eating These Diabetes-Healing Meals

Now that you know the superfoods that will heal your diabetes, you can begin to build your meals around them. Start with breakfast, which is the most important meal of the day—especially for diabetics—and add Greek yogurt, whole grains and grapefruit. If you need more inspiration and recipe ideas, browse Appendix C: Diabetes-Healing Breakfasts.

Build your snacks, lunches, and dinners around proteins like nuts, grass-fed beef, wild-caught salmon, and beans. Add in your choice of broccoli, romaine lettuce, or onions. Flavor your food with curry spices or olive oil and you will be on your way to better health. Your goal should be to add at least one superfood to each meal and snack you eat, and follow this simple formula for healing your diabetes:

- Choose nutrient-dense foods like whole grains, vegetables and high-quality protein.
- Reduce damaging fats.
- Eliminate starchy simple carbs like bread products.
- Avoid nutrient-poor processed foods.

By following this outline, your healing meals will keep your blood glucose at proper levels without overwhelming your insulin production. They'll also nourish and support your organs for healthy functioning.

## Feeling Full

The next time you choose your food, think about what we call the "fullness factor." Foods that have a low calorie to volume ratio (meaning they have few calories per gram) tend to fill you up faster (vegetables, legumes, unbuttered popcorn). Foods that contain large amounts of fat, sugar, and/or starch such as pasta, pizza and white bread have low Fullness Factors, and are much easier to overeat. Foods that contain large amounts of water, dietary fiber, and/or protein like fruit and nuts have the highest fullness factors. It's interesting to note how these two contrasting food groups roughly correspond to the GI and GL. We recommend that you go to NutritionData.com and do some comparisons on their easy-to-use calculators.

## **Patient Case Study: Dolores**

My name is Dolores. I live in Miami. I had been a diabetic for 14 years. I was taking three prescription medications. I had a heart attack and required an open-heart bypass operation. I felt tired, overweight, and depressed. I was very scared that I would have another heart attack.

My friend told me about how the 30-Day Diabetes Cure Plan had cured her diabetes. I followed the book's instructions and in just four weeks had lost 36 lbs, had twice the energy, and felt great. I was able to get off my prescription drugs completely. I just had to learn what to eat and what to do.

# CHAPTER 11

# THE DIABETES-HEALING POWER OF EXERCISE

*"The reason I exercise is for the quality of life I enjoy."*

—KENNETH H. COOPER, MD, MPH

AFTER DIET, regular physical activity is the most important tool in healing your diabetes. Even slow-paced activities, such as yoga, tai chi and walking, can have the same benefit. To achieve these impressive benefits, all you need is a minimum of 30 minutes of physical activity every day. Study after study shows that this is some of the best "medicine" for conquering diabetes.

## Regular Movement Energizes Your Health

Our bodies are designed to be in motion—this is when they work best. Physical activity is the key to unlocking optimal health and longevity because it's the driving force that powers all metabolic functions. Activity burns glucose and stored fat so you don't gain weight. It moves wastes and toxins out of your body. It thins your blood. It makes your cells more sensitive to insulin. And it pumps life-giving oxygen and nutrients to all your organs, including the most essential one: your brain.

We know of no other single endeavor that can come close to generating the positive benefits of being physically active. It keeps your muscles toned and strong, makes your heart pump more efficiently, strengthens your immune system, helps flush away excess cholesterol, maintains your trim profile, bestows self-confidence, fights frailty and discourages cancer. Study after study shows that being active brightens a person's mood, boosts intelligence, improves memory and makes you feel more fully "alive." In short, physical activity is a true anti-aging, anti-diabetes elixir. Wow! If they can ever bottle that, it would be the best-selling drug in history.

## *Not* Moving Produces the Opposite Effects

Inactivity, on the other hand, creates a stagnant environment inside you, and that is when health problems can easily develop. An active body is like a mountain stream that is constantly flowing: The water is always fresh and pure because movement oxygenates it and pathogens do not have a chance to establish themselves. But inactivity produces stagnant conditions, like a land-locked pond where algae overgrowth depletes the oxygen, pests and insects breed, fish die, and the water becomes putrid and full of disease-causing organisms.

When water does not move, it definitely dies. And the same is true for the human body—especially if you have blood glucose irregularities, because they multiply health problems very quickly. Here is how being a slug-bug shortens your life…

**Glucose inefficiency.** Remember, in a healthy metabolism, the carbs you eat are converted into glucose for immediate use as energy. Any glucose you do not burn immediately is stored for later use in your cells and liver in the form of fat. The hormone insulin oversees the conversion of glucose into fats (called triglycerides) and then unlocks the pathways to your cells so these fats can enter for storage.

If you are not sufficiently active to burn off that excess glucose, insulin is summoned to turn it into body fat. With chronically high levels of insulin your cells begin to ignore insulin's effect so that greater amounts of insulin are required to clear the bloodstream of glucose. The result is widespread insulin resistance and eventually Type 2 diabetes. Without physical activity (which naturally burns off the glucose in your bloodstream and keeps your cells sensitive to insulin), the insulin-producing beta cells in your pancreas eventually wear out from exhaustion and die. At this point, you will likely have full-blown Type 1 diabetes and will need insulin injections for the rest of your life. This degenerative progression can take many years to unfold—sometimes 10 or even as long as 20 years. (In its early stages, Type 2 diabetes can be symptom-free: Up to 33% of people with diabetes do not even know they have this "silent disease." But some 20% of those with early, undiagnosed diabetes already have retinopathy, a vision-robbing condition that can lead to blindness.)

During this undetected "stealth period," your body can suffer serious damage without you even realizing it. Chronically elevated levels of glucose and insulin in your bloodstream damage your arteries, accelerate the aging of tissues, organs, and skin (making you look much older than your years), and shorten your life by an average of two decades. Regular physical activity can help prevent this, but few people, doctors included, have been properly educated about its remarkable healing power.

**Poor circulation.** Circulation means movement of the blood. It is important because blood carries life-giving nutrients and oxygen to every part of the body—and healthy circulation provides the push. When an organ is deprived of these vital elements, or its supply is diminished, it becomes malnourished and sick. This is one of the most important causes underlying many of the serious complications that result from diabetes. It happens this way:

One component of your blood is tiny disc-shaped cells called platelets that carry twin receptors (similar to passenger seats), upon which two oxygen molecules ride. This is how oxygen travels through your body and nourishes it. When there's excessive sugar in the bloodstream, glucose molecules kick the oxygen molecules out of their seats and take their place. In effect, they hijack the blood cell and greatly diminish its oxygen-carrying capacity.

Diabetes is called a "wasting disease" for this very reason—because it deprives the body of the nutrients it needs for life and as a result the body wastes away. Forcing more oxygen into your bloodstream through the huffing and puffing of physical activity can break the stranglehold glucose has on blood cells, thus reversing the oxygen-nutrient deprivation that results. Has your doctor ever mentioned this to you?

# Complications from Not Moving

When blood cells cannot nourish distant parts of the body, such as toes and lower limbs, the eyes and the brain, they begin to die. In the case of fingers, toes and lower limbs, neuropathy can develop, possibly leading to gangrene, which requires amputation. When the eyes are deprived, vision loss and blindness can occur. And when the brain does not get a sufficient supply, dementia such as Alzheimer's disease often results. Poor circulation also can cause intense, chronic leg pain known as neuropathy. If avoiding these problems is not enough to get you moving, keep reading…

**Heart disease.** Excess glucose also makes blood platelets sticky, which leads to a thick, sluggish circulation. Slow-moving blood is responsible for a host of serious (and often life-threatening) cardiovascular problems. Sticky blood cells are more likely to clump together and adhere to artery walls, causing plaque build-up and blockages that trigger chest pain (angina), heart attack, and stroke. Thick blood is also more likely to clot. This is why people with diabetes have a stunning 400% higher risk of cardiovascular disease than non-diabetics.

When insulin becomes ineffective, it takes longer to convert glucose into fat for storage. Instead, the fats (triglycerides) hang around in your bloodstream and flood your liver. The liver then emits particles that move this fat into your arteries and smaller blood vessels. Once there, these fats become oxidized by free radical molecules and become very dangerous. They inflame the walls of your arteries and initiates plaque formation. So, it is not so much the carbs themselves that cause heart disease, but rather the body's inability to properly process the blood fats that result from all that circulating blood glucose.

Physical activity helps reverse all this by thinning the blood and speeding its flow. It also allows more oxygen and nutrients to reach distant limbs and nourish vital organs. In addition, besides making your cells more sensitive to insulin, physical activity also burns up excess blood glucose and stored fats, which facilitates weight loss.

**Dangerous inflammation.** Too much glucose and insulin flowing through your bloodstream is highly inflammatory. This is a bad situation because inflammation has been revealed as the causative factor underlying most of today's serious chronic and degenerative ills. The widely-respected physician Mark Hyman, MD, author of the book *Ultra-Metabolism* and former medical director of the world-famous Canyon Ranch health resort, gets right to the point when he says, "All the diseases that kill us in our society are related to refined carbohydrates and sugars—cancer, heart disease, obesity, diabetes, stroke, and Alzheimer's."[211] In every instance, people with diabetes or other blood glucose problems have a much higher incidence of these diseases.

Inflammation results when high blood glucose generates a barrage of free radical molecules that inflame and damage delicate tissue such as artery linings. Plaque is created when LDL (bad) cholesterol, triglycerides, and other blood fats try to patch up this damage. It is these plaques that are the main cause of artery blockages, chest pain, heart attack, and stroke.

There is a cancer connection as well. When you have too many free radicals in your body, they can overwhelm the antioxidants defending your DNA, damaging its genetic blueprint. This triggers cellular malfunctions, which cause tumor growths and cancer.

Performing physical activity (and eating a diet of antioxidant-rich foods) can prevent and even reverse inflammation and the health problems it causes.

**Unhealthy weight gain.** Too many sugary calories and fast carbs—and a lack of physical activity to quickly burn it off—can lead to rapid weight gain. And that extra body weight makes diabetes much worse. But it is a vicious cycle that can be broken. Studies clearly show that people with an "apple shape"—who carry weight around their mid-sections—have a far greater risk of developing insulin resistance and, eventually, diabetes.

An expanding waistline (not just weight itself, but where it is deposited) is now viewed as the single most important factor in the development of diabetes. In 2002, the International Obesity Task Force discovered that 60% of diabetes cases worldwide were due to this type of fat accumulation. (In Europe and North America the figure was closer to 90%!)[212]

Because the connection between belly fat and diabetes is so strong, it is a dead giveaway that diabetes is silently developing. Belly fat is clear visual evidence of a malfunctioning metabolism and a blood profile that is loaded with risk. With all the frightening health consequences at stake, you have to wonder why so many people continue to eat junky foods and skip exercise.

## Don't Blame Your Lack of Willpower

It may come as a shock to learn that your body is genetically programmed to hoard carbohydrate calories and store them in the form of body fat. This was nature's way of protecting us from starvation back in the early days of human development. But our ancient programming to conserve energy and calories has another dangerous aspect. It creates a kind of natural aversion to physical activity, which is why a lot of people say they "hate to exercise." Here is the explanation:

Tens of thousands of years ago, daily life was an arduous struggle. People wandered all day in search of food, hunting from sunup till sundown, often chasing wounded game for miles. There was no guarantee they would land that animal and be able to eat it. Early humans often expended more energy than the calories they ultimately ingested. This "deficit eating" was the rule of the day, and death from starvation or malnutrition was quite common.

In this scenario, calories were scarce and therefore precious, so energy had to be conserved. The human body evolved to become very efficient at converting and storing calories to body fat, which was later called upon for nourishment during times of scarcity. Wasting calories for frivolous activity could cost you your life, so people rested whenever possible (although because they had to be vigilant against many dangers, this did not often happen). Sleeping through the night was rarely possible and people lived on the brink of exhaustion.

Flash forward: Over the course of human development, this biological programming to conserve energy became part of our genetic make-up and remains with us today. This is why it feels so good to relax. And while it is true that physical activity often feels good, resting usually feels better.

## The Modern Predicament We Face

Why are we taking the time to tell you all this? Because we want you to understand the powerful forces you must overcome to get yourself into motion. Today we find ourselves in a double-whammy situation. We are still genetically-programmed to eat our fill (which we do, at almost every meal) and our bodies continue to store as many of those calories as it possibly can (even though the next meal is guaranteed in our culture). Most of us take every opportunity we can to rest—gym memberships and home treadmills aside. We have become creatures of comfort, as well, with most of us no longer facing hard physical labor day after day. Bottom line? The genetic forces that worked in favor of our ancestors' survival when food was scarce are now working against us, with deadly consequences.

While we cannot change our genetic programming, we can *outsmart* it. And that is the secret of our success with the 30-Day Diabetes Cure Plan. In addition to changing the way you think about food (and changing the foods you eat), it is time to change your attitude about physical activity, so it becomes something you like and *want* to do, instead of something you must force upon yourself.

## You Will Live Longer

Yes, walking will literally increase your lifespan. The National Center for Chronic Disease Prevention and Health completed an eight-year study of nearly 3,000 adults with diabetes to uncover the long-term impact of physical activity—specifically, walking—on death from diabetes, heart disease and all other causes.[213] This is what they found:

■ Walking lengthened the life of diabetics regardless of age, sex, race, body mass index, length of time since diagnosis, and presence of complications or limitations.

■ In addition, walking just two hours a week (that is less than 20 minutes a day) lowered the death rate from all causes by 39%. Walking three to four hours a week reduced mortality from all causes by 54%. *Wow!* This is not running two miles, or lifting weights, or taking aerobic exercise classes. Simply walking around your neighborhood, a park, the mall or a local track every day means a person with diabetes can live a longer, healthier and happier life.

■ Here is even more evidence: The Diabetes Prevention Program[214] showed that walking 120 to 150 minutes per week and losing just 7% of your body weight (12 to 15 pounds) can reduce your risk of diabetes by 58%. Time to put on those walkin' shoes and step out!

## Why Is Walking So Healing for Diabetes?

In addition to helping you shed extra pounds, walking actually increases the number of insulin receptors on your cells. Insulin, as you know, helps blood glucose move into cells, where it's needed to produce energy. And because physical activity has this amazing benefit of helping your body use insulin more efficiently, you might even be able to reduce the amount of medication you take—another reason to keep your doctor clued in on your progress.

As we will discuss in detail in Day 1 of Part 2, it is important to track your glucose levels as you increase your activity level. Especially if you take insulin, exercise can drop your glucose levels too much in the two hours after activity. Take control by tracking your glucose levels to learn just how more exercise affects your body. As you progress, your doctor will be able to wean you off added insulin, which is a sure sign of curing your diabetes!

## CHAPTER 12

# DEATH SENTENCE OR WAKE-UP CALL: HOW WILL YOU RESPOND?

*"It's always a wake-up call to get beaten."*

—USAIN BOLT, Olympic Gold Medal Jamaican sprinter

A DIAGNOSIS OF DIABETES definitely changes your life. But how long will that change last? And will it change you for the better or worse? The answer depends on how you respond to the challenge.

After reading the preceding chapters, you now know that you have a real choice. You can choose to live with Type 2 for the rest of your life, managing your symptoms with medications, and hoping for the best. Or, you can fully commit yourself to kicking diabetes out of your life, reclaiming your health and independence, and sticking around to enjoy the people you love and who truly love you.

Put simply: you can give up or you can fight back. You can leave everything up to doctors —or you can do your darndest to take control and beat this thing.

## Death Sentence or a Wake-up Call?

Jim would like to share a powerful story for those of you still unsure if you can make these changes in your life.

At a class for newly-diagnosed diabetic adults in a Milwaukee hospital, a mechanic named Roberto listened to a diabetes educator explain the medication options to a group of newly diagnosed diabetics. After an hour, he had had enough. "Tell the truth," he burst out. "Diabetes is a death sentence, isn't it? It killed my father and my aunt. You give us this advice, but all we're doing is slowing it down a little bit. Why don't you tell it like it is?"

Millions of people, including many diabetes professionals, agree with Roberto, even if they will not openly admit it. They secretly believe that Type 2 diabetes is a death sentence, a chronic, progressive, incurable disease that will slowly cripple and ultimately kill you. If you believe this, your life will certainly change. You will believe your life is over and you will find it hard to see the point in living. With this attitude, it is inevitable that you will become depressed and pessimistic.

After Roberto's class, another student named Juana approached him. "I used to think like you," she told him. "But it's not a death sentence. It's a wake-up call. Before I was diagnosed, I felt bad all the time and didn't know why. Once I learned how to eat better and take good care of myself, my whole life changed. Now I have more energy and better spirits. I play with my grandchildren. I work. I have more energy than my daughter does!"

You will find hundreds of stories like Juana's on diabetes blogs and chat forums, such as Diabetes Daily (*www.diabetesdaily.com/forum/*).

## Will You Panic—or Plan?

When you have diabetes, you are deluged with advice from everywhere: "Eat this." "Don't eat that!" "Exercise." "Take these supplements." And on and on. It is so easy to become confused and overwhelmed.

Bram and Ralph were able to beat Type 2 diabetes because they found plans that made sense for them—and they stuck with them. Ralph realized that sweets and junk foods put way too much strain on his body's insulin. By cutting them out, his body was able to heal. Bram did the same thing with a vegetarian diet.

Having a plan makes all the difference in the world. And this is why we created the 30-Day Diabetes Cure Plan. Our goal was to create a simple, foolproof, step-by-step roadmap for reversing Type 2 diabetes. Like following your car's GPS navigational system, you simply follow the directions each day and you will reach your goal. But our Plan only can work if you work it, as they say. Whether you succeed or not is entirely up to you.

## Awaken Your Warrior Spirit Now

To beat diabetes, the most important change you need to make is to *change your mind*. Type 2 diabetes is a disease of passivity. It results from eating the way the food companies say you should—and living for the values television says are important. It also might mean working long hours without taking breaks, or self-medicating your stress and feelings of powerlessness with sugar, carbs, alcohol, or creature comforts.

But if you stay passive when our modern culture is making it so easy for you to be sick, what do you think will happen? You will probably become even sicker. That is why we feel it is crucial that you arouse your "warrior spirit" and put up the fight of your life.

Modern society encourages us to take the easy way out at every opportunity. Corporations have turned us into consumers of everything: comfort…ease…leisure…convenience…and pleasure. As a result, we have become dependent on them for just about everything we need to survive. We have, as the old-timers used to say, "gone soft." Ultimately, this is the real reason diabetes and obesity have become global epidemics today.

It takes courage, effort, and willpower to go against the grain and eat right, exercise regularly, relax deeply, and say no to the toxic substances and habits that destroy your health and happiness. Most people fail to make the effort because they do not believe they are "worth it." This is why believing in yourself is the most important part of awakening your warrior spirit.

## This Is Your Chance

The saddest part of today's health statistics is the shocking rise of Type 2 among our children, a condition that hadn't affected them previously. According to the SEARCH for Diabetes in Youth study, the incidence of Type 2 among US adolescents has risen by 21% in the past decade.[215] Doctors are now seeing children as young as 10 years old with the telltale signs of diabetic complications, such as heart disease, high blood pressure, and diabetic neuropathy.

We simply cannot tolerate this. Our children and grandchildren are being turned into cash cows by Big Food, Big Medicine, and Big Pharma—and we must put a stop to it. We adults are the role models our children look to for cues on how to live and what to eat. If they see us spending our lives on the couch, compulsively consuming junk food, snacks, sodas, and beer, and passively surrendering to diabetes without a fight, how can we expect them not to do the same?

## Healing Yourself Will Help Heal Our World

Behavior is contagious—both good and bad. When people see their friends and family members engage in behaviors such as overeating, smoking, binge drinking and sedentary living, they are more likely to indulge, too. When someone in this circle decides to get well, shape up, and reach for a higher goal, his or her actions can trigger a positive effect on those around him. He is, in effect, helping to spread a "good health virus."

In this way, you can become a force for good health by healing yourself. Your example will encourage and inspire those around you to do the same. Family and friends who witnessed you transformation will ask: "How did you do it?" And, sooner or later: "Do you think I can do it, too?" This is how healing yourself can help to heal our troubled world.

Your fate does not depend on your doctor, or a bottle of pills, or some researcher working on a new cure for diabetes. Your health and future are in your own hands—right now. Whether you become a victorious survivor or another unfortunate statistic is completely up to you.

The most exciting adventure of your life (thus far) is calling. You can slay the dragon. You can free the hostage. You can save the day.

You can be a real hero. To your family. To your friends. To the world. And most of all, to that person in the mirror.

So, go for it. Please. While there is still time.

# Endnotes—Part 1

## Introduction

[1] Lin SX, Pi-Sunyer EX Prevalence of the metabolic syndrome among US middle-aged and older adults with and without diabetes—a preliminary analysis of the NHANES 1999-2002 data. *Ethn Dis.* 2007 Winter;17(1):35-39

[2] *http://www.diabetes.org/advocacy/news-events/cost-of-diabetes.html*

[3] Ibid

[4] *http://www.gallup.com/poll/156833/one-five-adults-smoke-tied-time-low.aspx*

[5] *http://www.diabetes.org/advocacy/news-events/cost-of-diabetes.html*

## Chapter 1: The Type 2 Diabetes Cure Right Under Your Nose

[6] *http://ndep.nih.gov/diabetes-facts/#howmany*

[7] Gregg EW at al. Association of an intensive lifestyle intervention with remission of type 2 diabetes. *JAMA* December 19, 2012, Vol. 308, No. 23 (*www.ncbi.nlm.nih.gov/pubmed/23288372*).

[8] *http://forecast.diabetes.org/surgery-apr2013*

[9] *http://www.merriam-webster.com/dictionary/cure*

## Chapter 2: What Is Diabetes, Anyway?

[10] *The Blood Sugar Solution* by Mark Hyman, MD (Little Brown, 2012)—p. 7

[11] *Wheat Belly* by William Davis, MD (Rodale, 2011)—pp. 99-100

[12] *The Blood Sugar Solution* by Mark Hyman, MD—p. 7

[13] Lakka HM, et al. The metabolic syndrome and total and cardiovascular disease mortality in middle-aged men. *JAMA.* 2002 Dec4;288(21):2709-16.

[14] Ott A, et al. Diabetes mellitus and the risk of dementia: The Rotterdam Study. *Neurology.* 1999 Dec 10;53(9):1937-42.

[15] Key T, Reeves GK, Spencer EA. Symposium 1: Overnutrition: consequences and solutions for obesity and cancer risk. *Proc Nutr Soc.* 2009 Dec 3:1-5.

[16] *The Blood Sugar Solution* by Mark Hyman, MD—pp. 10-11

[17] Targher G, Day CP, Bonora E. Risk of cardiovascular disease in patients with nonalcoholic fatty liver disease. *N Engl J Med.* 2010 Sep 30;363(14): 1341-50.

[18] Pan A, et al. Bidirectional association between depression and type 2 diabetes mellitus in women *Arch Intern Med.* 2010 Nov 22;170(21):1884-91.

[19] *The Blood Sugar Solution* by Mark Hyman, MD—pp. 10-11

[20] Ibid.

[21] Ibid.

[22] Emerging Risk Factors Collaboration et al. Diabetes mellitus, fasting glucose, and risk of cause specific death. *N Engl J Med.* 201: Mar3;364(9):829-41.

[23] Franco OH, Steyerberg EW, Hu FB et al. Associations of diabetes mellitus with total life expectancy and life expectancy with and without cardiovascular disease. *Arch Intern Med* 2007 Jun 11;167(11):1145-51.

[24] Garber AJ, et al. Diagnosis and management of prediabetes in the continuum of hyperglycemia: when do the risks of diabetes begin? A consensus statement from the American College of Endocrinology and the American Association of Clinical Endocrinologists. *Endocr Pract.* 2008 Oct;14(7):933-46

[25] Some marathon runners and endurance athletes harness this function by "carbo-loading" the night before competition. By consuming large amounts of simple carbohydrates (usually pasta), they are able to store extra glycogen that

is then released during extended periods of exertion. This, however, is not a wise strategy for non-athletes because it pushes up glucose and insulin levels and creates widespread damage in the body.

[26] Ginsberg et al. *J Cardiometab Syndr* 2009;4(2):113-9

[27] *http://www.ncbi.nlm.nih.gov/pubmed/11399122*

[28] F.B Hu, et al., Meta-Analysis of Prospective Cohort Studies Evaluating the Association of Saturated Fat with Cardiovascular Disease; *American Journal of Clinical Nutrition*—91 #3 (2010): 502-9

[29] D.C. Goff et. al., Insulin Sensitivity and the Rise of Incident Hypertension; *Diabetes Care* 26, no. 3 (2003): 805-9

[30] "Too Much Insulin A Bad Thing For The Heart?" *Science Daily—http://www.sciencedaily.com/releases/2010/04/100419233109.htm*

[31] *http://www.hopkinsmedicine.org/healthlibrary/conditions/adult/diabetes/diabetes_and_periodontal_gum_disease_85,P00349/*

[32] *http://ajcn.nutrition.org/content/76/5/911.full*

[33] *http://www.princeton.edu/main/news/archive/S26/91/22K07/*

[34] Deng Y, Scherer PE. Adipokines as novel biomarkers and regulators of the metabolic syndrome. *Ann NY Acad Sci.* 2010 Nov;1212(1):E1-E19. pp 400

[35] Lautenbach A, Budde A, Wrann CD. Obesity and the associated mediators leptin, estrogen and IGF-I enhance the cell proliferation and early tumorigenesis of breast cancer cells. *Nutr Cancer* 2009;61(4):484-91.

[36] Endogenous Hormones and Breast Cancer Collaborative Group. Endogenous sex hormones and breast cancer in postmenopausal women: reanalysis of nine prospective studies. *J Natl Cancer Inst* 2002;94:606-16.

[37] Johnson RE, Murah MH. Gynecomastia: pathophysiology, evaluation, and management. *Mayo Clin Proc* 2009 Nov;84(ll):1010-5.

[38] *http://www.news-medical.net/news/2007/12/18/33652.aspx*

[39] *http://www.ncbi.nlm.nih.gov/pmc/articles/PMC3020305/*

[40] *http://www.dukemedicine.org/news_and_publications/news_office*

[41] *http://circ.ahajournals.org/content/117/6/754.abstract*

[42] Ibid

[43] *http://www.diabetesforecast.org/2010/may/the-other-diabetes-lada-or-type-1-5.html*

[44] *http://www.ncbi.nlm.nih.gov/pmc/articles/PMC2769828/*

## Chapter 3: What Your Test Results Mean

[45] Garber AJ, et al. Diagnosis and management of prediabetes in the continuum of hyperglycemia: when do the risks of diabetes begin? A consensus statement from the American College of Endocrinology and the American Association of Clinical Endocrinologists. *Endocr Pract.* 2008 Oct;14(7):933-46

[46] Glucose tolerance and mortality: comparison of WHO and American Diabetes Association diagnostic criteria. The DECODE study group. European Diabetes Epidemiology Group. Diabetes Epidemiology: Collaborative analysis Of Diagnostic criteria in Europe. *http://www.ncbi.nlm.nih.gov/pubmed/10466661*

[47] Khaw KT, et al. Association of hemoglobin A1c with cardiovascular disease acute mortality in adults: the European prospective investigation into cancer in Norfolk. *Ann Intern Med.* 2004 Sep 21;141(6):413-20.

[48] McGlothin, P, Averill M. Glucose Control: The Sweet Spot in Longevity. The CR Way: Using the Secrets of Calorie Restriction for a Longer, Healthier Life. NY: HarperCollins; 2008:57-78.

[49] Bjornholt JV, Erikssen G, Aaser E, et al. Fasting blood glucose: an underestimated risk factor for cardiovascular death. Results from a 22-year follow-up of healthy nondiabetic men. *Diabetes Care.* 1999 Jan;22(1):45-9.

[50] AACE: CAD Risk for Prediabetes Similar to Diabetes—*http://www.diabetesincontrol.com/index.php?option=com_content&view=article&id=14598&catid=1&Itemid=17*

[51] Jessani S, et al. Should oral glucose tolerance testing be mandatory following acute myocardial infarction? *Int J Clin Pract.* 2007 Apr;61(4):680-83.

[52] The Lie That's Killing Us: Prediabetes *http://www.huffingtonpost.com/riva-greenberg/prediabetes_b_3023146.html*

[53] *The Blood Sugar Solution* by Mark Hyman, MD—p. 181

[54] U. Hoffmann, T.J. Brady, "New of New Imaging Techniques to Screen for Coronary Artery Disease," *Circulation* —108 (2003): e50-e53

[55] *http://www.mayoclinic.org/tests-procedures/magnetic-resonance-elastography/basics/definition/prc-20013647*

[56] *http://www.princeton.edu/main/news/archive/S26/91/22K07/*

## Chapter 4: The Terrible Complications of Type 2 Diabetes

[57] National Kidney Foundation A to Z Health Guide *http://www.kidney.org/atoz/content/diabetes.cfm* Accessed August 2013

[58] *http://ajcn.nutrition.org/content/86/2/285.full*

[59] *http://www.dukehealth.org/health_library/news/10205*

[60] *http://circ.ahajournals.org/cgi/content/abstract/117/6/754Imagine*

[61] *http://diabetes.niddk.nih.gov/dm/pubs/neuropathies/#peripheralneuropathy*

[62] *http://www.ninds.nih.gov/disorders/peripheralneuropathy/detail_peripheralneuropathy.htm*

[63] *http://www.cogenzia.com/the-global-impact.html*

[64] *http://www.neurology.org/content/77/12/1126.abstract*

[65] *http://www.nationalreviewofmedicine.com/issue/2005/12_15/2_advances_medicine01_21.html*

[66] *http://www.health.com/health/condition-article/0,,20189395,00.html*

[67] Tina K. Thethi, MD, Nana O. Asafu-Adjaye, MPH and Vivian A. Fonseca, MD "Erectile Dysfunction" *Clinical Diabetes* July 2005 vol. 23 no. 3: 105-113

## Chapter 5: What Your Doctor Isn't Telling You

[68] *http://www.msnbc.msn.com/id/21333262/print/1/displaymode/1098/*

[69] *http://www.ncbi.nlm.nih.gov/pubmed/9918487?dopt=Abstract*

[70] *http://www.prnewswire.com/news-releases/diabetes-diagnosis-treatment-and-drug-delivery-market-will-almost-triple-in-value-by-2016-says-idata-research-63589042.html*

## Chapter 6: Why Drugs Are Not a Solution

[71] Chang, Kenneth, et al. (2001). Diet and exercise are found to cut diabetes by over half. *New York Times*, August 9, 2001

[72] *http://www.nhlbi.nih.gov/health/prof/heart/other/accord/*

[73] Diabetes Study Partially Halted After Deaths by Gina Kolata published in *The New York Times*–Feb. 7, 2008

[74] Effect of intensive glucose lowering treatment on all cause mortality, cardiovascular death, and microvascular events in type 2 diabetes: meta-analysis of randomised controlled trials *BMJ 2011; 343 doi: http://dx.doi.org/10.1136/bmj. d4169 (Published 26 July 2011) Cite this as: BMJ 2011;343:d4169 http://www.bmj.com/content/343/bmj.d4169*

[75] *http://insciences.org/article.php?article_id=8521*

[76] Landmark ACCORD Trial Finds Intensive Blood Pressure and Combination Lipid Therapies do not Reduce Combined Cardiovascular Events in Adults with Diabetes *http://nih.gov/news/health/mar2010/nhlbi-15.htm*

[77] The Diabetes Dilemma for Statin Users by Eric J Topol, MD as reported in the *New York Times* published on March 4, 2012

[78] The ACCORD Study Group. Effects of combination lipid therapy in type 2 diabetes mellitus. *N Engl J Med*. 2010. Apr 29;362(17):1563-74. pp. 395 [B]

[79] The NAVIGATOR Study Group. Effect of valsartan on the incidence of diabetes and cardiovascular events. *N Engl J Med*. 2010. Apr 22;362(16):1477-90

[80] Haffner SM, et al. Mortality from coronary heart disease in subjects with type 2 diabetes and in nondiabetic subjects with and without prior myocardial infarction. *N Engl J Med.* 1998;339:229-34

[81] Taylor F, et al. Statins for the primary prevention of cardiovascular disease. *Cochrane Database Syst Rev.* 2011 Jan 19:CD004816. pp. 395

[82] Sirvent P, Mercier J, Lacampagne A. New insights into mechanisms of statin-associated myotoxicity. *Curr Opin Pharmacol.* 2008 Jun;8(3):333-38. pp. 396

[83] *The Blood Sugar Solution* by Dr. Mark Hyman—p. 30

[84] *http://www.sediabetes.org/gestor/upload/revistaAvances/25e-6-3(1).pdf*

[85] *http://en.wikipedia.org/wiki/Insulin_glargine*

[86] *http://www.diabetesincontrol.com/index.php?option=com_content&task=view&id=15280&Itemid=8*

[87] *http://www.cmaj.ca/content/early/2008/12/10/cmaj.080486.full.pdf*

[88] *http://health.usnews.com/health-news/diet-fitness/diabetes/articles/2008/10/30/consumer-group-seeks-fda-ban-on-avandia*

[89] Glucose control and vascular complications in veterans with type 2 diabetes. *http://www.nejm.org/doi/full/10.1056/NEJMoa0808431*

[90] Preventing Diabetes Complications: Are We Too Glucocentric? Mann D.M., M. Woodward, P. Muntner *Int J Clin Pract.* 2010;64(10):1024-1027

[91] *http://www.ncbi.nlm.nih.gov/pubmed/19236215*

[92] American Diabetes Association (2009). Medical management of hyperglycemia in type 2 diabetes: A consensus algorithm for the initiation and adjustment of therapy. *Diabetes Care*, 32: 193-203.

[93] Diabetes Prevention Program Research Group "Reduction in the Incidence of Type 2 Diabetes with Lifestyle Intervention or Metformin" *N Engl J Med* 2002; 346:393-403 *http://www.nejm.org/doi/full/10.1056/NEJMoa012512*

[94] *http://www.healthcentral.com/diabetes/c/110/159899/mimetics-pancreatitis/*

[95] *http://care.diabetesjournals.org/content/34/Supplement_2/S264.full*

[96] Nissen SE, Wolski K "Effect of rosiglitazone on the risk of myocardial infarction and death from cardiovascular causes". *N Engl J Med* 356 (24): 2457–71 (2007) *http://www.nejm.org/doi/full/10.1056/NEJMoa072761*

[97] Giles TD et al "Pioglitazone and heart failure: results from a controlled study in patients with type 2 diabetes mellitus and systolic dysfunction." *J Card Fail.* 2008 Aug;14(6):445-52. *http://www.ncbi.nlm.nih.gov/pubmed/18672190*

[98] David Willman "The Rise and Fall of the Killer Drug Rezulin" *Los Angeles Times* June 4, 2000. *http://articles.la times.com/2000/jun/04/news/mn-37375*

[99] Dan Brewer, M.D "Are Alpha-glucosidase Inhibitors Effective for Control of Type 2 Diabetes?" *Am Fam Physician.* 2006 Feb 1;73(3):433-434. *http://www.aafp.org/afp/2006/0201/p433.html*

[100] Diabetes in Control SGLT2 Inhibitor Approvals and Updates March 28, 2013 *http://www.diabetesincontrol.com/articles/diabetes-news/14415-sglt2-inhibitor-approvals-and-updates*

[101] *http://www.usatoday.com/story/news/nation/2013/01/08/diabetes-drug-heart-risk/1818801/*

[102] *http://www.dddmag.com/news/2013/01/diabetes-drug-may-pose-heart-risk*

## Chapter 7: Type 2 Diabetes Can Be Reversed: The Medical Proof

[103] *http://www.jameslindlibrary.org/illustrating/articles/the-introduction-of-successful-treatment-of-diabetes-mellitus-wi*

[104] *http://www.diabetes.ca/diabetes-and-you/what/history/*

[105] *http://diabetes.diabetesjournals.org/content/33/6/596.full.pdf*

[106] *http://care.diabetesjournals.org/content/11/2/201*

[107] Lindström, Jaana, et al. (2003). The Finnish diabetes prevention study (DPS): lifestyle intervention and 3-year results on diet and physical activity. *Diabetes Care,* 26 (12). *http://www.ncbi.nlm.nih.gov/pubmed/14633807*

[108] Roberts, Christian, MD, et al. (2005). Effect of a diet and exercise intervention on oxidative stress, inflammation, mmp-9, and monocyte chemotactic activity in men with metabolic syndrome factors. *Journal of Applied Physiology.* *http://Jap.Physiology.Org/Cgi/Content/Full/100/5/1657.full*

[109] Hu, Frank B., MD,et al. (2001). Diet, lifestyle, and the risk of Type 2 diabetes mellitus in women." *New England Journal of Medicine*, Volume 345:790-797, No. 11. *http://content.nejm.org/cgi/content/short/345/11/790*

[110] Chang, Kenneth. Diet and exercise are found to cut diabetes by over half. *New York Times*, August 9, 2001. *http://www.nytimes.com/2001/08/09/us/diet-and-exercise-are-found-to-cut-diabetes-by-over-half.html*

[111] Metabolic response of people with type 2 diabetes to a high protein diet by Frank Q. Nuttall, MD, PhD and Mary C. Gannon, PhD—published in *Nutrition & Metabolism* 2004, 1:6

[112] Yancy Jr., William S, et al. (2005) A low-carbohydrate, ketogenic diet to treat Type 2 diabetes. Published in *Nutrition and Metabolism*; December 1, 2005

[113] Westman, Eric C. (2007). Low-carbohydrate nutrition and metabolism. *American Journal of Clinical Nutrition*, vol. 86, no. 2, pp. 276-284. *http://www.ajcn.org/cgi/content/full/86/2/276*

[114] Lim EL, et al. Reversal of type 2 diabetes: normalisation of beta cell function in association with decreased pancreas and liver triacylglycerol. *Diabetologia.* 2011 Oct;54(10):2506-14.

[115] *The Blood Sugar Solution* by Mark Hyman, MD—p. 24

[116] Association of an Intensive Lifestyle Intervention With Remission of Type 2 Diabetes published in *The Journal of the American Medical Association*; December 19, 2012, Vol. 308, No. 23

[117] Look AHEAD Research Group, Wing RR. Long-term effects of a lifestyle intervention on weight and cardiovascular risk factors in individuals with type 2 diabetes mellitus: four-year results of the Look AHEAD trial. *Arch Intern Med.* 2010 Sep 27;170(17):1566-75.

## Chapter 8: 12 Common Diabetes Myths That Keep You Sick

[118] Vimaleswaran KS, Loos RJ Progress in the genetics of common obesity and type 2 diabetes. *Expert Rev Mol Med.* 2010 Feb 26;12:e7. doi: 10.1017/S1462399410001389. *http://www.ncbi.nlm.nih.gov/pubmed/20184785*

[119] Lichtenstein P, et al. Environmental and heritable factors in the causation of cancer—analyses of cohorts of twins from Sweden, Denmark, and Finland. *N Engl J Med.* 2000 Jul 13;343(2):78-85.

[120] *The Blood Sugar Solution* by Mark Hyman MD—pp. 21-24

[121] Ebbesson SO, Schraer CD, Risica PM et al. Diabetes and impaired glucose tolerance in three Alaskan Eskimo populations: the Alaska-Siberia Project. *Diabetes Care* 1998;21:563-9.

[122] Daniel M, Rowley KG, McDermott R et al. Diabetes incidence in an Australian aboriginal population: an 8-year follow-up study. *Diabetes Care* 1999;22:1993-8.

[123] Crawford EM. Death rates from diabetes mellitus in Ireland 1833-1983: a historical commentary. *Ulster Med J* 1987 Oct;56(2):109-15.

[124] Banting FG, Best CH, Collip JB et al. Pancreatic extracts in the treatment of diabetes mellitus: preliminary report. *Can Med Assoc J* 1922 March; 12(3): 141-6.

[125] *Good Calories, Bad Calories* by Gary Taubes

[126] *http://www.diabetes.ca/diabetes-and-you/what/history/*

[127] *http://www.medscape.com/viewarticle/782796*

[128] *http://www.joslin.org/about/elliot_p_joslin_md.html*

[129] Volek JS, Sharman M, Gomez A et al. Comparison of energy-restricted very low-carbohydrate and low-fat diets on weight loss and body composition in overweight men and women. *NutrMetab* (Lond); 2004 Nov 8;1(1):13 *http://www.ncbi.nlm.nih.gov/pmc/articles/PMC538279/*

[130] Volek JS, Phinney SD, Forsythe CE et al. Carbohydrate restriction has a more favorable impact on the metabolic syndrome than a low fat diet. *Lipids* 2009 Apr;44(4):297-309. *http://www.ncbi.nlm.nih.gov/pubmed/19082851*

[131] What If It's All a Big Fat Lie? by Gary Taubes; *New York Times*—July 7, 2002 *http://www.nytimes.com/2002/07/07/magazine/what-if-it-s-all-been-a-big-fat-lie.html?pagewanted=all&src=pm*

[132] Westman EC, Yancy WS, Mavropoulos JC et al. The effect of the low carbohydrate, ketogenic diet versus a low-glycemic index diet on glycemic control in type 2 diabetes mellitus. *Nutr Metab* 2008 Dec. 9, 5:36 *http://www.nutrition andmetabolism.com/content/5/1/36*

[133] *Wheat Belly* by William Davis, MD—p. 114

[134] Eric C Westman, MD, Is dietary carbohydrate essential for human nutrition? American Society for Clinical Nutrition—2002 *http://ajcn.nutrition.org/content/75/5/951.2.full*

[135] Manny Noakes, Paul R Foster, Jennifer B Keogh, Anthony P James, John C Mamo, And Peter M Clifton: Comparison of isocaloric very low carbohydrate/high saturated fat and high carbohydrate/low saturated fat diets on body composition and cardiovascular risk; *Nutrition & Metabolism*—Jan. 11,2006, 3:7 *http://www.nutritionandmetabolism.com/content/3/1/7/abstract/*

[136] *http://www.everydayhealth.com/diabetes/diet-the-foundation-of-diabetes-treatment.aspx*

[137] American Diabetes Association: Help for Diabetics? *http://www.healthy-eating-politics.com/american-diabetes-association.html*

[138] *http://senate.universityofcalifornia.edu/inmemoriam/johngofman.html*

[139] *http://www.dieheartpublishing.com/diet-heart-timeline*

[140] Ibid.

[141] Ibid.

[142] Ibid.

[143] *Why We Get Fat* by Gary Taubes; p. 182

[144] *http://www.dieheartpublishing.com/diet-heart-timeline*

[145] *http://www.forbes.com/companies/american-diabetes-association/*

[146] *http://www.diabetes-warrior.net/2011/02/08/19-million-paid-to-ada-by-bigpharma/*

[147] In Diabetes Fight, Raising Cash and Keeping Trust by Marc Santora; *New York Times*—November 25, 2006

[148] Ibid.

[149] *http://www.diabetes.org/donate/sponsor/national-sponsors.html*

[150] *The Cure For Diabetes* by Adam Campbell in *Men's Health Magazine*—November 3, 2006

[151] *http://www.pbs.org/wgbh/pages/frontline/shows/diet/interviews/willett.html*

[153] Ibid.

[154] Ibid.

[155] O'Kane, Maurice J., et al. (2008). Efficacy of self monitoring of blood glucose in patients with newly diagnosed type 2 diabetes (ESMON study): randomised controlled trial. *British Medical Journal*, 336: 1174-1177. *http://www.bmj.com/cgi/content/full/336/7654/1174*

[156] Gulliford, Martin. (2008) Self monitoring of blood glucose in type 2 diabetes. *British Medical Journal*, 336: 1139-1140. *http://www.bmj.com/cgi/content/full/336/7654/1174*

[157] Cost effectiveness of self monitoring of blood glucose in patients with non-insulin treated type 2 diabetes: economic evaluation of data from the DiGEM trial; *BMJ* 2008; 336 doi: http://dx.doi.org/10.1136/bmj.39526.674873.BE (Published 22 May 2008) Cite this as: BMJ 2008;336:1177

[158] Clar C, et al; Aberdeen Health Technology Assessment Group. Self-Monitoring of Blood Glucose in Type 2 Diabetes: Systematic Review. *Health Technol Assess*. 2010;14:1-140.

[159] Malanda UL, et al. Self-Monitoring of Blood Glucose in Patients With Type 2 Diabetes Mellitus Who Are Not Using Insulin. *Cochrane Database Syst Rev*. 2012 Jan 18;CD005060.

[160] Malanda UL, et al. Self-Monitoring of Blood Glucose in Patients With Type 2 Diabetes Mellitus Who Are Not Using Insulin. *Cochrane Database Syst Rev*. 2012 Jan 18;CD005060.

[161] Jessani S, et al. Should oral glucose tolerance testing be mandatory following acute myocardial infarction? *Int J Clin Pract*. 2007 Apr;61(4):680-83.

[162] Khaw KT, et al. Association of hemoglobin A1c with cardiovascular disease acute mortality in adults: the European prospective investigation into cancer in Norfolk. *Ann Intern Med*. 2004 Sep 21;141(6):413-20.

163 *Good Calories, Bad Calories* by Gary Taubes—pp. 189-190

164 *http://diabetes.diabetesjournals.org/content/45/Supplement_3/S45.full.pdf*

165 Yaffe K, et al. The metabolic syndrome, inflammation, and risk of cognitive decline. JAMA. 2004 Nov 10;292(18):2237-42.

166 de la Monte SM, Wands JR. Alzheimer's disease is type 3 diabetes—evidence reviewed. *J Diabetes Sci Technol.* 2008 Nov; 2(6):1101-13.

167 *The Blood Sugar Solution* by Mark Hyman, MD—pp. 28-29

168 The Myth About Exercise; *TIME* magazine (August 17, 2009)

169 Ibid.

170 Why the Campaign to Stop America's Obesity Crisis Keeps Failing by Gary Taubes; *Newsweek*—May 7, 2012

171 *Salt Sugar Fat* by Michael Moss

172 *Good Calories, Bad Calories* by Gary Taubes—pp. 86

173 Why the Campaign to Stop America's Obesity Crisis Keeps Failing by Gary Taubes; *Newsweek*—May 7, 2012

174 Philip R. Schauer, MD, et al. Bariatric Surgery versus Intensive Medical Therapy in Obese Patients with Diabetes; *N Engl J Med* 2012; 366:1567-1576 April 26, 2012 DOI: 10.1056/NEJMoa1200225 *http://www.nejm.org/doi/full/10.1056/NEJMoa1200225*

175 Lim EL, et al. Reversal of type 2 diabetes: normalisation of beta cell function in association with decreased pancreas and liver triacylglycerol. *Diabetologia.* 2011 Oct;54(10):2506-14.

176 *http://www.ncbi.nlm.nih.gov/pubmed/23161525*

177 *http://www.eatingdisordersreview.com/*

178 Luigi F. Meneghini, MD Early Insulin Treatment in Type 2 Diabetes Division of Endocrinology, Diabetes and Metabolism and the Diabetes Research Institute, University of Miami Miller School of Medicine, Miami, Florida. *Diabetes Care* November 2009 vol. 32 no. suppl 2 S266-S269 *http://care.diabetesjournals.org/content/32/suppl_2/S266.long*

179 *The Blood Sugar Solution* by Mark Hyman, MD—p. 29

180 *http://www.acpm.org* (Search "lifestyle medicine diabetes" for first PDF under Documents)

181 Some Cells in Pancreas Can Spontaneously Change Into Insulin-Producing Cells, Diabetes Researchers Show—*http://www.sciencedaily.com/releases/2010/04/100405091926.htm*

182 *http://diabetes.niddk.nih.gov/dm/pubs/insulinresistance/*

183 *http://www.ncbi.nlm.nih.gov/pubmed/18197184*

## Chapter 9: Start Reversing Your Diabetes Now

184 "What to Eat," Marion Nestle; p 17

185 "Plant-animal subsistence ratios and macronutrient energy estimations in worldwide hunter- gatherer diets," L Cordain, et al., *American Journal of Clinical Nutrition* March, 2000; Vol. 71, No. 3.

186 *http://www.webmd.com/diet/features/beware-empty-calories*

187 *http://myhealingkitchen.com/medical-conditions/diabetes/diabetes-make-it-worse/stay-away-from-sugar/*

188 *http://abcnews.go.com/Health/daily-sugary-drink-linked-heart-risk-men-study/story?id=15904276#.UIbM_xyCa2l*

189 *http://myhealingkitchen.com/featured-articles/the-alzheimer%E2%80%99s-epidemic/*

190 *http://www.naturalnews.com/041307_Aspartame_artificial_sweeteners_obesity.html*

## Chapter 10: The Diabetes-Healing Superfoods

191 *http://www.naturalhealthresearch.org/nhri/?p=76*

192 *http://www.ars.usda.gov/main/site_main.htm?modecode=12-35-00-00*

193 *http://care.diabetesjournals.org/content/25/10/1766.full*

194 *http://stroke.ahajournals.org/cgi/content/full/39/11/3079*

[195] *http://www.ncbi.nlm.nih.gov/pubmed/17983584*

[196] *http://jn.nutrition.org/cgi/content/abstract/136/11/2766*

[197] *http://www.parkhurstexchange.com/columns/cardiology/feb10_fish_oil*

[198] *http://www.ajcn.org/cgi/content/full/70/5/817*

[199] *www.consumerlab.com/results/omega3.asp*

[200] *http://www.medicalnewstoday.com/articles/250513.php*

[201] *http://lpi.oregonstate.edu/infocenter/minerals/chromium/*

[202] Ibid

[203] *http://umm.edu/health/medical/altmed/supplement/manganese*

[204] *http://www.news.cornell.edu/stories/2004/10/some-onions-have-excellent-anti-cancer-benefits*

[205] *http://onions-usa.org/all-about-onions/onion-health-research*

[206] Reduction in the incidence of type 2 diabetes with the Mediterranean diet: results of the PREDIMED-Reus nutrition intervention randomized trial. *Diabetes Care.* 2011 Jan;34(1):14-9

[207] *http://ajcn.nutrition.org/content/78/3/617S.abstract*

[208] *http://ajcn.nutrition.org/content/early/2010/10/20/ajcn.2010.29764*

[209] *http://www.lef.org/magazine/mag2001/sep2001_cover_curcumin_01.htm*

[210] *http://www.whfoods.com/genpage.php?tname=foodspice&dbid=68*

## Chapter 11: The Diabetes-Healing Power of Exercise

[211] Hyman, Mark. *Ultra-Metabolism.* New York: Atria, 2008.

[212] *http://www.health.com/health/condition-article/0,,20188164,00.html*

[213] *http://www.jacn.org/cgi/content/abstract/26/4/303*

[214] Orchard, MD, Trevor J., "The Effect of Metformin and Intensive Lifestyle Intervention on the Metabolic Syndrome: The Diabetes Prevention Program Randomized Trial," *Annals of Internal Medicine* (2005)

## Chapter 12: Death Sentence or Wake-Up Call?

[215] *http://diabetes.niddk.nih.gov/dm/pubs/statistics/*

# PART 2

## The 30-Day Diabetes Cure Plan

**PHASE ONE:**

**Blood Sugar "Boot Camp"**

Days 1 to 10

**PHASE TWO:**

Days 11 to 20

**PHASE THREE:**

Days 21 to 30

# HOW THIS PLAN WORKS

*"Although the world is full of suffering,
it is also full of the overcoming of it."*

—HELEN KELLER, educator and activist, 1880–1968

We hope you have found the introductory chapters helpful in understanding diabetes and what it takes to reverse it. Here, we offer an overview of our 30-day plan so you know exactly what to expect. First, let us briefly explain how we've structured the 30-Day Diabetes Cure Plan.

## Phase One: Blood Sugar "Boot Camp"

This is the strictest stage of the Plan. During the first 10 days, you are going to go "cold turkey" off all the diabetes-causing foods, beverages, and bad habits that have been making you sick and threatening your life.

For the next 10 days, you won't be consuming any sodas, sugary beverages, fruit juice, candy, or refined carbohydrates (including breakfast cereals, chips, cookies, ice cream, and energy bars). You will also abstain from bread, rice, potatoes, pasta, whole grains, and baked goods. No beer, wine, or alcohol of any kind. And you will eat no restaurant meals of any kind.

Before you freak out, know that you will be eating three regular meals a day, plus two healthy snacks if you feel the need for them. We want to reassure you that you will never feel hungry during this initial period—or ever—on the 30-Day Diabetes Cure Plan.

You will be enjoying a satisfying variety of delicious and filling foods, from meat, fish, and poultry to dairy, eggs, veggies, and cheese. Small amounts of certain fruits will also be allowed. Plus, your withdrawal from the diabetes-causing foods will be gradual over the next 10 days and you will be able to reintroduce many foods (though not all of them) in Phase Two.

During Phase One, you also will re-learn an essential skill, one with which you were born: how to distinguish between true hunger and mere appetite, the latter being a psychological desire for certain tastes.

If the cold-turkey approach to quitting certain foods seems harsh, let us explain here why research and Dr. Canfield's patients have found this to be the quickest, most effective way to halt the progression of diabetes and start reversing it:

**"Cutting back" just does not work.** Study after study shows that gradual withdrawal from cigarette smoking, alcohol dependency, and other drug addictions just does not work. The same is true for food addictions—and that is basically what people with diabetes and blood sugar irregularities have developed over the course of their lives. "Cutting back" is like giving a hungry wild cheetah a can of cat food. This only aggravates the animal's hunger, driving it to kill and eat anything it encounters. Your eating habits, along with the particular tastes, appetites, and desires you have developed over a lifetime of consuming food, are not unlike this ravenous animal, and they are not swiftly changed by gradual withdrawal.

Imagine asking a drug addict to limit himself to just one fix every 24 hours. Or allowing an alcoholic just one drink a day. Try telling a lifelong smoker she can have just one cigarette every 24 hours. It is impossible to succeed this way because consuming smaller amounts of any troubling substance simply feeds the desire for more.

**Think about eating just one potato chip.** Remember the advertising campaign "Bet you can't eat just one"? We absolutely do not want to set you up for failure—a sure thing with any slow withdrawal method—because it can lead to feelings of guilt, low self-esteem, and "justi-fication" for quitting the program entirely. In the long run, it takes far more willpower to limit your consumption of these disease-causing foods every day than to simply say *"absolutely no"* to them.

**Your body needs time to recondition.** We human beings are creatures of habit. And the older we get, the stronger these habits become—sometimes taking on a life of their own. If you are accustomed to curling up on the couch and munching an after-dinner snack while watching TV, your mind and body will come to expect this night after night. Many of our urg-es and habits are triggered by our subconscious and we generally obey them without question.

Saying no to the list of diabetes-causing foods for the next 10 days will break one of your enduring habituated patterns. It will also weaken your dependency on (and sometimes even an addiction to) certain strong flavors, whether it is sweet, salty, greasy, gooey, or alcoholic. While it may be challenging for the first few days, these bad patterns will diminish relatively quickly. With determination and commitment during these initial days, you will find yourself in charge of your subconscious habits and urges, instead of the other way around. And like many of our patients who have worked with our Plan, you will discover that this gives you tre-mendous confidence to keep moving forward.

Most importantly, Phase One will change you *internally*. That is because every night, during the eight hours you sleep, your body's biochemistry becomes a clean slate, returning to what we call "baseline." It is as though every morning you are given a new chance. Your goal in Phase One will be to maintain this baseline state by keeping taboo foods out of your system.

You will break the vicious carbohydrate craving cycle. Eating bad carbs creates the desire for more, and by eating more, you continue the cycle over and over, like an endless feedback loop. This is not just a psychological phenomenon. It is actually very physical. You see, when you eat a food that quickly breaks down into glucose—as all simple carbohydrates do—your pancreas triggers an insulin spike to quickly remove the sugar from your bloodstream. So, first you get a jolt of energy from simple carbs, but this is followed by an equally strong valley of fatigue…and hunger all over again as your bloodstream and brain chemicals actually *crave* more carbohydrates.

**Your blood sugar will normalize.** Cutting out these bad carbs during Phase One will re-lax the near-constant demand you have been placing on your pancreas. This means its insulin-producing beta cells can take a much-deserved vacation from being overworked. Quitting simple carbs will also re-sensitize your cells to insulin so they'll need less of it—even if you have Type 1 and take insulin injections. If you have Type 2, this re-sensitization will start to reverse the insulin-resistance in your cells. And that means your doctor can lower your dose of medication.

**You will lose weight without trying.** Before Phase One, when you fed your body all that glucose in the form of simple carbs, your body couldn't use it all. Anything extra was turned into fat and stored on your belly and hips. Eliminating bad carbs from your diet will not only halt the fat-storage process, but can reverse it. Without a constant supply of glucose-producing foods, your fat cells will be forced to release their contents back into the bloodstream, where they are reconverted into fuel for energy. That is why, by the end of Phase One, many people on the 30-Day Diabetes Cure Plan experience a loss of between two and six pounds. And that is *without dieting*.

You will be surprised how quickly these 10 days move along. And while the first few days may seem challenging, once you get beyond them, the rest of the 30-Day Diabetes Cure Plan is relatively easy. As your food cravings drop away, everything gets a lot easier.

During these first few days, if the going gets tough, we urge you to return to this introduction and re-read the description and benefits of Phase One. It will remind you of the importance of these first 10 days and firm up your resolve.

## Phase Two: Inside the Bubble

Phase Two is a bit like being a newborn in an incubator, where you are relatively safe from temptations and distractions that can undermine your progress.

Once you are able to eliminate your cravings for bad carbs and other diabetes-provoking foods, you will gradually reintroduce many of the foods you have come to enjoy—but in healthier versions. You will be able to add limited amounts of whole grains and potatoes… some desserts…and even alcohol in moderation. You should continue to restrict your consumption of bread, baked goods, all refined carbohydrate-based snack foods and commercial breakfast cereals because these foods can spike your glucose and insulin levels even higher than eating pure table sugar. And during Phase Two you will continue to avoid all restaurant dining.

The goal of Phase Two is twofold: To re-educate your taste buds so you actually enjoy and *desire* meals and foods that heal your diabetes and to incorporate more activity into your daily routine. The emphasis is on superfoods like beans, and legumes and a variety of activities, such as walking and yoga, which will get you moving more frequently.

Finally, because uncontrolled stress is particularly bad for people with diabetes, you will discover how to de-stress your nervous system and de-activate the hormones *cortisol* and *adrenaline*, which actually push your blood sugar to dangerously high levels.

You will also notice your weight loss is increasing more rapidly. By the end of Phase Two, most people lose between eight and 15 pounds—again, without even *thinking* about dieting or weight loss. If you are like the other people who have successfully employed this Plan, you will begin to notice that your clothes fit better. In fact, at this point, many people are able to slip into outfits they haven't been able to wear for years.

But more importantly, your weight loss is confirmation that you are well on your way to reversing Type 2 diabetes and insulin-resistance. In addition to losing weight, people who have Type 1 should be able to significantly reduce their insulin dosage (with their doctor's permission, of course).

## Phase Three: Ready for the Outside World

After 20 days on the 30-Day Diabetes Cure Plan, you will be ready for the real test: The outside world and its relentless temptations to eat and drink as you once did. After spending almost three weeks inside a "bubble" of protection while you learned to replace the foods and beverages that harmed your body with those that can help and heal it, you will be well prepared to snub the seductions.

During Phase Three, you will learn how to conquer the greatest seductions a person with blood sugar irregularities must face. You will discover proven strategies for surviving dinner parties, restaurants, travel, gas stations, airports, the food court at the mall—and even fast food menus. Phase Three will also introduce you to the specific vitamins and supplements that have been shown to be especially helpful for people with blood sugar problems.

## Meet the New You!

Think of this as your "advanced training." You will take your physical activity to another level by focusing on muscle building. You will gain valuable insights into the subtle ways some people sabotage their progress so you can avoid these pitfalls altogether. You will learn where to find friendly support for your new mission. You will read about special nutritional supplements that can help elevate you to the next level of natural glucose management—and possibly even support and repair your damaged beta cells. And you will see how easy it can be to add more lean muscle to your physique, which will help your body utilize insulin much more efficiently.

In just 30 short days, you are going to transform your mind, your body, and your biochemistry. You will go from being sick, feeling tired all the time, and relying on multiple medications…to being a "younger," stronger, leaner, healthier, and more energetic human being. How will you change? Let us count the ways…

1. Right off the bat, starting with Day 1, you'll see exactly how your favorite foods and beverages are affecting your blood glucose and insulin levels with "smart" self-monitoring. No more guesswork about what may be causing your spikes.

2. You will discover a wide variety of delicious foods that can reverse your cells' insulin-resistance, the root cause of Type 2 diabetes—plus the non-strenuous physical activities that actually increase your cells' sensitivity to insulin.

3. Your pancreas won't be flogged into producing as much insulin as usual, so it can rest—and this alone will protect the health and longevity of your beta cells, as well as your entire body.

4. Keeping you insulin levels low will naturally lead to automatic weight loss as your cells begin to empty out their stored fat, using it for energy.

5. Less sugary glucose in your arteries means they won't be so inflamed (the number-one way heart disease develops). And by consuming more antioxidant-rich foods and healing supplements, you will begin to repair the damage that past inflammation has caused. Result? In addition to healing your diabetes and insulin-resistance, you will also be reversing the process of heart disease…Alzheimer's…and quite possibly cancer at the same time.

6. Less glucose in your bloodstream will make your blood platelets less sticky, which can dramatically improve your circulation. At this point, more oxygen-rich blood and nutrients are reaching the tiny capillaries in your eyes, your brain, and your extremities. All of this greatly reduces the underlying problems that lead to the most horrific complications of diabetes—vision loss, dementia, and Alzheimer's, plus the horrible amputations that are so common when insulin and glucose are out-of-control.

7. Better circulation and nutrition also means more energy gets delivered to all parts of your body. As a result, you will feel better…have more pep…and find you are more lighthearted because the "happiness neurotransmitters" in your brain will be getting fed.

Bingo! In a relatively short time, your metabolism will be acting "normal" again, just as long as you do not go back to the crazy foods and lifestyle that triggered your disease in the first place. It is actually that simple and straightforward.

## And It Really Works!

Day-by-day—in a simple, systematic way—you will remove the diabetes-causing substances and habits that threaten your life and happiness. And, one-by-one, you will replace them with the health-building foods and behaviors that can repair, regenerate, and revitalize your entire being from head to toe.

By the end of our Plan, you may not be completely free of diabetes—but you *will* be well on your way and absolutely grounded in the diabetes-healing lifestyle that can conquer Type 2 and reverse insulin-resistance, while normalizing your blood sugar and hormone balance.

Those of you with Type 1 should find your need for supplemental insulin significantly reduced as your body becomes better able to utilize insulin. Best of all, your risk of nasty diabetic complications will be dramatically reduced.

## What If You Slip Up?

**We've planned for that, too.** We are only human, after all, and sometimes we fall back into old habits. If this happens to you, you will quickly recognize you are in trouble by the junky stuff you are eating again…by the tired, half-sick way you feel…and by the pounds and inches creeping back on your body.

Should the slip occur, just go back to Phase One and start with Day 1. It will be easier this time, because you have already followed our plan once. Stay there as long as you like, but at least until you get things back under control.

**Keep in close touch with your doctor.** If you fall off the wagon for a lengthy period, you may need help with medications temporarily until you can regain your balance. But keep in mind that you will never, *ever* be able to return to the lifestyle that upset your blood chemistry in the first place and damaged the beta cells in your pancreas as a result. The 30-Day Diabetes Cure Plan is not a magic bullet that allows you to go back to a life of junk food, sodas, sweets, and rich desserts. That path will always lead to diabetes and other serious health complications.

More than anything, the 30-Day Diabetes Cure Plan is a lifestyle—not a temporary fix. As they say in Alcoholics Anonymous: "It works if you work it." So work it, friends. We have every confidence you can.

## Make Your Doctor Your Partner in This

We strongly urge you to seek your doctor's help and support in implementing this program— especially if you are on any medications. *Never discontinue any medicines without your doctor's approval.* If you are self-administering insulin, your blood glucose reading will be your best guide as to the dose you need. But always advise your physician of your progress. We also recommend that you consult with a natural health practitioner to advise you professionally on using supplements.

Many doctors are skeptical of the power of natural healing, nutrition, and lifestyle modifications, so be sure to explain everything you are attempting on the 30-Day Diabetes Cure Plan to your physician. Your success could open his or her mind and perhaps even trigger a significant change in the way your doctor treats diabetes as a result. (Wouldn't that be nice?)

Occasionally, you will encounter a physician whose beliefs are so rigid that he/she refuses to entertain *any* unconventional or natural therapies. If this describes your doctor, you may want to reconsider whether this clinician is right for you.

Always remember: Your doctor works for you—not the other way around. If your physician is not supportive and cooperative, find one who is. Modern medicine is changing rapidly, so it shouldn't be difficult to locate a physician or health practitioner who is willing to incorporate new ideas, as long as they are not dangerous (or nutty).

In fact, the reverse is often true. Many doctors are *excited* when their patients make a commitment to getting well using steps like the ones in our Plan. The truth is, physicians just don't see that many patients who want to try. Imagine how depressing it is to try to save the lives of patients who aren't willing to lift a finger to save themselves. In many cases, doctors have to fight just to get a patient to take his or her medications. No wonder they get so discouraged.

## You Will Be a Hero to Everyone Around You

You are going to be a true and committed "diabetes warrior." You are going to fight for your health as if your life depends on it (because it does!). You are going to turn your condition around, starting tomorrow on Day 1 of The 30-Day Diabetes Cure Plan. You are going to inspire your doctor and your friends with your courageous example. You are going to be the poster child for self-healing. (Are you smiling at the prospect?)

You are also going to declare your independence from the greedy corporations that run the food, drug, insurance, and advertising industries, as well as our dysfunctional medical system. And in doing so, you are going to help *change the world*.

You have already read in Chapter 7 about the numerous studies that prove the effectiveness and superiority of simple lifestyle modifications over drug therapy. As we have previously pointed out, the deck is stacked against you. Everyone in the System will be pushing diabetes drugs on you, including TV ads, the American Diabetes Association, your local pharmacy, and, most likely, your doctor.

Corporations—especially drug companies and food manufacturers—are counting on Americans to take the lazy way out. They do not believe we are strong enough to take real responsibility for ourselves. They have watched us go soft in just two generations, and they do not believe we have got the grit to resist their junky foods and their sneaky undermining of democracy and our individual freedoms. This is your opportunity to prove them wrong.

## This Is Also Your Chance to Take Back Your Power

Diabetes is not a contagious virus you catch. It is not a genetic aberration (except in the case of Type 1). And it is not some unpredictable accident, like a car crash or falling off a ladder. Rather, 95% of all diabetes is something we bring upon ourselves. It does not begin in your blood or pancreas. Diabetes begins in your mind. And that is also where the real cure resides.

There is no doctor, drug, or treatment that has more power over this disease than you do. Saving your life requires *changing* your life. It means taking the next step up the stairway of evolved thinking and discovering a smarter, stronger, happier, and healthier you. It is like the line in the Bob Dylan song: "Them not busy being born are busy dying."

You are never too old to get better. And to keep getting better.

# DAY 1

# SMART MONITORING

*Don't worry about failures. Worry about the chances*
*you miss when you don't even try.*

—JACK CANFIELD, American author and motivational speaker

**Tip of the Day:** Knowing your blood glucose numbers means you can see how the foods and beverages you consume directly affect your blood glucose readings.

MONITORING YOUR blood glucose can be a powerful tool for managing diabetes. Here's how...

Imagine you are trying to land a plane...at night...in a snowstorm. Wouldn't you want some meters, lights, and gauges to tell you where you were and how fast you were going? Reversing Type 2 diabetes isn't as difficult as piloting an airplane at night, but it definitely helps to have some guidance. Self-testing your glucose levels will give you a control panel. Testing can show you how different foods, activities, medications, and stresses affect you. It can also tell you how well you are doing—or how close you are to crashing. Without testing, you are flying in the dark.

## "Smart Monitoring"

Most people, even those who test regularly, don't do so correctly. They test at the same times every day, usually in the morning and before meals. They don't keep track of their food, exercise and stress, so they can't relate their numbers to their diet and their life. Just checking a couple of times a day, at the same time every day won't help much. You'll have a nice sheet of numbers to show your doctor, but your day-to-day management won't change. You have to learn to use the test results to make healthy decisions.

A smarter way to do home glucose testing is to think like a detective or a scientist. You are investigating your own body and how it works. You want to pose questions about how exercise, food, stress, and medicine affect your glucose. Then you will use Smart Monitoring —our focus for today and a crucial tool for the next 30 days and beyond. Smart Monitoring means testing your glucose before *and* after a meal or activity and, based on the numbers, making a smart decision about whether it's helping or hurting your diabetes. Good record keeping is crucial, too!

## How Smart Monitoring Helps

Deb R. was taking seven pills a day for Type 2 diabetes, but her A1C's reached as high as 11% (a normal A1C is below 5.7%).[1] "My blood sugars were never under 200 (normal is below 125)," she says. "My doctor kept upping my dose and switching to stronger drugs. I weighed 200 pounds. No matter how I dieted or exercised, I couldn't lose weight. In October 2010, my A1C was 9.6, my triglycerides were 750, and my cholesterol was 220. My doctor told me I had to start insulin."

Deb went home to search online for an alternative. She saw an ad for *The 30-Day Diabetes Cure*. On December 12, 2010, Deb started the plan. A month later, she had lost 20 pounds. Although the book said she shouldn't change her medication without notifying her doctor, she quit taking Actos and *metformin*. She used Smart Monitoring to check her blood sugars regularly, and they were getting better.

"I'd forgotten to check back with my doctor about insulin," she says. One day his office called, demanding that she come in immediately. Deb remembers how eager she was to share her progress. But he refused to discuss it. He was angry with her for stopping her drugs and told her she had to start insulin right away.

"I told him I needed more time," she says. "And then I left." Deb was still taking meds for blood pressure and acid reflux, plus *glipizide* (a drug used to control blood glucose). But when she tried to refill her prescriptions, she found her doctor had cancelled them. He told Deb she couldn't get anything until she started insulin.

Deb found another doctor to provide a second opinion. Deb says, "She listened to everything I told her and was amazed at my results. I weighed 150 pounds. My A1C was 7.1, my triglycerides were 175, and the other tests were all normal." The doctor discontinued glipizide and Deb's blood pressure drug, lowered the dose of acid reflux medication, and halved Deb's metformin dose.

Deb is now down to 500 mg a day of metformin and plans to be off it in three months. Her dress size has dropped from a 16 to a 6. "It's so wonderful to be in control of my health and my life!" she exclaims.

## Think Like a Detective

OK. You've got your meter, your lancets, and test strips. Your mission is to find out what makes your glucose levels go up, and to figure out what you can do to bring them down. If your glucose is going too low, you need to investigate that, too. Glucose levels go up and down for reasons. Remember: They are just numbers, not value judgments. They are information you can use to help yourself. You only have to find the reasons for their being high. That's what "smart" monitoring is all about. Your glucose numbers enable you to determine the specific changes you need to make to your diet and lifestyle. And smart testing helps you make those changes faster and more effectively.

Once you have started controlling and reversing your diabetes, you will be able to cut down on testing—perhaps down to as little as once a week, just to be safe. While a single test can tell you what your blood glucose is at a given moment, it can't tell you how you got there. You need before and after numbers. To test in pairs, think of something you want to learn about your blood glucose. This could be anything, but most questions are about food and exercise. For example:

- **How does my usual breakfast affect my glucose?**
- **How does a brisk walk after dinner change my glucose numbers?**
- **Is there a difference in my blood glucose if I eat lunch with friends or eat alone?**

## Keep Accurate Logs

Like any good detective or scientist, you will need to keep records of your results. This way, you'll be able to compare results over time and see patterns that might not have been obvious from a one-week trial. The Success Planner includes a log where your results can be recorded.

Some important topics for your log records are:

- **Activities**—what, when, and how much?
- **Blood glucose**—what and when?
- **Insulin doses**—when and how much?
- **Foods**—what, when, how much?
- **Comments about emotions, stress, medications, etc.**

If you are injecting short-acting insulin, you should record the times and doses of your injections. This will teach you how much each unit of insulin brings down your glucose. However, we encourage all people with Type 2 to work their way off insulin as rapidly as possible. Most people can do this fairly easily with a diet like the one in our Plan.

## The Most Important Time to Test

When you are first learning your glucose profile, it helps to test at different times. Many people test at the same time every day, usually when they wake up and in the afternoon before dinner. Your blood glucose might look fine at those times, but you may be missing spikes that happen at other times.

The most important time to test is after meals. Usually two hours after your first bite works well. You can divide the day and your blood glucose results into three main categories: Fasting (in the mornings), pre-prandial (before meals) and post-prandial (after meals).

Remember, a normal reading 2 hours after meals is 140 or below. Yours may be higher, but you definitely want to be below 180 – and lower is better. If your reading is higher than you want, think about what you ate in that meal. How much carbohydrate was there, and how high was the glycemic load? Remember to consider the carbohydrate content of what you drank as well, and whether there was any exercise before or after the meal.

Note: You should test frequently when you are sick, because infection can raise glucose levels dramatically.

## Other Times to Test

Try doing occasional tests within two hours after key events, such as when something unusual happens, like a stressful meeting, taking an over-the-counter medicine, or eating a new food. You might want to test at different times in the evening before going to sleep a couple of times to see what is happening then.

You definitely want to test after exercise. And not just right after, but again one to two hours later, because blood glucose will continue to drop as muscle cells restore the glucose stocks they have burned. Once you know how exercise affects you—and you are sure that you won't go too low—you can test less frequently. Remember to log all test results and keep the records. Make copies for your doctor or diabetes educator.

### When to Test: A Checklist

- After meals
- After a stressful event
- After taking over-the-counter medicine
- After exercise
- In the evening before bedtime

## What Makes Blood Glucose Rise?

There is more to smart testing than just writing down your numbers. You want to use those numbers to understand what is happening with you—and why. How do you do that? How do you identify the problem? When glucose is up, there are many possible culprits.

## Things That Make Blood Glucose Rise

- **Food**—especially carbohydrates, and particularly refined carbs
- **Drinks**—especially juices, sodas, sports drinks, sweetened beverages, and alcoholic drinks
- **Stress**—emotional or physical
- **Infection**—such as flu, skin, or other infections
- **Inflammation**—especially gum disease
- **Hormone**—like the menstrual cycle
- **Medications**—for diabetes or not, prescription or over-the-counter
- **Reaction to having low blood glucose in the evening**—e.g. the Somogyi effect* in the morning (also called the "dawn effect")
- **Poor sleep or sleep apnea**
- **Inappropriate glucose dumping by liver**—can be due to what you ate or to other liver problems, such as fatty liver
- **Not enough basal insulin**—you might need some temporarily
- **Too much sitting around and not enough exercise**

## Avoiding Dips and Low Levels

If your glucose levels tend to run low, you should test your blood before driving any distance. If you are a bit low, you need to eat or take a glucose tablet. Most people rarely go low unless they are on insulin or a sulfonylurea drug such as *glipizide*, *glimepiride*, or *chlorpropamide*. These drugs push more insulin into your system. They can be dangerous, because you don't know exactly how much insulin will be coming in. If you have problems with lows, ask your doctor about reducing your medicines and doses.

The best way to lower blood glucose is to burn it off through exercise. But don't overdo it because this can drop your glucose level too low. By testing before and after different physical activities, you can see how far walking, running, or yard work (for example) will lower your glucose, so you can do it safely.

Medications also affect glucose levels—and not just diabetes medications. Even an over-the-counter pain medicine like *ibuprofen* or an antibiotic for an ear infection can significantly change some people's glucose levels. When you start a new medicine, you might want to test

---

*The Somogyi effect is an episode of high blood sugar—usually after breakfast—that follows an evening of low blood sugar

for its effect on your glucose. You should also read package inserts to see what the effects on glucose might be. If a drug seems to be raising (or lowering) your glucose outside the normal levels you've discussed with your doctor, ask your doctor or pharmacist right away.

Stress often raises people's glucose level. Stress also increases insulin resistance and causes the liver to release stored sugar (glycogen). This can happen quickly in a crisis—or it can occur gradually, when we feel threatened or worried about some life problem. When something stressful happens, checking your glucose can tell you if it is affecting your body or not. Not all stresses are mental or emotional. Infection or inflammation anywhere in your body will tend to raise blood glucose. In diabetes, the most significant infections are often in the feet or in the gums.

## Using Your Numbers to Guide You

Your glucose numbers are a guide. They can warn you if your glucose levels are getting too high or too low. They let you see right away how things in your life affect you for better or worse. But glucose readings only help if you use them to make healthy changes in your diet, lifestyle, and emotional states. This is why you want to keep a record of your diet, exercise, and stress, as well as your glucose numbers. It's hard to understand one without the other. When you test smart and keep logs, you will have the information you need to make healthy changes.

Then what do you do? First, try to identify patterns. Perhaps you can see the patterns your food or medications, sleep, work, or something else in your life have on your blood glucose levels. If you fail to see clear patterns in your numbers, you can ask your doctor or educator for help. Bring your records in and work with your professionals to come up with a plan. When you understand which factors are raising your glucose levels, you can then commit to doing things that keep numbers down—such as consuming less sugar, fewer sweets and starches, getting more physical activity, or whatever your logs tell you. You will probably see what is causing any low glucose levels you are experiencing. In some cases, your medication doses may need to be reduced.

Monitoring your blood glucose in a "smart" manner, following all the leads and clues, and then tracking down the probable villain might seem like a daunting task. And for the first few weeks it might be, because you will be doing a lot of testing. But within a couple of months, you will gain control and will not need to test nearly so much. By being a good detective, you can put diabetes behind bars where it will never threaten you again.

## Normal Glucose Levels

**Fasting**

NORMAL—70–90 mg/dl (4-5 mmol/L)

Prediabetes—100–125 mg/dl (5.5–7.0 mmol/L)

DIABETES—more than 125 mg /dl (7.0 mmol/L)

**Post-prandial** (2 hours after eating)

NORMAL—less than 140 mg/dl (7.8 mmol/L)

Prediabetes—140–199 mg/dl (7.8–11.0 mmol/L)

DIABETES—200 mg/dl (11.1 mmol/L) or more

**Hemoglobin A1C**

NORMAL—4.0–5.7%

Prediabetes—5.7–6.4%

DIABETES—more than 6.4%

## Smart Monitoring Tips

•**Let your hand hang down by your side for a while before testing.** Gravity will bring more blood to the hand. Place the finger on a sturdy surface like a table, so it doesn't shake or move when you push the button.

•**Buy the thinnest lancets that work for you.**

•**Use different sites.** Change fingers, and use different sides of the fingers. Keep track of where you've poked recently. You can probably find two or three spots on the inside of each finger and two or three on the outside. We don't recommend using your fingertip for this testing.

## Tapering Off Testing

As your glucose comes down and you've learned how your body responds, you can cut down on testing to as little as once a week. If you are on insulin, even basal insulin, you should test at least a few times a week. The insulin may have gone bad, or something else may have changed. If you use short-acting insulin, you will need to test more often to get your doses right. When you change medicines (even over-the-counter meds) or diet or make some other life change, it's best to test frequently again to see if your profile has changed. Testing with a plan will give you a clear picture of how your blood glucose changes. Then you need to figure out why it changes.

## Today's Action Steps

•Investigate how your lifestyle affects your blood glucose levels.

•Use Smart Monitoring to discover the answers.

•Log your food, activity, and stress levels regularly and accurately in your Success Planner.

•Use your blood glucose readings to help you make positive lifestyle changes—and to reinforce them.

**Extra credit:** List a few beverages you enjoy that do not contain sugar or alcohol.

# DAY 2

# SODA POP AND ALCOHOL SWAP

*"If there were a fountain machine*
*that dispensed destruction instead of soda,*
*would you grab an extra large cup?"*

—JAROD KINTZ, American author

**Tip of the Day:** There are diabetes-healing beverages that provide beneficial nutrients without upsetting your glucose levels and increasing your weight. In fact, they'll help you shed pounds!

ELIMINATING SODAS, alcohol, energy drinks, and fruit juices—all sugary drinks—is the single most important way you can begin to normalize your blood glucose so you can eventually get off your medications. Sodas and sugary beverages (even "diet" drinks, which we'll get to in a moment) are unhealthful in general, but they are especially devastating for people with blood glucose problems. Quitting all these sugary beverages will dramatically improve your blood glucose levels and allow your body to better utilize insulin immediately. So today you're going to put a stop to this.

Exactly what are you eliminating? Here's the list: All sweetened beverages, including carbonated sodas and diet sodas…"sports" and "energy" drinks…sweetened coffees and teas… fruit drinks, including those made from 100% juice…alcohol…and every beverage that contains high fructose corn syrup (HFCS).

But don't fret that this will leave you with only water and flavorless beverages to drink. There are plenty of diabetes-healing alternatives that provide beneficial nutrients while slaking your thirst—but without upsetting your glucose levels and increasing your weight.

Remember to use Smart Monitoring to investigate how these beverages—and eliminating them—affect your glucose readings. Frame a question around one of the drinks you are eliminating, or around one of the diabetes-healing swaps, and log your results.

## How Sodas Destroy Your Health

Cutting out soda pop and sweetened beverages will improve your blood glucose and general health almost immediately. That is because these super-sweet drinks are really harmful. Here's how…

**They immediately spike your glucose levels.** A simple test using the Smart Monitoring method will demonstrate this effect. This sudden rise in blood glucose triggers your body's insulin response. When glucose and insulin levels are chronically elevated (and this is precisely what happens when you drink sugary beverages), these cells eventually grow resistant to insulin's efforts to transport glucose inside, so your pancreas is forced to pump out still more of the hormone to get the job done. Not only does this drench your cells with insulin, causing excessive levels in your bloodstream, but eventually your pancreas will wear out and won't be able to produce any insulin at all. When this occurs, you will need regular insulin injections to stay alive.

**They make you fat.** When the liver, pancreas and cells throughout your body are fully stocked with glucose, insulin aids in transforming excess blood glucose into fat, which your body usually stores in the belly area (called visceral fat). Fat cells in these regions act more like glands that secrete enzymes that are highly inflammatory. This inflammation further increases insulin resistance. Even worse, it damages blood vessels, tissues and organs, which leads to serious complications such as heart disease and cancer. Some of the nation's top obesity researchers at institutions like Stanford, Harvard, and Yale have pronounced sodas and other sweetened drinks to be the leading cause of obesity today. Harvard's famous Nurse's Health Study found that women who drank sugary beverages such as soda or fruit punch increased their risk of weight gain and diabetes by a staggering 50%.[2]

**They age you faster.** Elevated levels of sugar and insulin in your bloodstream produce inflammatory waste products called *advanced glycation end products* (AGEs), which accelerate the aging of all tissues in the body. On the skin, they're seen as "age spots" and wrinkles—but this accelerated aging also occurs in organs. People with diabetes frequently appear 15 to 20 years older than their chronological age because *biologically* they are. But it is not diabetes that is causing AGEs to flourish. Rather, it is chronically high glucose levels caused by one factor: too much sugar (which sodas definitely contain).

**They weaken your bones.** Sodas (including seltzer) contain *phosphoric acid*, which leaches minerals from bones and leads to osteoporosis. This acid also inhibits your body's ability to absorb manganese. Low levels of this trace mineral significantly weaken the stabilizing ligaments that support joints, making them unstable and subject to increased risk of osteoarthritis, dislocation, and injury.

## Diet Sodas Are Just as Bad

Please don't think that diet sodas are a safer alternative. Instead of helping you lose weight, diet sodas actually cause weight gain by boosting insulin production, leading to excessively high insulin in your blood, which triggers greater fat accumulation and even more cravings for sugar. The science against the consumption of the artificial sweeteners in diet sodas is extremely disturbing…

•According to a study at the University of Texas-San Antonio, people who drank one diet soda daily were 65% more likely to be overweight than those who drank none. Drinking two or more diet sodas a day boosted the risk of obesity even higher.[3]

•A 2009 study published in *Diabetes Care* [4] found that drinking diet soda every day increases the risk of metabolic syndrome (another way of saying "prediabetes") by 36% and the risk of developing Type 2 diabetes by as much as 67%.

•Researchers at Purdue University discovered that consuming saccharin (Sweet'N Low) actually *contributes* to weight gain.[5] The FDA won't permit saccharin's use as a food additive because it has been linked to bladder cancer. Apparently adding it to soft drinks is somehow different. (We certainly don't understand their rationale.)

•Scientists at Duke University found that the sucralose in Splenda *increases* the likelihood of obesity,[6] while destroying many beneficial intestinal bacteria (known as probiotics).

•Aspartame, the sweetener in NutraSweet, Equal and Sugar Twin, has been linked to serious adverse effects, including a higher risk of cancer. When aspartame is broken down in the body, the neurotoxin (brain poison) methanol is produced, causing a range of neurological symptoms, from headaches to seizures. Aspartame, by the way, has been re-branded as AminoSweet, no doubt with the idea that uninformed consumers will think this carcinogenic chemical is a new "health food."

## How to Lose a Pound a Week
## Without Even Trying

It's hard to believe that Americans drink 56 gallons of soft drinks per person per year.[7] And research shows that drinking sodas increases your risk of obesity by a staggering 60%.[8] On the flip side, researchers have found that eliminating just one soft drink per day results in one pound *lost* per week. And that's without changing your diet or lifestyle in any other way. Remember, that's just from cutting out one daily soda—and you're going to give up *all* sugary drinks entirely. Imagine the results!

## Take Your Magnifying Glass Shopping

By examining food labels closely, you will begin to notice the mystifying variety of "camouflage words" used to hide the presence of added sweeteners, including corn syrup, molasses, sucrose, dextrose, lactose, juice concentrate, glucose, maltose, fructose, maple syrup, corn sweetener, natural sweeteners and, of course, high fructose corn syrup.

But you can save yourself the trouble by heeding this rule of thumb: The vast majority of food products that bear a label contain sugar. (Yes, there are some exceptions—and later we'll share our list of nutritious prepared foods that you can feel free to enjoy.)

## Are There Any "Good Sweeteners"?

Here's a question we get a lot: Is there a significant difference among such "natural" sweeteners as molasses and honey? The answer is yes. These do contain nutrients and important minerals, but your body responds to all sweeteners in the same way: By spiking your blood glucose and calling for more insulin to clear it from your bloodstream.

## Take a Short Break from Alcohol, Too

Everything you've read and heard about moderate alcohol consumption being good for your health is correct. A drink or two helps lower blood glucose, protects against heart disease and de-stresses your nervous system. Numerous studies confirm its place in a healthful diet—even if you have diabetes. (By the way, we define "moderate" as up to two drinks per day for men; and no more than one drink daily for women.)

But we want you to abstain from any alcohol for Phase One of the 30-Day Diabetes Cure Plan because alcohol is high in calories and sugars—and we want to get your blood glucose down to baseline. Also, excessive alcohol consumption is directly toxic to your liver and brain.

Moderation is key to healthful alcohol consumption, and it's just not possible to reverse diabetes or prediabetes if you're over-consuming. If you experience difficulty abstaining from alcohol for these first 10 days, it could be a sign that you have a dependency (and your blood glucose problems could be a direct result). This is a good opportunity to get professional help, if you do have a problem.

**The benefits of passing on alcohol.** Taking a short break from alcohol will accomplish two things. First, it will help make dramatic reductions in your glucose levels. If you're currently on medication, this will lead to a significant reduction in the dose you require. Second, it will reveal any hidden dependency you may have.

If you've been drinking too much, cutting back on your alcohol consumption (provided you don't have an outright dependency) will produce some immediate health benefits. You'll lose weight, improve your blood glucose, and feel better overall. You'll be able to manage your blood glucose more easily and you might even experience a surge in sexual desire. You'll think more clearly, your mood will brighten, and your relationships could improve. Long-term, you'll lower your risk of cancer, stroke, liver disease, and Alzheimer's. You'll be adding precious years to your life. And you'll dramatically reduce your chances of diabetic complications such as vision loss, kidney failure, and limb amputation.

## The Problems with Too Much Alcohol

Even moderate amounts of alcohol can cause your blood glucose to rise, a condition that makes diabetes symptoms worse. But drinking alcohol excessively can make your blood glucose plummet (hypoglycemia)—especially if you are taking diabetes medications that already moderate your blood glucose. This can cause a sudden swing to such low blood glucose that you might become dizzy, sleepy, or disoriented. You could confuse this with being drunk, but you won't get the right treatment if you're suffering from a hypoglycemic episode rather than excessive alcohol consumption.

**Alcohol prevents fat burning.** One of the benefits of changing your diet and lifestyle is that you lose weight. But alcohol consumption may work against this, according to the *Journal of the American Medical Association*.[9] Swiss researchers found that alcohol in the bloodstream slows fat metabolism by more than 30%. And if you're in the habit of enjoying chips or pretzels with your drink, these will drive up your blood glucose and insulin levels even higher.

## Leaving Alcohol Behind Can Help You Move Forward

*The 30-Day Diabetes Cure* has helped people on every continent fight Type 2 diabetes, including Milan G., of Ljubljana, Slovenia. Working as a sales representative for a multinational information technology consulting company resulted in constant exposure to the three S's: sugar, sitting, and stress. As Milan approached 60 years old, the consequences of his lifestyle showed up as hypertension, Type 2 diabetes, atherosclerosis, and prostate cancer. For five years, Milan took five different drugs daily to control his blood pressure, high cholesterol, heart disease, and Type 2 diabetes. The quality of his life was rapidly deteriorating. Milan realized he would have to fight to stay alive, and decided to turn his attention to his large daily prescription load. He began to take ownership of his health by researching and educating himself about his chronic health conditions. Meanwhile, Milan's doctor had begun to prescribe higher doses of *metformin*. Milan knew he had to improve his lifestyle and get off the medications.

When Milan found *The 30-Day Diabetes Cure* he knew it was what he was looking for: A step-by-step plan with clear action, medical explanations, and scientific reasoning. Milan feared his doctors would disapprove of his decision to get off diabetes medications, but they were supportive and encouraged him to continue. The hardest part of the plan for Milan was eliminating alcohol during Phase One. In fact, he spent three weeks trying to abstain for 10 days that the plan requires. "I experienced difficulty in abstaining and discovered that I actually had a dependency on alcohol," said Milan.

Despite this difficulty, Milan pushed ahead and The 30-Day Diabetes Cure Plan has worked like a charm for him. He's been off all of his medications for the past nine months, has lost more than 15 pounds, and he's feeling great. These days, Milan cooks for himself creatively, chooses foods wisely, and makes fitness an integral part of his life. "I'm still working on a few steps from Phase Two, which are crucial to me. I also return and repeat steps from Phase One when I see it necessary." Milan explains, "I now understand what author Jim Healthy means when he says: 'Good health is mainly a mind game.'"

In addition, when you consume alcohol, your liver goes into overdrive trying to clear it from your bloodstream, leaving all that glucose to be converted into body fat. Alcohol also reduces the amount of enzymes that break down triglyceride fats—and even encourages the production of more still triglycerides. So you end up with a liver that's so overtaxed by removing alcohol from your blood that it can't pay attention to your blood lipid levels. Your LDL cholesterol and triglycerides go up, increasing your risk for heart disease and added fat storage. (They don't call it a "beer belly" for nothing.)

Alcohol adds empty calories. Still need convincing? Alcohol, which is chemically similar to fat, has about seven calories per gram. Giving up sugary drinks and desserts will help you cut calories, but if you're still sipping two or more cocktails, beers, or glasses of wine daily, you won't make much headway. Incidentally, the sugar that beer is made from (*maltose*) has a higher glycemic index (GI) than table sugar and white bread. After fermentation, sugars known as *maltodextrins* are left behind. They too have a high GI score and cause an insulin response that leads to fat storage in your abdomen. All alcohol contains calories that get stored as fat, period.

## Why You Need to Eliminate Fruit Juice, Too

You might think that fresh-squeezed organic fruit juices would be acceptable because they provide a wealth of vitamins, minerals, antioxidants, and other super-nutritious compounds. However, fruit juice has virtually no fiber. Normally, the fiber portion of the whole fruit slows the conversion of fructose into glucose. With the fiber gone and because of its natural fructose content, drinking the fruit's juice has the same effect on your blood glucose as drinking a soda. From now on, treat fruit juice as you would soda: Avoid it. Eat whole fruit instead.

Two exceptions to the juice rule are unsweetened pomegranate juice that has been diluted by water or fizzy mineral water, and tomato juice or vegetable juice. The latter in particular can supply a super dose of nutritional benefits. All other juices and juice drinks should be avoided because they'll play havoc with your glucose levels.

## Keep Dehydration in Mind

•Diabetes can cause dehydration, a dangerous health condition that can lead to shock and death. When glucose isn't metabolized properly, the process of excreting it from the body requires extra fluid. If you're not adequately hydrated, this fluid is pulled from the tissues in your body. This is why excessive thirst and frequent urination are symptoms of impending or existing diabetes.

•Unless you're replenishing your body's fluids by drinking extra liquids regularly, you can cause a deficiency of essential electrolytes. According to the Mayo Clinic, the symptoms of dehydration include dry or sticky mouth, a decrease in urine, urine becoming concentrated and dark yellow, the absence of tears, sunken eyes, vomiting, diarrhea, and lethargy—or simply feeling "thirsty" most of the time.[10]

•The Diabetes Friends Action Network[11] advises that you drink at least 64 ounces of water or other liquids every day. This does not include soda or diet soda, fruity drinks, fruit juice or punch, sweetened coffee or tea, or alcoholic beverages. These drinks don't hydrate your tissues and cells, and they trigger a host of blood glucose problems.

•So how will you stay hydrated now that you've given up sodas, soft drinks, and fruit juice? It's easy. There are plenty of delicious and satisfying drinks that will actually help to heal your diabetes. In the following sections, you will learn how to incorporate pure water, black coffee and tea, and other diabetes-healing beverages into your healthful new lifestyle. These drinks will keep your cells hydrated and aid in stabilizing your blood glucose levels, all while providing satisfying, thirst-quenching replacements for soda and other sugary drinks.

## Good Ole Water Is Still Best

•Drinking plenty of water is still tops when it comes to staying hydrated without adding to your health troubles or weight. Get into the habit of carrying a bottle with you everywhere you go, and sip from it frequently. Fill a 32-ounce glass bottle with water or some healthful substitute (see our suggestions on page 182–183) first thing in the morning and keep it on the kitchen counter or your desk at work. If you're uncertain about the quality of your municipal tap water or your water pipes, it's wise to purchase a good quality water filter to avoid dangerous chemicals.

•Here's a tip for making sure you get enough water when you're out: Always order water in restaurants and drink a glass *before* your meal; it'll keep you hydrated *and* help curb your appetite. A slice or two of lemon gives it some flavor and offers a multitude of added benefits, from balancing stomach acids to getting more vitamin C.

•Be sure to avoid plastic water bottles—especially hardened BPA plastic. New studies are confirming older research, which links plastic to hormone irregularities. So use glass or stainless steel bottles for your portable water supply, and don't drink from plastic cups or bottles. (To be safe, don't store or microwave food in plastic containers or covered with plastic wrap, either.)

## Tea Protects Against Diabetes

Drinking tea—whether green, black, white or herbal—is an excellent habit to develop… especially for people with diabetes. Research reported in the *Journal of Agricultural and Food Chemistry* found that tea lowers blood glucose and inhibits the development of diabetic cataracts.[12]

•A five-year study in the UK[13] involving 17,000 participants discovered that those who drank three or more cups of tea (or coffee) per day were at a significantly lower risk for developing diabetes than those who did not drink tea.

•Other studies show that green tea also helps stabilize blood glucose and, especially important for people with diabetes who struggle with weight issues, produces a *thermogenic effect*[14], which stimulates the metabolism and helps to burn calories at a faster rate.

•Green tea also has been shown to improve kidney, liver and pancreatic function[15]—an essential benefit for people with diabetes. It also alleviates arthritis, protects the skin and eyes from disease, and improves gastrointestinal function. In fact, this delicious multipurpose beverage has also been used to manage allergies, prevent bacterial and viral infections, and to treat a variety of other diseases that stem from inflammation (including diabetes and cancer), as well as improve psychological health.

•The primary healing compound in tea is the polyphenol ECGC (*Epigallocatechin gallate*). Researchers have documented its positive impact in preventing heart disease, ability to enhance brain function, potential to inhibit tumor growth and benefit in losing weight.*

•According to a 2008 study, the same compounds that protect against cancer also reduce blood glucose spikes after eating (your doctor calls this post-prandial hyperglycemia) by inhibiting an enzyme called *alpha-glucosidase*. Black, green, oolong, and white teas all were noted to have this effect.[16]

## Beware of Tea Imposters

Clever marketing has given Americans a wide range of choices in drinks called "tea," although few of them bear any resemblance to the nutritious traditional beverage we're talking about. Iced tea in a bottle with added fruit "flavor" isn't an energy boost—it's a sugar rush.

To get the maximum healing benefits, drink tea that's brewed from the leaf or twigs of the plant. Look for true Japanese green tea, which is readily available in health food stores and Asian markets. Rich, fragrant black teas like oolong and other varieties of Japanese tea such as *matcha, sencha* and *gyokuro* all contain more ECGC benefits than Chinese tea (even if it's decaf). As noted above, white tea also provides ECGC benefits, while herbal teas are also healthy choices. If in doubt about how a variety of tea will affect your glucose levels, remember that you have taken control of this knowledge by using the Smart Monitoring method. Formulate a question involving the beverage in question and test in pairs to understand how that beverage affects you.

Steep your tea for three to 10 minutes in piping-hot water, but never boil the tea itself or you'll destroy its nutritional value. Drink within one hour of brewing for maximum benefits. One to three cups of tea per day provides plenty of diabetes-healing benefits, while also triggering liver enzymes that detoxify your body of accumulated poisons.

---

*http://healthyeating.sfgate.com/egcg-green-tea-8453.html*

## Get Back to Basics with Real Coffee

Brewed coffee—black, not loaded with cream, sugar, and flavorings—is actually highly beneficial for people with diabetes. Coffee contains magnesium, polyphenols, and a substance called *quinides*, all of which have been found to help regulate blood glucose levels and insulin production. Compounds in coffee also aid in the metabolism of sugar in the body. Multiple studies by Australian researchers reported in a recent article published in the *Archives of Internal Medicine*[17] show that drinking regular or decaf coffee can significantly lower the risk of developing diabetes. And research done at University of California-San Diego with people with prediabetes—whose levels of blood glucose were above normal, but not high enough to be defined as diabetes—found the coffee drinkers had a 60% lower risk of developing diabetes, compared with those who never drank coffee. According to the researchers, coffee has a "striking protective effect."

**Smart coffee choices.** If you think coffee should taste like a candy cane or apple pie with a huge dollop of whipped cream on top, you're not reaping coffee's health benefits. Instead, you're drinking a dessert that's loaded with over 300 calories, including 43 grams of sugar (not to mention that $4–5 price tag and a throwaway cup).

A smarter, healthier (and cheaper) solution is to get yourself a simple, drip-style coffee maker and brew a pot of coffee at home. Buy a sturdy thermos carafe (glass-lined stainless steel is best) and tote your java to work if you want. Skip the high-calorie additives and the non-dairy, chemical-laden creamers; instead, add soymilk or a small amount of milk (whole or low-fat).

If you're feeling more adventurous, try a French press carafe or a traditional Italian stove top espresso pot. Experiment with different types of roasts and blends from various coffee-producing countries. Just stay away from those unnatural flavorings like raspberry and caramel because they're usually sugar-based—and don't belong in a good cup of joe anyway.

For an extra zing with healing benefits, remember to sprinkle your grounds or coffee with a little cinnamon. This spice has been shown to reduce blood glucose levels. Why not do a Smart Monitoring experiment to see how adding a teaspoon of cinnamon to your drinks over the course of the day affects your glucose levels? Other spice possibilities include cardamom and even cloves, both of which aid digestion and provide other health benefits.[18]

## 7 Diabetes-Friendly Beverages

Water, black and green tea, coffee, and pomegranate juice are a sensible foundation for drinking healthfully as a diabetic. The 10 suggestions that follow will help widen your thirst-quenching horizon, reduce your soda habit, and satisfy your taste buds and thirst. Since you probably won't find these in any vending machine or convenience store, carry them with you in a small thermos so they stay cool.

## Pomegranate Power

With every rule, it seems there's usually an exception, and here are ours: The one juice people with diabetes should definitely make room for in the refrigerator is unsweetened pomegranate juice. Pomegranate juice has tons of benefits that stem from that rich, dark color—evidence of its powerful antioxidant, *anthocyanin*. Just don't drink it straight because it still contains fruit sugar. It is best enjoyed diluted with some tap or fizzy mineral water (try a 1:1 ratio to start).

What exactly do antioxidants do? They fight *oxidation*, a natural part of the respiration process. Oxidation causes metal to rust and fresh food to turn brown and spoil. It also can damage your blood vessels. In fact, oxidized LDL cholesterol clogs arteries, leading to heart disease and stroke. Damaged blood vessels in the eyes cause retinopathy and in the kidney they cause kidney disease. In the feet they cause neuropathy, infections, and gangrene, leading to amputation. Additionally, too many oxidized cells can damage your DNA and cause cancer. What causes oxidation in the blood? High blood glucose and insulin levels. The remedy? Antioxidants along with a diet that naturally lowers your blood glucose.

**1. Accessorized water.** Plain water too boring? Add slices of your favorite fruits and veggies—lemons, oranges, berries, cucumber, mint, or limes—to a pitcher of ice-cold water for a refreshing and flavorful drink. Carry your own supply with you wherever you go (use a glass bottle or stainless steel container to keep your beverage safe from plastics and chemical leaching).

**2. Chilled green or black tea.** Both are loaded with antioxidants to fight free radicals, as well as other nutrients. Flavor with lemon and/or ginger.

**3. Iced ginger or herbal tea.** Enliven with a little unsweetened pomegranate juice to taste.

**4. Low-fat milk.** The calcium in dairy products not only strengthens your bones, but studies show that it helps you lose weight by burning extra calories.

**5. Iced coffee.** But that doesn't mean a 16-ounce Starbucks iced café mocha with whipped cream (330 calories)! Instead, brew strong black coffee for its healing antioxidant and caffeine benefits. Mix with a splash of milk and pour over ice.

**6. Soy and almond milks.** Be sure to check the sugar content of prepared soy and almond milks, and choose the lowest you can find. (We think unsweetened soy milk is delicious!) Soy protein powder (again, read the labels to avoid high sugar content!) can be added to water for a tasty and nutritious drink.

**7. Fruit smoothies.** You can enjoy this treat any time of day: Mix a few frozen berries with unsweetened yogurt, water, and a pinch of cinnamon, cardamom, and vanilla extract in the blender.

# Jim Healthy's Power Smoothie Recipe

This smoothie is packed with protein, fiber, and nutrition. It's naturally sweet, whips up in minutes and is easily transported for sipping during your commute or later in the morning.

**Ingredients:**

1–2 cups berries (strawberries, blueberries, blackberries, and/or raspberries in any combination, fresh or frozen)

1 cup plain, unsweetened, full-fat yogurt with live cultures

2 tablespoons whey protein powder or spirulina powder

1 to 2 tablespoons of ground flaxseed

A few ice cubes (omit if you use frozen berries)

Water as needed to thin to desired consistency

**Instructions:**

Place all ingredients in blender and blend until smooth. Drink immediately or transfer to a thermos bottle for easy transport. (Be sure to perform a Smart Monitoring test about an hour or two after drinking this to see how it affects your glucose level.) You might also want to make a bigger batch and freeze the leftovers in ice cube trays. Transfer frozen "smoothie cubes" to zip-lock bags and store in the freezer. When needed, pop a few cubes into the blender, add some water to thin and you're good to go!

## Today's Action Steps

- Replace soda pop and other sugary beverages—including "sports" and "energy" drinks, sweetened coffees and teas, and fruit drinks, including those made from 100% juice—with diabetes-friendly beverages.

- Take a break from alcohol for the next 10 days (you'll be able to reintroduce moderate alcohol consumption after this initial period).

- Obtain a glass or stainless steel water bottle and consider purchasing a water purification system.

- Smart Monitor before and after to determine the effects of any beverage.

**Extra credit:** Learn to make a basic and refreshing fruit smoothie that can quench your thirst healthfully.

# DAY 3

# FRUIT SWAP

*"Taste every fruit of every tree in the garden at least once.
It is an insult to creation not to experience it fully."*

—STEPHEN FRY, English comedian, actor, and writer

**Tip of the Day:** Fresh fruit provides essential fiber and loads of vitamins, minerals, and antioxidants. It also can add a little sweetness to your life—if you don't overdo it.

A COMMON REFRAIN THAT DIABETICS HEAR is that all fruit is taboo. This outdated notion can make it more difficult for you to maintain a healthy diet while trying to reverse your diabetes. While some fruits that spike your blood sugar—such as watermelon, pine-apples, and bananas—should absolutely be avoided, most fruits and berries actually provide a wealth of essential nutrients and fiber. Fruits and berries also are rich storehouses of beneficial antioxidants. Antioxidants neutralize free radical molecules which cause inflammation in the body whenever present—and inflammation leads to a number of cardiovascular diseases and diabetic complications. Choosing fruits and berries high in antioxidants—such as blueberries, oranges, apples, and peaches—can help heal your body and reverse Type 2 diabetes.

Today, we will show you how to incorporate naturally sweet fruits and berries into your diet. Learn to appreciate fruit as a satisfying dessert and an excellent addition to your break-fast and protein smoothies. Just be sure to avoid the fruits that spike your blood glucose (listed below).

## What's So Great About Fresh Fruit?

Let us count the ways: Fruit contains lots of fiber for glucose management and toxin removal. It is loaded with nutritious antioxidants for neutralizing free radical damage and for healing inflammation. It is also one of nature's best sources of *phytonutrients* (plant chemicals that lower cholesterol and other blood fats, while promoting healthy blood vessels and brain cells). What more could you ask for? Well, there is more...

Fresh fruit is sweet and delicious, as well as readily available in every supermarket in America. Purchase "organically grown" whenever you can—especially berries, apples, and other fruits that, when conventionally raised, can contain high levels of pesticides. Organic frozen berries are an excellent option. Stock your freezer when they are in season and at their lowest price. If you have a local farmer's market—or access to a pesticide-free orchard or berry patch—you will be getting the cleanest, freshest fruit available.

When you eat a piece of fruit in its whole form, you also consume the fiber and micronutrients that slow down the conversion of fruit sugar (fructose) into blood glucose. This is why it is usually better to consume fruit in its whole, natural state—rather than just its juice. Another way to mitigate the insulin-spiking effect of fruit is to combine the fruit with a protein source. Protein sources such as nuts or nut butters, full-fat yogurt and cottage cheese also complement the flavors of fruits and berries. These combinations make for great breakfast and snack options. Use the Smart Monitoring techniques you learned on Day 1 to test the effects that different fruits have on your blood glucose. Avoid the following taboo fruits, which have a high Glycemic Index rating.

## Taboo Fruits

These fruits tend to have a higher Glycemic Index and should be avoided:
- **Pineapple**
- **Watermelon**
- **Papaya**
- **Banana**

## A Quick Reminder About Fruit Juice

Abstain from processed fruit juice, which has been stripped of its fiber, leaving the natural sugar in fruit juice (fructose) to speedily convert into blood glucose. As a refined carbohydrate, the sugar in fruit juice contributes to glucose and insulin spikes in your bloodstream. Testing your blood glucose before you drink fruit juice, and again approximately two hours later, will show you this effect.

## Other Forms of Fruit to Avoid

**Jams and jellies.** Except those made with *zero* added sweeteners and other ingredients, jams and jellies should not be consumed. Many "all-fruit" brands use grape or apple juice as sweeteners, and these are also off limits.

**Commercially canned and jarred fruits.** These have virtually no nutritional value because they've been peeled and heated and are packed in either sugary syrups or in natural juices, which are also high in sugar. Also, the natural acids in the fruit can accelerate the leaching of BPA or metals from the can into your food.

**"Fruity" desserts.** Pies, fruit-flavored yogurt, fruit sauces, and fruit syrups should be avoided because of their high added sugar content, as well as additives, chemicals, and fillers.

**Dried fruit.** This is problematic due to its concentrated natural sugar content—most dried fruits, with the notable exception of prunes, rank high on the GI. As well as the generally high sugar content, dried fruits have added oils, flavorings, and chemicals. A couple of pieces of naturally dried fruit are fine, though—think raisins or chopped prunes, apricots or dates added to yogurt or oatmeal. Just remember: *Moderation!*

## Put Down That Peeler

A large part of fruit's most beneficial antioxidants and anti-cancer phytochemicals lie in its skin, so eat the peel[19] on everything from apples to peaches, pears to kiwi. Kiwi? It's worth trying: Compounds in kiwi are said to ward off infections like *E. coli* and *staphylococcus*.[20]

## The Best Diabetes-Healing Fruits

Look for these highly beneficial fruits and berries on your next shopping trip. Fruits that are high in fiber but low in sugar are the best for diabetics and there are many good fruits to choose from. Remember that the key is to eat them fresh without any added sugars. Most are probably old favorites, but now you will learn just how they can help reduce your blood glucose and benefit your overall health. Test in pairs to monitor the effects of these healing fruits.

**Grapefruit.** Grapefruit is one of the best fruits out there because it has loads of vitamins and minerals. Grapefruits belong to the citrus family and that makes it great for combating colds, viruses, and certain forms of cancer. Grapefruit reduces excess sugar in the blood and eating as little as three grapefruits a week can help keep a person's blood glucose in check. Grapefruit also helps prevent arterial plaque buildup by flushing LDL cholesterol from arteries. If you peel and eat a grapefruit like you would an orange, you get a good dose of cholesterol-lowering pectin from the membranes.[21] Note that grapefruit can interact with prescription medication; consult your doctor before adding grapefruit to your diet.

**Oranges, lemons, limes, and tangerines.** All are loaded with vitamin C. The antioxidants in oranges help support the liver. Oranges also contain potassium, flavonoids, lycopene, and zeaxanthin. If consumed regularly, these nutrients help combat high blood pressure.

**Blueberries.** This little gem is packed with antioxidant vitamins. Specifically, blueberries contain anthocyanins, which are a type of flavonoid. The anthocyanins in blueberries are more effective antioxidants than those in other foods, such as dark chocolate, red wine, and tea. Anthocyanins can also be found in black currents, blood oranges, and eggplant. Keep these fruits in mind while shopping, as well.

**Apples.** They contain beneficial natural compounds that have been shown to lower the risk of prostate cancer as well as lower blood pressure. In red apples, these compounds include ellagic acid, hesperidin, and quercetin. Green apples contain chlorophyll, antioxidant vitamin C and lutein. To reap the most benefits from apples, try to eat both red and green varieties.

**Cherries.** These sweet and sour nuggets contain ellagic acid and quercetin, two nutrients that help eliminate toxins from the body. They also contain anti-inflammatory properties and have been linked to improved joint function for those suffering from arthritis.

**Green grapes.** These contain chlorophyll, fiber, zeaxanthin, folate, and vitamin C—nutrients that help to reduce blood pressure. Grapes also support the digestive and immune systems.

**Red grapes.** These small, sweet orbs contain compounds that have been shown to lower the risk of high blood pressure and heart disease. They are rich in fiber, antioxidants, and resveratrol. Red grapes and red wine both contain this restorative compound.

**Gooseberries.** These old-fashioned berries are rich in vitamin C and help reduce blood glucose levels.

**Strawberries.** These beauties are incredibly rich in the flavonoid called *quercetin*, which also produces strong anti-inflammatory effects.[22] Researchers at the Harvard University School of Public Health discovered that strawberries drive down levels of C-reactive protein (CRP), a blood marker for inflammation that is strongly predictive of a host of degenerative diseases. The Harvard scientists found that women who ate just 16 or more fresh or frozen strawberries per week lowered their CRP levels by 14%!

**Peaches.** These golden globes contain beta-carotene and a host of antioxidants that are good for lowering blood pressure. The natural beta-glucans and lignans found in this fruit fortify the immune system. In addition, eating peaches helps balance hormone levels.

**Avocados and olives.** Avocados and olives are often not thought of as fruits because they are not sweet. However, both are high in monounsaturated fat, a beneficial fat that helps modulate blood glucose.

## Combining Protein with Fruit

Your meals and snacks should have protein and healthy fat, as well as a healthy carbohydrate source. When enjoying fruits and berries, remember to combine them with foods containing protein and fats, such as cheese, nuts, yogurt ,or protein powder. This slows any rise in blood glucose. The Power Smoothie recipe from Day 2 is an excellent example of this.

Here are a few combination ideas:

- **Apple and cheese slices**
- **Berries and yogurt**
- **Fruit and nuts**
- **Fruit slices dipped in unsweetened almond butter**
- **Chopped fruit and cottage cheese**

## Today's Action Steps

•Fix yourself a delicious, diabetes-healing fruit snack. Incorporate healthful protein into small to moderate-sized portions of healing fruit, allowing your body to benefit from the bountiful nutrition of fruit without over-consuming sugars.

•Stock your kitchen with a supply of fruit and berries, then try out some delicious combinations.

•Choose one or two fruits to test using Smart Monitoring.

**Extra credit:** Prepare the Power Smoothie recipe provided in Day 2 and test in pairs to see how it affects your blood glucose levels.

# DAY 4

# TAKE A BREAK FROM SWEETS

*"Just when you're beginning to think pretty well of people,
you run across somebody who puts sugar on sliced tomatoes."*

—WILL CUPPY, American humorist

**Tip of the Day:** Breaking a sweet tooth habit is crucial for reversing Type 2 diabetes and saving your life.

BY ELIMINATING SODAS, SUGARY BEVERAGES, AND JUICES, plus the taboo fruits from your diet, you have already taken huge steps toward conquering the hold that sugar may have on you. Today, you will commit even further by taking a break from sweets entirely. While this may seem daunting, know that it only takes three to 10 days to break a sugar addiction! Use the Smart Monitoring method to give yourself concrete proof of the effects of sugar and refined carbohydrates on your glucose levels if you find your resolve weakening.

## Sugar Is Poison in the Amounts We Consume Today

Americans consume, on average, approximately 170 pounds of sugar *per person* per year according to the USDA. That's roughly a half-pound every single day. Compare that to 100 years ago, when the average sugar consumption was just four pounds per person *per year*.[23]

There can be no doubt that this overconsumption of sugar and sweeteners has led the way to the explosion of Type 2 diabetes in Western cultures. In fact, sugar is directly responsible for the staggering number of people suffering from severe health problems caused by diabetes. There are patients who require dangerous multiple medications, constant monitoring and frequent invasive medical care because they suffer horrific complications, a miserable quality of life and, eventually, premature death. And that is not to mention the tremendous financial burden these medical problems place on the world economy.

## Sugar Is the Most Sickening Food on Earth

There is absolutely no chance of reversing your diabetes or getting off your medications until you break this deadly addiction. So for the next 10 days of the 30-Day Diabetes Cure Plan, you're going to take a healing break from sugar in its many forms—be it candy, dessert, added sweeteners such as brown sugar, table sugar, and honey, or processed foods containing high fructose corn syrup or artificial sweeteners (even so-called "diet sweeteners").

On this fourth day, we want you to remember—if not memorize—these important points:

- Sugar damages your arteries, which causes nerve damage, tissue death, gangrene, and amputation.

- Sugar is the leading cause of heart disease.

- Sugar will steal your eyesight.

- Sugar is devastating to your hormone balance and metabolism.

- Sugar adds to your weight and girth.

- Sugar triggers dangerous inflammation throughout your entire body.

- Sugar represents a severe health risk. It leads directly to diabetes, cardiovascular problems, and cancer.

## Taking a "Sugar Break" Can Save Your Life!

We will not sugarcoat the truth: If you have a serious sweet tooth, taking a break from sugary desserts and snacks will be challenging. But it is absolutely essential that you do so—and it is entirely possible to beat this life-threatening habit. Thousands of other people with stronger cravings for sweets than you have succeeded in breaking their addiction. So you can, too, as you will soon see.

What's your motivation? Your life is at stake. Your future happiness hangs in the balance. We assure you, breaking your addiction to sweets will be a walk in the park compared with going blind…having your limbs amputated…suffering a heart attack…or receiving a cancer diagnosis.

## It Takes 3–10 Days to Break Your Addiction

That is usually all it takes to break sugar's hold on you—and to learn to love other deliciously satisfying foods that can help reverse your diabetes, instead of making it worse. Giving up sugar and sweets for a short time won't be as painful as you imagine. But if you don't believe you can make it 10 days without sugar, we urge you to stash this book away right now and don't retrieve it until you're really serious about reversing or at least improving your condition.

And if you're one of those people who thinks, "Life without sweets just isn't worth living," then please return this book immediately for a refund. Unless you are determined to break sugar's stranglehold on you, your future almost certainly *won't* be worth living.

## Cold Turkey Is the Fast Lane to Success

You might be wondering: "Why can't I just cut back on my consumption of sweets slowly?" Because it is stressful, painful, counterproductive, and almost always ends in failure. Gradual withdrawal of (or cutting down on) any addictive substance—from Camels and Coors to cocaine

—almost never works. People waste a lot of valuable time trying (and repeatedly failing) with this approach because they still have one foot in the "river of denial."

Look at it like this: If you crave sugary dessert foods to the point where you can't give them up for 10 days, you have a serious dependence on them. The only successful solution to this problem is to quit them. If you can do this, you will emerge a changed person. You will not need to eat doughnuts for breakfast and a vending machine snack cake to quell the mid-afternoon slump. You will not be that person who must have a bowl of ice cream every night in front of the TV.

Now you understand why diabetes medications are so popular, don't you? They offer the illusion that you can continue to eat all the sweets you want as long as you use glucose-lowering drugs to pump up your insulin or reduce your blood glucose. Sounds like the perfect plan, right? *Wrong.* Drugs won't stop the progression of diabetes or protect you from its horrific complications. Study after study confirms this.

## Understanding the Power of Sugar

There is no doubt that sugar can have a powerful hold on some people. A famous study involving rats showed that sugar was even more addictive than cocaine. When rats were offered the choice between cocaine and sugar water, over 90% of them chose the sugar! In addition, they were more motivated to work harder for a sugary reward than for the cocaine. We all know how powerfully addictive cocaine is. Could sugar actually be stronger? In our minds, there's no question.

And then there's the sugar-cancer link. In 1924, German scientist Otto Warburg was awarded the Nobel Prize for discovering that cancer cells use glucose as their primary fuel. Subsequent research shows that when cancer develops, blood glucose that should be used by the body for normal functions gets hijacked by cancer cells. This generates excess lactic acid, causing overwhelming fatigue in patients and a welcoming environment in which cancer cells multiply and form tumors.[24] When you have cancer, much of your glucose gets diverted to it, instead of your healthy cells. This deprives the body of the nutrition; and so cancer patients die from malnutrition. Is it worth it?

## You Will Thank Us for This "Tough Love"

Quitting sugar-laden foods is the first step in allowing your body and mind to break the carbohydrate-craving cycle. Here is what you are going to accomplish with this approach…

- We are changing your eating habits and rewiring your brain. Eating sugar leads to craving more sugar (known as "carbohydrate craving"). So abstaining from it temporarily will almost magically disrupt your sugar cravings—often as quickly as within 72 hours.

- Your internal metabolism will begin to change as well. Your need for insulin will be reduced, and the insulin your body does require will be used far more efficiently. You will be clearing your system of one of the most health-destroying substances.

- As you push on, day-by-day something miraculous will happen. The absence of all these sugary foods will begin to normalize your blood glucose. Your pancreas will say "Ah! I can relax" from the relentless drive to produce more and more insulin to process all that sugar—and your overtaxed beta cells will be able to take a well-deserved break.

- When you stop eating sugary products, your body's leptin response will come back online. (Leptin, as you'll recall, is the hormone that tells your brain when you've eaten enough—and also commands your metabolism to burn stored body fat when it needs fuel instead of signaling, "It's snack time again!") As a result, you will begin to lose weight without trying.

## You'll Experience Immediate Benefits

During these first 10 days, you will also learn to discern the difference between appetite and hunger. (Once we flush all the excess sugar from your system, the distinction will become much clearer to you.) *Hunger*, you see, is a genuine physiological need for nourishment. *Appetite* is a desire or craving for a specific food. Appetite has more to do with your brain than your stomach (and this includes all those advertisements and appetite triggers that surround us daily). As long as your appetite rules you, you will never be able to reverse your diabetes.

Believe it or not, your craving for sweets will actually weaken. Yes, you read that correctly. Not only will you lose your constant desire for sugary foods, but when you do take a bite of something overly sweet, you may not even like it. Your taste buds will have become more sensitized to the delicate sugars in real foods.

Your body will begin to regulate its sugar intake on its own because after this Phase One period, it will know when "enough is enough." This doesn't mean you won't be eating anything sweet for the rest of your life. You can and will—but you'll just be more moderate about it. There is a bounty of natural sugars in natural foods that are satisfying and will not produce abnormal weight gain or out-of-control blood glucose.

## Tips for Conquering Your Cravings Now

Here are some tips that you can employ when you get the yearning for something sweet…

**Smart Monitoring.** Don't take our word for it! Keep a log of what you eat and compare it with your glucose readings (before and after meals) for the week. You will see for yourself how any lapse affects your glucose levels.

**Begin with breakfast.** Never skip the most important meal of the day: Breakfast. Eating a breakfast built around a high-quality protein will help curb your sugar cravings throughout the day. Also, research has shown that skipping breakfast is associated with a higher risk of developing Type 2 diabetes.[25] Tomorrow, you will learn how to put together the top diabetes-reversing breakfasts.

**Hydrate.** Drink a large glass of water, a cup of hot or iced herbal tea or coffee, instead of reaching for sweets. Make sure there's no sugar added.

**Go nuts.** A small handful of mixed nuts (without the dried fruit usually present in trail mix) is a satisfying between-meals snack. The protein in nuts will perk up your brain, instead of triggering a crash the way candy does. Even better, nuts contain healthful monounsaturated

## The Real Healing Starts When Sugar Is Eliminated

Terrance (Terry) Cook was driving home with his wife late one night in 1998. Terry asked, "Where's all this traffic coming from?"

She said, "There's only one car in front of us."

"I was seeing 30 taillights," Terry says. His wife took the wheel, and he scheduled a doctor's appointment the next day.

Terry's doctor said, "Honey, you've got diabetes." Terry learned that his A1C was 8.4. He says, "She told me to eliminate all kinds of sugars and go to the pharmacy immediately." The doctor said Terry could lose his toes, fingers, and limbs. He knew he had to get his diabetes under control. But even with meds, he never got his daily glucose readings below 180. His doctor tried different medications. None worked.

Terry's doctor upped his meds. But over 14 years, his condition actually got worse. His mood worsened, too. "I was miserable," he says. Around this time, he heard of *The 30-Day Diabetes Cure*. He was skeptical about it.

Terry's doctor eventually told him that he'd have to go on insulin. Terry is terrified of needles. He says, "The doctor allowed me 90 extra days to try to get my sugars under control. I immediately bought *The 30-Day Diabetes Cure*."

He started the plan that very day, sticking strictly to the plan of passing on sweets. By Day 5 his blood sugar was below 200 (without medications). As days passed, the numbers got lower and lower. After 30 days, his average blood sugar reading was 121.

He calls himself a "happy camper" now, but he's surprised how many people he knows with diabetes. He tells everyone about his experience. "I know others can benefit by my example," he says. Word of his success has spread like wildfire through the casino where he works, getting 20 of his coworkers interested in *The 30-Day Diabetes Cure*. They fight over his book on lunch breaks.

"I wish I had this book 14 years ago," he says. "I had no idea how much better my life could be!"

fats that help heal diabetes. Just be sure the nuts you munch are unsalted and either raw or dry-roasted.

**Choose cheese.** In Europe, people like to finish a meal with a sampling of cheese instead of a sweet dessert. Choose stronger-flavored artisan cheeses because you won't need a big chunk. A portion about the size of your pinky finger should be plenty. The protein in cheese will also keep your hunger satisfied longer.

**Eat protein instead.** Withdrawing from sugar can make you feel tired, unfocused, or headachy in the beginning. Having a little protein can stabilize your blood glucose in a healthy way. Here are some suggestions: Try a hard-boiled egg, a quarter cup of chicken or tuna, a few raw nuts, a piece of cheese the size of your pinky, or a quarter cup of chickpeas with a little olive oil. Half a cup of plain full-fat yogurt or cottage cheese will fit the bill. So will a tablespoon of natural peanut butter with celery sticks.

**Crunch raw veggies.** Always keep a small baggie of cut fresh vegetables with you like celery sticks, radishes, carrots, and bell pepper strips. There's something about the crunchiness that satisfies. And if you pay close attention, you'll notice that these veggies are loaded with delicate natural sugars. The problem is your taste buds need the time to readjust. Coming off of a diet loaded with candy and sweets is like leaving a loud rock concert and not being able to hear your partner whisper "I love you" in your ear.

**Gargle and brush.** It's good dental hygiene—and it's a slick trick for thwarting sugar cravings. This usually is all it takes to dull the "I need sugar!" impulse. Try it, and while you're at it, floss.

**Never skip a meal.** Not eating three regular meals is like starving a wild tiger. It's going to eat anything it can get its claws on—and you're no different. When your hunger is raging, you grab the first thing in sight. Beginning your day with a diabetes-healing breakfast is the smartest way to keep hunger and cravings at bay. Plan ahead to have healthful meals at regular intervals throughout the day. And keep some healthful snacks handy just in case Mr. Hunger stalks you.

**Sip some hot soup.** There's something about a cup of soup that takes the edge off of hunger. And the majority of soups are good for you. When you have the urge for something sweet, turn to soup. Microwave for a minute or so and sip it slowly. It will satisfy your appetite and relax you at the same time.

**What do you really need?** Very often, the craving for a sweet treat is really an emotional need for something that's missing from your day—or your life. Maybe you're just bored…or tense…or anxious…or angry…or lonely (or all of the above). Sugar has drug-like effects on brain chemistry (which is why it is addictive), so something sweet is usually comforting. But the relief is only temporary. Like all mind-altering drugs, you need to keep taking it to feel the effect. Of course, this will not change your circumstances or problems—and constant eating increases your weight, lowers your self-esteem, weakens your willpower, and puts off until "tomorrow" addressing the source of your distress. Stop eating to make yourself feel better—and change what's really making you feel bad.

**In an emergency.** If you have a strong dependence on sweets and this temporary abstinence is unbearable, here's an escape hatch that can prevent you from completely breaking down and scuttling the entire plan: If your cravings are irresistible, allow yourself to suck on frozen grapes. They can provide the sweetness you're craving, and by having grapes rather than chocolate squares, for example, you're preventing yourself from taking the first steps down a dangerous slippery slope.

## Beware of Hidden Sugars

In addition to the 170 pounds of sugar the average American eats every year, we also ingest another 53 pounds of sweeteners that are added to our foods. Food manufacturers do this because refining and processing food (to make it last on supermarket shelves indefinitely) destroys most of its natural flavor. So to compensate, they add loads of sweeteners, sodium, and "flavor-enhancing" additives to make their products palatable. The problem is that this also makes them very unhealthy.

So, on this "giving-up sweets day," we also want you to develop an eagle eye for the sweeteners that food manufacturers sneak into their products. You may need to splurge on a magnifying glass, because these guys intentionally keep the type small on their ingredient lists and disguise the sweeteners they use with exotic names.

As many as 60% of all processed foods contain high-fructose corn syrup (HFCS), which is why today you'll also start to become an expert on reading labels. If you see a product that contains it, drop it like a hot potato.

Food manufacturers add sugar to just about every processed food imaginable—even foods that don't taste especially sweet—including ketchup, mayonnaise, canned soups, spaghetti sauce, salad dressings, frozen dinners, commercial peanut butter, seasoned potato chips, sports drinks, bottled tea, and so-called "energy" bars.

In order to back off from sugar right now, you may want to call a truce on eating virtually all prepared foods. We say "virtually" because some prepared foods—such as canned tuna, beans, and tomatoes that contain no added sugar—are healthful whole foods and are an integral part of our 30-day diabetes-reversing plan. From this day forward, read the label on anything you're thinking about eating, from a bag of frozen veggies to a jar of peanut butter.

## Never Eat "Diabetic" Food Products

A quick word here about the deluge of products marketed to diabetics. Go into any drugstore and you'll see shelves of "diabetic" candy and "sugar-free" snack and dessert products. Don't be fooled. These items are usually sweetened with sugar alcohols such as *xylitol, mannitol* and *sorbitol*—or one of the other artificial sweeteners we'll discuss in a moment.

Some of these artificial sugars are derived from plants, while others are manufactured in the lab from various sugar and starch molecules. Though they're not as sweet as table sugar, these artificial sweeteners still shoot into your bloodstream almost as quickly. They have serious downsides, as you'll soon read. And if you've ever had chronic gas, bloating, diarrhea, or intestinal upsets after eating one of these products, check to see if it contained one of these odd sugars, because they can produce unpleasant gastric side effects. They also can raise your blood glucose and keep you in a cycle of wanting/needing "fast carbs" for energy.

While diabetic candy and snacks may seem like a clever solution, the larger issue is that these products continue to promote a pattern of eating sweet snack foods that are lacking the diabetes-healing nutrients you'll get in whole, nutritious foods. We want to break this habit in Phase One and move you toward a diet that can reverse—or at least dramatically improve—your condition.

If you need proof of this, use the Smart Monitoring method to test in pairs and see exactly how consuming these falsely marketed foods affect your blood glucose levels.

## Never Underestimate "Big Sugar's" Influence

The American public is slowly becoming aware of the horrible health toll that consuming excessive sugar exerts on our health and that of our children—and manufacturers are beginning to run scared. In 2013, 60 food and beverage manufacturers spent a mind-boggling $30 million to lobby Congress, seeking government favors and protection for their unhealthful products. It was an increase of over $4 million over the prior year!*

Furthermore, they are beginning to churn out so-called "healthful" products such as energy drinks and vitamin water to keep us hooked on a steady supply of sugar and sugar-like substances. But these "sugar-free" products are loaded with highly refined chemical concoctions—not just sugar alcohols, but weird laboratory-manufactured sugar-derived molecules with natural sounding names that are anything but.

Because these giant food companies are so powerful, they are able to receive FDA approval for many of their products. But, generally speaking, the FDA is more concerned with the interests of these food companies than the consumers it's supposed to protect. It would take an entire book to expose the FDA's links to the corporate food lobby and the evidence that these lab-constructed sweeteners are, in fact, harmful to your health.

Remember, the diabetes industry would have you believe it is impossible to eat anything without some kind of sugar added. Why else would there be such a market for artificial sweeteners?

## What About Artificial Sweeteners?

We do not recommend artificial sweeteners in "diet" drinks and "sugar-free" food products because they confuse your body's ability to know when it is full. Even though they're

---

*http://www.opensecrets.org/lobby/indusclient.php?id=N01&year=2013

marketed as diet aids, these products actually *cause* weight gain, in direct opposition to their stated purpose. Artificial sweeteners don't trigger your body's "I'm full" response because they bypass the leptin response, and thus you end up eating more calories.

The outcome is that fake sugar in any form can increase the amount of calories you take in. In the US, consumption of artificially sweetened foods and drinks has increased exponentially over the past 25 years—and obesity and diabetes right along with it. Some research has even linked artificial sweeteners to depression, memory loss, fatigue, migraines, and seizures.[26]

The history behind artificial sweeteners should be enough to make you cringe: Aspartame (marketed as Equal, NutraSweet, AminoSweet, and Canderel) got its start as a Pentagon biochemical warfare agent.[27] Today, it's nearly ubiquitous throughout our food supply, appearing in more than 5,000 so-called diet foods, including gum, cereal, soft drinks, table-top sweeteners, jams—even over-the-counter medications.

It's shocking that more than two-thirds of adults in the US and about 40% of kids use aspartame, often as NutraSweet. Research already points to aspartame-produced adverse effects including Parkinson's-like symptoms—headaches, mood swings, memory loss, and seizures.[28]

From where we sit, there's a serious lack of long-term studies questioning the safety of the following artificial sweeteners. Their danger as carcinogens and links to various cancers are being ignored, downplayed, or purposely suppressed by their manufacturers and the FDA. For your health, steer clear of any product that contains the following...

- Saccharine (Sweet 'n' Low, SugarTwin)

- Aspartame (Equal, NutraSweet, AminoSweet)

- Sucralose (Splenda)

- Acesulfame-K (Sunette, Sweet One)

- Tagatose (Naturlose)

## Today's Action Steps

- Begin to break your dependence on sweets now. These include white cane sugar, white beet sugar, corn syrup, honey, molasses, pancake syrup (real maple syrup as well as the commercially produced syrups), brown sugar, and of course all artificial sweeteners.

- Eat a little extra protein and three regularly spaced meals (plus two healthful snacks in between) to weaken your craving for sweets considerably. Nutritious, balanced meals filled with protein, fresh whole fruits and vegetables, and good fats such as olive oil will satisfy hunger and provide your body with the energy it needs.

**Extra credit:** Prepare snacks for the rest of the week to have on hand so you'll be ready if your sugar cravings get strong. Try fruit and protein combinations, veggie snacks, or smoothies.

# DAY 5

# EAT BREAKFAST EVERY DAY

*"Never work before breakfast; if you have to
work before breakfast, eat your breakfast first."*

—JOSH BILLINGS, American humorist, 1818–1885

**Tip of the Day:** Eating a protein-rich breakfast will effectively stabilize your blood glucose levels and lessen your cravings for unhealthful snacks throughout the day.

BACK WHEN EARLY MORNING meant the start of back-breaking labor on the farm or at the factory, breakfast was the most important meal of the day—the one that "broke the fast" of a long night's sleep and fueled your tank with energy for the hard day to come.

Most of us do not toil long days in fields or factories anymore, but we still face stressful, energy-draining days juggling 21st-century pressures including commuting, work deadlines, complex family challenges, and an overscheduled calendar. There are children and elderly parents to care for, financial insecurities to overcome, and personal needs to look after too.

Living life and controlling diabetes is challenging enough when your energy level is less than abundant. And that is why breakfast is so important. Without a nourishing breakfast, your blood glucose drops and you experience powerful mid-morning cravings for the wrong foods, such as sugary muffins, flavored coffees, and processed snack foods. Swap these refined carbs for healing meals built around protein and breakfast superfoods. Use Smart Monitoring to learn which breakfasts are the best for your body.

## The Most Important Meal of the Day

Ask an overweight person if he or she eats breakfast, and the answer is usually no. Ask a fit, trim, healthy person and you will virtually always hear an enthusiastic "yes!" For people with blood glucose problems (especially), breakfast is the most important meal of the day. That's because it's important to stabilize your blood glucose and get your body's metabolic engine revved up as soon as possible after waking. But you have to be careful about the kind of fuel you pump into your tank in the morning…

## The Breakfast Superfoods

During Phase One of The 30-Day Diabetes Cure Plan, we want you to build your breakfast around lean-and-clean protein such as free-range chicken eggs, full-fat yogurt, cheese, milk, and other healthful dairy foods. Nuts, seeds, and certain soy foods are also good choices. These "breakfast superfoods" should comprise the majority of your meal. Remember: It's always easier to *add* good foods to your diet rather than to fight off your cravings for the bad ones. Here are some specific tips that will help get your day off to a roaring start...

**Protein for strength and stable blood glucose.** Your entire body—organs, brain, and immune system included—needs protein for healthy function. People who don't eat enough of it eventually feel weak and lethargic and can experience slow wound healing (a big risk for people with diabetes, who already have compromised circulation), hair loss, skin rashes, brittle nails, muscle loss, heart problems, depression, and anxiety. Protein from breakfast also stabilizes your blood glucose, slowing the rush of glucose from any carbs you might eat and keeping blood glucose from spiking too high or dropping too low.

Meats and fish provide essential protein. Choose small portions of lean chicken breast, Canadian bacon, or turkey sausage or even a piece of salmon or other fish (part of the traditional Asian breakfast). Avoid low-grade processed meats, such as greasy sausage and conventional bacon (choose the preservative-free variety instead). These low-quality processed meats are high in unhealthy fats, sodium, and are loaded with chemical additives and preservatives (including nitrates and nitrites), which are known carcinogens. Nut butters (peanut, almond and sesame) are also good choices.

Unprocessed soy foods are a fine option too, but avoid soy-based meat substitutes such as "soy bacon." Many questions remain about these types of *processed* soy products. It is best to enjoy soy as it has traditionally been consumed in Asia: Either as soybeans themselves (Japanese edamame) or in the healing fermented foods known as tofu, tempeh, and miso. Occasional use of soymilk and soy protein powder (without added sugars, of course) is okay as long as it is not a large portion of your diet.

**Whole grains.** In terms of getting your day started right, few foods can compare with whole grains. High in fiber, low in calories and good sources of protein, whole grains pack in a lot of nutrients. From oats and brown rice to millet and quinoa, whole grains are ideal hot breakfast cereals. Try enlivening a bowlful with fresh berries, raw nuts, and spices such as cinnamon and nutmeg. For more on the goodness of whole grains, see page 126.

**Egg-cellent eggs.** In the grocery, look for eggs labeled "omega-3 fortified," produced by hens allowed to range free and fed grasses and wilds herbs. These eggs have three to six times the omega-3s of other grocery store eggs, and omega-3s are definitely essential for both cardiovascular and mental health. Here are some other reasons why eggs have been called the perfect food:

■ Eggs are a weight-loss dream.[29] Two extra-large eggs contain just 160 calories and 14 grams of protein. In fact, researchers at St. Louis University found that people who ate eggs instead of a bagel (with equal calories) for breakfast ate *fewer* total calories at both lunch and dinner. The egg-eaters lost 65% more weight than the bagel-eaters.

■ Eggs are also a great source of the vision-protecting compounds *lutein* and *zeaxanthin*, and carotenoids, which are especially vital for people with diabetes, whose sight can suffer. Risk of cataracts and macular degeneration are both significantly lower in people who eat eggs regularly.

■ As a bonus, your new diabetes-healing breakfast might help you remember where you put the remote control. Eggs are an excellent source of *choline*, essential for proper brain development and function, including memory.

■ Eggs have been much maligned over the past few decades, accused of causing high cholesterol, clogged arteries, and heart disease. But researchers have long suspected the exact opposite is true, and new studies prove it. As reported in the *International Journal of Cardiology* in 2005, participants who ate two eggs a day for six weeks showed no increase in total cholesterol, no increase in LDL (bad) cholesterol and no narrowing of the arteries.[30]

If you are still feeling wary of eggs, remember you can use the Smart Monitoring method to investigate how eggs affect your blood glucose levels.

**Butter's back.** A little butter in the omelet pan makes for a heavenly breakfast, but remember when we were told that butter was bad and margarine was better? We now know that hydrogenated vegetable oils (trans-fats) like those found in many margarines are extremely damaging—and researchers are beginning to prove that the saturated fat in butter is a far better choice. According to a 2009 article in the *Journal of American Dietetic Association*, saturated fat seems to provide protection against weight gain.

Haven't we been told repeatedly to stay on low-fat diets to prevent obesity and cardiovascular disease? Well, Danish researchers who studied the links between eating different foods and their effect on waist size (which at certain measurements is a "red alert" for increased risk of insulin resistance, Type 2 diabetes, heart disease, and some cancers ) found that women who ate more butter and high-fat dairy products gained less weight around the middle than those whose diets were lower in saturated fat. Those who ate more red meat also had smaller waistlines.

The secret to reaping these benefits is portion control. Go easy on the butter and other high-calorie, saturated-fat foods like dairy products and red meat. Moderate consumption of goods fats will protect you. Overindulgence will work against your goals.

**Yay for yogurt.** Talk about a "living food!" Protein-rich yogurt is naturally fermented milk that offers a wealth of health benefits, starting with the stabilization and reduction of glucose levels. In addition, according to a study published in *Natural News*,[31] fermented foods such as yogurt have a lower Glycemic Index (GI) than unfermented food because they convert sugar into lactic acid, thus bypassing the glucose-insulin cycle.

For the very best results, choose yogurt made of milk from organically raised, grass-fed cows or goats. Absolutely avoid yogurt that has any added sugar or artificial sweetener (read labels carefully). Yogurts that contain fruit, cereal, cookie bits, or other flavorings are loaded with health-robbing sugars and chemicals. Most grocery store yogurts bear little resemblance to the ancient healing food that's been eaten throughout the world for millennia for longevity and health—but some stores now stock varieties of plain, unsweetened Greek yogurt, a dreamy thick concoction containing the live bacterial cultures that confer such remarkable healing properties. Again, read all labels to ensure no added sugar. Your local health food store is another source for this living food. Better yet, learn to make your own and save a bundle (see our directions below).

The calcium in yogurt is also great for weight loss. A study published in the *International Journal of Obesity*[32] found that obese men and women who ate three six-ounce servings of calcium-rich yogurt daily while on a reduced-calorie diet lost 22% more weight and shed 80% more abdominal fat than those who ate the same number of calories, but got just one serving of dairy products. The yogurt eaters lost an impressive 61% more body fat than the non-yogurt group.

**Got milk (and cheese)?** You should, because research published in 2005 in the *American Journal of Clinical Nutrition* found that eating a diet high in calcium foods boosts the metabolic burn-rate of body fat. Women from 18 to 30 years of age with normal weights were put on either a high-calcium or a low-calcium meal plan for a full year. The high-calcium women

## Homemade Yogurt

Making your own yogurt is easy, saves money, and you can use grass-fed cow's milk to boost the omega-3s. Ensure all utensils and bowls are extremely clean—any microbes can interfere with the yogurt's bacterial growth. It takes a little practice to make great homemade yogurt, but it's worth the effort.

Although you can buy specialty yogurt-makers, there's no need to clutter your kitchen with more appliances. I've found that using either a thermos bottle or a small beverage cooler is the cheapest and easiest way to achieve sure success with no fuss. To get started, you'll need:

1 quart organic whole or low-fat milk or organic soy milk (purchase by the gallon to save money)

yogurt starter (see below)

cooking thermometer—available at most grocery stores

2-quart saucepan

2 quart jars with lids

bath towel

Thermos bottle or a small picnic cooler

Optional: Organic powdered milk

First, be sure your pots and utensils are very clean and free of all soap residue. Both kitchen microbes and soap can interfere with the yogurt's bacteria growth. Next, you'll need a "starter" of the right bacteria cultures to get the yogurt going. My favorite yogurt starter is Probiotic Acidophilus by American Health. It comes in a brown bottle and is kept refrigerated in the Vitamin section of your supermarket or local health food. It costs about $12 for 30 tablespoons. (I keep mine in the fridge and eat a tablespoon straight from the bottle when my digestive system needs an extra boost.) One tablespoon of the acidophilus starter is all you need.

I also tried the Yogourmet starter, priced at $8 for a package of three starters. This product was totally acceptable. It has milk powder and three strains of bacteria. The end result was a nice thick and tangy yogurt that was a little firmer than the other types.

The cheapest starter of all (under $1) is a cup of good quality whole organic yogurt with "live active cultures" printed on the label. Look for specific bacteria that fight inflammation, such as the *Lactobacillus* strains and *Propionibacterium*. This method tends to produce yogurt that's a bit runny, but adding ⅓-cup powdered milk with the starter thickens the yogurt nicely. You'll only have to purchase a starter once because your own homemade yogurt will provide you with a continuous supply of starter. Just remember not to eat it all! One cup will provide all the cultures you need for the next batch.

**Instructions:**

**1.** Heat ¾-quart of organic, non-bGH milk in a saucepan to 170–180 degrees.

**2.** Turn off the heat and let the milk cool to 108–112 degrees.

**3.** Add the starter of your choice and stir.

**4.** Pour this cultured milk mixture into a thermos or a quart jar (see instructions below).

**5.** Let sit 4 to 8 hours, or until thickened. Do not bump, move, or otherwise disturb!

**6.** After it has thickened, store your finished yogurt in the refrigerator.

**The Thermos method.** This is the easiest method by far. Once the starter has been added to the milk, pour it into a wide-mouth, quart-size Thermos bottle. Cap it, wrap the thermos in a thick kitchen towel, and set it in a warm place. When the yogurt has thickened (4 to 8 hours), transfer it to a glass jar and store in the fridge.

**The cooler method.** After adding the starter to the warm milk, pour the mixture into a quart jar and set it in the cooler. Fill a second quart jar with boiling water, and nestle it right up against the yogurt. Cap the jars, cover them with towels and close the cooler. When the yogurt has thickened (4 to 8 hours), put it in the fridge.

This method works well for bigger batches. For a double batch, mix two quarts of milk and two cups of starter and pour the mixture into two glass quart jars. Fill two more quart jars with boiling water and nestle them in the cooler, right next to the yogurt jars. Top with a towel, and close the cooler.

**For the insatiably curious.** I can never follow instructions unless I know why I am supposed to do something a certain way. For those stricken with a similar affliction, here's the explanation:

Heating the milk to just below boiling kills off any "bad" bacteria that might interfere with the good bugs.

Cooling the milk to 108–112 degrees brings the temperature into a range that will help the good bacteria multiply. Any warmer, and you'll destroy the friendly bugs. Any cooler and they'll be shivering so much they won't procreate.

I say "do not disturb" because any rocking of the container interferes with the bacteria setting up and thickening the milk. So position the container in a place that's easy to access. Avoid jostling it while checking for progress.

**Yummy yogurt! My tests found that this simple method results in yogurt with a tangy, complex flavor.** This yogurt has a slightly tart bite and is creamier than store-bought brands, but still sturdy enough when making a sauce or dip. Adding the acidophilus gives it a sharper taste, while adding powdered milk mellows the tang and thickens the yogurt. Experiment with different batches until you get the texture just as you like it. Once you have created a yogurt you prefer, you can use one cup of it to start your next batch. After a few tries, you'll easily master the art of yogurt-making.

**To make a richer, thicker Greek yogurt.** Pour the yogurt into a muslin cloth hanging over a bowl. A probiotic-rich liquid will drain off. Do not waste it! Drink it—or add it to juices or smoothies. Scrape the Greek yogurt from the cloth after two hours and refrigerate.

Yogurt will keep for at least a week in the fridge. Remember to reserve one cup of your last batch to start your next batch. Consume at least one cup of yogurt daily and resupply your stash every few days so you don't run out. (For more diabetes-healing recipes, see pages 375–402.)

took in 1,000 mg to 1,400 mg per day from food sources, while the low-calcium group got less than 800 mg daily. Results? The high calcium group burned fat at 20 times the rate of the low calcium group! This is a true testament to calcium's fat-burning power. (Just don't try this with calcium supplements—it only works with calcium-rich foods!)

For maximum benefit, choose protein-rich milk, ricotta, and cottage cheeses made of milk from organically raised grass-fed cows or goats. You will reap the benefits of extra omega-3s while you enjoy a high-calcium food that boosts the metabolic burn rate of body fat.

# Start Your Day Off Right!

Still not sure how to break the bad breakfast habit? Give yourself extra time in the morning by waking up a little earlier than usual. (This may require calling it an evening no later than 10 p.m.) Prize this morning respite as "me time" and savor it by sipping a hot cup of tea or fresh brewed coffee. Or sit quietly, meditating on just being in the present moment.

Be sure your kitchen is neat, clean, and well organized when you wake up. Remember: "Healing takes planning; illness just happens." (You might want to write that down and post it on the door of your fridge.) Below are a few suggestions for a healthful, protein-centric breakfast. For several tasty diabetes-healing breakfast recipes, see Appendix C on page 375.

**Veggie scramble.** Warm some butter or pure olive oil in a skillet and sauté chopped onions, garlic, tomatoes, broccoli, asparagus and/or green peppers—whatever you like or have on hand. Then whisk a couple of omega-3 eggs in a bowl and pour over the vegetables. Add a tablespoon of plain yogurt so the eggs stay soft—and a bit of grated cheddar if you like—folding no more than three times (no stirring!) to keep the eggs fluffy. Option: Sauté the veggies first and set aside. Pour the whisked eggs and yogurt into a mildly hot pan. Add the veggies and cheese and fold over into a perfect omelet. Here are some other options:

**Go Mexican.** Warm some canned refried beans or black beans with melted cheese and tomatoes. Serve beside two or three eggs any style. Enjoy with a dollop of salsa and plain Greek yogurt.

**Asian-inspiration.** Have miso soup or scrambled tofu with veggies. Also enjoy a small dish of edamame (boiled green soybeans) with your tofu.

**Grass-fed morning.** How about three ounces of (high in omega-3s) ground grass-fed beef for breakfast? Sauté the meat with onions, garlic, and fresh oregano and add canned or fresh tomatoes for an extra morning veggie.

# Diabetes-Healing Breakfasts "On the Go"

If you can't manage to cook in the morning, consider these quick—and healthy—possibilities.

**Make the veggie egg scramble the night before, cool and refrigerate.** The next day, heat for a couple minutes in the microwave and enjoy.

**Protein power.** Cook and peel a few hard-boiled eggs. Keep them covered in the fridge and in the morning enjoy one with a piece of Parmesan cheese the size of your little finger.

**Smoothie time.** Remember that Power Smoothie recipe from Day 2? Smoothies are a quick and easy way to get a balanced and nutritious breakfast. They can even be made in advance so you have smoothie breakfasts for an entire week ready and waiting every morning!

**Yogurt with chopped nuts** and sprinkled with cinnamon.

**Celery sticks** with almond or peanut butter.

**Chopped almonds in ricotta cheese.** Add a shake of unsweetened cocoa powder and/or cinnamon.

**Cook a big batch of steel-cut oats** to eat as part of your breakfast throughout the work week.

## Today's Action Steps

•Eat a protein-rich breakfast every day, replacing fast carb breakfasts (toast, waffles, pancakes, etc.) with the diabetes-friendly foods mentioned above.

•Combine protein and good fats to provide sustained energy while helping to heal your diabetes.

•Use Smart Monitoring to determine which breakfasts make you feel the best and most effectively stabilize your blood glucose levels throughout the day.

**Extra credit:** Make your own yogurt using the recipe suggested on page 203.

# DAY 6

# CLIMB OFF THAT COUCH!

*"Those who think they have not time for bodily exercise
will sooner or later have to find time for illness."*

—EDWARD STANLEY, Earl of Derby, 1826–1893

**Tip of the day:** Just a few minutes of activity each day will stabilize your blood glucose
and insulin levels as well as enhance your mood.

THE OLD ADAGE, "When you stop moving, you start dying" is absolutely true. Bad things
begin to happen to your body and brain when you stop being physically active. This is especially true for people with diabetes and prediabetes. If you are not already active, today is the
day you will incorporate some physical activity into your diabetes-healing plan. Begin with a
very simple activity that you are sure you can do, such as walking or yoga, which will provide
your body with the blood glucose-lowering benefits of moderate exercise. Make a commitment to yourself to be consistent so you can build this workout into a regular daily habit. Use
Smart Monitoring so you can see the effect that physical activity has on lowering your blood
glucose.

## Start Walking Today!

Walking is the easiest way to rescue yourself from the dangers of a sedentary life. Nothing is
easier or better for you. Walking helps you manage your weight, lowers your glucose levels
naturally, controls blood pressure, and decreases your risk of heart attack. It also boosts your
"good" cholesterol, lowers your risk of stroke, and protects against hip fracture.

Need more reasons to start walking? How about less stress, improved sleep, stronger muscles and bones, elevated moods, and a better sex life—all worthy of pursuing on their own but
especially vital if you want to increase your life span and the quality of your life by healing
your diabetes.

Remember the powerful tool of Smart Monitoring you have to use in your fight against
diabetes. Test your blood glucose before your activity and again immediately after. Test your
blood glucose again one to two hours later, because blood glucose will continue to drop as
muscle cells restore the glucose stocks they have burned. Once you know how exercise affects
you, and you know you do not go too low, you can test less often.

# Small Steps: The "Kaizen" Secret of Success

Of course, it is neither necessary nor advisable to start out with an overzealous flurry of activity. The most important first step of any exercise program is to create a new habit—and the best way to do this is by utilizing what the Japanese call "kaizen." The term literally means "continuous improvement."

Kaizen is about building good habits so they become incorporated in your daily life. Recognizing that habits must be nurtured, kaizen is based on the principle of starting small. In fact, it recommends that you start with the *smallest* action that you are absolutely sure you can perform and commit to.

For example, if you want to start a running program, yet you have not run in a long time—*or ever*—kaizen suggests that you start by walking. This is a very practical approach because if you have been inactive for a long period of time, running for 30 minutes is going to be painful and difficult. In fact, it will be so painful and difficult that most people quit on the spot and never attempt it again.

Kaizen takes a much smarter (and more successful) approach. It realizes that repetition is the basis of building a habit and that "slow and steady wins every time." So, in the beginning, kaizen asks you to commit to a habit that you are 100% sure you can perform—no matter how "stupidly simple" it appears. For example, if you have doubts that you can commit to 30 minutes of walking per day, ask yourself what you are absolutely sure you can commit to. For some people, this will be walking for a mere five to 10 minutes. For others, it might be walking to the mailbox and turning around. People who feel they have no willpower at all might only be willing to commit to putting on their walking/running shoes and lacing them up. That's it. And believe it or not, that is enough to start.

You see, the whole idea is to get a good habit started. Putting your walking/running shoes on at the same time of the day for a week or so will give you the encouragement to take the next step—which might be walking out to the mailbox and turning around. Doing this for a while can encourage you to walk around the block. Once you do this, it is just a matter of slowly increasing your time and distance until you are walking for 30 minutes or maybe an hour. Smart testing in pairs will reinforce this new habit and help you find the best starting place for your new exercise regimen.

The kaizen approach is very wise and practical. It realizes that the most important factor in achieving success is building success-oriented habits. Neuroscientists tell us that every time we perform a repetition, we actually create and reinforce a "groove" in our brain—and this groove makes it easier to continue with the good habit. That is the power of kaizen. Remember: Mighty oaks grow from tiny acorns.

# From Small Steps to Running a Half-Marathon

Motivational speaker and publisher of *Success* magazine, Darren Hardy likes to tell this story to illustrate the power of kaizen:

One of the women that worked for me—her name was Beverly—just returned to work after having her second child. She was having a hard time losing her "baby weight" and was chatting with a friend who just signed up to run a half-marathon. I overheard Beverly saying how much she wished that she could run a half-marathon.

"Beverly, you could run a half-marathon," I said. "Oh, there's no way," she replied. "I get winded just going up a small flight of stairs."

So I said: "Beverly, if I could show you how to run a half-marathon with little or no pain during the process, would you take me up on it?"

"That's impossible," she replied. "The very *idea* of a half-marathon gives me pain." "Okay," I told her, "I will create a plan that will have you running a half marathon in nine months—and you will never experience any pain." "You're on," she said. And here's the plan I created for her:

I asked Beverly to get in a car and map out a one-mile loop around her house. Then I asked her to walk this loop just three times over a period of two weeks. And she did that easily.

Then I told her to walk it three times per week for an additional two weeks. And she had no trouble doing that.

Then I told her to start a slow jog until you become breathless. "As soon as you become breathless, just walk the rest of the way," I said.

Using this technique, Beverly was able to jog a quarter of a mile. In a short time, she was able to jog a half-mile. It took her three weeks to get up to three-quarters of a mile; and almost two months before she could run a full mile.

Now, a half-marathon is more than 13 miles. And if it took Beverly two months to run a mile, you're probably thinking that she isn't ever going to make 13 miles. But you'd be wrong.

I asked Beverly to just increase her distance by ⅛ of a mile each time she went out for a jog. That's only 300 steps. Well, at the end of six months, she was running nine miles. And at the end of nine months, she was running 13½ miles. Result? She ran her half-marathon.

Since then, Beverly has run four *full* marathons—and she lost 50 pounds in the process. Running is her new passion and she can't wait to lace up her Nikes. It has changed everything in her life. She looks fantastic...has energy to spare for her kids...she's sexy and attractive to her husband...and she is loaded with self-confidence! *That's the power of kaizen!*

## Walk with Your Own Style

Here are some tips if you're just starting out:

**Start with a stroll.** If you are not used to exercise, use the kaizen approach by walking slowly for the first three to five minutes. This prepares your heart, circulation, and muscles for their new activity, sending the message that says, "We are starting to move." This is the best way to avoid shin pain and foot discomfort. After a few minutes of gentle strolling you can pick up the pace for another five to 15 minutes until you feel a little sweat emerging. Slow down again for your last five minutes to let your body relax and cool off. That is really all there is to it!

**Set your personal pace.** This is not an Olympic event—it is just a pleasant walk, a break from work and stress, a little time outside after sitting at your desk or being cooped up inside for hours. It does take practice to find your personal walking speed, so it's important to start with a slow pace and gradually increase it so you are walking slightly faster than normal for you (but without any discomfort). If you can talk out loud without becoming out of breath and maintain that for 15 to 20 minutes, you have hit just the right pace. Remember, this is not about speed. A faster speed puts stress on your knees and we do not want that until they become stronger. If your knees do get sore or swell after a walking session, rest with an ice pack on them for a few minutes—and next time, do not walk as fast or for as long.

**Watch your stride.** More important than your speed is the length of your stride and how much you swing your arms. This is how you turn a walking rhythm into your own diabetes-healing dance. To make your walk more brisk, swing your arms with your stride—a longer stride will stretch out those long muscles and get your heart pumping.

**Time or distance?** A time goal usually works better for beginners than shooting for a certain distance. You will always be successful within your allotted time frame, whether you need to walk a little more slowly, combine periods of brisk and slow walking, or even add a few rest breaks to breathe deeply and get the oxygen flowing.

Once you begin your commitment to walking, you can start out with as little as 10 minutes and then gradually extend that to 30 minutes. You do not need to walk any longer, because 30 minutes is the life-saving, diabetes-healing magic number. Most of the people that we know who walk often love it so much they forget about time (and please do not worry if this happens to you). It is not bad for you to walk longer and farther, just make sure your feet and legs feel comfortable throughout your walk.

**How much is enough?** A mere 30 minutes, three or four days a week, is your basic goal. Plus, you do not even have to do your 30 minutes all at once! You can accumulate exercise throughout the day. Three short walks of 10 minutes each give you the same health benefits as a single 30-minute walk. That is just a quick stroll in the morning on your way to work or school, another at lunchtime, and one more when you get home. If that sounds easy, that is because it is: Walking is the simplest and most effective form of life-saving exercise you can incorporate into your daily life. What is most important, though, is to make a habit of walking at least every other day. Once you begin to enjoy your walks, you can walk five or six days a week. When you exercise regularly, your body learns a new skill, so you steadily become stronger, more capable—and more motivated to continue your newfound habit.

**Ask the pros.** If you have not exercised for a while and have questions about what is safe for you, ask a person who has experience with exercise and diabetes. Your local health-care providers and fitness professionals are all good sources for referrals and information. Remember that you are not alone. Most people who exercise regularly say they needed information and reassurance when they started. The most important thing is that they started, and that's what you can do for yourself by beginning today. Make a commitment now to developing this new habit. You will be losing weight, improving your blood glucose, and lowering your triglycerides and "bad" cholesterol without drugs.

## Tap into the "Compound Effect"

It is a fact of life: The longer you do something, the longer you are more likely to do it. We humans, after all, are creatures of habit.

If you reach for a cigarette every time you feel stressed or need to relax, that is what you will always do. If your first act when you get home from work is to pop a cold beer, you will look forward to that all day and will keep doing it. If you watch TV on the couch every evening accompanied by a bowl of ice cream, missing even one night will make you irritable, sad, and uncomfortable.

Habits are like automatic behaviors. They do not require us to be very conscious. There are no decisions to be made. And no willpower is needed. We just keep doing the same thing over and over, until one day we encounter the accumulated consequences of our actions. We may discover that we have added 50 pounds to our weight. We may receive a cancer diagnosis. We may have a heart attack.

The good news is that healthy habits, such as regular physical activity, can become just as automatic. All it takes is getting started and sticking with it for a minimum of seven days. After that, the power of habit begins to take over—and it gets easier with each passing day. The habit has a power of its own.

It does not take much time or effort for an exercise program to have a positive effect on your hypertension and overall health. Overcoming your genetic impulse to conserve energy by climbing off that couch will reward you quickly.

Remember to drink plenty of water before, during, and after your workout. This will keep your body hydrated and assist the removal of toxins from your body.

Start off slowly with your exercise routine. Warm up your body for five to 10 minutes before you really get going. While exercising, you want to aim for activity that puts your heart rate at 65% to 85% of your maximum heart rate. To calculate your maximum target rate, subtract your age from 220. If you are 50 years old, your maximum heart rate is 170, so you should aim for 110 to 145 beats per minute.

## Walking Works Wonders

Ex-Air Force Engineer and Vietnam vet Bob R. realized that his blood sugar was in big trouble—and he knew that his diet and lifestyle were to blame. By the time he was discharged from the Air Force, Bob's diet came mostly from the frozen food section of the supermarket and he had a bulge of fat around his middle that wouldn't budge. He had witnessed his parents' struggle with diabetes, and knew that prescription medications weren't the way he wanted to go.

In early 2008, Bob's blood sugar spiked to 235. He discovered *The 30-Day Diabetes Cure* and knew it was the perfect plan for him. "The first six days on plan were the toughest," Bob admits. "I started the plan on a Monday morning, and by the time I got to Saturday, someone gave me a blood-sugar test strip. When it read 81, I said, 'Yeah! This is the way to go!' Once I got the sugar out of my system, everything changed really fast."

Since beginning *The 30-Day Diabetes Cure*, Bob reports that he feels stronger and full of energy. He has learned the good taste of real food and notices how he responds to different foods. His favorite new dish is bean soup. "I bought a big stainless steel pot, tomatoes, onions, some seasoning, and hot sauce—and I taught myself how to make an excellent soup," he says with pride. He walks six to seven days a week and uses resistance training to maintain his muscles. He loves his body's physical changes. "The biggest thing I noticed was that I lost the bulge around my middle," he beams. "The only time I didn't have that was when I was training in the mountains with the Air Force!"

What keeps him going? "Once you see the proof that you're doing the right thing, that's all the motivation you need," he says.

## Are You Still on the Couch?

Does the idea of doing even three 10-minute walks a day seem out of reach? You are in luck! Walking in quick spurts, then slowing down, and then walking quickly again provides its own benefits. Also known as *interval walking*, this approach dramatically improves triglyceride levels even better than cardio or aerobics. How long do you have to walk fast? You can start improving your metabolism with just 45-second bursts! Just make sure you breathe a little harder and get that little bead of sweat on your forehead after a few intervals.

You can thumb your nose at those buffed up weightlifters and treadmill junkies, because you could live longer than they do with just 30 minutes a day...or 10 minutes three times a day...or 45-second interval walking. Coupled with eating the right foods and losing weight, healing diabetes is as easy as stepping outdoors.

**Where should you walk?** Maybe you feel completely ready to start walking right this minute but you cannot think of a good place to go. Let's say your neighborhood has bad sidewalks, no street lamps, or no park. Maybe you don't feel safe outdoors alone, even in the daytime. Or your urban sidewalks are so busy you can't set a comfortable pace. That can really put a damper on your enthusiasm. A study published in the *Annals of Internal Medicine* shows that simply having a good environment may mitigate the risk of Type 2 diabetes because it creates a community of active people.* In a nutshell: Finding a place with safe sidewalks, parks, and attractive public green spaces can help you reverse this disease.

If you live in an unsuitable neighborhood, make it your personal challenge to find a nearby park, walking track, or safer neighborhood that you can use for your walking territory. Sometimes local schools will let you use the athletic field. Contact your city council representative and advocate for a new park, an improved lot, or a public greenbelt. The research on the importance of regular walking is on your side. You deserve it. And your life depends on it.

**Listen up.** Many people enliven their walks by listening to music or audio books on their iPods or MP3 players. Music puts rhythm in your stride and makes the time pass quickly. Listening to an audio book allows you to improve your mind while you are healing your body. Consider your walk to be personal "me time" for de-stressing and relaxing. You can download your favorite music at iTunes online. Or you may prefer listening to a good book. Choose from thousands of bestsellers and classics available through Audible (*www.audible.com*). Listening to books is a great way to increase your intelligence and boost your vocabulary. Many audiobooks, especially novels and works of fiction, are read by very talented actors who can transport you into their own private world of imaginable drama. This is a great way to nourish your body and your mind. By listening during the one-hour walk, you could easily "read" 30 or more books in a year. Imagine what that could do for your IQ!

## Staying Motivated

Developing a new habit can be challenging, but there are many things you can do to remind and encourage yourself to get your body activated.

**Be consistent.** Try to go through your exercise at the same time every day. If you are a morning person, take your walk after your morning cup of hibiscus tea. If you have a busy work schedule, utilize your lunch break every day, or hit the gym every day on your way home.

**Prepare yourself.** Set out your walking shoes and clothes each night before bed. Have your gym bag packed and ready to go before you go to bed each night.

**Find a buddy.** Having an exercise friend for support and company will make this exercise routine even more meaningful. Building up your community around a healthy lifestyle is a good idea. Just remember to rely on yourself and your own motivation; if your friend bows out of your activity every now and then, don't let it stop you.

**Accessorize.** Dress in layers that can be removed as exercising raises your body temperature. Wear gloves and cover your ears if it is chilly outside. Sunglasses will protect your eyes

---

*http://archinte.jamanetwork.com/article.aspx?articleid=773622

from harmful sunrays, dust, and pollen. A fanny pack to hold your ID, cell phone, and water will free your hands for unrestricted movement. Comfortable and supportive shoes will also benefit your body in your new exercise habit.

**Log your time and readings.** Keeping track of your progress will keep you motivated. You can use a pedometer to track the number of steps you take during your walk. Or, you can record your distances. Also, be sure to monitor your blood pressure and log those readings in your Workbook.

**Keep getting better.** As you build up your strength and stamina, try for a landmark that extends your walk. Increase your pace or practice a session of yoga. Change the location or difficulty of your workout if you need to add a little interest.

## Today's Action Steps

•Step out of your home or office for a 10-minute walk—or even just around the block.

•Commit to doing this every day for the next week.

•Remember the Nike slogan: "Just do it" if your mind starts churning out excuses. There is tremendous power in breaking your inertia. Don't think about tomorrow or the next day. Just take it "one day at a time." When you can trust your commitment to this action, take it to the next level.

•Remember, willpower is like a muscle. The more you work it, the stronger it gets. Use it or lose it.

•Use Smart Monitoring—remembering to test your blood glucose before, immediately after, and again two hours after your exercise routine—to track your progress, keep motivated, and figure out how a particular exercise affects you.

**Extra credit:** Find a walking buddy and decide on a regular time and place that you'll walk together.

# DAY 7

# CARBOHYDRATE SWAP

*"The breakfast slimes, angel food cake, doughnuts and coffee, white bread and gravy cannot build an enduring nation."*

—MARTIN H. FISCHER, American physician, 1879–1962

**Tip of the Day:** Swap "fast carbs" for "slow carbs" to stabilize your blood glucose and heal your diabetes.

IN ADDITION TO GIVING UP SODAS, one of the single most important steps you can take to *quickly* lower your blood glucose and reduce your weight is to stop eating bread, baked goods, and other "fast carb" foods made from the refined flour of wheat and other grains. This includes bagels, muffins, pancakes and waffles, flour tortillas, breadsticks, pizza crust, noodles and pasta, white "minute" rice, dinner rolls, instant mashed potatoes, burger buns, flatbread, crackers, cookies, and chips. "Oh, no!" you might gasp. "I *love* all those foods. I thought you said this wasn't a 'diet!' You promised there wouldn't be any *deprivation!*"

This 30-day plan is all about changing your habits from hurtful to helpful. Test in pairs if you doubt the devastating effects of these fast carbs. Before you eat one of these snacks, test your blood glucose. Two hours later, test your glucose levels again. Are they elevated? See for yourself!

## No, This *Isn't* a Diet

"Dieting" means restricting your calorie intake until you reach your goal, with the idea that you can somehow return to your old eating habits once you've reached your goal. This is why 95% of all diets fail. And we're not going to let you set yourself up for this type of failure.

Instead of dieting, you'll be making important lifestyle changes—with the emphasis on *life*—because the foods you're giving up on The 30-Day Diabetes Cure Plan are quite literally "killers" to you. You won't be returning to eating like you once did (and believe us when we say, *You won't want to*).

# Carbs Are Important!

Your goal is not to eliminate all carbohydrate foods—just the ones that get your blood glucose in trouble. What you want is a carbohydrate that will enter your bloodstream *slowly* (because it still contains its natural fiber content) so it won't trigger an overproduction of insulin.

But let's not turn eating into a science project—that will kill not only your motivation but also your enjoyment faster than a raspberry Danish hits your bloodstream. A good rule of thumb is to *generally choose a whole food*, rather than one that has been commercially refined and processed. On this eating plan you will not be giving up satisfying and delicious meals. Instead you are going to be loading up on meals that contain slow carbs such as fresh vegetables, beans, and legumes—and combining them with plenty of nutritious protein foods, such as grass-fed beef, organic milk and dairy products, and free-range eggs. And here's a bonus: In the next 10 days or so, you can expect to lose between eight and 13 pounds while you are eating slow carbs!

# Carb Craving Is a Physical-Biochemical Phenomenon

"Carbohydrate craving" is a very biological phenomenon. As you have already learned, when you eat a fast carb food, your body breaks it down into glucose very quickly. This sudden spike in blood glucose triggers a surge of insulin, which, if it is functioning properly, pulls the glucose out of your bloodstream.

Because glucose is the main fuel for your body and brain, this quick exit causes a sudden drop in your energy level. Deprived of fuel, your brain feels foggy and your body feels tired. You may have the urge to nap so your brain can consolidate the neurochemicals required for clear thinking and concentration.

But what happens if you cannot take a snooze because you are at work or behind the wheel in traffic? Your brain will call for fast glucose in the form of carbohydrates. In short, you are hungry again—for a very specific kind of food. You want a candy bar. Or chips. Or a soda. And you *really* want them. That is a biological carbohydrate craving. Continually satisfying this powerful urge upsets your body's basic metabolic functions and leads to permanent damage in the form of diabetes. Breaking this vicious cycle is absolutely essential to restoring your body's healthy management of glucose.

# Breaking These Cravings Is Relatively Easy

All you do is reach for a "slow carb" food instead of a fast carb. Crunch a raw carrot topped with almond butter instead of a candy bar. Bite into an apple and cheese rather than a cupcake. Substitute sipping a cup of green tea for slurping a soda. Your brain will get its glucose in a slow, steady supply. And your insulin will not be aroused because it won't need to deal with a big barrage of blood glucose.

Your mind might be thinking, "Hey, I really wanted a candy bar" or "This doesn't taste as good as a mouthful of chips." That's because it is easy to become habituated to certain flavors and foods. As we've stated, it simply takes time to break an old habit and establish a new one—usually 21 to 30 days (and that is why most drug and alcohol rehabilitation programs last for 28 days).

If powerful addictions like drugs and alcohol can be reversed in such a short time, curing your body's craving for carbohydrates is a cinch. Just follow our suggested daily steps and you will succeed.

Yes, the first two or three days will be the toughest, while your body chemistry starts to adjust. But after that, it gets much easier. After a mere three to 10 days or so, your craving for these foods will be greatly diminished, if not all but gone. Most people who stick with our Plan, lose their desire for these fast carbs *completely*—and that's when their blood glucose really starts to normalize and the pounds melt off.

## The Secret of Our Plan's Success

How is this possible? Do they have superhuman willpower? Not at all. These folks are ordinary people just like you, who've lived with powerful carbohydrate cravings all their lives. Yet, they've been able to let go of their appetite for them because they've substituted "brain power" for willpower.

You see, willpower says, "No." And guess what happens when you try to resist strong desire? Most people rebel because no one likes to be denied. Brain power, on the other hand, uses *knowledge* to de-energize a craving. These ex-diabetics developed the ability to recognize an "appetite" when they feel it arising. Instead of acting unconsciously or habitually, they use *awareness* to notice what's going on in their mind. They are able to recognize when their habituated appetite is being stimulated by a picture, memory, or seeing the actual food itself, rather than having a genuine hunger for nourishment and sustenance.

## Here's How It Works

Think of what you experience when you see a doughnut, for example. You remember how good the last one tasted: The sweet sugary glazing…the fatty, doughy texture when you chewed it…the satisfaction as you swallowed it down with a splash of sweet, hot coffee. Yum!

But now, these memory-trigger sensations are entering your conscious mind before you impulsively act. You're not blindly ordering the doughnut without realizing what you're doing. You're watching all this unfold. You now have awareness of the process that used to occur unconsciously over and over. And what gave you this new awareness? Your knowledge of the *consequences*—and your commitment to fighting for your health and life.

You see, it's much easier to stop eating certain foods when you know exactly how they are harming you. Once you step out of the shadows of ignorance and denial, it's difficult to continue a habit that you know is slowly and surely killing you. Providing your body with healing carbohydrates instead will ease your hunger and retrain your appetite.

"But what about cigarette smokers, alcoholics, and drug users?" you might wonder. Their cravings aren't mere habits; they are powerful physical and chemical addictions, much different than what you are experiencing. And yes, even dependencies such as those can be (and are) broken by developing awareness and realizing the harmful consequences of these actions.

## How Fast Carbs Affect You

So, what's so bad about white bread, processed foods, snacks, and desserts?

They instantly raise your blood glucose. Your body responds to the fast carbs in white-flour foods such as bread and pasta as if you just ate pure sugar. Your glucose spikes up, the insulin response is triggered, and fatty triglycerides are formed and stored around your belly. A steady diet of toast, breakfast cereal, waffles, pancakes, sandwich bread, burger buns, dinner rolls, breadsticks, bagels, crackers, cookies, and cake makes your cells *resistant* to all the insulin that keeps getting pumped out to handle the glucose, until your pancreas burns out from overproduction.

Insulin resistance (prediabetes) turns into Type 2 diabetes and suddenly you're taking medications that make you feel really lousy (not to mention their cost). Unless you change your eating habits, the next thing you know you are injecting yourself with insulin several times a day. When that happens, your risk of a sudden heart attack or stroke skyrockets. You also are in danger of going blind…having your digits and limbs amputated one by one…and developing Alzheimer's. Believe me, it is hard to enjoy doughnuts day after day when you're really aware of how much they're harming you.

**They trigger inflammation.** Fast carbs create inflammatory proteins called cytokines, which regulate the body's inflammation response. More inflammation is the last thing you want in your body because it worsens insulin resistance and raises your risk of practically every serious chronic and degenerative disease, including diabetes. Inflammation also makes your joints and muscles painfully sore. It causes your arteries to clog up with plaque. It destroys brain cells. And it raises your risk of all cancers. Sure, you can pretend to ignore all of this as you chomp on your morning doughnut or bagel. But that won't stop the inflammation one bit.

They are loaded with damaging fats. Most processed foods, including buns, rolls, breakfast cereal, soft breads, crackers, and chips contain refined vegetable oils, such as soy, corn, cottonseed, or canola, which are high in omega-6 fatty acids. They often contain trans-fats (labeled as "hydrogenated oil" or "vegetable shortening"). Omega-6s deplete your body's storehouse of omega-3 essential fatty acids—which are anti-inflammatory fatty acids—resulting in higher inflammation throughout the body (more about this on Day 9).

So, with commercial baked goods such as burger buns, snack cakes, and dinner rolls, you're getting a double-whammy: A spike in glucose from the fast carbs and more inflammation due to the excessive omega-6 content. Too much omega-6 also elevates your levels of triglycerides and cholesterol—increases insulin resistance…impairs normal cellular repair…and raises your risk of diabetic complications.

Although there has been some progress by food manufacturers, trans-fats—the unhealthiest fats ever invented—are still present in baked goods, crackers, and snack foods, and are also frequently used to deep-fry restaurant foods such as French fries, fried chicken, fish and chips, and most fast food. Trans-fats oxidize LDL cholesterol, turning it "bad" and making it more likely to damage your arteries and cause the formation of artery plaque. These Frankenfats also reduce the levels of HDL, the protective cholesterol. A study of 80,000 women which was published in the *American Journal of Clinical Nutrition* found that increasing the intake of trans-fats by only 5% results in a 37% increase in the risk of heart disease—for which people with diabetes already have a higher risk. So before you take a bite, ask yourself: Is it worth it?

**They lack fiber.** When you're fighting diabetes, fiber is your best ally. High-fiber carbohydrates (such as beans and vegetables) contain fewer calories than starchy carbohydrates and fill you up faster because the fiber component isn't digested. Fiber is the *roughage* component of vegetables, fruits, whole grains, and beans that give these foods their bulk. Because the ratio of calories-to-volume is so high, you can eat until you're full without gaining weight—in fact, you find yourself *losing* pounds steadily by eating these foods. For example, an apple is more filling than a half cup of apple juice that contains about the same calories. (In the days ahead, you'll learn much more about fiber and how to use it to reverse your blood glucose problems.)

Refined carbs, such as bread products, are the black sheep of the carbohydrate family. Because they've had their bulk and fiber removed, they're a more concentrated source of calories. And since their volume has been reduced by processing, it is easy to eat more of them before your stomach tells your brain, "I'm full." That's just one reason they're so fattening: We simply eat more than we should.

A bigger problem results when many of these refined carbs are combined with other high-calorie ingredients, as in the case of bakery goods. When white flour is mixed with eggs, oil, milk, and sweeteners, its calorie content jumps, but its volume (the amount it takes to fill your stomach) increases only slightly. The sugar combined with the refined flour carbs also triggers an instant spike in your glucose levels. As you now know, this signals the release of insulin, which unfortunately facilitates the rapid conversion of carbohydrates into fatty triglycerides. Translation? More belly fat!

**They may trigger hidden allergies.** Bread products are loaded with gluten, a protein found in wheat, rye, oats, and barley, which can be difficult to digest and cause inflammation of the intestines. A full-blown allergic reaction to gluten is called *celiac disease*. Doctors are beginning to realize that millions of Americans (as many as one-in three) may have an undiagnosed sensitivity to, or outright intolerance of, gluten. Symptoms include fatigue, weakness and general achiness, abdominal bloating, and chronic diarrhea. Gluten intolerance has also been linked to osteoporosis, anemia, cancer, lupus, multiple sclerosis, and other autoimmune diseases, as well as psychiatric and neurological conditions such as depression, migraines, and schizophrenia, according to the *New England Journal of Medicine*.[33] You may not even suspect you have gluten intolerance until you start paying attention to how you feel after eating gluten foods. Eliminating these foods is the first step to improving your health and well-being, especially if you suffer from an already debilitating disease like diabetes. But even if you don't have gluten intolerance, these fast carbs will spike your blood glucose and insulin rapidly. Use your smart monitoring techniques to see the proof with your own eyes.

**They poison your pancreas.** The refined flour that most commercially processed baked goods are made with starts its life as wheat, a whole grain, but in the refining process, the nutritious bran and wheat germ are removed to give the flour a finer texture and longer shelf life. In order to make it a more appealing white color instead of its natural brown, chlorine gas (a known toxin) is used to bleach it. When chlorine gas comes into contact with wheat, it forms a byproduct called *alloxan*, a substance that actually damages the pancreas by destroying the beta cells that make insulin.[34]

Scientists are well aware of the dangers of alloxan. They actually use it to induce diabetes in laboratory animals because they know that it will destroy the insulin-producing function of the pancreas and allow high blood glucose to get out of control. If you eat white flour products, you are ingesting this toxic substance and harming your pancreas. What can protect you from this insidious poison lurking in so many common foods? Two things…

■ Stop eating white flour products. It is as simple as that. We hope we've conveyed clearly enough that white flour is literally poisoning your pancreas.

■ Second, take 400 IU of vitamin E (mixed natural *tocopherols*) every day. Scientists believe it can protect from the dangers of alloxan. Since this powerful antioxidant has a host of other protective benefits, we think it's a good way for you to start reversing the damage alloxan can cause as well.

**They take the place of nutritious healing foods.** If you are consuming a lot of bread-based foods, you're probably eating fewer of the diabetes-healing superfoods we've covered in-depth in Chapter 10. Remember: You always have the choice. The next time you reach for a piece of toast, a thick sandwich, a plate of pasta, a dinner roll, a cupcake or brownie, a Danish or morning muffin, ask yourself: "What could I be eating instead that would help *heal* my diabetes and blood glucose problems—instead of making them worse?"

Today, you will be swapping in delicious, super-nutritious foods that are proven to lower your blood glucose…reduce your inflammation…help you lose weight naturally…slash your triglycerides, cholesterol and blood pressure…give you more energy…perk up your moods…improve your general health…and lengthen your life. Not a bad trade-off, is it?

## "Speed Healing" by Cutting Fast Carbs

Charles C. nearly died of acute pancreatitis in 1979—an episode that eventually led to diabetes. Though pancreatitis compromised his pancreas and beta cells, his body could still produce insulin. Charles was diagnosed with diabetes in 1996, and spent years maintaining decent A1C scores through medication and a rigorous exercise program. But in 2008, blood tests showed that Charles' kidney function had suddenly fallen from about 75% to 50%. His kidneys were apparently failing—and fast.

By the beginning of 2012, Charles was taking a whole medicine cabinet worth of drugs for his diabetes, and feeling terrible. One day, a small ad popped up on his computer screen for *The 30-Day Diabetes Cure* and he studied the website. "The whole approach left the healing process in my hands," Charles says. "That's what convinced me to buy the book."

He began the life-changing 30-Day Diabetes Cure Plan in March of 2012. The hardest change for him was cutting out bread, cereal, and pasta, his favorite comfort foods. In early September of 2012, just six months after starting the plan, Charles took his first A1C test since ditching almost all his medication the previous May, and the result was a 5.9, down from 7.3. His kidney function also improved from about 50% of full capacity a year before to about 65%. Charles's doctor called him his "role model" and promised to buy *The 30-Day Diabetes Cure Plan* for his wife, who was prediabetic.

Charles is the author of *Zen and the Art of Diabetes Maintenance*, published by the American Diabetes Association in 2003. He thinks it's fortunate for diabetics everywhere that *The 30-Day Diabetes Cure* has made his book obsolete. As he says, "Now diabetes maintenance is out, and diabetes *curing* is in."

## How to Tell a Fast Carb from a Slow Carb

Fast carbs. Slow carbs. Good carbs. Bad carbs. Simple carbs. Complex carbs. Perhaps you've heard all these terms tossed around, but maybe you aren't sure what they mean—or how to tell one from the other. So let's clear the air: The issue is the speed at which your body is able to break down any food into energy-providing sugar in your bloodstream.

Fast carbs are highly refined grain products that have a simple, short chain of natural sugar molecules, which convert *quickly* into glucose in your bloodstream. Fast carbs are also called "simple carbs" because of their simple chain of molecules.

Slow carbs contain fiber and other components that *slow down* the food's conversion to glucose in your bloodstream. Slow carbs have a more complicated molecular chain, which is why they're also called "complex carbs."

## The Worst Diabetes-Causing Fast Carbs

- White bread, toast, bagels, English muffins, breadsticks
- Fruit juice, soda, energy drinks, and all sweetened beverages
- Waffles, pancakes, French toast
- Pastries, coffee cake, muffins, donuts, cupcakes, cake, cookies
- Candy
- Jams and jellies, especially those with added sugar or sweeteners
- Boxed breakfast cereals
- Instant hot cereals, including instant oatmeal
- Tortillas—corn or white flour
- Fast-food fries and hash browns
- White "minute" rice

**Other foods to avoid,** because they are high in sugar or other sweeteners, dangerous oils and/or processed flours (and low in fiber and nutrients): Snack cakes, energy bars, marshmallows, candy, flavored gelatin and pudding, commercially flavored and sweetened yogurt, potato chips, corn chips, pretzels, crackers, ice cream, and pie.

Today, you will swap the refined and junky fast carbs of yesterday with the healing, slow carbs of your diabetes-free tomorrow. In just a few short days, your appetite for quick and unhealthy fast carb snacks will be replaced with genuine hunger for the flavors and textures of vegetables and whole grains.

## Beware of Gluten-Free Foods

While gluten sensitivity and celiac disease are serious concerns, it is important to not let yourself get tricked by business ploys that capitalize on the current "gluten-free" fad. If you do have any form of gluten sensitivity, you should avoid wheat, barley, rye, and foods containing these grains. However, avoiding these products will not benefit your health at all if you aren't gluten sensitive. And if you have diabetes or prediabetes, you should avoid them regardless (unless they are truly 100% whole grain products) because they will increase your glucose levels.

The reason for this is the same reason you are avoiding all processed foods in general: Refined products are stripped of natural fibers, fats, and other nutrients that slow the digestion of food. In short, gimmicky gluten-free products may actually spike your blood glucose more quickly than the gluten-containing options. This is because other starchy refined carbohydrate "flours" have simply been substituted for the wheat flour.

## Using the Glycemic Index

Fast carbs rank very high on the Glycemic Index (GI), a system devised to determine how fast or slow a food enters the bloodstream and raises your blood glucose level. In general, foods with a high glycemic index are fast carbs and should be avoided.

Another way to determine whether a food is a fast carb is its glycemic load (GL), which not only gives its GI rating, but also tells how much carbohydrate is actually in the food. Here's where the science can get a little confusing, because a food might have a high GI number, but a small amount of actual carbohydrate in relation to its fiber (which slows it down).

That means that some whole foods, like carrots or potatoes (which are high in fiber), might have a high GI number, but a low GL ranking. The GL reveals the true impact a food has on your glucose metabolism.

The GI and GL of over 100 foods are listed in Appendix B, beginning on page 370. It's a useful point of reference as you move forward with this Plan.

## Are Whole Grains for You?

Whole grains are living foods and therefore have a limited shelf life. That's because they contain oils, fats, and vitamins that go rancid (the result of the oxidation process that "spoils" any living food). To extend the shelf life of these foods, manufacturers remove the living elements of these foods, rendering them lifeless. This may be good for their profit margins, but it's terrible for human health because these refined foods are devoid of nutrition and life force. To overcome this, manufacturers "fortify" refined foods with synthetic vitamins; but this is a far cry from their normal state. In a classic research study, researchers fed rats a diet of white bread exclusively. The experiment ended when all the rats died from starvation and malnutrition, proving that white bread and white flour can't sustain life, let alone promote optimal health.

Complex carbohydrates such as whole grains, on the other hand, haven't had their nutrients removed by the refining process, which strips away the nourishing "whole" in whole grains. Whole grains can be viewed as rooms in a house, each with a different function. For example…

**The bran,** or outer coating of a whole grain, is like the walls and roof of a house—the protective layer that defends the inside from environmental assault. When you consume a whole grain with its bran intact, you get loads of fiber and more than 60% of the grain's minerals. And just as the bran protects the plant material inside, it protects your cells with its generous quantity of micronutrients.

**The germ** is the part of a whole grain that would sprout, given the right conditions (which isn't good for storage purposes). The germ is packed with B vitamins, vitamin E and health-giving micronutrients. Like a child in our house, it wants to be fed (that's what the endosperm does). A note about the germ: Most refined grains including white flour have not only had the bran stripped away, but the germ as well!

**The endosperm** is like the pantry in our whole-grain house, filled with starchy calories to feed the hungry young germ. This endosperm portion of the whole grain is nutritious when eaten along with the bran and the germ, as nature intended. But eaten alone—as it is in fast-carb foods such as white bread—it acts like sugar in your bloodstream, offering negligible nutrition and a lot of calories.

## Top 11 Most Healthful Whole Grains

1. Rye
2. Barley
3. Quinoa
4. Spelt
5. Whole wheat
6. Amaranth
7. Buckwheat
8. Oats
9. Brown rice
10. Millet
11. Farro

## Whole Grains Can Be Diabetes Fighters

Whole grain foods can be "diabetes fighters" because they're packed with fiber, which slows digestion and sends a steady flow of glucose to your bloodstream at a rate your metabolism can handle. This is precisely how you will control and eventually reverse your Type 2 or pre-diabetic diagnosis—by having *balanced* blood glucose, instead of the peaks (hyperglycemia) and valleys (hypoglycemia) caused by a glucose rush from fast carbs.

The natural fiber in whole foods is essential for controlling your blood glucose. Fiber makes weight loss easier and, at the same time, lowers insulin resistance, allowing your own natural insulin to do its job better. As your blood glucose drops, so does your weight—and this can help you reduce or even eliminate medications. And when it comes to fiber content, whole grains are full of it.

The best thing about whole-grain fiber is that it works quickly to stabilize blood glucose imbalances and improve insulin sensitivity. Whole grains work their magic by helping your cells reverse their resistance to insulin. This is because whole grains digest slowly, requiring less insulin, which helps prevent the toxic buildup of glucose (and excessive insulin) in your bloodstream. As you already know, the more responsive (sensitive) your cells are to insulin, the better able they are to metabolize glucose and the less likely you are to develop full-blown diabetes. Improving your body's sensitivity to insulin will also help reverse your diabetes. Plus, this approach is vastly superior to the results you get with drugs that artificially lower your glucose. Healing diabetes involves achieving the right balance of blood glucose to insulin so your entire endocrine system works in harmony, just the way it was designed to. Drugs can't mimic or force that kind of balance.

A word of caution: Some diabetics find that whole grains actually increase their blood glucose. You may be one of them, so it is important to use your Smart Monitoring techniques to see. Just remember to avoid gluten-containing whole grains, if you have even a slight gluten intolerance because this can increase inflammation in your arteries.

## The Whole Truth About Whole Grains

There's a lot of exciting research on how diets rich in whole grains prevent—and even reverse—diabetes…

■ In a UCLA study that allowed obese men to eat as much food as they wanted as long as most of it came from high-fiber fruits, vegetables, and whole grains, the guys lowered their blood glucose levels by 7%, cholesterol by an average 20%, and their blood pressure dropped too. They also walked for up to an hour daily.[35]

■ According to a 10-year Harvard Medical School study of 75,000 women, 97% of the women who ate whole-grain foods avoided diabetes entirely.[36]

■ A similar eight-year project by the Black Women's Health Study of 59,000 African-American women (an ethnic group twice as likely as white women to develop diabetes) confirmed the power of whole grains. Those eating whole grains such as wheat, oats, barley, rye, wild rice, and brown rice prevented dangerous swings in their blood glucose, thus effectively and dramatically reducing their risk of diabetes.[37]

■ You can reduce your diabetes risk by 40% just by replacing a few fast carbs with slow carbs like whole grains, the same Harvard study showed. This means substituting brown rice for white rice, and slow-cooked Irish oatmeal (or any of the diabetes-healing whole grains listed on page 225) over any boxed ready-to-eat breakfast cereal.

## Why Comforting Carbs Make You Feel Good

Whole grains are nature's most healthful "comfort foods." They're warm, chewy, tasty, and filling, providing lots of pleasure and satisfaction without the empty calories of processed fast carbs. These slow carbs are most beneficial when eaten *moderately* and consistently. Italian researchers noted in *Diabetes Care* in 1991[38] that while diets high in carbohydrates throw blood glucose and metabolism into chaos, the problem is easily resolved (especially for people with diabetes) when those carbs are rich in dietary fiber. You'll reap the benefits long after mealtime is over, too. Researchers at the Creighton Diabetes Center in Nebraska found that when people ate a breakfast cereal made with fiber-rich barley, their rise in blood glucose after eating was significantly lower than when they ate oatmeal—already one of the best slow carbs you can eat. That's because barley is particularly high in a type of fiber called *beta-glucan* that is uniquely effective at slowing down digestion.

The point here is that eating a *variety* of whole grains is important, but portions matter too. Because of their roughage, whole grains help you feel "full" much faster than refined carbs like commercial breakfast cereals. This means you won't need a large serving to satisfy your hunger. Many people following our Plan find that a half-cup serving of any whole grain is plenty. Some start with even less. But bite for bite, whole grains provide more nutrients and fiber—with fewer calories—than any other food group. Are you starting to see how grains play such an essential part in controlling your glucose levels and your weight simultaneously?

## Beginning Your Whole-Grain Odyssey

Whole grains at any meal—for instance, brown rice, a hearty mushroom-barley soup, or a small slice of a true 100% whole grain bread—are easy to incorporate into your daily diet. They also make eating a lot more enjoyable because they add variety. Enjoy old favorites such as oats, barley, and brown rice a few times per week. But don't hesitate to experiment with new whole-grain foods. The variety of whole grains is phenomenal, making this a way of eating you can stay with for life. Try cooking up a large batch of whole grains and freezing it in individual portions for later use. For a wealth of diabetes-healing recipes, see pages 375–402.

**Whole-grain hot cereals.** Slow-cooked real oatmeal (look for varieties labeled as steel-cut oats, and Irish or Scottish oats), wheat berries, or, if you're gluten-sensitive or just looking for a change, brown rice, millet, quinoa or buckwheat all make excellent breakfast choices. You might want to try what Jim does at home: Prepare a large batch on the weekend and store it in the fridge so you can quickly scoop out and heat a portion in the microwave on weekday mornings. You might even prepare half-cup portions in small bowls, sprinkle them with cinnamon, and pop them into the fridge to make things easier for you in the morning! If you like, add toppings like fresh berries, nuts, flax, a few raisins, or unsweetened yogurt (both soy yogurt and dairy yogurt have beneficial probiotics).

Choose whole grains and hot cereals that have longer, slower cooking times (20 to 40 minutes). Avoid all instant or quick-cooking hot cereals because they've been processed to within an inch of their lives and offer no more fiber than white bread. Many packaged instant hot cereals also contain added sweeteners and artificial flavorings. *Yuck.*

**Don't forget the cinnamon.** Less than half a teaspoon daily significantly reduces blood glucose levels in people with Type 2 diabetes, according to a study conducted by the US Agricultural Research Service.[39] Cinnamon works by stimulating the insulin receptors on cells, improving your body's response to insulin. So be sure to sprinkle some on whatever whole grain cereal you're enjoying!

**Homemade granola.** Homemade granola (when you control the ingredients) is delicious eaten with yogurt and fresh fruit. There are abundant sources for recipes. Just remember: Use a small amount of good fats including coconut oil, olive oil or even butter. Skip any sweet ingredients that are more candy-like than nutritious. A few raisins or a little honey/molasses to sweeten a large batch of granola is just fine.

**Baking without sugar or white flour.** A home-baked muffin made with buttermilk and carrots, pumpkin, or zucchini is a good occasional treat as long as you use true whole-grain flours, eliminate the sugar, and include real butter or coconut oil, instead of shortening. Unsweetened applesauce is a perfect substitute in any recipe calling for vegetable oil, which you're avoiding because of its "bad fat" omega-6 content. As a bonus, applesauce provides sweetness and extra moistness without adding sugar or extra oils. You can also add a few raisins for sweetness.

As for flour, there is a world of whole-grain flours to discover. Start by looking for Bob's Red Mill brand at your grocery (or online). This company offers high-quality flours made from whole oats, garbanzo beans, and even black beans. You can quickly make your own brown rice flour by whizzing some uncooked brown rice in a coffee grinder. Same for oat flour. Don't be afraid to experiment. If you suspect that you are allergic or sensitive to wheat, look to gluten-free cookbooks. Because gluten-intolerant people can't eat wheat, these cookbooks offer a wide range of substitutes that fit perfectly with our plan.

*Pasta?* **Yes, pasta!** Some manufacturers have gotten smart—they've heard our message about fast carbs and responded by transforming white-flour pasta into whole-grain versions. A good example is Racconto whole-grain pasta, offered both in health food stores and mainstream groceries. Their "8 Whole Grain" series of pastas is made from whole grains including rye, barley, brown rice, buckwheat, kamut, spelt, and millet. Two ounces of their pasta contains just 190 calories and is delicious. This is comfort food we highly recommend! If your local store doesn't carry this brand, order it online. Spaghetti squash also makes a yummy pasta substitute.

**Eat real food.** Remember to eat foods as close to their natural state as possible. Slow-cooked, old-fashioned oatmeal is a much better choice than a store-bought oat bran muffin, which includes refined flour, lots of vegetable oil, and way too much sugar or other sweeteners. Slow-cooked Irish oats, on the other hand, is one of nature's perfect diabetes-healing superfoods. It is hearty, satisfying, loaded with healing nutrients, and chock full of fiber, which slows the release of glucose in your bloodstream, requiring less insulin and providing a steady flow of energy all morning long. Top it off with some fresh berries, yogurt, ground flaxseed, and cinnamon, and you will have the perfect diabetes-healing breakfast.

**What about fiber powders and mixes?** We are big fans of eating whole foods so you can reap the benefits of all their nutrients—good fats and vitamins, minerals and antioxidants, proteins and carbs. We feel the same way about fiber. When eaten in foods such as whole grain, veggies, and fruit, it produces a natural, synergistic effect in the body. Instead of opening up a jar of fiber supplement that works on your intestines, we prefer you eat foods naturally high in fiber. This way, you get the benefits of lower blood pressure, stabilizing blood glucose, effortless weight loss, plus added nutrients that come with it. Tastes better, works better, and is better!

## Smart Monitoring

Remember to log your meals and test in pairs in order to understand how your new dietary habits are affecting your body. Consider trying one or two new whole-grain breakfast cereals and testing your blood glucose levels to determine which grain helps your glucose levels stay in the healthy range. Logging your meals and testing in pairs will help you find patterns and keep on track with your new and healthful lifestyle.

### Today's Action Steps

- Stop eating fast carbs right now and substitute with healthful slow carbs.

- Go through your pantry, cupboards, and fridge and get rid of any refined carbohydrates.

- For today, have eggs or a whole-grain cereal for breakfast and full-fat yogurt with berries mid-morning. You can enjoy vegetable or bean soup with a big salad for lunch. Choose lean protein with plenty of vegetables for dinner.

- Use Smart Monitoring to discover which slow carbs heal your body most effectively.

# DAY 8

# ADD DIABETES-HEALING VEGETABLES

*"Every patient carries her or his own doctor inside."*

—ALBERT SCHWEITZER, German physician and philosopher, 1875–1965

**Tip of the Day:** Vegetables are high in fiber and healing nutrients. You can't go wrong with them because they keep your blood glucose in balance, help you lose weight, and nourish every cell in your body. Starting today, you are going to include two servings of veggies with every meal. (Sorry, French fries don't qualify.)

WHEN IT COMES TO DIABETES-HEALING SUPERFOODS, fresh vegetables top the list. They're loaded with vitamins, minerals, antioxidants, and fiber, plus other phytonutrients that have overwhelmingly positive effects on your blood glucose, your metabolism, and your cardiac health. As healing foods, they are virtually unbeatable.

How do vegetables provide so much healing? For one thing, they are incredibly low in calories, meaning you can eat your fill without gaining weight. And because they are rich in all-important fiber, they slow down the digestive process so glucose is metabolized slowly. That means they provide your bloodstream with a steady supply of energy, instead of spiking it up and down like a roller coaster. On top of that, their fiber scoops up cholesterol, fats, toxins, and waste products and escorts them out of your body.

Making vegetables the main focus of your meals helps you lose weight without trying, lowers insulin resistance and allows your pancreas to catch its breath. As you begin to fill your meals with these healing vegetables, keep track of your blood glucose progress by using Smart Monitoring.

## The Weight Loss Connection

Many vegetables also have high water content—especially cucumbers, celery and tomatoes—which helps hydrate your cells and fill your stomach with their volume. Eat all the vegetables you want. They will fill you up and trigger your "I'm full" hormone, signaling your brain to stop eating. This metabolic message tells you when to push the plate away; but it is often bypassed by over-consuming sweetened and processed foods, much to the detriment of your waistline and your health.

230

# Why, Exactly, Do Diabetics Need Vegetables?

Nutritionists and dieticians (and moms, of course) often remind us to eat our vegetables, but most of us have only a vague understanding of *why* they are so good for us. Here are some specifics…

**Heart and circulation health.** Cruciferous vegetables, including broccoli, cabbage, cauliflower, bok choy, and broccoli sprouts are all high in *sulforaphane*, which plays a major role in healing blood vessels harmed by inflammation.

People with diabetes are nearly 500% more likely to develop cardiovascular diseases such as heart attack or stroke. But according to the Mayo Clinic, sulforaphane encourages the production of enzymes that reduce the damage to blood vessels caused by high blood glucose, thus helping to minimize the devastating effects of diabetes.* And UK researchers publishing in the journal *Diabetes* wrote that sulforaphane in broccoli and other cruciferous veggies not only helps boost the immune system and support the liver's job of detoxifying your body, but also protects against oxidative stress.

Oxidative stress is a term for the damage done to cells, tissues, and blood vessels by Reactive Oxygen Species (ROS) molecules, which include free radicals. Sulforaphane combats oxidative stress by activating a certain protein in the body called *nrf2*, which is able to switch on genes that actually increase the body's production of its own antioxidants and detoxifying enzymes. In lab tests, sulforaphane was found to double the activation of the protein nrf2 and reduce ROS free radical molecules by an astonishing 73%.[40] All this from enjoying a serving of broccoli or its cruciferous cousins! Broccoli sprouts contain even higher sulforaphane concentrations.

Here is more good news for your heart. Folic acid (also known as folate) is one of the B vitamins that are so helpful in preventing blood vessel damage, thereby reducing the risk of heart attack and stroke. In a study of more than 150,000 women, those who consumed folic acid (found in romaine lettuce, spinach, asparagus, cauliflower, and beans) significantly decreased their risk of high blood pressure and cardiovascular disease that can develop as a result.** Both complications are quite common among people with diabetes.

**Protection with vitamins.** Just one cup of broccoli delivers about 116 milligrams of vitamin C, almost twice the recommended daily amount for adults. Bell peppers, mustard greens, zucchini, celery, asparagus, fennel, parsley—and of course many fruits—are all powerful sources of vitamin C.

According to the Linus Pauling Institute[41], even small amounts of vitamin C can protect against the damage done by free radicals and ROS that results from metabolic irregularities, as well as exposure to pollution and toxins (damage that can lead directly to diabetes, cardiovascular disease and/or stroke).[42]

*http://articles.mercola.com/sites/articles/archive/2008/08/23/broccoli-reverses-diabetes-damage.aspx
**http://whfoods.org/genpage.php?tname=disease&dbid=15

**Veggies protect your eyesight.** Your body uses beta-carotene to make vitamin A, another powerful antioxidant that's particularly protective of your vision. Damage to the retina (retinopathy) is one of the serious consequences of diabetes. Besides broccoli, sweet potatoes, carrots, kale, and spinach are all bountiful sources of beta-carotene.

Another important eye-protector is the antioxidant *lutein*, a carotenoid your body coverts into *zeaxanthin*. Lutein not only neutralizes oxidative damage done by free radicals and helps prevent atherosclerosis, but it also improves eye health, according to a study published by the *Journal of the Science of Food and Agriculture*.[43] This is good news for people with diabetes, who are at much greater risk for developing not only vision-destroying retinopathy, but cataracts and macular degeneration. Leafy greens such as romaine lettuce, kale, and spinach are excellent sources.

**More mineral help, too.** Broccoli, romaine lettuce, onions, and tomatoes are good sources of the trace mineral chromium, used to manufacture glucose tolerance factor (GTF), which helps break down blood glucose. Chromium drives down your blood glucose, cholesterol and triglyceride fats, which greatly reduces your risk of cardiovascular disease. Chromium aids in the metabolism of glucose by actually re-sensitizing the insulin receptors on the surface of your body's cells. Many people who consume the typical Western diet are chromium-deficient thanks to all the refined carbohydrates, such as white sugar and white flour, they consume. These foods are not only low in chromium; they also deplete it from your body. People with Type 2 diabetes have especially low levels of chromium

Romaine lettuce (a great alternative to bread for wrapping around sandwich ingredients) is high in manganese, a mineral that helps you metabolize fats and carbohydrates. Manganese is also essential for good blood glucose management. And it's a component of manganese superoxide dismutase (Mn-SOD), the antioxidant that neutralizes free radicals and repairs the damage they cause. Manganese also helps protect against the oxidation of LDL cholesterol, preventing the buildup of plaques in your arteries, which is the major cause of heart attack and stroke. Other leafy greens are also loaded with manganese, among them mustard greens, kale and chard, as well as spinach, garlic, and green beans.

Fill up on greens and you'll never be manganese-deficient, which up to 37% of Americans are these days because of eating all those fast-carb refined foods, according to researchers at the University of Maryland.[44] Curiously, some research has found that people with diabetes have much lower levels of manganese than normal, but it's not known whether this is a cause or an effect of diabetes. And it really doesn't matter. What is important is that you up your intake.

Romaine lettuce, by the way, is also very high in vitamin K, which prevents arterial plaque and may also improve insulin resistance. In a recent three-year study published in *Diabetes Care*,[45] researchers found that vitamin K decreased insulin resistance in men over 60.

## Top 10 Ways to Enjoy Vegetables

**1. Salads, all mixed up.** Start with romaine or red and green leaf lettuce. Grate in carrots, chopped cucumbers and bell peppers. Toss in a few nuts and seeds (lightly toasted pine nuts, pumpkin seeds, almonds, or walnuts are delicious and add beneficial fats, protein, and other nutrients) as well as a quarter cup crumbled feta, goat, or bleu cheese. Slice in a hard-boiled egg. Whisk a tablespoon of extra virgin olive oil with a few drops of balsamic vinegar or lemon juice. (Add some Dijon mustard and fresh herbs if you'd like.) You have just made a perfect dressing. Avoid bottled dressings altogether—they include unhealthy polyunsaturated oils such as canola or safflower, along with sugar and artificial flavorings.

**2. Steam your vegetables.** Lightly steam finely chopped vegetables such as broccoli or Brussels sprouts. Drain the water and add a tablespoon of extra virgin olive oil or butter. Your veggies will be perfectly *al dente*: Crunchy, bright green and delicious.

**3. Try a one-bowl meal.** Add steamed veggies to brown rice, toss in some chopped cooked chicken breast or salmon, a tablespoon of olive oil or coconut oil, a dash of soy, and your favorite spice mix. Enjoy!

**4. Snack on raw vegetables.** Keep sliced carrots, celery, bell peppers, broccoli, and other veggies on hand for a quick snack. Spread celery with peanut butter or low-fat cream cheese. Dip broccoli in hummus. Plain yogurt with minced garlic and other spices also makes a great dip.

**5. Pick a pita pocket.** Whole-grain pita bread can turn a healthy salad into a hearty sandwich. Toss a variety of finely chopped vegetables and lettuce with a slivered hard-boiled egg or any leftover cooked meat you might have, such as roasted chicken or fish. Add a spoonful of hummus, garlic-flavored yogurt, or a splash of extra virgin olive oil along with your favorite seasonings. Now tuck into half a pita pocket for a salad you can eat with your hands.

**6. Juice it.** A high-quality juicer can turn a whole crisper drawer of fresh vegetables into a nutritious meal-in-a-glass. Tomatoes, carrots, lettuce, spinach, cucumbers—even parsley and celery (which can reduce high blood pressure)—can be juiced together for a high-vitamin, low-calorie midday boost in a glass. Experiment to find a recipe that works for you. Just remember to go for variety every time. Straight carrot juice, for instance, will be very high in natural sugars and could overwhelm your bloodstream. But you can add carrot and sweet raw beets to juiced greens and other veggies for sweetness and flavor. Use a juicer that doesn't separate out the pulp; otherwise you'll be missing out on its benefits.

**7. Step up and sauté.** Lightly sauté chopped leafy greens such as spinach, kale, and collard greens in olive oil and garlic over low heat. Serve over quinoa, millet, or buckwheat. Or use light olive oil (not extra virgin), peanut oil, sesame oil, or coconut oil to sauté the vegetables. Toss in a few tofu cubes, shrimp, or strips of skinless chicken breast and dress with a splash or two of low-sodium *tamari* (wheat-free soy sauce).

**8. Do the mash.** Cube cauliflower florets and/or turnips sliced and steam on the stove. If you're feeling bold, add minced garlic or Japanese *wasabi* (the green Asian horseradish served with sushi). When soft, add some butter and mash with a fork. Serve alongside baked chicken or a small piece of grass-fed steak. Yum!

**9. Make slaw.** Shredded carrots and broccoli stems, purple and green cabbage, even zucchini, all make excellent additions to salads or mixed up on their own without any lettuce at all. Whisk yogurt with herbs for dressing. Or combine extra virgin olive oil with rice wine or cider vinegar and toss to blend.

**10. Experiment.** Discover. Be adventurous. Vegetables are enormously versatile—they can be baked, broiled, steamed, sautéed, or just chomped raw. They're the ideal accompaniment to just about everything: Meat, fish, brown rice and other whole grains, and beans. Enjoy them the way they do in Asia and the Mediterranean countries—as the star of the plate, with animal protein in the supporting role.

## Buy Locally Grown Produce

Vegetables grown on giant agribusiness truck farms—even when labeled as organic—are often transported over long distances, sometimes halfway around the world. They're washed with chlorine and may be treated with other chemicals to prolong shelf-life. While these practices may benefit industrial growers, they do not do much for your health. Choosing locally grown produce from your local farmer's market whenever possible is better for your health and your local economy. Veggies and other goodies you buy locally will not only taste better, they will be healthier for you because they are far fresher. Make sure they are 100% organically raised. Of course, if you want to take ultimate control, grow your own!

### Today's Action Steps

• Make a point to eat vegetables several times a day—the more frequently, the better.

• Commit to two servings (½ to 1 cup each) of vegetables with each meal. The more you eat, the better your blood glucose and general health will be. Don't be afraid to eat your fill; their high-volume, generous fiber content and low-calorie roughage will more than satisfy your hunger *without* increasing your weight. In fact, you will actually shed pounds without dieting.

• Track your progress by testing in pairs. As you increase the amount of vegetables you eat each day, you will be able to look back at your Success Planner and see how your Smart Monitoring numbers are improving. You can also use testing in pairs to find the vegetables that stabilize your blood glucose most effectively.

**Extra credit:** Discover new ways to include vegetables for breakfast. For example, learn to make your own vegetable omelets, veggie and egg burritos, and Eggs Benedict with spinach and salmon. Search cookbooks and the Internet and dare to be creative!

# DAY 9

# SMART PROTEIN SWAP

*"Calories from protein affect your brain's appetite control center,
so you are more satiated and satisfied."*

—MARK E. HYMAN, MD, holistic doctor and best-selling author

**Tip of the Day:** Choose lean and clean protein sources for optimal health.

OUR BODIES NEED PROTEIN to build and repair nerves, tissues, bones and to create new cells. Protein also helps our bodies generate hormones and amino acids. But the kinds of protein we choose to eat can either harm or heal our blood glucose levels. Today, you will discover the junkiest protein sources in your diet and learn to replace them with top-quality "clean" protein, such as wild Alaskan salmon, free-range meats, eggs and dairy, whey or spirulina protein powder.

## All Meat Is Not Created Equal

Some meat is of a terrible quality—filled with hormones, antibiotics, preservatives, and other harmful chemicals. This is especially true for processed meat products—including cold cuts, conventional bacon, greasy sausage, plus junky hot dogs. These products may not spike your blood glucose, but they definitely aren't good for your arteries, heart, and general health.

Equally bad for you are animal products that come from large factory farms where animals are penned up in crowded conditions that are a breeding ground for disease. They are fed an unnatural diet designed to speed up production of meat, eggs, and milk. These animals are routinely injected with antibiotics and hormones to unnaturally speed the animal's growth so that its body can turn a profit more quickly. Scientists are now experimenting with altering the genes of factory-farmed animals. This type of protein is not good for your health and contributes to the inflammation associated with diabetes. We urge you to instead opt for naturally raised meats that contain healthful fats. Grass-fed beef is high in omega-3s, essential fatty acids (EFAs)[46] that lower inflammation and are beneficial for cardiovascular health.

You can avoid these bad-for-you animal products by reading labels carefully. Look for "grass-fed," "hormone-free," "organic" and "free-range" on labels. This will usually protect you from purchasing inhumanely raised animal products. Ask questions of your butcher and fishmonger. Learn where your food comes from. Get to know small, health conscious, compassionate ranchers who will sell their products directly to you from the farm.

In addition to being a clean source of protein, naturally raised grass-fed and free-range animal products are high in anti-inflammatory omega-3s, the essential fatty acids that improve your health. Shop for fish that is "wild" or "wild-caught," and avoid anything that is "farmed." Ask your butcher for fish and seafood that has not been factory farmed or altered in any way. Purchase your animal proteins when they are as fresh as possible.

Stay away from protein sources that are preserved, canned, or processed. This includes deli meats, hot dogs, conventional bacon, sausage, jerky, canned meat and meat products, plus sandwich meats. Besides containing poor quality animal sources, these products usually contain chemicals and preservatives such as nitrates and nitrites, which have been linked to cancer (nitrates and nitrites are known carcinogens). Canned meats and the meats used in products such as canned chili and soup should also be avoided.

## Shop for High-Quality Eggs and Dairy

Just as all meat is not created equal, the same is true for eggs, milk, cheese, and yogurt. As part of your diabetes-healing plan, you're going to move away from poor quality eggs and dairy products and toward the products that stabilize your blood glucose and insulin levels.

As you have already seen, eggs are an excellent, inexpensive source of protein—especially when they come from free-range chickens that are fed an organic diet and allowed to peck at omega-3-rich grasses, weeds, and wild herbs. New findings about eggs add to the positive nutritional image of eggs. Once regarded as a food to avoid, numerous research studies have concluded that eggs can be eaten without raising blood cholesterol levels.[47]

Milk and dairy products from pasture-fed cows are also good sources of omega-3 fats. When shopping, look for organic, hormone-free milk, yogurt, cheese, cottage cheese, sour cream, butter, and other dairy products. Not only are they more flavorful, but they are also much better for your health.

## Why Animal Protein?

Animal protein sources are complete proteins, meaning that they contain the full range of amino acids, which are the building blocks and repair agents of your body's muscle tissue. These sources include meat, fish, seafood and poultry, as well as eggs and milk and some products made from milk. While it is possible to have a healthy diet without animal products, it is important to realize that plant proteins are incomplete, lacking in some of the essential amino acids. However, it is possible to combine incomplete plant proteins with other complementary plant proteins to create a complete protein, and therefore a healthy diet.

## What to Do if You Are Vegetarian

If you choose to live a vegetarian lifestyle, it is important to teach yourself how to combine two or more incomplete complementary proteins to create a complete protein and assure your body gets all the nutrition it requires. The combination of beans and rice is the best-known example of pairing two incomplete plant proteins to create a meal that provides all the essential amino acids.

Here are some effective pairings of plant proteins that create all the essential amino acids:

- **Beans and brown rice**
- **Beans and corn**
- **Soybeans and rice**
- **Hummus and whole grain pita bread**
- **Chickpeas and rice**
- **Tofu and sesame seeds**
- **Barley and lentils**
- **Peanut butter on multigrain toast**
- **Oatmeal and soy milk**
- **Toasted cheese with whole wheat bread**
- **Cornbread and beans**
- **Farro with crumbled feta**

## Protein Powders

If you are concerned about getting enough quality protein in your diet, you might want to consider a protein powder. Made from sources such as spirulina (blue-green algae), soy and protein powders are a quick and easy way to increase your daily consumption of protein. Add a scoop of powder to yogurt or almond milk for a quick, protein-rich drink. Delicious, high protein fruit smoothies that make a great breakfast or afternoon pick- me-up are another way to add in healthful protein to your diet. (The Power Smoothie recipe in Day 2 is a perfect example of this.)

Protein powders vary greatly in quality and ingredients. Read labels to assure you are getting a quality product with no added chemicals or sugars as some brands heavily incorporate sugar in their powders.

## Today's Action Steps

- Remove all junky protein sources from your diet.

- Buy only organic, free-range eggs, milk, cheese, and yogurt.

- Speak with your butcher and request grass-fed, hormone-free chicken and turkey, bison (buffalo), and beef. The website *www.eatwild.com* is an excellent resource for finding local sources of grass-fed and hormone-free products.

- Purchase wild Alaskan salmon (either fresh or canned) and other quality seafood products. Our favorite source is available at VitalChoice (*www.vitalchoice.com*).

**Extra credit:** Empty your fridge of all cold cuts and lunch meats—and promise yourself that you will abstain from them from now on.

# DAY 10

# HEALTHY FAT SWAP AND OIL CHANGE

*"Health is the thing that makes you feel that now
is the best time of the year."*

—FRANKLIN PIERCE ADAMS, American writer, 1881–1960

**Tip of the Day:** Bringing high-quality fats and oils into your diet will support your immune system and balance your hormones—and they won't make you gain weight, either.

YOUR TASK FOR TODAY IS TO CLEAR YOUR KITCHEN of all refined vegetable oils and any foods containing them or trans fats. Swap these harmful fats for healthful oils such as coconut, cold-pressed extra virgin olive oil and—yes!—good ole butter. We also will explain why you should not be afraid of saturated fats and how you can discover the best sources of omega-3 fatty acids from both animal and plant sources.

## Meet the Good Fats

Back in the 1930s, a Harvard graduate and dentist named Dr. Weston A. Price took a trip around the world. His mission was to study indigenous cultures and observe the effects that their natural diets had on their health. He discovered that, although native populations in various parts of the world ate very different foods, they all seem to display some interesting similarities in their diets and their general health. Dr. Price learned that all healthy populations had at least one source of saturated animal fat and protein in their diets. Many of these diets contained at least 10 times the animal fat recommended by more "civilized" cultures today, yet these populations did not suffer from the heart disease, diabetes, digestive problems, cancer, or obesity rates plaguing their "modern" cousins. In fact, these conditions did not exist at all in these indigenous cultures.

Contrary to what you may have been told by doctors, health experts, and the media, saturated fats are *essential* for good health. Here is what they do:

- Help your bones absorb calcium.

- Support your immune systems.

- Provide essential strength to cell membranes.

- Help balance your hormones.

239

- Contribute to a healthy nervous system.

- Lower lipoprotein (a), or Lp (a), a significant factor in the development of heart disease, and raise HDL, the protective cholesterol.

- Protect the liver from toxins, including alcohol.

- Help the body utilize essential fatty acids—especially omega-3s.

## Excellent Sources of Healthful Fats

Try adding the following foods and ingredients into your meals and recipes because they are concentrated sources of healthful fats and/or beneficial cholesterol:

1. **Avocado (including its oil)**
2. **Raw nuts and seeds**
3. **Cold water wild-caught fish**
4. **Organic cage-free eggs**
5. **Organic free-range chicken**
6. **Grass-fed beef**
7. **Virgin coconut oil**
8. **Organic red palm oil**
9. **Cold-pressed olive oil**
10. **Butter (made from hormone-free milk from pastor-grazed dairy cows)**

Be sure to consume saturated fats from whole foods that have been minimally processed. These beneficial cholesterols and fats contribute to healthy blood glucose and insulin levels. The danger comes when we consume fats that have been damaged in the refining process by heat, oxygen, and man-made chemicals.

## The Truly Bad Fats

Along with Dr. Price's observation that native populations do consume saturated fats, he noticed that these populations had an absence of sugar and polyunsaturated fats. Avoid polyunsaturated fats and trans fats at all costs. These fats are extremely inflammatory and diabetes-hurting.

**Polyunsaturated fats.** These fats spoil (oxidize) easily and must be treated with care. Polyunsaturated vegetable oils should never be heated or used in cooking because they become unstable and are prone to oxidation. This can lead to free radical damage and blood pressure-hurting inflammation. We advise that you reduce your consumption of polyunsaturated fats found in margarine, salad dressing, and vegetable oils—including corn, canola, cottonseed, flaxseed, grape seed, safflower, soybean, and sunflower. This includes margarines that are supposed to be heart-healthy, such as Smart Balance and Benecol.

**Trans fats.** These fats are by far the worst fat for your heart and blood vessels—yet they are hidden in a large percentage of US food products under coded names such as "partially hydrogenated vegetable oil" and "vegetable shortening." You can recognize them as being solid—a property achieved by passing hydrogen into cheap vegetable oils at room temperature—but they are also hidden in many processed foods.

These "Frankenfats", as they are called, are commonly found in many processed foods, including commercially baked goods, icing, margarine, and snack foods—such as potato chips, cookies, crackers, and microwavable popcorn. They are even commonly used in some vegan products. Trans fats are also widely used in fast foods and fried foods, such as french fries and fried chicken. We recommend you avoid them entirely.

## Heat Stability or "Smoke Point"

When oil begins to smoke when heated, it is a sign that it has a low smoke point and is therefore not stable or recommended for high heat. The oxidation that occurs at these temperatures will create free radical molecules in your body that are highly inflammatory.

Coconut oil is ideal for high-heat cooking because it remains stable when heated. Olive oil, on the other hand, becomes unstable and therefore unhealthful when heated to a high temperature. For this reason, olive oil is one of those healthy fats that are best consumed raw, and should only be heated in light sautéing.

## On to Phase Two!

Even though you are just on Day 10 of the 30-Day Diabetes Cure Plan, you're already starting to turn the ship around: Your diabetes and blood glucose problems now should be in reversal! Your Smart Monitoring should confirm this. And by now, you know which foods raise your glucose levels—and which ones don't.

These seemingly small steps you're taking are having a big effect. Keep going. Don't let anything slow the momentum you're building as you make more healthful food choices. If you slip, we are here to catch you. Just get back up, dust yourself off, and return to the foods and beverages that aren't raising your blood glucose levels.

Remember that Smart Monitoring your own blood glucose and comparing the results to your food and activity log provides you with the most powerful knowledge: Concrete numbers that show you how specific foods and activities affect your own body. Use it regularly until you know which foods and beverages are your friends!

## Today's Action Steps

- Remove any harmful cooking oils from your home. This includes vegetable oils like corn, canola, cottonseed, flaxseed, grape seed, safflower, soybean, and sunflower.

- Purge your pantry and fridge of commercially baked goods, icing, margarine, and snack foods like potato chips, cookies, crackers, and microwavable popcorn—anything that contains health-damaging oils.

- Buy healthful cooking oils, such as coconut oil, peanut oil, and ghee (clarified butter) that have a high smoke point.

- Purchase extra virgin olive oil, which is ideal for use in salads.

- Read labels on food products like mayonnaise and salad dressing and avoid anything that lists harmful fats.

# DAY 11

# EASE STRESS

*"Worrying is like a rocking chair.*
*It gives you something to do,*
*but it doesn't get you anywhere."*

—AUTHOR UNKNOWN

**Tip of the Day:** Dealing well with stress will help you heal your diabetes.

WHEN JAPANESE RESEARCHERS checked blood glucose levels in diabetics right after a large earthquake, they found that the stress had spiked their blood glucose significantly. Levels were highest of all in those who lost property and family members.[48]

Because stress is a stimulant, it causes glucose to be released into your bloodstream and triggers hormones that upset glucose levels. Plus, when you are stressed, you probably will not eat right or exercise. Use monitoring to test this effect the next time you know you are about to have a stressful experience, such as a congested commute to work or perhaps a meeting with a financial advisor.

## High Stress Equals Higher Blood Glucose

Stress is a major risk factor for heart disease, heart attacks, and irregular heartbeat rhythms. People with diabetes are already at risk for heart disease, giving you yet another reason to get a handle on your stress. Uncontrolled stress boosts your blood glucose because it is the job of the stress hormones (adrenaline, epinephrine, and cortisol) to ensure you have enough energy (in the form of blood glucose) to fuel the "fight-or-flight response." By pumping out stress hormones in the blood glucose during an urgent situation, such as a mugging, you're able to act fast and survive.

But a steady diet of lower-level, chronic daily stress causes your body to churn out *cortisol*, the "worry hormone," which in turn spikes your blood glucose and triggers unconscious eating patterns. If you have an angry boss or troubled relationship, chances are they are making your blood glucose issues worse. In fact, constantly living in a stressful state can literally wear you out. Researchers at Tel Aviv University in Israel studied a large group of healthy professionals to evaluate the consequences of work stress on their health.[49] Their results should be a red flag to anyone with diabetes. They discovered that people with the highest level of burnout during the five-year study were 84% more likely to get a diagnosis for diabetes. Samuel Melamed, MD, who directed the research, explained that burnout inter-

243

feres with the body's ability to metabolize blood glucose properly.[50] Eventually your adrenals cannot keep up and burn out.

## Stress Triggers Bad Habits

Living with diabetes is stressful enough, involving a state of heightened alert about what to eat, whether you are making the right health decisions, and being fearful about how you will manage food choices at the next company function or family dinner. Add this to any minor or even major emergency and your glucose can skyrocket.

Then there are all those conscious and unconscious responses to stress: Skipping meals or overeating…snacking on unhealthy foods…eating more sweets and processed foods…not getting sufficient sleep…drinking extra alcohol…or turning to tranquilizers or recreational drugs. They're all particularly dangerous when you have a blood glucose imbalance.

Many of us have been living with chronic stress for so long that we're not even aware of the "background anxiety" in our lives. Highly adaptable, we humans continue to adjust to whatever's in front of us—working longer hours, over-scheduling our lives and those of our children, letting ourselves be swept up in a frenzy of overstimulation. Today you'll start to address this threat to your well being.

## Which Stress Factors Can You Control?

You really are in charge of more stress-provoking situations than you might think. In fact, feeling out of control is the underlying basis for most stress. Remember you have the Smart Monitoring method to help you take control of your blood glucose levels. Here are some other easy ways to address this problem…

**Write it down.** Even if you're not a list-maker by nature, now's a good time to write down what stresses you out—meaning anything that causes you worry, fear, anxiety, nervousness, or tension. If your first response to this is "I don't have time for this!" then make "lack of time" number one on your list. The truth is, identifying the stressors in your life is non-negotiable. If you can't make time for this important exercise, that's proof enough that your stress level is at an unhealthy high. Bonus: While you're working through this process, you might actually find some stressors you can eliminate right away.

**Stop watching so much news.** It is not an overstatement to say most news outlets follow the "if it bleeds, it leads" playbook. If you keep your TV on with a constant stream of bad-news programming, your stress levels will definitely rise. Find a calm news channel and watch an hour to catch up. Or get the news in your local paper while you take a nice hot bath. Or read it online, but do not dwell on bad news. If a particular issue is upsetting you, take action—write, contribute, or volunteer. Just don't let a flood of bad news wreck your health.

**Sort it out.** Once you have identified your stress sources, determine which ones you can immediately address. Work toward eliminating some. Do you really need to take the bus all the way home—or could you get off earlier and release some of your after-work tension with a short walk? Some stressors just require a new method. (Yes, your kids actually *can* help with dinner, rotating assignments like setting the table, making a salad, or loading the dishwasher. In the process, you will be helping them organize their lives too.)

**Limit your drive time.** Cooperate with other parents to carpool, so you are not driving every single day. Bundle your driving errands for one day a week if possible—shop, pick up the cleaning, and buy groceries on the same day. Plan appointments for car maintenance, doctor visits, and other must-do's with plenty of off-days in between, so you are not feeling rushed all the time. Once in a while you need to stay home and re-group. Do it as often as possible. Remember, this is *your* life, and it is filled with choices.

**Unclutter your life.** Sort your mail and "to-do" list into three piles: *Must Do Now, Do Later, and Forget About.* Recycle the *Forget About* mail immediately. Then open and organize your *Do Later* pile. If "now" means now, sit down and take care of it immediately: bills, phone calls, forms to be filled out, etc. Procrastination creates extra background stress. Believe it or not, actually dealing with tasks as they pop up is much less stressful than letting them accumulate in your psyche or on your desk.

**Learn to say no.** As in, "Sorry, I just cannot make those cookies for the bake sale." Or, "I would love to help you, but I cannot do it this week—maybe next time." Or, "It is a good cause, but I cannot volunteer right now." Saying no and not overly obligating yourself is saying yes to your health and peace of mind. Remember, healing your diabetes is your top priority now, more vital than being the perfect mom or wife…dad or husband…friend…or employee. (Without good health, you cannot be any of those in the long run anyway.)

**Make some "me time."** Taking care of your health requires making time for yourself. That means taking the time to cook and eat well…exercise properly…get enough sleep…lose yourself in a hobby…study quietly…and just relax. If you are thinking, "Yeah right, who has time for that?" it is another signal that you are overscheduled and overstressed. If you do not make time to take care of yourself now, when will you ever get around to it?

## Are Stress-Provoking People Making You Sick?

**Your doctor.** Seeing your doctor is enormously important, but if you find your doctor visits stressful and less than satisfying, ask yourself these questions: Am I getting enough personal care and attention? Am I arguing with my doctor over my decision to control my blood glucose with diet and exercise, instead of medication? Are my appointments with "whichever doctor is available" instead of one person who knows me and works with me as I progress? Do I have to wait a long time before my consultation or exam? If you are unsure about whether your doctor visits are causing you stress, go ahead and test in pairs around your next appointment.

If any of these issues are causing you anxiety, it may be time to start researching alternatives and following through. Join a diabetes support group and ask members for recommendations. Search your community for properly credentialed alternative physicians, such as naturopaths or certified nurse practitioners (your local health food store may have a newspaper or magazine devoted to alternative health and this is a good resource). Many doctors who include alternative modalities in their practice are also open to managing diabetes through lifestyle rather than medication. Interview potential candidates until you find one who will serve your needs. Remember, you're paying your doctor and he/she works for you. If you are not getting the care you want, find another doctor.

**Creditors.** Financial problems are one of the biggest stressors, and these days it is rare to find any working person who does not carry this burden. It is easy to feel panicked and scared about your financial security, but doing so just amps up your stress levels. Instead, take action by pulling together your financial information and getting some professional advice. Most cities have free financial counseling centers or offer support via state offices, community colleges and other noncommercial endeavors. Letting anxiety burn like a flaming torch is not helping you heal. Address your financial woes with maturity and commitment so you can weather these uncertain times with grace. Steer clear of hucksters promising "credit relief"—they descend on vulnerable homeowners and credit card debtors like vultures on wounded prey.

**Family members and coworkers.** Parent and sibling disagreements can last for decades. Negative coworkers can make your workday miserable. Navigating difficult romantic relationships and life partnerships can generate constant stress. Even some friendships become a burden. Sometimes, stressful relationships can be eased by simply becoming less available, but for others a swift, clean break is preferable. In general, committed relationships that have become stressful can benefit from the guidance of a professional counselor. If this sounds like your situation, don't put it off. Remember: You need calm strength to heal your diabetes. Ask a therapist for advice in steering you toward independence and *away* from problems that are unsolvable.

Also consider this: Close relationships are always affected when someone has a chronic illness. Your personal health challenges may be making life harder for those around you. Be compassionate and open-minded. Make time for conversations in which you let the other person talk about how your health situation has affected him or her. Listen up and avoid the temptation to be defensive. Many times, just talking honestly has a healing effect and actually brings people closer.

## Your Stress-Relief Tool Kit

You will never be able to eliminate all the stress from your life, but you *can* relieve it. Here are some of the best ways to de-stress your nervous system and reverse the harm it causes you…

**Meditate.** One of the best ways to unwind and renew your calm vitality is to "check out" for a few minutes with meditation. In addition to immediately relaxing you, meditation lowers your heart rate and blood pressure, reduces the adrenaline and cortisol in your bloodstream, and sharpens your mental functions and creativity.

Consider meditation a "time out" from your problems, worries, fears, and racing thoughts. (Do not worry—they will be there when you return.) Schedule an uninterrupted period of 10 to 20 minutes daily and create a comfortable place to sit without distractions. Close your eyes and bring your focus to the rhythm of your breathing, mentally counting each out-breath until you reach 10 (when you get to 10, start over). When your mind wanders (and will it ever!),

## Meditation Can Give You the Support You Need

Jane B. was overweight as a child. With her first baby, Jane "gained like crazy" and never lost the weight. As time went by, her weight continued to climb, topping out at 213 pounds. She was diagnosed with Type 2 diabetes through a routine blood test and put on medication, but Jane made the decision to take herself off *metformin*.

With no medication, no blood sugar monitoring, and no lifestyle changes, Jane's pulse hit 108 (a bit above normal) and stayed there or above for two weeks. She returned to the doctor, who wanted to put her back on medication, but Jane begged for another chance to control her blood sugar and insulin levels without drugs. Her doctor gave her a month, warning, "If you keep on this path, you'll be on dialysis in five years or less."

Jane discovered *The 30-Day Diabetes Cure*. With the holidays approaching, and with her role as the family cook, Jane was hesitant to start a new lifestyle. Still, she asked herself an important question: "If I don't bite the bullet and do it now, will I ever?" Jane made the hard decision to start the 30-day plan on November 16. Once she began, "It was not hard," Jane says. "I followed the plan to a tee and lost 23 pounds in the first 30 days…right through the holidays!"

Since completing *The 30-Day Diabetes Cure Plan*, Jane walks more easily and rides a stationary bicycle. She's taken up meditation to cope with job stress, and she's also learning qi gong. Jane's weight is down to 145 pounds now. She's off all diabetes medications. In fact, her doctor told her recently that he no longer considers Jane to be a diabetic.

gently return it to focusing on your breathing and begin counting again. Do not turn this into another achievement project. The whole idea of counting is simply to distract your mind, which exists in the past and the future. The point of meditation is to be in the present moment, the now. As your mind quiets, your body will begin to relax.

You may find that in this peaceful mind-state, solutions to problems simply bubble up unrequested. A meditation break helps you face the rest of the day with a feeling of harmony and balance, and this sense of relaxation will extend throughout your day. Sleep may also come more easily if you meditate just before bedtime.

Regular meditation produces amazing benefits on the body and brain. As Deepak Chopra, MD, reports in his book *Ageless Body, Timeless Mind*:

"We now know that meditation may actually reshape the brain, modify our responses to daily situations and train the mind…In terms of aging, the most significant conclusion (about meditation) is that the hormonal imbalance associated with stress—and known to speed up the aging process—is reversed. This in turn slows or even reverses the aging process, as measured by various biological changes associated with growing old. From my experience with studies on people using Transcendental Meditation, it has been established that long-term meditators can have a biological age between five to 12 years younger than their chronological age."

In short, science has proven that meditation helps slow the aging process.

**Exercise.** Are you someone who just can't sit still? Try meditating in motion. Some people find it easy to lose themselves in physical activities that involve repetitive movements, such as walking, running, swimming, or cycling. To enter a meditative state during exercise, simply focus on your breathing or the rhythm of the movement itself. In no time, your mind will calm down and you'll enter the present. Try this today on your walk.

**Spend time outdoors.** Fresh air, green trees, and the peaceful natural world are all powerful healers. In fact, researchers discovered in the early 1980s[51] that hospital patients whose windows looked out onto nature healed better (and faster) than those whose view was a brick wall. Today's hospitals are being designed with these principles in mind. You can take advantage of nature's de-stressing effect by walking outside in the park, down a tree-lined street or just by leaving your home for your own green backyard or garden.

**Relaxation.** Relaxation reduces the wear and tear that daily life can exert on your body and your mind. By consciously focusing your concentration on relaxing, you can lower your blood pressure and heart rate, boost your immune function, reduce muscle tension, relieve chronic pain, and increase blood flow to your muscles. Mayo Clinic doctors recommend these three relaxation techniques…

**Autogenic relaxation.** This technique uses a word, phrase, suggestion, or mental image to help you relax and let go of muscle tension. In a comfortable position, repeat any of these phrases to yourself over and over: "I am perfectly relaxed…I am living in harmony and balance…I am healing my diabetes by becoming more and more relaxed." Imagine a peaceful visual setting and then focus your concentration on your breathing.

**Progressive muscle relaxation.** This focuses your awareness on different muscles, tensing each one for a few seconds and then relaxing it, keeping your awareness on your body instead of allowing your mind to wander. Start by flexing your toes for 10 to 20 seconds, then release. Next, move to your ankles…then your calf muscles…then your knees…and so on. Move progressively up to your scalp, focusing on as many individual muscles as you can.

**Visualization.** This involves taking an "internal journey" to a peaceful imaginary place, engaging as many of your senses as you can. Visualize a beautiful scene, such as a sunny beach or flower garden. Create the scene with as much detail as you can, and place yourself in the scene. Feel the warm sun on your back, smell the flowers, hear the surf rolling in. It's a mini-vacation in your mind.

Relaxation takes practice. While your body shifts from "go-go-go" to "stop-and-rest-a-while," you'll find your mind wandering and you may notice all sorts of twitches in your muscles and itches on your skin. Relaxing well and deeply is a learned skill, but don't let it turn into a stressful accomplishment. Just take your time, breathe slowly and deeply, and give yourself a much-needed break. You will feel better soon.

**Biofeedback.** If you need support in learning to relax, locate a biofeedback therapist. Research psychiatrists at the Medical University of Ohio in Toledo divided diabetes patients into two groups, with one receiving biofeedback and relaxation training and the other getting educational information about the disease. People in the biofeedback group reduced their blood glucose by a remarkable 11%, while the blood glucoses of those in the education group actually *increased*. Conclusion: "Patients with Type 2 diabetes could significantly improve blood glucose control through the use of biofeedback and relaxation training," said the researchers.[52]

Biofeedback's easy and actually fun. You're hooked up to a monitor that senses stress in your body through skin temperature or muscle tension. A beep or flashing light notifies you when you're stressed. By modifying your breathing and calming yourself, you teach your body how to turn off the signal. After mastering this technique, you can replicate it in real-life situations.

**Prayer.** The calming effects of prayer rival those of meditation, relaxation and biofeedback. Praying for healing assistance and forgiving your enemies really works and plenty of unbiased scientific studies prove it. What's important is that you remember to pray when you need it most—and this requires you to notice when you're stressed.

If you belong to an established religion—or even if you don't, but feel drawn toward one—go to church, temple, mosque, or ashram and seek help from its spiritual director. You needn't adhere to a religion's tenets to reap the benefits of contemplating your problems in the context of the greater spiritual universe.

**Counseling.** To keep stress, depression, and anxiety from overtaking your life, think about getting help from a trained therapist who specializes in mental health issues. Be wary of those who want to write you a prescription without taking the time to offer you other options. Studies show that antidepressants are *rarely* effective. Talking with a therapist to gain perspective and control over stressful issues can help you keep a grip on your core problems without resorting to drugs.

## Today's Action Steps

- Reduce or eliminate as many stressors in your life as you can.

- Neutralize stress with an effective stress-management technique that's best suited to your personality and temperament.

**Extra credit:** Right now, put down this book and close your eyes. Breathe deeply and rhythmically, counting your exhales until you reach 10. Keep going if you feel relaxed. Congratulations! You've just had your first healing meditation session!

# DAY 12

# SMART LUNCH SWAP

*"Let me tell you the secret that has led me to my goal.*
*My strength lies solely in my tenacity."*

—LOUIS PASTEUR, French chemist and microbiologist 1822–1895

**Tip of the Day:** Swapping fast food meals and snacks at lunch with simple healthy choices will stabilize your blood glucose and help heal your diabetes.

WHEN YOU DOWN french fries or chips and a soda with your lunch, you are pumping a massive dose of fast carbs into your bloodstream and weakening the power of your insulin. Result? Elevated blood glucose, weight gain, chronic inflammation, and insulin resistance. The Smart Monitoring method can show you just how much damage these meals do to your blood glucose.

## Is Fast Food Worth It?

Even though the big fast-food chains *pretend* to be introducing less destructive lunch menus, the three most popular menu items have remained constant over decades: hamburger, fries, and a soda. You may suspect that fast food is one of the main causes of today's diabetes and obesity epidemics—and you're right. Here's why…

**Fast food wrecks your blood glucose.** We have already discussed the dangers of fast carbs, sodas, breads, buns, and baked goods. The same holds true for the massive servings of French fries and the football-sized baked potatoes loaded with imitation cheese sauce, sour cream, bacon bits, and fake butter. The fast-food industry has been highly successful at turning the humble potato into a high GI, high-fat, high-calorie, low-nutrient fat bomb that raises your blood glucose, your calorie intake, and your risk of cardiovascular disease and diabetes *without* any of the health benefits you'd find in a small baked potato with a sensible pat of butter.

**Fast food is brimming with bad fats.** You will learn a lot more about the difference between good and bad fats later in this Plan, but here's some advance information:

The bad fats that the fast food industry uses prolifically (such as polyunsaturated vegetable oils made from corn, soybean, safflower, sunflower, and canola), plus the trans fats in shortening and margarine, are *extremely* damaging to your heart and arteries. Trans fats raise LDL (bad) cholesterol levels, lower HDL (good) cholesterol, and lead to the build-up of arterial plaque and heart disease (the number one killer of people with diabetes).

These unhealthy oils raise triglyceride levels, increase insulin resistance, impair cellular repair, and amplify your risk of diabetic complications. The average fast food lunch is extremely high in these dangerous fats. A Big Mac has 29 grams of fat and a large order of fries has another 25 grams. Contrast that to the one gram of fat in a turkey sandwich on whole wheat bread. Kind of a no-brainer, isn't it?

**Fast food is high in calories.** That means weight gain. All fats are high in calories—about nine calories per gram, or more than twice the amount of calories in carbohydrates or protein. (When measuring at home, figure about 120 calories per tablespoon of any oil.) That big juicy burger with all the trimmings contains 540 calories, and more than half of them come from the fat alone. French fries have another 500 calories. Add the 310 in a large soda and you've topped 1,000 calories for a *single meal*. That is more than half the total calories the average person should eat in an entire day!

- To maintain a healthy weight try to get no more than 1,500 to 2,000 calories per day (the low end for women, the high end for men), and even less if you're overweight and trying to shed some pounds and inches. It is, therefore, easy to see how quickly fast food can get you in big trouble.

**Fast food is full of salt.** More than 75% of the salt we consume daily comes *not* from the saltshaker, but from hidden sodium in prepared and processed foods. Fast food is, unsurprisingly, laden with high amounts of sodium. That Big Mac also has over 1,000 milligrams of sodium, the fries another 350.

- Read the labels on any soup can, box of stuffing mix, bottle of salad dressing, jar of spaghetti sauce, bag of chips, or frozen dinner and you'll be shocked at how much sodium is in there—Campbell's Chicken Noodle Soup: 890 mg, 37% of your suggested daily requirement; Ragu Spaghetti Sauce: 540 mg, 22% of your suggested daily requirement; Marie Callender's Frozen Chicken Pot Pie: 857 mg, 36% of your suggested daily requirement.

- Why is there so much salt in fast food and processed foods? Simple: Salt masks the inferior taste of poor-quality food. And we've been conditioned to add salt to every meal in order to "bring out its flavor." But good quality food already has flavor of its own; yet we can't get those delicate sugars and unique tastes because we're so used to all that salt.

- But here is the kicker: Too much sodium in the bloodstream (without enough potassium to balance it out) elevates your chances for a sudden stroke or heart attack—and people with diabetes are *already* at higher risk of these because of their blood glucose and insulin imbalance. That is the main reason one of the first prescriptions your doctor may give you when you're diagnosed with diabetes is blood pressure medication.

**Fast food is poor-quality food.** If all these calorie and sodium numbers aren't scary enough, understand that the meat in your fast food burger comes from industrialized factory feedlot operations. This ground beef is often an amalgamation of edible meat and scrap trimmings from various feedlot sources—one burger can come from literally hundreds of animals. Highly susceptible to dangerous *E. coli* and *salmonella* bacteria (not to mention the very real possibility of mad cow disease), the animals that produce these meat products are routinely treated with antibiotics and growth hormones.

- Setting aside both the environmental devastation wreaked by these "factory beef" operations (feedlot waste products are a major source of greenhouse gas emissions) *and* the thorny question of the heartless, inhumane treatment of these animals, what about the actual nutritional quality of this meat?

- According to the *Journal of Animal Science*, grain-fed beef from factory feedlots contains 300% more fat than grass-fed cattle—and this is mostly of omega-6 fatty acids, which are inflammatory in your body. The high amount of beneficial omega-3 fatty acids found in pasture-raised beef (in amounts that rival some fish varieties) is practically nonexistent in feedlot cattle. And vital nutrients, such as vitamin B and vitamin E—plus essential minerals like calcium, magnesium, and potassium—are greatly depleted in feedlot beef. No wonder red meat has gotten such a bad rap in medical and nutritional circles. But it is not red meat *per se* that is bad for you (properly raised, it is actually a very healthful food), it is the quality that really counts. That is true about all food.

## The High Cost of Cheap Food

Sure, grabbing a fast food or deli lunch is convenient—and it is certainly cheap. If you are pressed for time (and who is not these days?), the idea of cruising through a drive-up window or stopping for a quick bite with co-workers can be irresistible. But who wants a lunch that's going to make you feel bad, look old, have bad blood glucose, and shorten your life? *Not you!*

The truth is, that 99-cent burger is way more expensive when you factor in paying for the medical care it ultimately necessitates, not to mention the environmental cleanup and waste disposal for all the packaging. And what about the damage agribusiness does to our farm economy?

The old saying "There's no such thing as a free (or cheap) lunch" is absolutely true. You see, *you* pay all the hidden costs in the form of taxes and higher insurance premiums. Our federal government doles out generous farm subsidies in the billions to agribusiness corporations that produce enormous quantities of meat, milk and sugar…to corporations that grow mile after mile of soybeans and wheat for feeding cattle (whose natural food is *grass*)…and to corn growers whose crops are turned into high fructose corn syrup and corn oil. They may call it a "farm" subsidy, but you can be sure that little of those mega-dollars are going to small family farmers struggling to raise high-quality organic food.

Furthermore, your city and state tax dollars pay to dispose of all the packaging that fast food is wrapped in at your local landfill. And your taxes pay for the heart attack and stroke patients without health insurance who show up at the emergency room of your towns' hospitals.

These agribusiness subsidies and hidden taxes permit fast food corporations to charge artificially low prices that don't reflect the actual costs of their products. That $5 lunch might seem like a good deal at first glance, but when you look closer, you're really paying a lot more—*especially* if it gives you diabetes or heart disease.

## *"But I Crave Fast Food!"*

It's true. Many people actually have powerful cravings for fast food. Some scientists have even shown that it's physically addictive. But the *real* reason fast food is so appealing to the masses is that it combines three components our brains are programmed to feast upon: Fat, sugar, and salt.

You see, back in the days when our ancestors were constantly foraging for food, calories were in short supply. And locating salt, a mineral our bodies need for essential functions, was extremely difficult (except for those who lived near the sea). In fact, salt was so rare it was used as money for a period of history.

When food was hard to come by, survival also meant seeking out foods with the highest caloric content. As a result, we developed a strong appeal for sweet and fatty foods. When early humans happened upon a bramble of wild berries or killed an animal, they gorged themselves because the next meal was uncertain.

Thus, our brains became hardwired for sweets, fats, and salt—and this programming stays with us today. Just for a moment, visualize the last gas station or convenience store you were in—remember rack after rack of sweet, salty, fatty snacks and other packaged foods? Today, we're literally surrounded by an abundance of cheap, fatty, high-calorie foods. Ironically, the "survival programming" that's been hardwired into our brains over millions of years of evolution could now be the cause our extinction—unless we commit ourselves to outsmarting it. And that's what the 30-Day Diabetes Cure Plan is all about.

## It's a Minefield Out There!

Promise yourself right now that you'll say "no" to fast food for lunch. We assure you the next few weeks on this Plan will be easier *without* restaurant food. One-third of the total calories in the American diet comes from restaurant food—with fast food accounting for about 10% or more. In fact, 16% of Americans are hard-core "fast foodies," meaning they eat convenience food or fast food an average of three or more times a week.* You definitely do not want to be one of these statistics. On any given day, more than 80 million Americans are eating fast food for one or more meals.

That's why we believe "there is no place like home" when it comes to a healthful, diabetes-reversing lunch. You are much better off in a controlled environment—your own kitchen—so you can be certain you are eating the healing foods that will stabilize your blood glucose, help you lose weight, and keep you from being tempted by familiar greasy fast food aromas that you may have grown up with.

*http://www.gallup.com/poll/163868/fast-food-major-part-diet.aspx

In a couple of weeks, when you are more educated about healthful eating—and you have broken the hold these destructive foods have on you—you will be able to go out for lunch, have dinner with friends, and even enjoy a party or a pot-luck with confidence and know-how.

In fact, if you can conquer the desire for a fast food lunch today, you have eliminated one of the biggest stumbling blocks to healing your diabetes. So the question now is: What do you eat instead?

How can you step outside the lunch "box" and rethink the whole midday meal concept? What are your options when you say no to the ubiquitous fast food industry and all their seductive ads and "value menus?" Where do you turn when you say no to the office peer pressure and ask yourself: "What kind of lunch is going to make me healthier, slimmer, sharper, more productive on the job, and feeling better about myself?" Suddenly, a new world of lunch possibilities opens up!

## The Smartest Source for Lunch Is Your Home

Of course, when you are rushing out of the house in the morning on your way to work, the last thing on your mind is "What am I going to have for lunch?" But if you are trying to balance your blood glucose or lose weight (or both), eating a good, safe diabetes-healing lunch can make a huge difference in how you feel all afternoon long, not to mention your long-term health. Below are a few tips to help you get started. For several tantalizing diabetes-healing lunch recipes, see Appendix D on page 387.

**Brown bag it.** Your most healthful (and frugal) strategy is to bring your food with you. That way you are *certain* of what you will be eating. Even so-called "healthy" lunch places, like the salad bar or deli at your natural foods grocery, harbor foods that contain too much salt, sugar, and disguised fast carbs.

Your homemade diabetes-healing lunch can be quick and easy if you are pinched for time. All you need are a few small containers and a little time to pack them the night before to make sure your lunch will contain foods you *know* will heal your body, instead of hurting it. Perhaps some celery sticks stuffed with cream cheese or almond butter. Sliced grilled chicken or steak from last night's dinner. A real salad. Chopped veggies, which you can eat raw. Or a little bit of everything above. (We told you there would be no deprivation on our eating plan!)

You might have a baggie of mixed nuts, or maybe a slice of tasty artisan cheese and a hard-boiled egg. How about some yogurt or ricotta cheese? You can include a piece of fruit… or have a one-bowl meal of brown rice mixed with vegetables and some rotisserie chicken…a whole-grain pita pocket stuffed with chopped veggies, hard-boiled egg, and crumbled feta or goat cheese…a whole-grain tortilla wrapped around whatever's left from last night's dinner with some fresh tomatoes and grated cheese inside. (Mmm! Warm it up and you have one satisfying lunch.) The variety is endless, as well as delicious. Most importantly, you'll be healing your diabetes with every delicious bite.

**Pack it yourself for portion control.** One of the primary advantages of bringing your lunch from home is your control over your portion sizes. Restaurant food is notorious for too-big-to-finish servings—and yet we somehow manage to force ourselves. We finish it because we are paying for it, and because wasting food is just not in our genetic make-up.

And let's not forget the entire concept of "super-sizing," which started in the mid-1990s and has led to a complete and utter distortion of appropriate meal sizes. This profit-motivated "up-sell" strategy has been so successful that it's everywhere these days. In fact, we don't even know what a normal portion is anymore.

Researchers at the University of Minnesota examined the effects of different meal portion sizes on energy intake. Participants were given a pre-packaged box lunch every day at work for two months in either small or large sizes. They were told they could eat as much or as little as they wanted. The small lunch was a very satisfying 767 calories, the large one a hefty 1,528 calories.[53]

It turned out that those who got the bigger lunch consistently ate nearly 300 calories more than those given the smaller lunch. And, not surprisingly, those who ate more also gained weight: Two pounds, on average. That's 12 pounds a year, and you can do the math on that rate of weight gain over just a few years! This is a perfect example of how today's supersized portions work against our better judgment.

**Be prepared.** Today we are going to suggest a wide variety of easy and satisfying take-to-work lunches you can put together in a snap. The trick is setting up things in advance to save precious time, especially on busy mornings. Once you learn how to stock your fridge and pantry, half the battle is won. And when you start preparing diabetes-healing dinners regularly, making your lunch out of creatively inspired leftovers won't take any time at all. Let's look at what you want to include in the typical diabetes-healing lunch:

## Veggies Rule!

The more ways you can fit vegetables, cooked or raw, into your noontime meal, the better you will feel later in the afternoon and the *faster you will reverse your diabetes or prediabetes*. Here are a few ways you can enjoy the ultimate good carb:

Fresh in salads or lightly steamed, veggies are loaded with phytonutrients, antioxidants, vitamins, and minerals. They are the centerpiece of our diabetes-healing diet—and they travel well. You can even buy carrots and other vegetables already peeled and sliced in small packages, for mornings when prep time is limited. Sliced carrots, sweet bell peppers (red, yellow, and green) and cucumbers are easy to carry along anywhere. Just rinse, toss in a container or baggie—and you're ready to go. Try a light sprinkle of sea salt on peeled cucumber. Add peanut butter or cottage cheese to your celery sticks for a nutritious treat. (The protein will slow the breakdown of the carbohydrates even further—and satisfy your hunger longer.)

Chopped broccoli and cauliflower contain abundant antioxidants and the anti-inflammatory chemical *sulforaphane*. (Remember: Inflammation always makes diabetes worse.) Make these cruciferous vegetables the centerpiece of a salad or raw veggie medley—or steam them and splash with a tablespoon of extra virgin olive oil. In a few more days, you will be adding them to a container of brown rice you cooked the night before (or make a bigger batch on the weekend and portion it out for lunches and dinners during the week).

**For perfectly steamed vegetables with high-quality protein:** Steam the vegetables the prior evening and then mix the steam vegetables with leftover salmon, skinless organic chicken breast, or turkey sausage in a bowl. The result is an ideal diabetes-healing lunch, something you will look forward to all morning. Add a pat of butter or a drizzle of olive oil and you're good to go.

## Protein Keeps You Going

You need protein at lunch—just like you do at breakfast—to maintain the strength and stamina to get through the tasks of your day with energy and vitality. You don't need a lot of it, though, and you certainly don't need a quarter-pound slab of poor-quality ground beef from questionable sources. Here are our choices for the best sources of protein for a midday meal…

- **Chicken and turkey** can be added to salads, or chopped up and mixed with brown rice. Use whole-grain bread for a sandwich—but you can also skip the bread entirely and enjoy thin slices of chicken or turkey wrapped in lettuce leaves. Be sure you are eating real meat, though, and not processed and prepared "lunch meat."

- **Beans** are a terrific protein source and ideal for people with diabetes because they are a low-calorie, high-fiber choice. Buy canned, unsalted organic beans like garbanzos, kidney beans, white beans, or favas; rinsing them thoroughly and draining before adding to salads or chopped vegetables. Try also tossing them gently with a half-tablespoon of extra virgin olive oil and shake in a few herbs. You'll never miss that noontime burger. Buy refried beans (be sure to choose organic and fat-free varieties to avoid the unhealthy oils) to make a perfect south-of-the border lunch with chopped tomatoes and grated cheddar cheese. Just skip the chips!

- **Wild salmon, either fresh or canned,** is loaded with omega-3 essential fatty acids, an important anti-inflammatory compound. (Most canned salmon is wild Alaskan salmon, making it a convenient choice for a healthful lunch.) Canned salmon can be made into a number of delicious dishes, including salmon patties, salmon loaf, or salmon salad—all of which work perfectly as yummy lunchtime choices.

- **Hard-boiled eggs** are a super-easy lunch food. Peel and eat them out of hand, or make an easy and nutritious egg salad with onion, celery, cilantro, plus a little olive oil and vinegar. Or chop them up with vegetables and leafy greens. Eggs from free-range, pasture-fed hens are naturally high in omega-3 and other nutrients. Lots of people are keeping hens today in places you might not expect—even the city and suburbs. Check around for a source of ultra-fresh eggs. (You might make a few new friends in the hunt.)

■**Don't forget yogurt.** This go-to food can be eaten for breakfast, lunch, as a refreshing snack, or even dessert. Mixed with nuts, berries, or whole-grain granola, yogurt is a terrific lunch option. Just remember to buy live-culture yogurt that's unsweetened and unflavored. Mix in your fresh fruit for a sweet flavor. Completely avoid sugary grocery store yogurts loaded with fruit mixes and other add-ins such as cookie bits or cereals. Even worse are the yogurts with artificial sweeteners.

## Add a Diabetes-Healing Beverage

What to drink instead of that habitual soda? Return to Day 2 if you need a reminder of healthy drink options. In a nutshell, enjoy tap water or mineral water with a squeeze of lemon. Have tea—green or black tea, hot or iced—or brewed coffee. Or just enjoy a glass of ice-cold milk!

Remember to avoid all sodas, fruit juices, and sweet teas. The taboo list also includes flavored coffee drinks, flavored milkshakes and drinks, processed protein drinks and commercial smoothies, yogurt drinks or juice blends (they're all high in sugars and calories). However, you can mix up your own diabetes-healing versions of these drinks at home. Refer to the Power Smoothie recipe in Day 2 for a perfect new habit.

## Diabetes-Healing Lunches Begin with Smart Shopping

Here is another old saying that is absolutely true: "If you do not buy it, you cannot eat it." Improving your eating habits begins with shopping smarter. Try to follow these pointers…

**Never shop hungry.** Plan your shopping trip in advance, making sure you eat a healthy meal before you go. You'll be in much better shape to resist temptation along the way. (And supermarkets have plenty of psychological tricks up their sleeves!)

**Shop from a list.** Make a meal plan of menus for an entire week that's built around the diabetes-healing superfoods covered in Chapter 10. Shop strictly from your list to avoid "impulse purchases." (This is also an excellent way to reduce your weekly food bills.)

**Stick to the perimeter.** That's where you'll find fresh produce and the dairy case, plus the meat and fish. "Trouble foods" are stocked in the interior aisles, with the worst and often most expensive foods at eye-level (or wherever your kids can reach them). Brace yourself for the sale items stocked on the outside ends of each aisle. These are high traffic areas and temptation is almost always lurking there.

## Today's Action Steps

•Sit down and plan a week's worth of diabetes-healing lunches, based on the information you just learned.

•Just like breakfast, structure your midday meals around vegetables and protein—they will stabilize your blood glucose and control your hunger.

•Create a shopping list from your lunch menus and head for the supermarket. Don't forget to eat a good diabetes-healing meal before you leave the house.

•Spend a little time each evening preparing the next day's lunch, so you can grab it and go.

**Extra credit:** Make a commitment to pack your lunch each night for a week to get yourself into the habit. Do not go to bed without your lunch being ready to go for the next morning.

# DAY 13

# SNACK SENSIBLY, IF YOU MUST

*"Enough is as good as a feast."*

—JOSHUA SYLVESTER, English poet, 1563–1618

**Tip of the Day:** Establishing good snacking patterns will make an extraordinarily positive difference in your health.

IF YOU'RE EATING PROPERLY—and by this we mean three regular meals a day which feature protein, healthy fats, and carbohydrates—you shouldn't feel the need to snack between meals. If you're not consuming refined carbs at mealtime (which elevates glucose and stimulates insulin release) insulin never spikes very high and quickly fades from your bloodstream. This is great because insulin's absence allows the fat that is stored in your fat cells to be released and converted into essential fatty acids (EFAs) between meals. These EFAs actually serve as a food supply between meals and while you're sleeping. Your body literally feeds on its stored fat, which is exactly what you want it to do when you're trying to lose weight. But this won't happen if your meals contain sugary carbs and refined grains which stimulate insulin release—or if you're snacking between meals.

Most people feel the need to snack because they skip breakfast or lunch—or make poor choices for these meals. For instance, a breakfast of pancakes and syrup will spike your blood glucose and call out insulin to lower it. In doing so, insulin clears your bloodstream of glucose which makes you hungry again in about an hour or two. The result is that your brain feels tired and foggy—and your metabolism demands more glucose for energy. The next thing you know you're at the vending machine, dialing up a candy bar and a soda. This is certainly no way to reverse diabetes or lose weight.

## But If You Must Have a Snack

If you've been in the habit of snacking regularly in the past, this habit may die slowly. So let's talk about some of the positive aspects of between-meal snacks:

Between-meal snacking can help keep your energy balanced, which means your blood glucose will remain stable. *But these must be healthful, low-glycemic snacks*. This is a very important caveat. Eating the wrong snacks or too much of them, and you'll be undoing the positive progress you've made so far. With that in mind, today we'll talk about sensible snacking. Be sure to rely on Smart Monitoring after your snacks to see how your blood glucose levels are affected.

# The Perfect Snack

The perfect snack combines a protein, a healthful fat source, and low-glycemic carbohydrates (such as vegetables or whole grains), and should never exceed 100 to 150 calories.

Here are some examples:

**Nuts and seeds.** These snacks are rich in fiber, essential nutrients and healthy monoun-saturated fats—and they will not spike your blood glucose. Always reach for the raw, unsalted varieties. Nuts and seeds are high in fiber, vitamins, minerals, and antioxidants. Seven grams of fiber reduces the risk of stroke by 7%. Their portability and versatility make nuts a great snack food. Nuts are also a high-protein food. Ounce for ounce, nuts contain nearly twice as much protein as lean meat.

In a Harvard University study, nuts were shown to reduce the risk of developing cardio-vascular disease and Type 2 diabetes by helping to control glucose levels and improving the body's insulin response.[54] The study involving 83,000 women showed that those who fre-quently ate walnuts, almonds, peanuts, pecans, cashews, pistachios, Brazil nuts, hazelnuts, pine nuts, or macadamia nuts were 27% less likely to develop diabetes than women who rarely ate nuts. As an added benefit, the women who ate nuts also tended to lose body fat.

You can munch nuts out of your hand, add them to stir-fried dishes, sprinkle them on your salad, and mix them with yogurt and berries. To enjoy nuts and seeds in another form, purée them in your food processor and make your own nut butter to use as a dip or spread for your veggie slices. Even try adding a few nuts to your veggie drink.

Make sure you purchase peanut and other nut butters without anything else added (you should be a well-practiced food label reader by now)—and avoid added sugar, oils, and salt in packaged nuts. Also avoid packaged trail mix that includes added candy or dried fruit. Limit yourself to one or two dried apricots or date pieces, sliced and mixed into yogurt, or a spoon-ful of raisins or dried cranberries (and make sure the dried fruit has no added sweeteners).

It is best to buy organically grown raw nuts. If you want, you can lightly toast them in a dry frying pan over very low heat or in your oven at 350° for eight to 12 minutes. Keep nuts in a tightly sealed glass jar in the refrigerator, to prevent their natural oils from going rancid. Do not buy roasted nuts because they lose their potency when subjected to high heat and often have added salt and oils. Remember to keep nut snacking to a small handful, or no more than two tablespoons of nut butter daily.

**Peanuts.** Although technically a legume, peanuts contain *oleic acid,* the same healthy fat found in olive oil. Peanuts are high in vitamin E and a great source of antioxidants. A study published in the journal *Food Chemistry* found that peanuts contain high concentrations of the antioxidant polyphenol *p-coumaric acid*. Slow roasting (170 degrees for 20 minutes) can increase the levels by 22%.[55]

Peanuts are also high in *resveratrol*, an antioxidant found in red grapes and red wine and linked to the French Paradox, which maintains that eating a diet high in certain fats, the way

# And the Perfect Nuts Are...

**Almonds.** These nuts are especially good at keeping blood glucose levels under control. According to a study published in the *Journal of Nutrition*,[56] their high antioxidant content helps neutralize free radicals caused by chronically high glucose levels. And a study published in the medical journal *Metabolism*[57] reported that almonds not only have a low GI but actually help lower the GI of the entire meal eaten. They're also rich in the antioxidant, vitamin E.

Try almonds lightly toasted and sprinkled on yogurt, or buy natural almond butter and spread it on celery sticks. Whole-grain bread or sliced apples are delectable snacks when spread with a little almond butter. Have a few almonds between breakfast and lunch to keep your energy and blood glucose stable.

There are more health benefits worth knowing, too. The monounsaturated fats in almonds also help lower LDL cholesterol and reduce the risk for cardiovascular disease. According to a study published in the *British Journal of Nutrition*[58] eating almonds instead of other fats reduced LDL by 8% to 12%.

**Walnuts.** These nuts are exceptionally high in omega-3 essential fatty acids—and have the lowest ratio of omega-6 to omega-3 of any nut (4.2 to 1). Numerous studies show that a diet rich in omega-3s helps prevent the blood clotting and plaque build-up that can lead to atherosclerosis. And omega-3s also improve the ratio of HDL[59] cholesterol to LDL cholesterol, while reducing inflammation. Walnuts and apples are a classic combo eaten by hand or mixed into yogurt with a generous sprinkle of cinnamon—and it's a fantastically healthful snack.

- Eating antioxidant-rich nuts also lowers your risk for coronary heart disease. According to a study conducted by the University of Oslo, walnuts, pecans, and chestnuts are also exceptionally high in antioxidants.[60]

- Another study published in the research journal *Phytochemistry*, identified 16 different antioxidant polyphenols in walnuts they describe as "remarkable."

- Four large studies, including the Adventist Health Study, Iowa Women's Study, the Nurses' Health Study, and the Physician's Study, found that those who ate nuts at least four times a week lowered their risk for coronary heart disease by an amazing 37%.[61]

the French do, can actually benefit your heart. According to a study published in the *Journal of Agricultural and Food Chemistry,* resveratrol improves blood flow to the brain by as much as 30%, significantly reducing the risk of strok.[62]

**Dressing up fruits and veggies.** Fresh veggies or fresh fruit plus cheese equals great snacking. Try sliced apples with a pinky-sized piece of sharp cheddar, celery sticks with cottage cheese or peanut butter, pears and bleu cheese, or raw broccoli with goat cheese. These fiber-plus-fat combos are endless and so are the nutritional benefits. Fruits and veggies are the ultimate slow carb foods because their fiber slows down carbohydrate breakdown into blood glucose. The result is that you receive a steady-sustained supply of energy. The protein and good fats digest even more slowly, so you feel full sooner and hunger is abated for longer. In addition, a protein snack will perk up your brain and mental functions.

**Dipping permitted.** Making your own hummus is as easy as opening a can, and this yummy dip brings together several healing foods: chickpeas, olive oil, and the sesame-seed "butter" called *tahini,* along with lemon juice and garlic. Yogurt also makes a perfect base for a dip—add herbs, a dash of hot sauce, and some curry powder (all of which are beneficial for healthy blood glucose). Another satisfying dip can be made by seeding and dicing cucumbers, stirring them into yogurt with fresh chopped mint, and cracked pepper. These dips are perfect with raw carrot sticks, bell peppers, celery and/or radishes.

**Sweet surprise.** It's hard to call dark chocolate a guilty pleasure when you realize how good it can be for you. A small square of high-quality dark chocolate (containing at least 75% to 85% cocoa solids) is quite healthful in small amounts of about 150 calories due to the cacao bean's antioxidants, called *polyphenols.* Of particular importance to diabetics was the news in 2012 from researchers from San Diego State University. They conducted a small controlled study that showed eating dark chocolate has positive effects in lowering blood sugar levels and "bad" cholesterol levels and increasing "good" cholesterol levels.[63]

**Popcorn.** Popcorn is a *bona fide* whole grain that is loaded with fiber. Reject microwave popcorn. It is bathed in toxic chemicals, artificial flavors, and excess salt. Movie theatre popcorn is also off-limits due to its high omega-6 oils and salt content. Buy your own popcorn (organic is best) and pop it in an inexpensive air popper or on the stove with a drizzle of olive oil. In place of salt, add chili powder, garlic powder, dry mustard, cinnamon, or herbs like basil or oregano. Pack some in a sealed container and take to work for a snack.

**Other snack suggestions.** Other savory snacks to keep your blood glucose stable while providing a bounty of healing nutrients include:

- A few canned sardines in olive oil or a forkful or two of canned salmon with a smear of cream cheese on whole-grain crackers.

- A hard-boiled egg.

- Half a cup of plain yogurt.

- Cottage cheese with cinnamon.

•Peanut butter on celery stalk.

•Warmed refried beans as a dip for raw veggies.

Let your imagination run wild!

| The Top Blood Glucose-Friendly Snack Substitutions ||
|---|---|
| **Instead of** | **Choose** |
| **Chips** | Air-popped popcorn (with olive oil and parmesan cheese) |
| **Cookie** | Apple slices and five walnut halves |
| **Candy bars** | Four prunes and four almonds |
| **Ice cream** | Yogurt with berries, chopped nuts, and cinnamon |
| **Granola bar** | One tablespoon peanut butter, plus a teaspoon of raisins |
| **Nachos** | Baked potato skins with spinach or broccoli slices, onion, and cheese |
| **Milkshake** | Smoothie with plain yogurt, berries, and flaxseed |
| **Popsicle** | Ten tart, fresh cherries |

## Junky Snacks That Masquerade as Health Food

Assume that virtually every snack food—in a bag or packaging or stocked in a vending machine, convenience store, or snack-food aisle at the grocery store—has HFCS or other added sweeteners, plus trans fats, polyunsaturated vegetable oils like soybean or canola, refined white flour, excessive salt, and myriad chemicals used as preservatives, stabilizers, dough conditioners, artificial colors, and artificial flavors.

Most so-called energy bars (including granola bars) are high in processed soy products (much harder for the body to metabolize than traditional soy foods such as miso and tempeh, and possible hormone disrupters), as well as sweeteners, like highly concentrated fruit syrups, and refined carbohydrates such as rice "crisps."

"Yogurt-covered" raisins and dried banana chips are sweeter than candy. Rice cakes may be low in calories, but they are really just another refined and processed fast carb. Cheese-flavored or spice-flavored "puffs" are nothing more than damaging fats filled with air, fake colors and added flavors. "Natural" potato chips are potatoes minus their healing fiber that have been fried in polyunsaturated oils and salted for maximum fulfillment. Even innocent-sounding "whole-grain" pretzels and crackers turn into a rush of sugar in your blood.

**Always avoid HFCS (High Fructose Corn Syrup).** The most popular sugar substitute is HFCS, the sweetener of choice in soft drinks and snack foods.

Dr. Robert Lustig, Professor of Pediatrics in the Division of Endocrinology at the University of California, San Francisco, has discovered a number of subtle differences from regular cane sugar in the way our bodies respond to HFCS.[64] Chief among them is that HFCS calories are stored immediately as fat in a much higher ratio than plain old sugar. Nearly one-third of HFCS calories do not even line up to be converted into energy, they move directly into fat storage. It also creates a range of waste products for your liver to process that ordinary sugar does not.

## Be Prepared

Having your refrigerator stocked with sliced vegetables, veggie juice, boiled eggs, and homemade nut butter will make grabbing a healthful snack easy. Never leave home without carrying a supply of healthful food. This is one of the biggest traps that people fall into. If you are unprepared when hunger strikes you will reach for anything. Always travel with your own supply of food and water (or a beverage). A small baggie of mixed nuts travels well. So does a hard-boiled egg, chunks of cheese, and raw veggie slices. If you keep good snacks on hand, you will not be tempted to ruin your health with fast food and "fast" carb snacks.

## Today's Action Steps

- Prepare tomorrow's mid-morning and midday snacks tonight. For example, slice up some veggies, boil some eggs, and put some nuts into bags to grab on your way out the door.

- Remember to aim for the ideal snack, which contains 100 to 150 calories and includes fat and protein with a fiber-rich complex carbohydrate.

- Write a shopping list for items that will comprise these healthful snacks.

- Remember to use Smart Monitoring to find out which snacks agree with you best.

**Extra credit:** Make a snack plan for the next week. Obtain all the ingredients you need, remembering to prepare ideal snack combinations of high-quality protein, fat, and slow carbs. Continue to test in pairs to track your progress.

# DAY 14

# RESPOND, INSTEAD OF REACT

*"How people treat you is their karma; how you react is yours."*

—WAYNE DYER, PhD, author and motivational speaker, 1940–2015

**Tip of the Day:** The practice of controlling your temper and emotions will help keep your blood glucose steady.

IN ORDER TO CONTROL your emotions and to reduce the stress in your life, it is important to train your mind to respond thoughtfully, instead of reacting out of anger or frustration. Today you are going to learn effective "hesitation techniques" that can help you collect yourself before you speak or act. This is not easy, so do not be afraid to ask for professional help if you think you need it.

## Resist the Impulse to React

When faced with stress, it is common for people to "react" rather than "respond." Reacting is impulsive. It is what you do or say before you think things through. The problem with reacting is that it is associated with anger, anxiety, and fear, which can negatively affect your glucose level. To react is the first instinct—the first line of psychological defense. But, if reacting, rather than responding, becomes a habit, your relationships and health suffer. When we become reactionary we are allowing other people and circumstances to control us. When we respond we are steering our own course.

## Tools to Help You Respond

**Breathe.** You do not always have to give someone an answer right away. Sometimes, it is best to take a deep breath and count to 10 before you say or do anything.

**Blend logic and emotion.** You want to acknowledge your emotions, but also balance them with rational thoughts and facts.

**Ask yourself important questions.** The key question is: "Am I reacting?" Just asking yourself this can calm you down and stop the reactive cycle, giving you the clarity you need to say and do the right thing. Other helpful questions include: "What am I so afraid of?" "Why am I allowing this situation to upset me?" "Am I safe now?" "How would an impartial third party describe this situation?"

**Recognize that you always have choices.** Reactive emotions interfere with your ability to think clearly. When you realize that you always have choices, you can remember to consider them *and the consequences* they bring before moving forward with any words or actions.

**Improve your internal vision.** Hindsight is 20/20. If you have had a reactive emotional episode, review it afterward when you are feeling calm. By seeing exactly how and when you chose to let fear or anger control you, you can learn from your experience and imagine other more peaceful ways you could deal with a similar situation in the future. This mental rehearsal helps you see how past reactions could be changed into healthier responses in the future.

**Remain calm.** The best crisis managers (emergency management officials, firefighters, emergency room personnel) are trained to stay calm by practicing a variety of scenarios so they can respond rather than react. Mental rehearsal helps these professionals stay cool and calm under pressure. They learn to be in charge of themselves so that they can also help others.

## Signs You Have an Anger Problem

- Explosive, uncontrolled outbursts
- Domestic violence
- Controlling behavior
- Rages at work or on the road
- Depression or anxiety (may indicate introverted anger)
- Alcohol or drug dependence (may cover up an anger problem)

## When to Ask for Help

Reactionary emotions produce adrenaline. In this way, emotional outbursts actually give our bodies a chemical "rush." Some people can become addicted to the drug of adrenaline produced by emotional outbursts.

If you find yourself frequently in conflict, experiencing dramatic mood swings, blaming others for your experiences, slamming doors, crying, yelling, or otherwise creating drama; or, if you have difficulty maintaining friendships, you might benefit from having a professional help you learn to respond rather than react.

## Consider Counseling for Anger Management

The goal of anger management counseling is to help you feel less worked up when things go wrong. Counseling can help you manage your feelings and figure out the real reason for your anger. Anger management counseling has so many benefits that it's worth looking into if you feel out of control. Just look at some of the things it can help with...

- Examine and understand the "hooks" for your anger

- Look at your own unhealthy beliefs attached to your anger

- Rethink some of the beliefs about anger in your family

- Understand how anger affects your close relationships

- Take responsibility for your own anger

## Today's Action Steps

- Imagine a situation that upsets you. Now think of at least five ways you could respond rather than react to this situation.

- Learn to buy yourself time to cool down by counting, observing, and breathing.

- If you know ahead of time that you're about to go into a stressful situation, use Smart Monitoring to see how well you handle your temper.

- Ask for help when you need it.

# DAY 15

# STEP UP YOUR ACTIVITY LEVEL

*"Now before I work out, I think, 'I love exercise,' and it works."*

—ASHLEY TISDALE, actress

**Tip of the day:** Being consistently active is some of the best medicine for diabetes.

IN PHASE ONE of this plan you discovered just how much of an excellent low-impact exercise walking is. Today it is time to push to a higher level of fitness by adding more time, distance and challenging physical activity to your exercise routine. The more you exert your body, the stronger and more capable it will become. Consider increasing the difficulty and intensity of your daily walking program. Or learn how to activate your body by learning new activities. Smart monitoring is a valuable tool for choosing the best exercise routine for you.

## Getting Stronger

Notice how easy your daily walk has become. This means your muscles and lungs have adjusted to a greater amount of exertion. Have you noticed an impact on your blood glucose readings? Now you are ready for a longer distance or faster pace. This means you might be ready for an additional weekly class or a class of higher difficulty. Remember to use Smart Monitoring by testing your blood glucose before, immediately after and again two hours after your exercise program. If you prefer to stick with walking, here is a great way to increase the intensity of your daily walking program.

## Take Walking to the Next Level

**Add trekking poles.** Using walking poles began as a summer training tactic for cross-country skiers. They caught on with hikers and quickly spread from Europe to the US. There are many kinds of walking poles, including carved wooden walking sticks, lightweight bamboo poles, and lightweight aluminum "trekking" poles that can be adjusted for different conditions (shorter for walking uphill and longer for downhill). The added fitness benefits of walking with poles include...

■ A total body workout, because your upper-body muscles are used as well as your legs. Research at the Cooper Institute in Dallas found that using walking poles increases calorie burn by about 43%. It is estimated that an hour walking with poles burns about 400 calories compared to only 280 calories walking without them, depending on body weight.[65]

- They help propel you, which means you're burning more calories than usual even as the support given by the poles makes it feel easier.

- Poles assist with balance and pace. Visualize a four-legged animal and its steady front-back walking rhythm. Perfect balance can make vigorous walking feel easier. And if you're hiking on uneven terrain, the extra support can really come in handy.

- They also relieve stress on your knees, hips, and other weight-bearing joints. This is important because people with diabetes also have higher rates of osteoarthritis (due to sugar-induced inflammation). Our favorite walking poles (by far!) are made by Keenfit.

**Log your progress.** Tracking your progress can be a considerable motivator. Smart Monitoring is an important part of this tracking. A great place to start logging your walking and exercise experience is to record the amount of time you walked. You can also note the distance if you know it. If you use a pedometer, you can record the number of steps you took. Also, include your route, the weather, and walking companions, if any. If daily recordkeeping does not

## Changes for the Better Will Come

Albert L. sits at his computer all day, typing translations and studying the Bible, getting up occasionally to grab a snack. His sedentary job and his sweet tooth probably caused his Type 2 diabetes, he speculates. And, he says, "My ancestors are Italian, so I ate a lot of pasta and other highly processed, white-flour foods."

Albert was diagnosed with Type 2 diabetes in 2007. His doctor said Albert would have to take medication for the rest of his life. But the medication wasn't controlling his blood sugar, and his A1C was an unhealthy 6.6. "I have a lot of faith," he says, "but I was beginning to give up. I felt so frustrated. And I was worried that I'd be dependent on drugs for the rest of my life."

Then he stumbled upon *The 30-Day Diabetes Cure.* Albert used both his strong religious faith and his inner strength to follow the plan. "I couldn't just pray for help with my bad eating habits, I had to change my diet and promise myself to stick to the plan."

Once he made up his mind, it wasn't difficult. In fact, it was fun to introduce new foods into his diet. Day by day, he tracked his progress and insights in a journal, which helped him understand his behavior. His wife supported him wholeheartedly.

Albert struggled with getting more physical activity. "When I started exercising and didn't see fast results, I was discouraged," he admits. But once he began eating better, the benefits of exercise kicked in. "I looked and felt 10 years younger!" he says. After he experienced these early improvements, there was no stopping him.

Albert now walks regularly, he's eating healthier, and he feels great. Today, he is completely off his medications. "I've never been happier!" Albert says with a grin.

interest you, set aside time each week to catch up with your accomplishments and goals. Your walking log will be a fitness diary you can read months or even years from now. You will be amazed to see how much you have changed your life and your health.

**Try a pedometer.** A pedometer is a device that counts your steps. (If numbers inspire you, fancier models also calculate mileage, calories burned, and distance covered. Some include a time/date and/or stopwatch feature.) There are many brands, so shop for one that has the features you like. Small and comfortable, they can be worn all day to keep track of how many steps you've taken—and to motivate you to take even more.

- Park in the farthest corner of the lot at work, when shopping or for appointments. This will easily add hundreds of steps to your pedometer, and extra minutes to your daily walking time.

- Add a brief walk to your breaks and lunches at work. The fresh air will improve your mood and attention as well as help metabolize glucose. Walk the few blocks to your local shops or from one errand to the next instead of driving.

- Ask a friend to walk with you. This can be quality time, which is becoming rare in our fast-paced world.

- Give your dog an extra daily walk. One study showed that dog owners get nearly twice as much exercise as people without dogs. Don't have one? Get one! It is also true that 40% of pet dogs are overweight because they are not walked enough. Plus, one of the most common complications of dog obesity is—you guessed it—canine diabetes.

- Be a little less efficient at home and work. Make several trips up and down the stairs, not just one. Carry grocery bags into the house one at a time to cover more ground. Take the long way around, whether it is from house to garage, or from your office to the restroom. Choose the stairs over the elevator. Skip shortcuts to increase your total steps.

**Step out with a group.** If walking solo does not inspire you, join a walking group (or start one yourself). Walking with others has many benefits. In some towns, it is safer than walking alone. Group walking also relieves boredom, is more motivating, and offers the chance to socialize and make new friends. For people who are naturally drawn to groups, it can increase commitment to a walking routine. Here are some ways to keep your group engaged…

- Set regular times to walk as a group. Regardless of who shows up…walk!

- Establish group goals and make time for everyone to announce how they are doing with their goals.

- Periodically meet to cook/share healthy recipes, like those you will find in this book.

- Share articles and books on walking. Remind each other that walking can reduce stress, help prevent heart disease, improve sleep, help maintain or lose weight, and help heal diabetes or reduce the risk of developing it.

- Invite a personal trainer to teach you how to improve your form and the effectiveness of your workout.

- Share ideas for interesting new walking routes.

**Turn on the tunes.** The evidence is undeniable: Music helps you walk faster and farther (and makes your walking a lot more fun!). A study published in 2002 by Ohio State University researchers found that people who listened to music while walking traveled four more miles per week than the control group who didn't use music.[66] Music helps distract you from the tedium of exercise, makes it more pleasurable, and also increases your respiration and heart rate. Most of all, playing music you love provides motivation. Just be certain you are not missing any safety cues—like traffic noises.

**Walk for charity.** You can help others while you are helping yourself by walking for a worthy cause. Charity walking events are great ways to meet others who share a cause.

## Take 10,000 Steps a Day

Studies show that walking 6,000 to 10,000 steps a day provides the ideal health benefits. This is the equivalent of walking almost four miles or about one hour. You can probably work up to that distance faster than you think. If that sounds like a lot of steps, it may surprise you to learn that the average sedentary couch potato already takes 3,000 or more steps just getting through a normal day. So doubling or tripling the amount of steps they take is not really a big deal. Remember, these steps can be accumulated throughout the day—while you are doing chores around the house or moving around your office—and not just on one long, dedicated walk.

A pedometer is useful because it keeps count of your steps during the day and displays your total. This comes in handy because it gives you a goal to shoot for and shows you your progress any time you want to check. So if you are short of your 10,000-step goal by late afternoon, you can reach your target with an evening stroll.

By walking 10,000 steps a day, you will easily lose 10% of your body weight, with extremely good effects on your glucose metabolism. If you are prediabetic, 10,000 steps will significantly reduce your risk of getting diabetes. Here are some clever tricks for hitting that magic number…

## Choosing a New Activity

The best exercise is the one you will stick with. If you are ready to branch out from your walking routine, take a look at the following list of ideas for new ways to increase your fitness. Choose an activity that you will enjoy and look forward to. That's the best way to ensure it becomes a habit. Here are some suggestions for activities that will boost your fitness:

**Try a group sport or sport for pairs.** Increasing your interactions with other people is an important aspect of maintaining healthy blood pressure. Combining your quota of both physical activity and human interaction is an efficient way to heal your high blood pressure. Some adults enjoy playing tennis, racquetball, soccer, and basketball.

**Individual sports.** These also are wonderful ways to improve your health. Some examples include walking, running, swimming, and cycling. Each of these offers opportunities to increase your activity level.

**Sign up for an exercise class.** Having guidance in your exercise routine can be helpful. Going to class and exercising with others can help your blood pressure continue to improve. It also has the benefit of helping you meet like-minded people who will encourage you on the road to better health. Taking a fitness class, such as Spin, yoga, dance, Pilates, and step, might give you the opportunity to meet a new friend who can become a new exercise companion, or who will simply support your progress.

**Include the kids.** For those with small children, boosting your activity by joining in with them has a triple benefit: It gets you both more active—and it brings you closer together. Instead of taking your kids or grandkids to the park and watching them play, get up and join them. Push them on the swings, boost them up to the monkey bars, and catch them at the end of the slide; try throwing or kicking a ball around. Some kids enjoy roughhousing and playing chase.

**Channel your "inner youth."** Was there a sport or activity that you thoroughly enjoyed when you were younger? Getting involved in this activity again might be just the right type of activity for you. The body had "muscle memory." This means if there was an activity or sport that you used to do—even if it was many years ago—your body will remember and regain its fitness much faster from the old activity than doing a new activity. If you have a child, god-child, grandchild, niece or nephew in your life, consider including them.

**Get a pet.** Having a pet can help you increase your activity level, especially if you are willing to step out of your comfort zone. According to the American Heart Association, having a pet—particularly a dog—reduces a person's risk of heart disease. If you do not currently have a dog, consider getting one. Dog owners are 54% more likely to get the recommended level of physical activity compared with people without dogs.[67] Studies also show that pets have a positive effect on your body's reaction to stress, including a decrease in heart rate, blood pressure and adrenaline-like hormone release when a pet is present.

If you do have a pet, assess the activity level you are currently giving your pet—and consider whether it can be increased. Try walking your dog farther than usual, or even jogging together. Prolong your playtime a little longer than usual. Even grooming your dog counts as physical activity. All of this adds up to lower blood pressure and better health.

Cat owners can also increase their level of activity through grooming and playing together. Try walking around the house dragging a string and watch your cat give chase. Buy a cat toy on a stick and bounce it around the room, keeping yourself moving the whole time. Consider yourself lucky if you have a horse, as this provides lots of opportunity to increase your activity in an enjoyable, companionable way.

**Make an activity date.** Try swapping "active dates" for sedentary standards such as dinner and a movie. Active date ideas include ice skating, flying a kite, taking a hike, strolling downtown, and dancing. You could even replace your sedentary dates for dancing lessons. Tango, salsa, merengue, and foxtrot are all social dances that can help add movement to otherwise inactive date nights.

**Turn housework into "exercise."** Swap less active household chores for those that require large muscle movements, like vacuuming, sweeping, and mopping. Negotiate with family members or housemates to take over those household chores that keep you moving from room to room.

**Get in the dirt.** Step up your activity by doing your own gardening. Caring for flowers and edibles, mowing the lawn, pruning trees, and raking leaves are satisfying ways to add more activity to your life than before.

**Spin your wheels.** Another great way to burn calories and get in shape is by *spinning*. This is a cardiovascular workout done on a stationary bike that can be adjusted to simulate riding uphill on flat ground. Some spinning bikes have an onboard computer that tracks your mileage, speed and distance—and even a heart monitor to keep track of your heart rate and calories burned. Here's what's great about spinning:

- It's safer than riding a bicycle on the road. You aren't limited by the weather or the time of day. It's easy on your weight-bearing joints (unlike jogging). And it burns a lot of calories (a 30-minute spinning session can burn 500 calories, melting away extra pounds). Gyms and health clubs usually offer spinning classes run by highly motivating trainers who incorporate warm-up and cool-down periods, as well as plenty of heart-healthy routines in between.

- It's aerobic and anaerobic. As an aerobic activity (meaning it increases your heart rate) spinning strengthens your heart muscle and lungs. Its anaerobic attributes include burning energy from stored fat and building muscle endurance, particularly in your legs.

- You're in control. You can adjust resistance levels, regardless of what an instructor or video recommends, in order to progress at your own pace.

- Group support. Spinning classes offer camaraderie and support as well as a sense of accomplishment and self-confidence. It's an opportunity for commitment, endurance, follow-through, and mental strength. (Of course, you can purchase your own stationary bike to use at home.)

**Hit the pool running.** Water-walking is even more low-impact than spinning, but it's a solid workout. It's easy on your joints because water's buoyancy reduces your body weight by 90% (really helpful if you're overweight). But because water is 800% more dense than air, it creates resistance that burns serious calories and strengthens your legs and core muscles as you walk, whether it's in the shallow end or the deep end (with a flotation belt). The deeper the water, the more strenuous your workout—and the more weight you'll lose.

Water-walking is so beneficial that it's the first physical activity elite athletes use when rehabbing after an injury or surgery. Ditto for patients in European hospitals immediately following joint replacement. It's also the therapy of choice for injured racehorses!

With water's buoyancy neutralizing the wear-and-tear pressure that gravity exerts on your joints, water-walking helps the surrounding muscles get strong enough to take up the slack. Plus, being in the water is comfortable for people who resist physical activity. You'll never again say "exercise hurts too much."

Here are some of the benefits of water-walking:

■ Puts less stress on your heart. While some exercises boost your heart rate, if you have health challenges, you may not want too much added stress on your heart, even while you're building new levels of endurance. Studies show that the exercising heart rate in water is up to 20 beats-per-minute *lower* than on land.

■ Builds muscle tone and strength. Shallow-water aerobic exercise builds real muscle strength—the kind that keeps you strong and active. One study showed that untrained women who performed shallow-water aerobics for just eight weeks achieved significantly greater gains in several strength areas compared with the land-based control group—even though the aqua aerobics routine included no specific muscle-strengthening exercises.[68]

With all that it has going for it, isn't it time you hit the pool? Plenty of public pools and gyms now offer aqua aerobics and aqua-step classes. Some people like having an instructor and find it fun to work out in a group, although water-walking can be as simple as taking a stroll up and down a lap lane. To find a class near you, contact your local YMCA, YWCA, or fitness center.

## Make the Most of Your Time in the Pool

If you are not big on swimming, the pool can still be your favorite workout arena. Besides water-walking, there is also a wide array of aqua exercise equipment, including aqua-steppers, aqua-cycles, and water workout stations. Check out *www.activeforever. com/water-exercise* for a glimpse. For water shoes (we recommend them for better traction), aqua barbells, flotation belts, aqua joggers, go to *www.waterworkout.com*. For the ultimate in aquatic exercise luxury, you must see the underwater treadmill at *www.active forever.com* or *www.hydrowork.com*.

## Make Time for Healing Exercise

I understand that you are busy. In fact, very few people have hours of free time just waiting to be filled with exercise. The reason healthy people exercise every day is because they make time for it. Even if you go from dawn until dark managing your home, family, and business, you can reserve 10 minutes three times a day in your schedule for a brisk walk. All it takes is your commitment. Once you get into the regular habit and feel the positive benefits, it will be easier to expand that time to do even more.

If your health condition limits you to a short walk once or twice a day, you will still be better off than sitting on the couch. Physical activity gets your blood flowing, which improves circulation. Keeping your blood moving, your heart pumping, and your limbs swinging freely slows the production of inflammatory chemicals and limits the damage that free radicals can do.

Physical activity is not "optional" for people with diabetes. Consider it medicine that you must take every day in order to stay alive. But unlike most medicines that merely manage your symptoms, physical activity can actually heal the underlying cause of your condition and reverse it. That is just another way of saying "cure!"

### Today's Action Steps

• Increase your activity level by adding more distance and difficulty to your current routine.

• Make a commitment to take at least 10,000 steps every day starting now.

• Choose a new activity to try, whether as an individual or in a group.

• Use Smart Monitoring—remembering to test your blood glucose before, immediately after, and again two hours after your exercise routine—to track your progress, keep motivated, and figure out how a particular exercise affects you.

**Extra credit:** Visit a nearby health club or your local YMCA/YWCA and sample a spin class or try water-walking today. Most clubs will issue you a free temporary pass (sometimes good for up to a week) if you tell them you're investigating becoming a member. There is no reason not to do it!

# DAY 16

# CONQUER SELF-SABOTAGE

*"Be faithful in small things because it is in them that your faith lies."*

—MOTHER TERESA, 1910–1997

**Tip of the Day:** Reaffirming your commitment to get better will help you combat self-sabotage.

DID YOU THINK *The 30-Day Diabetes Cure* worked like a diet? That it was something you could stick with for a while, get "well" on, and then discard for your old patterns of eating and activity? By now you know this plan does not work like that. This is a new way of living that can actually save your life. Poor food choices and lack of physical activity are what cause diabetes—and reversing these habits is the way to heal it.

## How to Handle Discouragement

Have you stopped paying attention to your eating plan for days at a time? Did you decide to ignore your blood glucose when those cookies came out at work? Have you given in to some of your old cravings? Do you feel you're drifting back to the habits that got you in trouble in the first place? If you've "fallen off the wagon," the best way to regain your footing is to start again at Day 1. Repeating Phase One will put you on an even keel and bring your blood glucose and metabolism back into balance.

Do not feel discouraged. This is perfectly normal—after all, none of us is perfect. Trial and error is one of the most effective methods of learning. Most importantly, you have noticed that you are getting off track and you will correct your course as soon as possible. In the words of Nelson Mandela, "The greatest glory in living lies not in never failing, but in rising every time we fail." The old Japanese proverb, "Fall seven times, stand up eight," reiterates this wisdom.

Going back with the knowledge of where your weaknesses lie will help you meet them head on when they pop up again. Here are some tips to take with you…

## We Are What We Repeatedly Do

Aristotle said it, adding, "…Excellence is not an act, but a habit." Thousands of years later, scientists at Duke University confirmed this realization. They found that while people like to

276

*think* they are in control of what they do, nearly half of all daily actions occur in the same location every single day.[69] In short, humans are creatures of habit—for better or worse.

"Many of our repeated behaviors are cued by everyday environments, even though people think they're making choices all the time," says Wendy Wood, PhD, James B. Duke professor of psychology and neuroscience. "Most people don't think that the reason they eat fast food at lunch or snack from the vending machine in late afternoon is because these actions are cued by their daily routines, the sight and smell of the food or the location they're in. They think they're doing it because they intended to eat then, or because they like the food."[70]

Consider the positive side of this: You get up, use the bathroom and brush your teeth because you are in the bathroom. It is a habit based on location—and a good one. People who struggle with establishing good habits can apply this insight. Example: If you get the urge to eat while watching your favorite TV program, you should consider moving the TV. That's right: Put it (or yourself) in a new location. Other possibilities include getting yourself a stationary bike and pedaling while you watch and taking up a craft, such as knitting or drawing, to perform while watching TV. These create new habits that don't include a bowl of ice cream (like the couch did!). Sounds kooky, but it really works.

## The Top 10 Commitment-Busters

You might be sabotaging your own best efforts by…

1. Keeping junky food in your home or office, so you can "sneak" a treat.

2. Creating "special food rules" for various occasions, like birthdays, holidays, or celebration dinners.

3. Letting others sway your eating or activity schedule. Just because your mother-in-law wants you to eat her coffee cake doesn't mean you have to.

4. Giving in to "stress eating." After a hard day, it's easy to reach for a junky snack (especially if it's around the house).

5. Not recognizing that judgmental comments from family or friends over your new approach to diabetes are based on ignorance or their own insecurities.

6. Skipping your 30 minutes of daily walking because you "do not have enough time."

7. Not reminding your family that you need their support in order to succeed.

8. Forgetting to snack regularly (and healthfully) twice a day.

9. Still eating or drinking anything with sugar in it.

10. Skimping on sleep (one of the most healing aspects of your life).

# How to Get Back on Track

Changing your old unhealthy habits is central to our 30-day plan. But your new approach to eating and exercise won't happen without real effort and focus from you. Try these tips to get back on track...

**Recognize your motivation.** If you need motivation, re-read our Special Report, *Dodging Diabetes Complications*, where we describe the terrible toll that unchecked diabetes can take.

**Write it down.** Put pen to paper and create a week's worth of diabetes-healing menus—from breakfast to dinner. Now make a grocery shopping list.

**Declare your intentions.** Tell everyone you know about your decision to follow *The 30-Day Diabetes Cure*—your partner, children, friends, and co-workers. Declaring your intentions ups the odds you will follow through. Put a reminder on the fridge too—just for yourself!

**Get cookin'.** Dedicate an hour of time to make a double-batch of vegetable soup, three-bean chili, or a week's worth of Irish oatmeal. Portion it into meal-size containers and freeze some for later. Do this again with a new recipe two days from now. When hunger propels you, you will reach for these diabetes-friendly meals just as easily as you once reached for a bag of chips. Trust us, you will.

**Find a sponsor.** In AA, a sponsor is someone who has experience in the recovery process. That experience comes from his or her ability to bounce back from "slips" and learn from them. A sponsor (or mentor) provides support and encouragement "one day at a time." Ask a friend who has diabetes to work through this program with you. A great resource is your local Diabetes Support Group, where you can seek out a mentor who can provide guidance.

**Log it in.** You may think you have made little to no progress in changing your eating and exercise habits, but is that really true? Here you are at Day 16. You've hung tough for more than three weeks. You have learned a bunch. You are fighting the good fight. So acknowledge your progress and accomplishments. Remember that testing in pairs and comparing your blood glucose reading to your meals and activities is one of your most powerful diabetes-fighting tools.

**Recognize triggers.** All habits have at least one trigger. Is it the donut box at work? Dessert after a meal? The aroma of french fries? The stronger the trigger, the more powerful the habit. To break the hold these triggers exert, you first have to recognize them. Then you can create your own positive replacement habits. For example, when the donuts appear (as you know they will), make sure you have an apple and some walnuts to munch on. As for the post-meal expectation of dessert, enjoy an orange, yogurt with berries and cinnamon, or a small square of dark chocolate. Create replacements you can learn to love.

**Be mindful.** Old habits haunt us, but being mindful focuses you on the present. Use the one-meal-at-a-time approach and make a healing choice *right now*. "For lunch, I will have my yummy rice and veggies." Do not think about what your co-workers are eating. Eat well in the moment, consistently, applying your new food choices one meal at a time.

**Replace.** If old bad habits are ganging up on you, arm yourself with specific replacements. For instance, if a cold soda beckons at your local gas station, make sure you have got a nice pomegranate spritzer along for the ride. If you crave a mid-afternoon sweet, reach for your healthy snack bag and enjoy a dried fig, or a couple of dried apricots or prunes, along with a small piece of cheese or five almonds. Never be far from your stash of healthy snacks.

## Reject Negative Self-Talk

Negative self-talk is a real speed bump on the path to progress. Do you tell yourself you will never be able to stick with a plan like this for life? Or that you simply hate walking for 30 minutes every day?

Stop creating self-fulfilling prophecies. There is reason for hope from Duke University on this very subject. Researchers there say the older we get, the wiser we become emotionally—and that includes not letting negative thoughts and feelings dominate.[71] One easy solution is to replace negative thoughts with positive ones. The more you do it, the easier it gets. If you think you are a negative self-talker, try these positive self-talk tips…

- When you feel yourself thinking or saying something negative, say "stop" out loud and affirm the opposite. "I cannot eat a healing dinner because I did not shop for food" becomes "Stop! I have a can of beans in the pantry, olive oil, and an onion, so I can make a yummy meal."

- Modify your wording to use less powerful phrases. "I can't find a way to stay on the eating plan" changes to "it is challenging to stay on the eating plan." Then, explore ways to make it less challenging and you will be able to add "…but I am getting better at it."

- "This will never work" becomes "how can I make this work?" Imagine the possibilities when you shift your mindset.

- Be optimistic—even if you are not! Count your successes every day and record them in your journal. Healing breakfast? *Check.* Diabetes-healing snack at 10:30? *Check!* Walked at lunch? *Double check!* You are on your way to being more optimistic already.

- Draft a few positive affirmations and repeat them aloud or to yourself daily. Repetition is key. Create sentences phrased as if they're true right now. You can use these or write your own: "I am reversing my diabetes with every step I walk." "I am healthier with every bite of this delicious chili." "I feel peaceful and happy with my decision to stick with this plan."

- Jot down your affirmations and post them strategically on the bathroom mirror, refrigerator, pantry door, and workplace drawer.

# Are You Your Own Worst Enemy?

We did not say it would be easy, but we know you *can* do this. You *can* reverse your diabetes. You *can* get off your medications. You *can* reduce your insulin. You *can* avoid the deadly complications of diabetes. Most important is whether or not you believe it.

Henry Ford said: "If you think you can do a thing or think you can't do a thing, you're right." Everyone has a little voice inside telling us what we *cannot* do. Making choices every day about what you eat is not difficult unless you believe it is. It is not any harder to go to the grocery store and buy fresh vegetables and a piece of wild Atlantic salmon than it is to pick up cookies, ice cream, a six-pack of Coke, and frozen pizza. A homemade salad loaded with fresh vegetables and beans, sprinkled with nuts and soft savory cheese crumbles and some cold sliced chicken breast is a snap! Your shopping list for this salad is:

- **Pre-washed organic baby spinach**
- **One red bell pepper**
- **Red onion**
- **A can of kidney beans**
- **Raw walnuts**
- **Cheese**
- **Deli cooked chicken breast**

By buying double the ingredients, you can toss together another one on the weekend.

Now consider the alternative: Eating a feedlot burger with an order of greasy fries, washed down by a HFCS-loaded soda handed to you by a clerk who may or may not have remembered to wash his hands after using the bathroom. The choice is easy.

When we're trying to recover from diabetes, we frequently meet the same obstacles that gave us the disease in the first place. Over and over, we are encountering the many ways in which we are our own worst enemy—instead of being our own best friend. In politics, this is called voting against your own best interests.

# More Tips to Succeed

**Exercise to curb your appetite.** Researchers from the University of Colorado in Denver found that exercise diminishes hunger and appetite. That's one of the many reasons why regular physical activity is so important.[72]

**Eat green.** Our meal plan is definitely good for your general health, as well as your diabetes. For instance, women who eat more folate-rich foods (one of the B vitamins) have 50% less chance of getting colorectal cancer than women who don't eat their folate foods, say researchers at Hallym University College of Medicine in South Korea.[73] You have our permission to "pig out" on broccoli, greens, oranges, and beans—all great sources of folate. Stay on your healing path and you'll conquer cancer at the same time!

**Use Smart Monitoring.** Testing in pairs is one of the most powerful tools you have. It allows you to know for certain just how different foods and activities are affecting your blood glucose levels. A high reading reminds you just how unhealthful processed foods are for you. A healthy reading rewards you for sticking to your diabetes-healing habits.

## How to Get Out of a Rut

Step away from negative influences (and people) that stand in the way of your goals. Did your mother tell you that snacking would spoil your appetite? Does her voice still whisper as your hunger grows and dinner looms? Be sure you nail those hunger pangs twice a day with healing snacks (along with filling, diabetes-healing meals). Remember the hormone ghrelin? It signals that you're hungry now and then quiets down after you eat. So go ahead and enjoy a handful of pistachios (it takes half an hour for ghrelin to know you've eaten and send the "satisfied" signal).

Is a well-intentioned friend offering up "expert" advice? It is *not* true that nibbling on low-cal rice cakes is better than having a thumb-sized portion of parmesan cheese and an apple, no matter what he/she says. Gently remind your advice-giving pal that you are on a doctor-created plan and that you love your new food choices. Even invite him/her to join you.

Remember that fiber is your best friend. High-fiber foods are slow-carb foods. Eating them for meals and snacks ensures that your body will be powered with a steady fuel supply. As a bonus, fiber digests more slowly, so you will feel fuller longer. If you haven't picked up the habit of eating fiber foods, start now.

Muscle burns calories. Muscle burns an astonishing 12 times more calories than fat. Have you added the extra exercise from Day 15? Literally lift yourself out of the doldrums by getting a pair of weights and starting to build muscle. Your newly lean body will keep you inspired to stay on the plan.

### Today's Action Steps

- Decide now to eliminate anything that is sabotaging your success.
- Pick up a pen and plan your meals and snacks for the upcoming week.
- List your successes so far, and declare tomorrow a chance to start fresh.
- Test your blood glucose right now, so you can use Smart Monitoring with your very next meal or activity.

**Extra credit:** Choose one self-sabotaging behavior you recognize in yourself and decide how you can transform it. Have you not walked yet? Hit the road right now. Have you not planned dinner? Go cut up a plate of raw veggies to snack on while you create your menu. Do you know what is for breakfast tomorrow? Hard-boil a few eggs so you will be ready in the morning. It truly is that easy!

# DAY 17

# ELIMINATE TOXIC FOOD INGREDIENTS

*"Education, whatever else it should or should not be,
must be an inoculation against the poisons of life and adequate
equipment in knowledge and skill for meeting the chances of life."*

—HAVELOCK ELLIS, British physician and writer, 1859–1939

**Tip of the Day:** Minimize your exposure to toxins and strengthen your liver to help heal your diabetes.

PROCESSED FOOD MANUFACTURERS add lots of unhealthful ingredients to their products. These chemicals are used to extend the shelf life of their products, add color and texture, improve flavor, boost their profits, or create food cravings in you. What these questionable ingredients are not designed to do is to nourish your body. In many cases, these artificial ingredients can be quite harmful to your health. Learning to read labels carefully will help you avoid ingredients that raise blood pressure and diminish your health.

## Protect Your Health

The easiest way to protect yourself and your family from toxic ingredients is to avoid as much processed food as you possibly can. Foods that come directly from nature don't have an ingredients list. An egg is an egg. An almond is an almond. Water is water. Because of this, some nutritionists say that the most healthful foods are "single ingredient" foods. See the evidence yourself by using Smart Monitoring as you add nontoxic foods to your meals and snacks.

Still, there are times when you might want to use certain processed foods. While we don't recommend that you make a habit of this, there are some processed foods on the market that contain organic and healthful ingredients. Go ahead and monitor how eating toxic foods affects your blood glucose levels by testing in pairs. When consumers demand healthy ingredients in our foods, food companies will get the message and provide us with better products.

## Top 10 Worst Toxic Food Ingredients

Here is an at-a-glance list of the 10 "worst of the worst" food product ingredients, in our opinion (not necessarily ranked in order of the harm they do). Read labels carefully. Do *not* purchase or consume any products that contain these substances.

1. **Agave nectar**

2. **Artificial food coloring**

3. **Aspartame and other artificial sweeteners**

4. **BHA and BHT (preservatives)**

5. **High fructose corn syrup (HFCS)**

6. **Monosodium glutamate (MSG)**

7. **Potassium bromate**

8. **Recombinant bovine growth hormone (rBGH),** used in milk and other dairy products

9. **Refined vegetable oils** (including those made from corn, safflower, soybeans, and canola)

10. **Sodium nitrite and sodium nitrate**

To follow are in-depth descriptions of each toxic ingredient listed above, why it is thought to be harmful, other names it may masquerade as ("A.K.A"), and in which foods the ingredient(s) may be found.

## Agave Nectar

**What it is: This highly processed sweetener is derived from the agave cactus plant.** Most agave sold in the US comes from Mexico.

**Why it is harmful: Many consumers believe agave nectar is a healthful sweetener, but it is anything but.** Agave nectar contains the highest amount of fructose (55%–97%) of all the commercial sweeteners, including HFCS (which averages 55% fructose).

Contrary to what many health experts and the majority of consumers believe, fructose is not inherently evil. In fact, fructose is the natural sugar found in fruits and vegetables. The health problems associated with fructose arise when it is extracted from fruits and vegetables and isolated from the fiber that slows its digestion. This allows a person to over-consume fructose easily. For example, the amount of fructose in a can of soda or glass of juice is equal to the amount in approximately 10 to 12 apples or oranges.

Overconsumption of fructose has been shown to increase insulin resistance, the precursor to Type 2 diabetes. The liver converts fructose to fat. Fructose, consumed in quantities greater than 25 grams a day (the equivalent of five teaspoons), has been shown to elevate uric acid levels, which causes chronic, low-level inflammation throughout the body, and may cause gout. It is also a main cause of fatty liver disease. Fructose overconsumption also leads to weight gain, elevated blood glucose and triglycerides, and high blood pressure.

**A.K.A.:** Agave syrup

**Found in:** Ice cream, energy bars and cereals, ketchup and other sauces and condiments. Agave is also sold by itself as a "healthy" sweetener.

# Artificial Food Coloring

**What it is:** Food product manufacturers add dyes to make bland products look more appealing.

**Why it is harmful:** Artificial food dyes were originally synthesized from coal tar—and now they are derived from petroleum. They have long been controversial and are one of the most widely used additives in food products today. Many food dyes have been banned because of their adverse effects on laboratory animals. Studies have confirmed that nine dyes currently approved for use in the US raise health concerns.

According to the Center for Science in the Public Interest's (CSPI) study on food dyes, "The three most widely used dyes, Red 40, Yellow 5, and Yellow 6, are contaminated with known carcinogens. Another dye, Red 3, has been acknowledged for years by the Food and Drug Administration to be a carcinogen, yet it is still in the food supply."[74] CSPI further reports that these nine food dyes are linked to many health issues including hyperactivity, ADHD, allergic reactions, and cancer.

A large-scale study conducted by the British government found that a variety of common food dyes, as well as the preservative sodium benzoate, increased hyperactivity and behavioral problems in children, while also decreasing their attention spans. The study was published in 2007 in the British medical journal *Lancet.*[75]

While the European Union has mandatory labeling regulations in place to inform consumers of the health risks, the US has no such labeling requirements at this time.

**A.K.A.:** Caramel color, FD&C Blue #1, Brilliant Blue FCF, Bright Blue, Blue #2, Ingtotine, Royal Blue, Red #3, Erythrosine, FD&C Red #40, Allura Red AC, Yellow #5 and #6, FD&C Green #3, Fast Green, Sea Green, as well as other names.

**Found in:** Beverages, candy, baked goods, cereals, energy bars, puddings, jams, bread, macaroni and cheese, deli meat, frostings, condiments, fast food, ice cream, sherbet, sorbet. These dyes are also added to meat and fish to make them appear "fresher."

# Aspartame

**What it is:** One of the most commonly used artificial sweeteners.

**Why it is harmful:** Aspartame is an excitotoxin, which is a neurotoxic chemical additive shown to harm nerve cells by overexciting them, sometimes to the point of cell death. Regularly consuming excitotoxins destroys significant numbers of brain cells and can lead to serious health problems, including neurological disorders. (The two other common excitotoxins used in food are *monosodium glutamate* MSG and *l-cysteine*, which is used as a dough conditioner.)

Aspartame and *aspartic acid* are also believed to be carcinogenic. They produce neurotoxic effects such as headaches, dizziness, blurry vision, and gastrointestinal disturbances.

Aspartame contains *10-percent methanol*, which is broken down by the body into the toxic by-products formic acid and formaldehyde.[76] Formaldehyde is considered to be a potent nerve toxin and carcinogen, which may explain why aspartame accounts for more reports to the FDA of adverse reactions than all other foods and food additives combined.[77]

**A.K.A.:** NutraSweet, Equal, Canderel, Spoonful, NatraTaste, AminoSweet, and others.

**Found in:** Over 6,000 products contain aspartame, including diet and sugar-free sodas and drinks, sugar-free chewing gum, yogurt, breath mints, instant breakfasts, frozen desserts, juice beverages, and gelatins. Common in products labeled "lite," "diet" and "low-fat."

**Avoid its cousins:** Splenda (sucralose), Sweet'N Low (saccharine).

## BHA and BHT

**What it is:** Butylated hydroxyanisole (BHA) and butylated hydroxytoluene (BHT) are preservative chemicals used to prevent oxidation and extend the shelf life of many grocery items.

**Why it is harmful:** BHA and BHT are *oxidants*, which form potentially cancer-causing reactive compounds in the body. The International Agency for Research on Cancer considers BHA to be possibly carcinogenic to humans. The State of California has listed it as a known carcinogen.[78]

**Found in:** Packaging materials, breakfast cereals, sausage, hot dogs, meat patties, chewing gum, potato chips, beer, butter, vegetable oils, cosmetics, and animal feed.

## High Fructose Corn Syrup (HFCS)

**What it is: This is a highly processed sweetener made from cornstarch.** The starch is separated from the corn kernel, and then converted into corn syrup through a process called acid *hydrolysis*. To turn the corn syrup into high fructose corn syrup, some of its glucose molecules are converted into fructose molecules by exposing the syrup to an enzyme produced by bacteria.

**Why it is harmful:** Nearly all HFCS is made from genetically modified corn, which creates health concerns of its own. HFCS contributes to weight gain, obesity, and the development of Type 2 diabetes.[79] It is the number one source of calories in the US diet.

HFCS also is a major contributor to cardiovascular disease, arthritis, insulin resistance, and elevated triglycerides and LDL (bad) cholesterol. In 2009, mercury was found in nearly half of all samples taken of HFCS.[80] The HFCS came from three different manufacturers, including popular brands such as Quaker, Hunts, Kraft, Yoplait, Nutri-Grain, and Smuckers. Mercury is a heavy metal and is considered a potent brain toxin. The presence of mercury-contaminated caustic soda in the production of HFCS is common.[81] Americans consume an average of more than 20 teaspoons of HFCS per day per person.[82]

**A.K.A.:** Corn sugar, glucose/fructose syrup, high-fructose maize syrup inulin, iso-glucose, and fruit fructose.

**Found in:** HFCS is inexpensive, and as such is often the preferred sweetener used by the processed food industry. It's found in soda, sports drinks, sweet teas, sweetened juices, salad dressings, breads, cookies, cakes, crackers, cereals, yogurts, soups, lunchmeats, pizza sauce, and condiments such as ketchup.

## Monosodium Glutamate (MSG)

**What it is:** MSG is one of the most common food additives. It is an amino acid used as a flavor enhancer in processed foods. It is also used by some restaurants.

**Why it is harmful:** Like aspartame, MSG is an excitotoxin, shown to harm nerve cells. Regularly consuming excitotoxins such as MSG can lead to serious health problems, including neurological disorders. (L-cystene and aspartame are two other excitotoxins to avoid.) Regular consumption of MSG also stimulates the appetite, contributing to weight gain and obesity.

**A.K.A.:** MSG is often a component in many common ingredients, including hydrolyzed vegetable protein, hydrolyzed plant protein, vegetable protein extract, yeast extract, glutamate, glutamic acid, sodium caseinate, textured protein, and calcium caseinate.

**Found in:** Processed foods such as salad dressings, low-fat yogurt, canned meats, frozen entrees, potato chips, canned soups and powdered soup mixes, canned stews, entrees, and crackers.

## Potassium Bromate

**What it is:** Potassium bromate is a form of bromide. It is used as an additive to increase the volume in some breads, baked goods, and flours.

**Why it is harmful:** Potassium bromate is banned in the European Union, Canada, and several other countries. It has been shown to cause cancer in animals. Bromide is also known to disrupt the endocrine system.[83] The state of California requires that all baked goods made with bromate carry a cancer warning label. However, it is not regulated throughout the rest of the US. Since 1991, the FDA has asked bakers to voluntarily cease its use.

**A.K.A.:** Bromic acid, potassium salt, bromated flour, "enriched flour."

**Found in:** Most commercial baked goods in the US. It's also common in flour and baking mixes. It is also an ingredient in some mouthwashes and toothpastes.

## Recombinant Bovine Growth Hormone (rBGH)

**What it is:** It is a genetically engineered version of the natural growth hormone produced by cows, created by the Monsanto Corporation. rBGH is used to hasten lactation and boost milk production in dairy cows.

**Why it is harmful:** In the US, milk containing rBGH is not required to be labeled. Milk from cows who have received rBGH contains high levels of insulin-like growth factor (IGF-1), excess levels of which have been implicated as major causes of breast, colon, and prostate cancers.

Dairy cows given rBGH have an increased risk of mastitis. When a cow has mastitis, pus and blood are secreted into the milk. Cows are given antibiotics to try to prevent or treat mastitis. This leads to antibiotic resistance, which is tied to the spread of virulent staph infections such as MRSA. These germs and the antibiotics used to treat them can also get into the milk. Hormones in food have also been linked to the onset of early puberty for girls.

Consumer protest encouraged such companies as Dannon, General Mills, Wal-Mart, Starbucks, and Publix to phase out dairy products containing the hormones rBST and rBGH, though it still appears in dairy products in the United States.

**A.K.A.:** Recombinant bovine somatotropin (rBST).

**Found in:** Dairy products that aren't specifically labeled "No rGBH or rBST."

## Refined Vegetable Oil

**What it is:** There are many different kinds of commercially refined vegetable oils, including soybean oil, corn oil, safflower oil, canola oil, and peanut oil.

**Why it is harmful:** Intensive mechanical and chemical processes are used to extract the oil from the seeds of plants. The refining process also uses chemical solvents and high temperatures. The oils are then typically deodorized and bleached. This refining process removes the natural vitamins and minerals from the seeds and creates a product that has been shown to easily oxidize and become rancid, leading to the formation of free radicals, which are linked to cancer, rapid aging, and other health concerns.

Refined vegetable oils, unlike extra virgin olive oil, are also high in omega-6 fatty acid, which neutralizes the benefits of omega-3s in your diet, and causes inflammation in the body. The oxidation effect has also been shown to contribute to DNA damage, elevated blood triglycerides and impaired insulin response. Additionally, many refined vegetable oils are hydrogenated. This process creates trans fatty acids, which are known to contribute to heart disease and some cancers.

**A.K.A.:** Partially hydrogenated vegetable oil, cooking oil, shortening, margarine.

**Found in:** Many, if not most, processed foods and baked goods such as crackers and granola bars. They are also sold as cooking oils and margarines.

## Sodium Nitrite and Sodium Nitrate

**What they are:** These two closely related chemicals are used to preserve meat. They are present in most canned meats and in many dried meats, lunch meats, and bacons.

**Why they are harmful:** When added to meat, the nitrates are readily converted to nitrosamines, which are associated with an increased risk of certain types of cancers. This chemical reaction occurs most readily at high temperatures. In a 2007 analysis, The World Cancer Research Fund revealed that consuming 1.8 ounces of processed meat every day increases your cancer risk by 20%.[84]

**A.K.A.:** Soda niter, chile saltpeter.

**Found in:** Cured meats, bacon, ham, salami, corned beef and hot dogs, pate, pickled pig's feet, canned meat (Vienna sausages, deviled ham), smoked salmon, dried fish jerky.

## Today's Action Steps

- Become a careful label reader. Keep an eye peeled for any and all of these toxic ingredients while shopping.

- Remove any processed food products from your cupboards that contain any of the 10 harmful ingredients listed above.

- The next time you go shopping, seek out real food, including fresh and frozen organically grown vegetables, lean and clean proteins that are cage-free, pasture-raised and free range, and dairy products that are labeled "organic" and hormone-free. "Vote" with your dollars by refusing to buy any food products that contain unwholesome and toxic ingredients.

- Monitor your progress by testing in pairs. See how eating wholesome foods containing no toxic ingredients improves your blood glucose levels.

# DAY 18

# EAT MORE BEANS AND LEGUMES

*"What moved him most was a certain meal on beans."*

—ROBERT BROWNING, English poet, 1812–1889

**Tip of the Day:** Beans are the *perfect* food for people with diabetes because they regulate blood glucose and improve your body's insulin response. You can eat your fill without gaining weight. In fact, the more you eat, the more weight you will lose!

BEANS AND LEGUMES are the world's most powerful diabetes-healing superfood. No other single food packs the diabetes-reversing power that they do. Beans are extremely low in calories, high in protein, packed with fiber and versatile enough to be enjoyed at every meal of the day. They are also inexpensive. Now *that* is a superfood!

Beans increase insulin sensitivity, lower blood glucose levels, add precious fiber, and fill you up on fewer calories. Eat beans as often as you can—at least one serving daily—for maximum diabetes, blood pressure, and weight loss benefits. Beans can be eaten at breakfast, lunch and dinner—and even as a snack. Add them to soups, serve them as side dishes, and toss them into salads. The more often you eat them, the faster your blood glucose will normalize and your diabetes will reverse. We promise!

But don't take our word for it. Remember that you are in charge of monitoring your blood glucose by testing in pairs. Track how beans are stabilizing your blood glucose and record your progress using Smart Monitoring.

## The Healing Power of Beans

Remember when we discussed the remarkable healing attributes of fiber in whole grains on Day 7? Today we will share the details about bean fiber because knowledge is power and the more clearly you understand the power of beans, the more likely you are to start eating them regularly. Fiber is the indigestible part of plant foods, commonly called *roughage*. Because it is not digested, it has no calories. Yet, it keeps you feeling full because it is bulky and literally "fills you up." Fiber is the ultimate weight-loss food: You could stuff yourself with fiber (not that we recommend it) and not gain a pound. And because high-fiber foods contain so few calories, they actually make weight loss easy—without dieting or ever feeling hungry. Understand that beans contain two types of fiber, insoluble and soluble, in perfect balance for healing diabetes.

**Insoluble fiber** is dietary fiber that does not absorb, or dissolve in, water. In plain speak it is the roughage that fills you up without many calories, facilitating weight loss. This action is essential for people with diabetes because shedding weight lowers insulin resistance and allows your natural insulin to do its job better. (If you have Type 1, decreasing your body's insulin resistance usually allows you to lower your dosage of synthetic insulin.) Losing weight via a fiber-rich diet also helps drive down high blood glucose, which can reduce or even eliminate your need for medications. This roughage component of fiber also reduces your body's use of insulin by slowing the rate at which you absorb carbohydrates (an action that also prevents surges in blood glucose). By contrast, a diet of sugary, fast-carb, low-fiber foods creates a chronic demand for insulin. Over time, the pancreas' ability to manufacture insulin weakens, and more glucose stays in the bloodstream. The resulting condition, known as insulin resistance (or pre-diabetes), is the most common cause of Type 2 diabetes.

**Soluble fiber** is dietary fiber that, when mixed with water, forms a substance like a gel and expands. It is found in foods such as beans and oatmeal and produces several extraordinary benefits for people with diabetes. This type of fiber delays the emptying of your stomach (helping you feel full longer), slows down your digestion of sugars and starches, and controls blood glucose spikes in the process. Soluble fiber's "magic gel" is beneficial in so many ways. Like a sponge, it soaks up cholesterol, triglycerides and other blood fats and escorts them to the colon so they can exit the body before they have a chance to clog up your arteries. By decreasing the level of blood fats, soluble fiber also reduces your risk of heart disease, the main complication of diabetes. Plus, some studies even show that fiber helps reduce the risk of certain cancers—especially colon cancer—by speeding the removal of toxic wastes from the body.

**Packed with pectin.** Another big bean benefit is the high pectin content. Pectin is yet another type of fiber that helps sensitize your cells to insulin. It actually helps insulin uptake by producing extra insulin receptors on cells. (No drug is able to achieve this!) These additional insulin receptors are like extra "doorways" that make it easier for insulin to move out of your bloodstream and into your cells. Boosting insulin receptors on cells is one of the keys to reversing diabetes naturally. Plus, pectin reduces your risk of heart disease by lowering cholesterol levels.

**Stashed with resistant starch.** "Starch" is the most essential fuel for the human body. It is the component of carbohydrates that metabolizes into glucose as the body digests it. All plant foods contain starch. But not all starches digest at the same rate. The fast-carb starch in cold breakfast cereals and white-flour baked goods moves into your bloodstream as rapidly as pure table sugar, because it is quickly broken down into glucose in the small intestine and released immediately. "Resistant starches," on the other hand, literally resist digestion. These include beans, barley, brown rice (and even white potatoes, especially after they have cooled a bit). Resistant starch foods bypass breakdown in the small intestine and are thus broken down at a slower rate. As a result, they cause a far slower and lower rise in blood glucose and insulin—and, incredibly, less fat storage after you eat them. In fact, some resistant starch is never turned into glucose at all.

**Burn off more body fat.** People who eat resistant starches such as beans burn more body fat, which is crucial for weight loss and controlling diabetes. An Australian study found that people eating meals that included a mere 5% of resistant starch (a small amount of beans would do the trick) increased the rate at which their bodies burned fat by an amazing 23%.[85] And this effect lasted for 24 hours afterward!

## The Amazing Health Benefits of Beans

Eating resistant starch foods, especially as beans, produces some other surprising health benefits as well, including…

- **Improves insulin sensitivity,** whether you are using your body's own insulin or injecting it. Either way, this is an important way eating beans helps heal your diabetes.

- **Improves glucose tolerance the following day** (also known as the "second meal effect"). Research confirms this sustained, slow-absorption effect even a day after you eat resistant starch foods.[86]

- **Produces more satiety (the feeling of "fullness") with less food.** An obvious and welcome benefit when you're trying to control your eating!

- **Blocks your body's ability to burn carbs** and prevents the liver from using carbs as fuel. Instead, your body burns stored body fat and recently eaten fat.

- **Shuts down hunger hormones.** Animal studies show that resistant starch prompts the body to churn out more leptin, the "I'm full!" hormone. Eating a meal that includes resistant starches like beans triggers a hormonal response to shut off hunger.[87] Result? You end up eating less.

- **Lowers cholesterol and triglyceride levels.** Who wouldn't welcome this as an alternative to drugs?

- **Promotes helpful bacteria,** while suppressing bad bacteria and their toxic by-products. Great for your immunity!

- **Encourages bowel regularity** and discourages constipation.

- **Produces the protective compound called *butyrate*,** which helps shield you from colon cancer.

## The #1 Anti-Diabetes Food

When it comes to resistant starch foods, beans top the list by far. Along with non-starchy vegetables, they have one of the lowest Glycemic Load ratings of all the slow carbs. Although the type of bean and its preparation method affect the amount of resistant starch available to you (canned beans contain less than reconstituting your own), the starch in beans is evenly divided between slowly digested starch and resistant starch.

This makes them the perfect food for people with diabetes or those who want to lose weight—or both! But what about the "gas" they produce for some people? Enzyme products such as Beano increase the digestibility of beans and can reduce their gassiness. If gas is a problem for you, try starting with a quarter-cup serving of beans sprinkled with Beano and work your way up to half-cup portions several times a day. Given time, many people find they digest beans without any gas at all.

### How Beans Helped Beverly Heal

Beverly L. and her husband have been full-time RV-ers for 13 years. This nomadic life, full of quick food and sweet treats, has taken a toll on Bev's health.

One night in 2009, Beverly ate a large piece of cherry pie a la mode. Later that night she got up 10 times to use the bathroom. The next day she saw a doctor. Her fasting blood sugar was a whopping 268. She was diagnosed with Type 2 diabetes. She went home and cried, imagining all the health problems she would face.

She thought just losing weight could help her, so she enrolled in Weight Watchers. After losing 15 pounds, Bev realized she couldn't continue forever. So she took *metformin* and stopped caring about what she ate. Her blood sugar crept as high as 156. She finally said to herself, "Bev, you've got to make a change." She'd heard about *The 30-Day Diabetes Cure*, but was skeptical. She ordered the book anyway and gave the plan a try.

In the past, Bev and her husband had dined out most nights—usually on burgers, fries, and the like. Bev started cooking her own "meals that heal" from *The 30-Day Diabetes Cure*. "There's hardly a day I don't have beans on the stove," she says proudly. She has emptied her cabinets of foods, beverages, and snacks that harm her blood sugar. She keeps no white flour or sugar in the RV. She's proud of her new food choices, even in social situations. At campground cookouts, her meals are the healthiest. At bingo, Beverly snacks on organic peanut butter and celery sticks or carrots and hummus.

If Beverly can beat diabetes while living on the road, anyone can beat it.

As an added benefit, beans are loaded with beneficial antioxidants. The pigments that give berries their bright colors also occur in the beans thanks to anthocyanins. Anthocyanins help control blood glucose and limit the damage diabetes causes to blood-vessel walls.[88] And black beans contain levels that rival that of berries!

## Reduce Drug Doses

People with Type 2 diabetes who boost their consumption of high-fiber foods actually improve their blood glucose to the point where they can reduce their drug doses, according to a study published in the *New England Journal of Medicine*.

During the research, participants ate 24 grams of dietary fiber from food every day for six weeks. (If that sounds like a lot, you'll get this much fiber from a mere one-cup serving of beans.) Over the next six weeks, patients doubled their fiber consumption by increasing the amount of high-fiber foods they ate. At the end of the 12 weeks, they had dramatic blood glucose improvements (and in their cholesterol levels too).[89]

## Fight Genetic Predisposition

High-fiber foods are so powerful they can defeat a genetic tendency toward diabetes. "It appears that adult-onset diabetes is largely preventable," says JoAnn Manson, MD, an endocrinologist at Brigham and Women's Hospital in Boston. "This is one case where heredity is not destiny."

Her study examined 6,000 adults for eight years and focused on several known risks for heart disease, a serious danger for people with diabetes. Dr. Manson's study found that people who eat more high-fiber foods are likely to have a lower body mass index (BMI), lower blood pressure, and less homocysteine—all major risk factors for heart attack and stroke.*

An active lifestyle and fiber-rich diet can greatly lower a genetic susceptibility to diabetes. Scientists at the National Institute of Diabetes and Digestive and Kidney Diseases discovered that the rate of diabetes among Mexican Pima Indians—who eat a traditional diet of low-fat unprocessed beans and corn tortillas—is 85% *lower* than that of Pima Indians living in Arizona, who tend to favor a higher calorie, low-fiber Western-style diet. The Arizona Pimas have the highest diabetes rate in the world, with a stunning 50% of tribe members between the ages of 30 and 64 suffering from Type 2.[90]

"Our results show that having a genetic predisposition to the disease doesn't mean that you'll develop Type 2 diabetes," says Leslie Schultz, PhD, who worked on the study. "If you can control your lifestyle, you can control, to a large extent, whether or not you develop the disease."[91]

---

*http://jnci.oxfordjournals.org/content/92/8/597.full

## Why You Can't Always Trust Conventional Medicine

Despite these impressive scientific studies about fiber, the ADA and a majority of physicians continue to under-recommend the amount of dietary fiber a person with diabetes should consume. Their suggestion—a meager 24 grams—is ridiculously inadequate. Every healthy adult needs at least *twice* that amount to prevent and reverse medical conditions such as hypertension, cardiovascular disease, obesity, and cancer, among others. And people with diabetes would benefit from even more.

Yet the average American consumes a scant 14 grams of dietary fiber a day—even less than the amount doctors are recommending. If you're eating a 2,500-calorie diet, you need a minimum of 35 to 40 grams of fiber every single day. And if you have diabetes, you should push this amount even higher—ideally 50 grams. How do you do it? Just follow the eating plan in this book and go to pages 375 to 402 for diabetes-healing recipes plus other helpful information about preparing delicious high-fiber meals.

**The SAD bottom line:** This is another clear example of how you can follow your doctor's orders religiously, take every drop of medication prescribed, eat the official ADA-recommended diabetes diet (which isn't very different than the Standard American Diet, appropriately abbreviated as SAD) and still succumb to this disease and its horrible complications. Not so on the 30-Day Diabetes Cure Plan. We want to see Type 2 people off medications *entirely*. In the case of injectable insulin, following this plan can lower your dosage to a minimal amount. This is the *only* way to kick this disease out of your life, improve the way you feel day-by-day, and live to see your grandkids grow up!

## The More You Eat, the More You'll Heal, "...So Eat Some Beans at Every Meal!"

That is the last line of a little ditty that every kid knew (at least when Jim was growing up) which began: "Beans, beans: Good for your heart..." As you have just read, beans *are* good for your heart—but they're even better for your blood glucose. The more you eat, the more you will heal. So, starting today, we want you to eat some beans at every meal. You won't need a heaping portion. A half-cup serving two or three times per day is perfect.

You already know that this relatively small amount of beans will produce enormous benefits. Beans are your best food friend, whether you are lowering your blood glucose, whittling your waistline, or trimming your grocery expenses. They are low in fat, full of nutrients, high in protein, loaded with fiber, and low in cost. They can be prepared in a myriad of styles and cuisines, so they always add variety to your meals. Eating beans every day will strengthen your diabetes-healing program immensely.

## Make Friends with Beans

Beans are members of the legume family, which includes lentils, split peas, string beans, and all dry beans. Black beans (20 grams of fiber per cup!) and red kidney beans (16 grams of fiber per cup) top the list for total fiber and resistant starches. Lentils and chickpeas (garbanzo beans) rate very low on the Glycemic Index, making them stars of the legume family in terms of stabilizing blood glucoses.

Start with your old favorites and then investigate the more exotic types you're not familiar with. There are more than 13,000 varieties of beans to choose from, so this could become quite an adventure! Here are some of our favorites: Adzuki beans, black beans, black-eyed peas, fava beans (also called broad beans), butter beans, calico beans, cannellini beans, chickpeas (also called garbanzos), edamame (green soybeans), Great Northern beans, Italian beans, kidney beans, lentils, lima beans, mung beans, navy beans, pinto beans, soy beans, split peas, white beans.

Test in pairs to take control of your glucose levels. Find out how the addition of beans to your daily diet stabilizes your blood glucose, and which types of beans have the best affect on your body.

## Beans at Breakfast

Beans are a breakfast staple in Mexico and in the southwestern part of the US. Perhaps you already eat beans with breakfast, but if not, today is a good time to start. Pinto and black beans are easy to incorporate into your breakfast because they pair so deliciously with most hot, savory breakfast items such as eggs, vegetables, avocados, and cheese. They also taste good with whole-grain tortillas. Add a huge scoop of salsa, which will give the dish even more flavor and double as a serving of vegetables.

If you are not already a bean-eater, you may need to start small because of their high fiber content. Try a small serving of black beans or refried beans as a side dish, and then build up to making beans your main dish.

The cheapest and easiest way to add beans to your breakfast is to make a batch ahead of time and store them in your fridge or freezer to be used as needed. Beans are easy to prepare from scratch—simply sort, soak, and boil. Season your beans to taste by adding a bit of salt, herbs, or spices.

Alternately, you can open a can of refried black beans, heat a half-cup portion and enjoy with scrambled eggs and some avocado slices for healthy fat. You may wish to sauté some tomatoes, onions and spicy chilies in butter or olive oil, add them to a serving of beans and melt a little grated cheese on top.

## Beans for Lunch

Bean burritos (use only 100% whole-grain tortillas, such as Ezekiel brand), bean soup and bean salad are all good lunch options. Bean burritos and bean soups are delicious served piping hot. If you are packing a lunch and cannot heat your beans, try bean salads with lettuce and chopped vegetables tossed in olive oil and vinegar. A small container of beans, or a bean burrito, makes for a portable lunch. If you have not yet become comfortable with the idea of beans as a main dish, try eating a small scoop alongside your regular lunch.

## Beans for Dinner

Beans and legumes shine at dinnertime because there are so many ways to prepare and enjoy them straight from the stovetop, crockpot, or the oven. Each food culture has its own distinctive recipes for beans, uniquely seasoned with spices typical of the region. These cultural flavors mean you can eat beans in many ways, without tiring of them. It also means that whatever your food preference, you can flavor your beans to reflect it.

If you like Mexican food, add cilantro, onion, chile (green or red), and cheese. If you enjoy Indian food, flavor your kidney beans or lentils with curry powder and garam masala. For a Moroccan flair, choose lima beans flavored with cumin, cinnamon, and pepper. The goal is to find the beans and flavors you enjoy so this new habit will become a lifestyle change that will continue to keep your blood pressure low for years to come.

## Snack on Beans and Legumes

Few people think of beans as between-meal snacks, but edamame, hummus, and various bean dips can help you eat your way to healthy blood pressure.

**Edamame.** These are green soybeans that are harvested while still young. They grow as pods with peas inside. They are eaten by squeezing the beans out with your fingers, making them great for days when you need a portable snack that is easily eaten straight from a container. Edamame is available at most grocery stores and can be purchased either frozen or fresh. Edamame requires little effort to prepare. Simply boil or steam and then sprinkle them with salt.

**Hummus.** This popular Middle Eastern favorite consists of mashed garbanzo beans (chickpeas) mixed with a spoonful of tahini (crushed sesame seed paste), lemon juice, olive oil, and sea salt. This dip is a healthy snack on its own, but becomes even more nutritious when paired with sliced fresh vegetables (called crudités).

**Bean dip.** Dips can be made from any kind of bean you choose. All healthy bean dips are basically mashed beans with seasoning. A creamy consistency is easy to attain with a blender or food processor. Add a little bit of extra virgin olive oil and lemon and season to taste. For a creamier bean dip, try mixing in plain Greek yogurt. Eat with whole grain pita triangles or raw, sweet red bell peppers and other sliced raw vegetables.

# Other Resistant Starch Superstars

Try out these other insoluble fiber rich foods to increase the healing of your diabetes:

**Bananas** (slightly green)

Resistant starch content: 6g per banana

Serving suggestions:

- Slice and mix with yogurt and oatmeal for breakfast.

- Dip in yogurt and roll in chopped nuts before freezing for a snack or dessert.

- Dice and toss with lemon juice, salt, sugar, and onion to make tangy banana chutney.

**Potatoes and Yams**

Resistant starch content: 4g per half cup

Serving suggestions:

- Serve cold potato salad tossed with olive oil and herbs as a side dish.

- Add chilled, chunked skin-on red potatoes to a salad.

- Puree sautéed yams, onion, and carrots to create a soup.

**Barley**

Resistant starch content: 3g per half cup

Serving suggestions:

- Sprinkle onto garden salads.

- Mix into tuna, chicken, or tofu salad.

- Add to chilled lentil salad.

**Brown Rice**

Resistant starch content: 3g per half cup

Serving suggestions:

- Order sushi with brown rice.

- Mix cooked brown rice with milk, raisins, and cinnamon for breakfast.

- Add to chilled marinated cucumbers as a side dish.

## Corn

Resistant starch content: 2g per half cup

Serving suggestions:

- Add to a taco salad, burrito, or quesadilla.

- Sprinkle into salsa or vegetarian refried beans.

- Make fresh corn relish with red bell pepper and onion.

## Today's Action Steps

- Stock your kitchen with a variety of beans.

- Start eating beans at every meal.

- Add beans in the morning, pack them for lunch, and build your dinners around your favorite beans and spices. Try snacking on edamame, hummus, and bean dips.

- Include some of the suggestions above in your next meal.

- Use Smart Monitoring to track the effect of beans on your blood glucose levels.

**Extra credit:** Try at least one new bean you have never tried before. Use Smart Monitoring to test the effect eating these diabetes-healing superfoods have on your blood glucose levels.

# DAY 19

# PRACTICE CONSCIOUS DINING

*"An ungrateful man is like a hog under a tree eating acorns,
but never looking up to see where they come from."*

—TIMOTHY DEXTER, businessman and author, 1748–1806

**Tip of the day:** Taking your time at the table will help you eat appropriate serving sizes, digest your food better, and deepen your gratitude and appreciation.

TODAY, YOU ARE GOING TO BEGIN PRACTICING CONSCIOUS DINING to slow down your meal and minimize overeating. You will see how to make mealtime more of a sensual, pleasurable experience by applying all five senses while you eat. One way to do this is to chew slowly, placing your fork down after each bite. You will learn how to minimize distractions and focus just on eating. The goal today is to replace mere "eating" with relaxed, conscious dining. Use Smart Monitoring to compare your blood glucose levels after a rushed meal versus a relaxed one.

## Slowing Down

Americans have become accustomed to eating quickly, often on the run. Too many of us are used to eating in a car, at a desk, or while walking from one place to another. Although on-the-go eating is sometimes unavoidable, more often than not it is simply a habit. When this habit is replaced with slow, conscious dining, we reap the benefits of more enjoyment from our food—and we eat less of it.

## Dine—Don't Just Eat

There is a big difference between eating and dining. All animals eat to sustain their bodies. But eating with awareness and conscious enjoyment turns this basic act of survival into an opportunity to add social grace and appreciation to our mealtimes.

It is no coincidence that people who describe their eating habits as "dining" also tend to have fewer issues with weight than those who eat on the run. When we make our meals small celebrations, we are more likely to chew, taste, and savor our food. Eating slowly and with more awareness allows our bodies the opportunity to extract more nutrients from our food; and it also allows intake-regulating hormones to signal when we are full rather than eating past full.

## Prepare Your Own Meals

Cooking for oneself also adds to the pleasure. Take time to plan, shop for, and prepare your own meals. This way, you will have complete control over your menu, the ingredients, and the healthfulness and flavor of your meals. This is a period of transition where you will move toward more healthful foods and learn to prepare them in ways you find more personally satisfying. Although the ultimate responsibility for your new food choices lies with you, it is helpful to bring those close to you along on your new journey. Friends and family can help you succeed in your new, healthier lifestyle. When preparing your own meals:

- **Take time to plan your meal ahead of time.**
- **Give yourself enough time to prepare your meal.**
- **Cook with your spouse, children, roommate, or friend.**

## Keep the Conversation Pleasant

Dining with others can sometimes encourage heated discussions that can turn divisive or even confrontational. Whether you are dining with friends or family, keep the conversation pleasant and light so as not to lose your focus on slow, mindful eating. Mealtime should be relaxed and fun, whether with friends, or with a spouse or children. Limit criticisms, business details, nagging, and lectures so that you and your fellow diners can concentrate on mindful eating. This can be difficult if you have children who refuse to eat what is served to them or who are causing trouble at the table. Still, it is best to focus on enjoying your meal and let other things go, if possible. Redirecting conversation can be artfully done, always remembering to keep it light, fun, and pleasant.

## Train Yourself to Recognize When You Are Near-Full

Check in with your stomach often. Eat only when your body is hungry. There is a difference between physical hunger and emotional eating, stress eating, addictive eating, eating from boredom, or appetite. Practice recognizing true hunger from appetite (the craving for a specific food or flavor) by following these steps (which are useful when battling food cravings between meals):

- **Close your eyes.**
- **Breathe deeply.**
- **Place a hand on your stomach.**
- **Focus your attention on your digestive system.**
- **Ask yourself if you are actually hungry, or if you are just thirsty.**

Often, people reach for food when they are, in fact, thirsty. Never deprive yourself of the food and nourishment your body and brain need. Skipping meals, low caloric intake, imbalanced meals, and nutrient deficiencies can damage your metabolism and may lead to binge eating.

People are so accustomed to eating until we feel "full," that it has become a habit. We suggest you experiment with calling it quits when your stomach feels 75% full. Many people find that they have more energy after mealtime when they do this. That means they can go for an after-dinner stroll around the neighborhood instead of retreating to the couch to let their food digest. If you can master this, you'll reap all sorts of benefits—not the least of which is weight loss and weight control. Try it!

## Focus on Your Meal

**Treat your senses.** Creating a meal comprised of foods that represent a variety of colors, shapes, textures, and flavors enhances your dining experience. Really notice your food. Feast your eyes on your meal before you take your first bite. Engage as many of your senses in the process as possible. Eat slowly and mindfully.

**Give thanks.** No religious affiliation is needed to appreciate the earth, the farmers, plus all the other people who helped make your meal possible. When someone is gracious enough to cook for you, always thank the chef, even when that chef is you. Remember that there are millions of people around the world who cannot eat because they do not have food. Feel your gratitude with every bite.

**Digestion begins in the mouth.** Slow down and really enjoy the flavors and textures on your tongue. Enzymes in your saliva begin the digestion process. Thoroughly chew every bite in order to facilitate full extraction of taste and nutrients.

**Enjoy your food.** Really taste and experience a single sunflower seed or bean sprout. Get in the habit of letting both food and beverages spend a little time in your mouth. We spend so much time avoiding certain foods or viewing food as the enemy that we forget it can be pleasurable and healing at the same time.

### Today's Action Steps

- Plan, create, and enjoy a wonderful dining experience as often as possible, beginning with at least one meal today.

- Pay attention to detail. Set the table. Create a relaxing atmosphere and start dining instead of just eating.

- Practice conscious dining by focusing on your meal and enjoying your food. Slow down and try to make your meal last for 20, or even 30, minutes.

- Recognize when you have eaten enough.

- Use Smart Monitoring to discover whether slowing down at meal times helps your glucose levels.

# DAY 20

# CONSIDER A DETOX PROGRAM

*"The first wealth is health."*

—RALPH WALDO EMERSON, American essayist and poet, 1803–1882

**Tip of the Day:** Fortify your body against toxins and detox in order to feel your best mentally, emotionally, and physically.

TOXINS ARE EVERYWHERE: in our water, food, air, and soil. Fortunately, following *The 30-Day Diabetes Cure* will give you one of the best detox programs around. You can also do a lot to boost the power of your liver and skin to help cleanse your body.

## You Don't Need a Detox "Diet"

Detox diets are all the rage in some corners, but we feel that most people don't need one. Let us remind you that you are already following one of the best there is. So keep up the good work. I do not recommend fad detox "cleansing" diets and fasting regimens because they dramatically disturb metabolism—and may even do long-term damage. People with diabetes need a steady source of nutrients to support blood glucose, so avoid these quick fixes. It is essential for you to reject any dietary protocol that could overstress your body's metabolism.[92] But here is what you can and should do to reduce your body's toxic load…

## Help Your Liver Do Its Job

Next to the pancreas, the liver is the most important organ in a diabetic's body. Your liver is your body's filter for toxins. It is simply an amazing toxin clearinghouse! All blood leaving your stomach and intestines flows first to the liver, which metabolizes nutrients and sends them off where they're needed. At the same time, it breaks down chemicals as it cleanses your blood of toxins such as alcohol and any chemicals you have ingested, absorbed, or inhaled. (The liver filters up to two liters of blood every minute.)

Pathogenic bacteria from the bloodstream is also screened by your liver, helping you resist infection. The bile your liver secretes helps break down fats in the blood so they can be absorbed for nourishment or stored for energy later. Your liver also produces cholesterol needed to carry fats through the body, for the creation of hormones and to keep the walls of your cells strong and healthy.

So be extra kind to your liver! Given its role in cleaning up your body's toxic load, you should not overload it or keep it too busy with one task (like clearing out alcohol by drinking); otherwise, it is not available when you need it to filter other environmental toxins.

## Detox Herbal Helpers

Chemical pollutants, exhaustion, poor eating habits, and chronic allergies can cause your liver to go sluggish. It is fine to use herbs to help the detox process along. After all, people have been doing it for thousands of years. Remember, though, that as your liver gets assistance from herbs in clearing the junk from your body, the toxins themselves will move through your bloodstream on their way out the door. This can cause temporary fatigue, a little malaise, nausea, or even a mild skin rash. (These are common symptoms that detoxification is occurring.) Start gently on low doses of detox herbs so you do not have any extreme results. Here are some of our favorites…

**Milk thistle.** This plant remedy has been used for more than 2,000 years[93] to protect the liver from damage and help it regenerate healthy cells. Multiple studies show that milk thistle is effective in protecting the liver from environmental toxins, including long-term alcohol use, plus pharmaceutical and over-the-counter drugs. Milk thistle's magic lies in the seeds that hold its active ingredient, *flavonolignans*, which actually alter cell membranes so that only tiny amounts of toxins can enter liver cells. It also stimulates protein synthesis for regeneration and repair of liver cells. In addition, these seeds contain essential fatty acids that serve as anti-inflammatory compounds in the liver.

Professional herbalists and alternative practitioners often recommend milk thistle as an herbal tincture for liver cleansing and healing—but you can also benefit from the capsule form. By stimulating the flow of bile through the liver, digestion improves along with elimination.

Visit a naturopath, clinical herbalist, or natural pharmacy for guidance on taking milk thistle. Generally, tinctures and extracts sold in natural foods stores can be taken by the dropper, added to a small amount of warm water. Start with one dropper once or twice a day and gradually increase it to two or three until you experience results. Milk thistle is often combined with licorice or dandelion, which also support liver health.

**Burdock.** This is another thistle herb used to cleanse the blood by helping your kidneys filter out impurities. Use a tincture of burdock along with milk thistle to ensure that toxins released from the liver do not hang around in your bloodstream very long.

**Turmeric.** Called the "king of spices," this Ayurvedic herb has long been used for liver cleansing. Its active ingredient is *curcumin*, a potent anti-inflammatory and antioxidant. Remember that your liver produces bile to move out toxins? Turmeric speeds the flow of bile and its toxic load. If you do not want to purchase supplements, just locate some organic turmeric and start sprinkling it on everything from eggs to chili. And while you are using it to boost liver function, you will also be boosting brain power. A study published by the *American Journal of Epidemiology* looked at the link between curry consumption (curry is made with turmeric) and brain function in older Asian adults. The researchers found that those who ate the most had the lowest rates of cognitive decline.[94]

There's even more good news if you are concerned about Alzheimer's (and people with diabetes should be, because they are at much higher risk). According to the *Journal of Neuroscience Research*, curcumin actually inhibits amyloid proteins from forming in the brain. These proteins are a hallmark of Alzheimer's.[95] Turmeric also helps with arthritis and prevents infections and also cancer. So, shake it on liberally!

## Your Skin Releases Toxins Too

Your body's largest organ is your skin—and it is a frontline detoxifier too. Just as skin absorbs toxins, it also purges them, releasing toxins in perspiration and body oils via sweat glands and oil glands. Sweat can even move out heavy metals such as mercury and oil-based toxins like petroleum products, which occur in many cosmetics. In keeping with the idea of a gentle detox, avoid extremes such as extended stays in any hot environment, which can be downright dangerous. Sweat it out in short spurts while keeping your cool by following these tips:

- Work up a sweat by exerting yourself with vigorous exercise regularly to stimulate perspiration and detoxing.

- Sweat in a sauna, steam room, or hot tub to open up pores and warm your body, which helps mobilize even more toxins to exit via the skin. Just a few minutes in any of these, with lots of fresh cool water afterward to replenish your liquid reserves, can be remarkably effective in releasing toxins through the skin.

- Drink a liberal amount of fresh water throughout the day to support normal perspiration, which also eliminates unfriendly chemicals.

## Today's Action Steps

•Commit to clearing toxins from your body by using *The 30-Day Diabetes Cure* as your main detox program.

•Support your body's natural detox system by drinking lots of fresh water and exercising until you sweat.

•Strengthen your liver with milk thistle and turmeric. And keep eating high-fiber foods to maintain good elimination.

•Discuss with your doctor testing your body's level of toxins.

•Use the Smart Monitoring system of testing in pairs to find out how the steps suggested today affect your blood glucose levels.

**Extra credit:** Schedule time for yourself in a sauna, steam room, or hot tub today.

# DAY 21

# SLEEP LONGER AND BETTER

*"Sleep that knits up the ravelled sleave of care*
*The death of each day's life, sore labour's bath*
*Balm of hurt minds, great nature's second course,*
*Chief nourisher in life's feast."*

—WILLIAM SHAKESPEARE

**Tip of the Day:** Establishing good sleep patterns will make a positive difference in your health.

WHEN DID SO MANY OF US forget how to get enough sleep? One of the most important self-healing functions of the human body, good sleep, is being completely disrupted by the 21st-century trio of over-commitment, over-stimulation, and overwork. We pay dearly for our constant physical and mental stress with shorter nights and less restful sleep. Studies show that a majority of Americans are walking through their day sleep-deprived. And that is making us sick.

## Skip Sleep and This Is What Happens

On Day 11, we explained the link between stress and insulin resistance. Sleep deprivation places enormous stress on your body and by so doing worsens insulin resistance. This in turn boosts your risk of developing diabetes and increases its severity if you're trying to manage the condition.

Women who slept just five hours a night were 250% more likely to have diabetes compared with those who got seven or eight hours, a study published in the *Archives of Internal Medicine*[96] reports. In other research, scientists looked at healthy young men who slept only four hours a night for six nights in a row. Their findings were shocking: Insulin and blood glucose levels of these young guys mirrored those of people with prediabetes. You read that right. In just one week of disturbed sleep habits, they developed a prediabetic condition. This is what's going on inside you when you're sleep deprived...

**Your cortisol levels skyrocket.** In a 2001 study published in *Journal of Clinical Endocrinology & Metabolism*[97], researchers showed that chronic insomnia leads to high levels of the stress hormone *cortisol*, in addition to hyperactivity of stress-response pathways in the brain.

Cortisol release is intended as a temporary energy-booster, activated during the fight-or-flight response to get you out of real danger quickly. It triggers a rush of glucose so you get an immediate burst of energy. But cortisol is also released during the drum-drum-drumbeat of chronic everyday stress, cranking up your cravings for fast carb foods, which lead to weight gain. High cortisol levels also suppress your immune system and disrupt blood glucose metabolism. The solution is to sleep longer (and better) to keep cortisol levels lower.

**Your appetite becomes out of whack.** Here's another major disruption caused by lack of sleep—appetite regulation. A delicate hormone balance normally keeps your appetite in check: The hormone leptin is responsible for signaling your brain: "I'm full, stop eating." *Ghrelin* is the hormone that tells your brain, "I need fuel. Let's eat." When you're deprived of consistent restful sleep, according to researchers at University of Chicago, leptin drops by some 18% (so you don't know when to stop eating) and ghrelin shoots up (making you feel even hungrier) by almost 30%. This is how sleep deprivation triggers overeating.[98]

**You'll put on weight.** Researchers at the Stanford School of Medicine found that sleep-deprived subjects had an increase in Body Mass Index (BMI) *regardless of their diet or exercise activity*. Interpreted, this means that no matter how closely you watch your food intake or how much you exercise, less sleep will increase your weight regardless.[99]

## Prescription Sleeping Pills Aren't the Answer

Getting into a pattern of healthy sleep—eight or nine hours with minimal interruptions—takes a little know-how and some new "sleep skills." Sleeping pill manufacturers, on the other hand, are counting on you not wanting to go through the trouble. They're not interested in what might be contributing to your inability to sleep. They simply want to sell you a pill that will knock you out. But at what cost? These drugs disrupt your natural metabolism, leading to unpleasant side effects and the very real possibility of addiction.

Statistics show that 10% of the US adult population has trouble sleeping, with three out of 10 individuals experiencing occasional sleeplessness. According to the National Sleep Foundation, only 56% of Americans say they get a "good night's sleep" on a typical work or school night. As more and more American's struggle to get enough sleep, the sleep aid business has skyrocketed. Spending related to sleep has increased 8.8% annually since 2008, reaching about $32 billion in 2012.*

What else do you get along with this artificially-derived sleep? Next-day drowsiness, depression, memory loss, and addiction. Those are just a few examples of how these chemical intrusions disrupt your delicate metabolic processes. More bizarre are the stories of sleep-walking, sleep-eating, sleep-cooking, and even sleep-driving that people on these heavily advertised sleep drugs have reported. In 2007, the FDA required strong warnings on the packaging of many sleep meds because of these dangerous side effects.

---

*http://business.time.com/2012/08/15/dont-nap-on-this-why-the-business-of-sleep-will-keep-booming/

# Be Aware of Your Sleep Habits

We encourage you to become more aware of your sleep habits and to begin making positive changes in your life that can contribute to peaceful, restful nights. By doing this, you'll be lowering your blood glucose, increasing your insulin sensitivity, and healing your diabetes. The first step to good sleep is to realistically assess your own sleep patterns so you can identify the reasons you're not getting a good night's sleep. Here's what we recommend…

**Smart monitor your sleep.** Test your blood glucose levels after a sleep-deprived night. Then try testing after you've had a good night's sleep. Do you notice any changes to your blood glucose levels? What do these changes tell you?

**Keep a journal.** As simple as it sounds, just keeping track of how many hours you sleep (or don't sleep) and how you spend the last few hours of the day can help you make important changes. On page 91 of your Success Planner, the companion workbook you received with this book, jot down sleep-related issues, such as what you ate for dinner, how much coffee or tea you had throughout the day, whether you drank alcohol, what you watched on TV, how late you worked, or what thoughts dominated your evening conversations. These can all affect the quality and quantity of sleep, as can napping during the day.

**Deal with stress effectively (again).** Before doing anything else, go back to Day 11 and revisit our discussion on stress. Worry, anxiety, and fear fuel sleepless nights. So do relationship issues, being overcommitted, and having financial problems. If you haven't addressed the stresses in your life yet, you need to do this now so you can start sleeping well for your health's sake. Unraveling the underlying causes of your sleeplessness puts you on track to resolve it, instead of just covering it up with a prescription.

**Make healthy lifestyle choices.** While it's true that some medications or illnesses contribute to sleep disturbances, in general sleep problems are caused by external activities interfering with your metabolism. That means changing your habits can most likely lead to positive improvements in your quality of sleep.

# Take Time to Wind Down Naturally

One of the most effective means of ensuring a night of deep sleep is to set aside time to unwind before getting into bed. These low-impact ideas can help create a calm transition from your busy day to a quiet night of restful sleep. Read on for some specific tips…

■**Limit coffee/tea consumption to one or two cups before noon, and none after that.**
Caffeine is a stimulant and can take several hours to fully metabolize, but everyone responds differently to caffeine. One person's afternoon pick-me-up is another's insomnia, so adjust your intake according to your own responses—or eliminate caffeine entirely. Testing in pairs will help you understand the effect caffeine has on you. Of course, sodas and "energy drinks" are already off-limits, because they are high in sugar (another stimulant). Alcohol is another known sleep-disrupter, which is one more good reason to limit your total consumption to one or two drinks with dinner.

■**Stop work-related activity two hours before bedtime**. This includes computer use, reading files, making calls, texting, checking (and responding to) email. People who work at home may find it difficult to unplug, but even people who commute to an office often find it nearly impossible to separate home-life from work activity in today's tight economy. This incessant involvement with work not only deprives you of family life and "me time," but it's also stressful. And this constant mental activity keeps your brain too revved up to sleep. Give yourself a break by taking time off work in the evening before bed.

■**Turn off the TV and computer.** Changing your TV/computer/video viewing habits might be one of the most important ways to ensure a peaceful night's sleep. Stop watching the news close to bedtime, and tune out anything else that is mentally stimulating. Instead of being discouraged by the nightly crime report, use the last couple of hours of the evening for rote, calming tasks.

■**Take up calming activities in the evening.** Find evening activities that are calming, such as reading, writing in your journal, or just listening to quiet music. Sort your laundry, clean the kitchen, prepare tomorrow's lunch. Jim likes to make the rounds in his house, checking every room, putting things in order, and closing the curtains in a meditative mind state. Remember, you don't have to be doing something all the time. Sometimes just making a to-do list relieves you of the feeling you have to accomplish everything now. Evening is also a good time to practice gentle yoga, meditation, and other relaxation techniques.

■**Reset your inner clock.** If you're in the habit of staying up past midnight and yet get up at dawn, it's time to reset your inner clock. To do this, give your body all the necessary bedtime cues much earlier than usual: Put on your PJs, brush your teeth, and pretend it's bedtime a couple hours earlier than you usually retire. Keep your house quiet and the lights low so your body can adjust by winding down naturally. If you have a social life that keeps you out late several nights a week, it's time to reassess the value of that versus the damage your lack of restful sleep may be doing to your health.

■**Count backwards from 100.** Here's how Jim falls asleep every night: Once in bed, he closes his eyes and begins breathing consciously, counting each exhale backwards from 100. He focuses his mind fully on this activity and nothing else. It's a rare night that he makes it to 80.

■**Other possibilities.** Exercise revs up your metabolism, so do it early in the day, not in the evening. Take a bath in the evening to de-stress, detox, and relax. Sip a warm glass of milk (which contains calming calcium as well as slow-digesting fat and protein) 30 minutes before going to bed. Chamomile tea is another time-tested calming influence.

■**Calm yourself back to sleep.** If you wake up in the middle of the night and can't get back to sleep, get out of bed for a while and putter around your house. Don't watch TV or turn on the computer, though. Instead, read a poem or a calming novel. On those rare occasions when this happens to Jim, he sits quietly and meditates until he's sleepy again.

# Sleepy Supplements

Sometimes a supplement taken regularly over time can help reset your body's natural sleep rhythms. There are a wide variety of herbs, vitamins, and minerals that help support sound sleep and target different sleep-related problems. That's why it's best to understand your own sleep patterns and stress levels *before* trying supplements.

Most supplements work best over time, so do some research. Choose one that reflects your own experience, and give it a few weeks to see if it works before stopping or switching to another. Take the lowest recommended dosage, notify your physician of whatever you're taking, and follow our guidelines for buying quality supplement products. Here are the most effective that we recommend…

**GABA (***gamma-aminobutyric acid***).** This neurotransmitter (brain chemical) has a calming effect. Some even call it the brain's "natural Valium." Low levels of GABA can lead to anxiety symptoms, palpitations, and irritability, all of which can result in disrupted or poor-quality sleep. Eating complex slow carbs increases the amino acid *glutamine*, which is a precursor to GABA. Other foods that can help increase your natural stores of GABA include almonds, bananas, brown rice, broccoli, spinach, and whole-grain oats. You can also take GABA supplements (500 to 1,000 mg spread out through the day with meals).

**Taurine.** This amino acid also works in the brain to calm anxiety as well as irritability and restlessness. It works by inhibiting the release of adrenaline, the "fight-or-flight" hormone released during stress. (Bonus: Taurine also improves insulin sensitivity.) A component of meat, eggs, dairy products, and shellfish—taurine is particularly beneficial to eye health by protecting the cornea from UV ray damage and preventing macular degeneration. It's also beneficial for cardiovascular health (it lowers blood pressure and cholesterol). You should be getting plenty of taurine in your diet if you're eating animal protein, but if you want to try a supplement to see if it helps you sleep, take 500 to 1,000 mg before bed and on an empty stomach.

**5-HTP.** *5-hydroxytryptophan* is an amino acid that's a precursor to serotonin (one of the "feel good" hormones) and is also involved in tryptophan metabolism. Serotonin and tryptophan are both involved in resolving stress and anxiety. When in balance, they promote a restful night's sleep. 5-HTP has become a go-to supplement for mild depression, and it's sometimes recommended for sleeplessness as well. Follow the dosage directions on the label.

**Tryptophan.** This amino acid is the one food writers like to mention around Thanksgiving in articles about people falling asleep after eating their turkey dinner. Turkey (like all protein sources) is high in tryptophan, which works with serotonin and melatonin to help you get enough sleep and also move through your day with a sense of harmony and balance. Follow dosage directions on the label and take tryptophan with vitamin B6 for maximum effectiveness.

**Melatonin.** This is Mother Nature's "sleep hormone"—but your body's production of it decreases with age and stress. It's often recommended as a supplement to combat jet lag. In a normal metabolism, levels of melatonin rise in the evening, stay high during the night and then drop around dawn. The amount of light you're exposed to affects your body's production of melatonin, so when the winter days are short and dark, melatonin increases, often making us feel sleepy or depressed during the day. People who work at night can find it hard to sleep during the day because their melatonin levels drop just when they need more to help them get to sleep. Melatonin can have powerful effects on your metabolism and may cause next-day grogginess. Effective dosages vary widely, so we recommend you work with a trained practitioner in trying it.

**Vitamin B6: This vitamin specifically counteracts high levels of the stress hormone cortisol.** If you have chronically high cortisol levels (waking at 2 am, 4 am, and 6 am is a common symptom) take 50 to 100 mg of vitamin B6 before going to bed. But remember: No supplement can halt cortisol release as well as learning to deeply relax can.

## Today's Action Steps

•Adjust your pre-bedtime ritual to include at least a few of the suggestions above.

•Replace your sleep-disturbing habits with a new "deep sleep" routine to help calm your mind and wind down from the activity of the day.

# DAY 22

# ADD YOGA

*"Blessed are the flexible, for they shall not be bent out of shape."*

—ROBERT LUDLUM, American novelist, 1927–2001

**Tip of the Day:** Yoga offers both physical and emotional benefits by providing gentle physical activity at a calming, meditative pace.

IT'S TIME TO UNPLUG. It's time to deepen your relaxation. It's time to focus your energy on healing not only your body, but also your mind and your heart. It's time for some "time out." To remember to breathe deeply. To release your hold on all the problems of the world. And to bring your entire self back to a state of natural balance and harmony. It's time to heal with yoga.

## Yoga for Your Health

Yoga is a gentle "mindful movement" practice that's tailor-made for people with diabetes—both for its positive physical effects, as well as for superior stress relief. As a physical exercise, yoga offers muscle toning, flexibility, and cardiovascular benefits at a calm, gentle, no-impact pace, making it ideal for people with chronic illness. Various movements and postures (called *asanas*) serve to stimulate different organs, including your liver, kidneys, and adrenal glands, which results in more effective natural detoxification within your body.

Yoga movements also stimulate the vagus nerve, which extends from your brainstem all the way down to your abdomen, carrying vital information to and from the brain. The vagus nerve is responsible for controlling your heart rate, breathing, and the entire digestive system, among other essential functions. Stimulating the vagus nerve usually causes the heart rate to slow, one of the first steps in stress reduction. Regular yoga practice can tone your heart muscle, banish depression, boost energy levels, and balance your hormones and blood chemistry. Test in pairs and find out how adding regular yoga practice affects your blood glucose. Test before, immediately after, and again two hours later to get the best idea of how yoga practice affects your blood glucose levels.

## Studies Prove It

The Center for the Study of Complementary and Alternative Therapies at the University of Virginia Health Systems reviewed more than two dozen scientific studies on yoga for Type 2 diabetes.[100]Their research revealed impressive healing benefits of yoga for people with diabetes, including lowering fasting glucose and after-meal glucose by 33%, plus decreasing A1C by up to 27%. Other benefits included lowering total cholesterol by 20% and LDL (bad) cholesterol by up to 8%, while pushing up HDL (good) cholesterol by up to 4%. Decreases in body weight (up to 8%) were also shown.

Researchers at Ohio State University found that regular yoga practice can significantly lower inflammation.[101] Fifty women participated in the study—half had just begun to practice yoga and the other half had been at it twice a week for two years. Blood samples were taken after yoga practice, light treadmill walking, and during a stress test. All the women who didn't regularly practice yoga had 41% higher levels of pro-inflammatory cytokine IL-6, a substance that increases dangerous inflammation in the body.

Keeping a regular schedule of moderate exercise such as yoga helps your body use blood sugar more effectively, serving as a sort of natural "active insulin." Increased physical activity pumps more blood into your muscles and puts glucose to work as fuel. More efficient use of blood sugar also makes your system more responsive to insulin. As you begin to reduce fat and build muscle, your entire cardiovascular system operates more efficiently as well, cutting your risk of further illness and complications. This will result in more stable blood glucose levels, which you can measure by testing in pairs.

## Yoga for Stress Relief—and More

The physical benefits are only one part of yoga's appeal. Yoga is all about balance, both outer and inner, and that balance is what can free you from stress. Yoga calms the mind because it requires concentrated attention, not just on body postures, but also on your breathing. This union of breath and body brings about a peaceful state of mind, as well as a more efficient and healthy body.

Another important aspect of regular yoga practice is its emphasis on mindful living (paying close attention) in a larger context. This isn't just reserved for your body and your breath during poses. The cultivation of mindfulness also extends into your everyday behaviors and choices. You've already learned the powerful health impact that comes from making good food choices and by understanding exactly what's in most of the processed foods you once ate. You've started paying closer attention by reading labels and expanding your awareness of the choices available to you. And you're learning to distinguish between a craving, appetite and genuine hunger. Yoga helps you extend this practice by reinforcing it through a steady commitment to mindfulness in all aspects of life.

Mindfulness is yet another key to reducing stress, because just as paying close attention to your good health becomes habitual, so too does control over your responses to stress-producing circumstances, whether spontaneous, chronic, or avoidable.

## Yoga Can Cure Cravings, Too

In July of 2005, Deborah T. felt faint at work and headed for the restroom. On the way, she blacked-out, fell, and broke her ankle. After a few days, she noticed one of her toes was turning a dark color—a sign of poor circulation. Several years later, Deborah found herself prediabetic, suffering from neuropathy, and overweight. "Although I have several family members with prediabetes or diabetes, I never really saw it coming," she says. What changed Deborah was going on *The 30-Day Diabetes Cure Plan.*

Deborah committed to exercising to get her blood sugar in check. These days, she walks or jogs about two miles a day and has made yoga and meditation a part of her daily routine. When she's feeling the urge for a cookie or some chocolate, her meditation practice helps her to analyze why she wants certain foods. "Whenever I feel a craving, I do yoga," she says. She's found alternatives to satisfy her sweet tooth. Green tea with stevia is her favorite.

Her new dietary staples are vegetables, oatmeal, eggs, and beans. She loves apples, oranges, strawberries, and other fruits for dessert. She stopped eating bread and other gluten-containing foods to help reduce inflammation. "That one step made me feel like a different person," she adds.

"I took my health into my own hands. I researched and researched," she says.

Her work has really paid off. Deborah has successfully prevented herself from developing full-fledged diabetes, her neuropathy was stopped in its tracks, and she has lost 70 pounds since starting *The 30-Day Diabetes Cure.* "I honestly feel like a new person!" she beams.

## Embarking on a Yoga Practice

Although yoga is a 5,000-year-old practice, it was perhaps inevitable that our contemporary culture would embrace yoga as a popular fitness activity. Yoga studios offer an alternative to weight lifting, aerobics, and conventional gym exercises—but all can be complementary in a comprehensive, integrated fitness program.

Practicing yoga with a class can provide motivation, support and added commitment. But if joining a class at your local yoga studio seems a daunting prospect, you may want to search out a private teacher for a few sessions to get you started. Learning yoga privately with individual attention may help you create a positive new ritual to start your day, in the privacy of your own home. Yoga specialists who focus on therapeutic yoga for specific health conditions will have a better understanding of the challenges you face with diabetes. To locate someone near you, go online and Google "private yoga instruction" and the name of your town. You could also visit a local yoga studio and ask if instructors offer private sessions—many do. Or just start your practice at home by following a DVD.

## Primers for Your Practice

**Keep it calm and gentle.** Leave the "power yoga" classes to others. You're seeking a gentle and calm form of yoga to heal your diabetes, such as Integrative Yoga Therapy, Vini-yoga, and Integral. Avoid upside-down postures if you have retinopathy. Shoulder stands, head stands, and even forward bends can increase pressure in the eyes. If you have questions about this, ask your ophthalmologist before starting. Diabetics with neuropathy or foot problems will want to take extra care to position themselves near a wall so that support is readily available. It's also wise to get a pair of thick-soled shoes to protect your feet and toes against injury.

**Consult your doctor about your medications.** Like the new food choices you've been making, you'll find that yoga does lower your blood sugar. That's a beneficial effect, but if you're taking medication, ask your doctor to adjust your drugs to accommodate your new health status.

**Eat smartly before your practice.** It's often recommended that you not eat for several hours before practicing yoga; but again, if you're taking medication, this may upset both your blood sugar and your energy levels. Follow your own diabetes regimen, eat something light (such as a vegetable and protein snack combination), and there won't be a problem.

**Get started today.** The free beginner's guide that accompanied your purchase of this book (titled *Healing Diabetes with Yoga*) contains a dozen basic yoga postures for people with diabetes, complete with photos (of Jim!) and instructions.

## Today's Action Steps

- Pick up an instructional yoga DVD and ease into your practice in the comfort of your home.

- Research local yoga studios and sign up for a class.

- Use Smart Monitoring to see how your blood glucose levels stabilize after a yoga session. As with other exercise routines, remember to test your blood glucose levels before, immediately after, and again two hours after your yoga practice.

**Extra credit:** Put on some comfy clothes and look through the basic yoga postures in the Special Report *Healing Diabetes with Yoga*. Pick just one and try it right now. Add a new one every day until you can perform the entire series.

# DAY 23

# REDUCE DEPRESSION AND BOREDOM

*"Hope is the thing with feathers*
*That perches in the soul*
*And sings the tune without the words*
*And never stops at all."*

—EMILY DICKINSON, American poet, 1830–1886

**Tip of the Day:** It is possible to roll back your "diabetes blues"—or prevent them entirely —by changing your routine in a few important ways.

HERE'S A DEPRESSING STATISTIC: The incidence of depression among people with diabetes is two times higher than in the general population.[102] It's easy to see why this is the case. Diabetes is a difficult medical condition to live with. Type 2 patients are told to constantly monitor their glucose levels, watch their diets, exercise more, and lose weight. This relentless demand for self-monitoring and self-control can take a serious toll on mental health. Many live in constant fear of heart disease and other complications. There's the energy-draining discomfort of physical symptoms and the difficulties of overcoming them (not to mention side effects from those drugs, too). Then there's the sense of not having control over your body or your life. Who wouldn't be depressed?

The sad fact is that people who have diabetes *and* depression often forget to test themselves, take their medication on time (if at all), exercise or eat at regular intervals. As depression becomes more severe, they're likely to give up their treatment regimen entirely.

## What It Means to Be Clinically Depressed

Depression can be traced to a chemical imbalance that affects not only how you face your day, but also how you think about yourself and your world. The brain has over 300 neuropeptides that allow you to function. Most important are serotonin, GABA, acetylcholine, and dopamine. Serotonin, the neurotransmitter (brain chemical) responsible for good moods, feelings of confidence, security, relaxation, calmness, and emotional balance is usually involved. Low levels of it can affect your sleep patterns and concentration…your interest in work and daily activities…your relationships and family life…even your sex drive.

Decreased serotonin plays a key role in the development of depression as well as anxiety, fatigue, insomnia, low self-esteem, low levels of concentration, plus a host of illnesses that stem from chronic depression. In a way, this diagnosis is less about your low moods than it is about a "depression" of your serotonin levels.

In addition, symptoms of depression or brain-chemistry imbalance can include such eating disorders as anorexia (under-eating), overeating that leads to excessive weight gain and bulimia (routine binge eating and purging).

## The Link Between Diabetes and Depression

The pharmaceutical approach to depression (including antidepressants such as Prozac and Paxil) attempts to concentrate your existing serotonin in an effort to boost its effectiveness. What these drugs *don't* do is increase your brain's levels of serotonin. In fact, some studies show they may actually *reduce* your natural serotonin levels over long-term use.

Certain foods, on the other hand, play a major role in maintaining brain chemistry, and can actually help your brain make enough serotonin so that you feel better and more emotionally stable, even in the face of discomfort or crisis. We'll describe some specific "mood foods" in a moment, but first, it's important to understand that brain chemistry works on the same principles as the rest of your body's chemical make-up. When functioning normally, your entire body is like a finely tuned race car. Every engine part relies on all the others in a delicate dance of cooperation and synergy. If an air hose has a slight blockage, over time the entire engine will suffer from a lack of adequate circulation. If there's a malfunction in your blood glucose chemistry, it's quite likely that a brain chemistry imbalance will follow.

When you lack the proper nutritional components to support the conversion of one chemical to another in the brain, you end up with a chronic imbalance in your brain chemistry as well as the rest of your metabolism. Result? Debilitating disease and serious depression.

Here's another twist to that concept: Depression is one of the indicators of the possibility of *developing* diabetes, meaning a scientific correlation between mental/emotional health and blood sugar metabolism is apparent—but the depression may actually come first. In a 2004 study at Johns Hopkins that tracked more than 11,000 middle-aged adults over six years who initially were not diabetic, scientists found that symptoms of depression actually predicted a later diagnosis of Type 2 diabetes. And a Kaiser-Permanente study of almost 1,700 people found that those with diabetes were more likely to have been treated for depression within the six months before their diabetes diagnosis—and that 84% of diabetics reported having "depressive episodes" earlier in their lives.[103]

## The Diet-Depression Connection

Poor diet can predict a risk for depression and other mental illnesses in the same way it does for heart disease. That's what a study published in the *British Journal of Psychiatry*[104] found. Another research project reported in the *American Journal of Psychiatry*[105]analyzed the dietary habits of more than 1,000 women, ranking them according to their psychological symptoms.[106] The women whose diets mirrored our 30-day plan—high in vegetables and fruit, meat and fish and whole grains—showed a correspondingly lower incidence of depression and anxiety. Women who had a higher incidence of depression and anxiety partook of a diet of fried foods, fast-carb refined grain products, sugary foods, and beer—the very same eating habits we've been urging you to abandon in order to heal your diabetes.

**Foods that depress your serotonin.** Since you began *The 30-Day Diabetes Cure*, we've been encouraging you to abandon the foods that caused your blood sugar imbalance: Sugar and sweets, sodas, fast carbs, high fructose corn syrup, trans fats, and refined vegetable oils with excessive omega-6 fatty acids and not enough omega-3s. Why? Because these foods encourage rampant inflammation, damage blood vessels, create dysfunction in your blood-sugar metabolism, increase your risk of heart disease and stroke, kidney failure, blindness, and limb amputation; and shorten your life span. These same foods also depress your serotonin levels and can trigger depression.

**Other factors that deplete serotonin.** Equally harmful to serotonin are chronic stress… excessive use of stimulants such as caffeine…alcohol and other drugs of abuse…cigarette smoking…and insufficient sleep. Depressed levels of serotonin in turn continue to disrupt sleep (because serotonin is required to create *melatonin*, the sleep hormone). And of course, lack of sleep can cause you to be even more depressed, more stressed, and to gain weight through overeating.

That's how low serotonin triggers junk food binges. In an effort to relieve stress and comfort your brain, you begin to crave fast carbs to stimulate a serotonin rush. Unfortunately, this only makes you feel good for a short time before your blood glucose plunges again. Like a junk food junkie, you keep coming back, trying to "self-medicate" with fast carbs and creating even more serotonin spikes and dips.

## Foods that Raise Your Serotonin—and Your Spirits

Follow the nutritional advice outlined in *The 30-Day Diabetes Cure* and you'll be choosing foods that boost your serotonin levels naturally to help stave off both depression *and* your recurring cravings for junky foods.

Foods that contain the amino acid *tryptophan* (including turkey, which is why you feel like dozing off after Thanksgiving dinner) are especially good for elevating serotonin levels in the brain. Tryptophan is not produced by your body—you get it strictly from food sources. Serotonin production is also supported by B vitamins, calcium, magnesium, omega-3 essential fatty acids, plus the essential fatty acid omega-6 (when taken in the right proportion to omega-3).

Where do you find these serotonin-supporting substances? Besides that Thanksgiving turkey, these vitamins, minerals, amino acids, and essential fats are found in naturally raised meats, eggs, fish, and dairy products—plus whole grains, leafy green vegetables, soy foods, nuts, and seeds. All of these are staples of our 30-day eating plan. Stick with the foods we've been recommending and you'll be improving your brain chemistry and your moods will brighten as a result. Your sleeping patterns will improve. You'll feel calmer and less anxious. And your ability to cope when faced with stress will surprise you.

## Supplements That Combat Depression

A supplement regimen can be integral in treating depression. Consult a natural practitioner to determine the supplements and doses that are best for you. Below are detailed descriptions of the supplements that we believe are the most effective at combating depression...

**Tryptophan.** A 1992 study reported in the *International Journal of Neuroscience*[107] confirms that tryptophan can stimulate the proper function of serotonin in the brain, thus alleviating mild depression. (Many antidepressant drugs work to increase the amount of serotonin in the brain, usually by preventing the serotonin from being depleted.) Tryptophan actually increases serotonin levels, and has the advantage of doing it without the adverse side effects associated with antidepressant drugs. Tryptophan should be taken on an empty stomach so it won't compete with other amino acids for absorption. We recommend taking vitamin C and a B-complex supplement along with tryptophan to facilitate the formation of serotonin. (But speak with your doctor before increasing your vitamin C intake.) The recommended dose is 500–1,000 mg taken at bedtime because it also helps induce sleep.

**5-HTP.** Serotonin is made from the amino acid *5-hydroxy tryptophan* (5-HTP), which itself is made from tryptophan. As you've just read, not getting enough tryptophan can cause depression. And while eating tryptophan-rich foods is often helpful, some people occasionally need supplemental help. More than 25 clinical studies comparing 5-HTP and SSRI antidepressants showed that this supplement is just as effective—and sometimes even better.[108] Other studies show that 5-HTP helps induce sleep and limit appetite as well as improving mood by increasing serotonin. You must be careful, and better yet, have your levels tested and a natural practitioner determine the right dosage—by raising serotonin, you can lower your dopamine and feel tired. You need to balance both.

**Folic acid.** Studies show that people are more likely to be depressed when they have low blood levels of B vitamins—particularly B6, B12 and folic acid—or high blood levels of the protein *homocysteine* (which, interestingly, signals the presence of inflammation and a deficiency in those three B vitamins). Coincidentally, these people are also less likely to feel better after taking antidepressants. Having a high homocysteine level actually doubles a woman's risk of developing depression. But there's good news: The higher your level of homocysteine, the more likely folic acid will work for you. Studies have shown that patients treated with folic acid improved their Hamilton Rating scores (a standardized measure of depression symptoms) by more than 50% after 10 weeks compared with those taking antidepressants.[109]

**Fish oil.** Numerous studies show the omega-3 fatty acids in fish oil (particularly its EPA, or *eicosapentaenoic acid*) are beneficial for mild depression.[110] In fact, EPA seems to be a natural antidepressant, and that's confirmed by six double-blind clinical trials that showed significant improvement with fish oil. If you're not already taking fish oil every day, we urge you to start—especially if you're feeling depressed.

Shop for a product that contains 500 mg DHA/EPA (300 mg DHA and 200 mg EPA). Take one or two capsules daily. Larger doses of fish oil can decrease the effectiveness of some glucose-lowering drugs and cause your blood glucose to rise, so always talk to your doctor before starting a new supplement. Use fish oil with caution if you're on the blood glucose-lowering medications *glipizide* (Glucotrol and Glucotrol XL), *glyburide* (Micronase or DiaBeta), *metformin* (Glucophage), or insulin. Excessive omega-3 supplementation may increase your need for these medications.

## The Big Boost from Exercise

Numerous studies also show that regular physical activity elevates serotonin levels enough to prevent and chase away mild depression.[111] As you'll recall, on Day 11 we suggested specific ways to de-stress your nervous system. Often, these steps dramatically improve depression and sleep problems. Incorporating a few of yesterday's exercise suggestions will start you on the right path.

## Eliminate Boredom

Boredom results from habitual, mind-numbing behaviors and routines. It's the opposite of pleasure, passion, adventure, education, and perpetual growth. When life lacks excitement, food fills the void. When eating is a person's central entertainment, big trouble ensues.

Chronic boredom numbs the senses and encourages destructive compensating behaviors such as overeating, alcoholism, smoking, plus recreational drug use and prescription drug abuse. When you're bored, your brain desires these quick fixes because it's either screaming, "Make me feel alive!" or "Please stop the pain!"

"Virtual reality" is replacing the real thing—but living our life through others isn't satisfying us. Our senses are being numbed by lack of stimulation. One tragic result is that eating has become our chief source of pleasure and entertainment. Food serves as a powerful mind-altering drug that blunts our day-to-day pain.

## Pick Up Healthy Habits

We believe it is vital for all of us—and particularly for those suffering from depression—to become passionate about something and pursue it with ardor. So, today, we're going to re-set your GPS for a new destination, one that takes you outside your comfort zone and pushes you toward new horizons.

**Get outdoors.** Simply climbing off the couch and getting outside is a great way to become more active. The cloistered habitats we have created are increasingly removed from the beauty and healing power of the natural world. So, if you're feeling down in the dumps, perk yourself up by going for a walk, taking a hike, or participating in some other physical activity outdoors.

**Take a short sunbath.** Lack of sunlight can be a factor in the development of depression. Melatonin, a neurotransmitter that helps control sleep, may overproduce in people who spend too much time indoors or in the dark. This can cause fatigue, lethargy, and depression. Poor indoor air quality may also affect mood. Spending just a few minutes outside each day can help relieve depression.

**Develop a social network.** People suffering from depression tend to isolate themselves, but this can further increase depression. Reach out to a friend whose company you have been missing, or invite a family member to visit. Even picking up the phone and having a meaningful conversation with a friend or family member can reduce feelings of isolation. (Sorry, Facebook doesn't count.) Participating in a community event or volunteering for an organization you support are more ways to reduce your isolation and perk yourself up.

**Develop positive self-talk.** People suffering from depression often have negative thoughts about their worth, capabilities, and value. It is important to understand that you can change these negative thoughts with a little practice. Thinking about yourself in a positive way will actually make you feel better about yourself and can reduce depression. Start by becoming more aware. Sit quietly and listen to your inner self-talk. Note how you feel about yourself and your abilities. Pay special attention to your attitudes. If you notice a lot of negative thoughts, make a plan to transform them. Don't be afraid to ask for professional help if you feel you need it.

**Practice deep breathing.** There is a strong link between depression and a lack of oxygen to the brain. When we slump, it is difficult to fill our diaphragm with air. Our breathing becomes shallow and our brain may actually be deprived of the optimal amount of oxygen needed. Shallow breathing also signals the brain that we may be in danger, thus causing even more anxiety. Deep breathing breaks this cycle.

**Continue your adult education.** Another way to get out of the house, interact with more people and engage your mind is to sign up for an educational class. This could be anything from a woodworking class at your community center to a history class at your community college. Follow an old passion or discover a new one, while making new friends at the same time.

**Spend time with animals.** Interacting with animals reduces stress and depression. Perhaps you want to commit to a pet of your own, or maybe a better fit would be volunteering at your local animal shelter. Consider volunteering at a horse rescue center or pet-sitting for a friend. Hanging a bird feeder will provide the simple pleasure of watching your local birds.

All of these suggestions for optimizing your mood will help in your journey to better health. By increasing your activity level and social interactions, and by consuming foods rich in mood-enhancing nutrients, you are also improving your blood glucose level and increasing the quality of your life.

# The Power of Volunteering

Your actions have a direct and powerful effect on your physical health, emotional wellbeing, and the lives of those around you. Every positive action, however small, increases your ability to create more happiness for yourself and others. Studies back this up, too—volunteering regularly can decrease depression, make you happier, and lengthen your life![112i]

There are many ways you can commit your time to help others. Offer to babysit a child for an hour or two for a busy parent, or volunteer in a classroom at your local elementary school. Choose an organization you support and begin to volunteer regularly. Find community events or organizations to volunteer for, such as your local library or church.

# Clear Out the Junk

It's amazing how giving away old junk can make you feel lighter and less depressed. It really can transform your living space, as well as your "inner space." Clear out the old "stuff" that's been holding you back. You've made conscious choices about diabetes. Now be mindful about the things in your new life that support your health—and throw away anything that might be a distraction or obstacle.

Start by tossing out those "plus-size" clothes that are now too big on you. Get rid of left-over prescription medications your doctor has taken you off of. You can't sail to your next destination until you've lifted the anchor that's keeping you moored in the harbor. Here are 10 ideas to get you started…

**1.** Give away all those diet books that failed you.

**2.** Donate movies and CDs to the library or a women's shelter.

**3.** Take old clothes and kitchen utensils to your local community thrift shop.

**4.** Let go of people in your life who add nothing but drama, stress, or misery to it.

**5.** Stop picking at old wounds and endlessly rehashing injustices. Forgive everyone in your past who has ever wronged you. Release every resentment, anger, and bitterness in you. Remember that "to forgive is to set a prisoner free and discover that the prisoner was you." (Lewis B. Smedes, author and theologian).

**6.** Free yourself from the endless loop in which you're always the "innocent victim" of someone else's thoughtlessness.

**7.** Decide you'll never again utter the words "I can't" (even before you fully consider whether you actually can).

**8.** Clean out the basement. Then the attic. Then the garage. Celebrate your new "lightness" that comes from not being bogged down by all this stuff anymore.

**9.** Stop listening to the "tape" in your head that defeats you. Change your internal discussion into something positive.

**10.** Catch yourself when you complain about problems and see how you can become part of a solution instead.

## Today's Action Steps

•Eat foods that boost your serotonin levels.

•Think of something you can become passionate about and immerse yourself in it.

•Pick up a good healthy habit (or two).

•Start clearing out the clutter in your life—in whatever form it may be.

**Extra credit:** Walking outside boosts your serotonin. Put on a comfy pair of shoes and walk around the block or explore your neighborhood.

# DAY 24

# ADD A SUPPORT SYSTEM

*The "I" in illness is isolation; and the crucial letters in wellness are "we."*

—MIMI GUARNERI, MD, cardiologist

**Tip of the Day:** Support groups, trusted friends and family, a skilled therapist—all can help build and maintain your good health.

DIABETES CAN MAKE you feel isolated and alone. That is why it is so important to build yourself a support network of people who understand what you are going through and can help you when you need it. You can find support in a friend's kitchen over a cup of tea, in a therapist's office, and even online. The key is to create a support system that is right for you. Use Smart Monitoring to record the positive effect a good support system can have on your blood glucose level.

## Lean on Support Groups

Since Alcoholics Anonymous started up in the 1930s, numerous support groups have emerged for just about every dysfunction imaginable. These types of groups are valuable for a number of reasons…

**End of isolation.** Nobody wants to be alone with a problem. People who go to self-help/support groups find real strength in being with others facing similar challenges.

**Boosting motivation.** Just hearing others describe how they are dealing with something —such as sugar cravings—can motivate you to do the same.

**Shared understanding.** While friends and relatives may have good intentions, they do not really know what you are going through unless they have gone through it themselves. A diabetes support group, on the other hand, provides compassion and real-life wisdom from people who have "been there."

**An accepting environment.** You can talk about pretty much anything in a support group without being judged or embarrassed. That is hard to find in the outside world.

**"Living the solution, not the problem."** The best meetings are not pity parties or complaint-sessions, but are energized by people who share ideas and solutions.

**Peer support.** Well-run groups share personal experiences and practical strategies, instead of being told what you *should* do. Newcomers are welcomed warmly. Do not be shy. (Remember, everyone was new once!)

**New trusted friends.** Many people become good friends with the people they meet in support groups.

**Low-cost anonymity.** Many groups are offered at low or no cost. Members use first names only to ensure privacy.

**The salt of the earth.** Some of the best-adjusted and friendliest folks on earth attend support groups regularly. These members honor first-timers as VIPs. You should feel warmly welcomed to whichever group you choose.

## P.S. on Support Groups

■ Experienced group members tend to recommend that you "take what you need and leave the rest." Translation: You will not find everything you hear to be immediately applicable to your situation. But do not disregard it. Group wisdom may be helpful later on, as your needs and situation change.

■ Some diabetes groups function under the premise that it is an incurable condition. You know better, of course. Maybe you will share what you have learned. If you sense a lack of openness, that is a sign this is not the group for you.

■ Choose well when you select a group, looking for a balance of newcomers and veterans coping with diabetes. Different perspectives add to the mix. Many groups have leaders —and the best ones keep domineering members in line while encouraging shy members to open up.

■ Steer clear of groups that charge a lot of money, push you to abandon your medical treatment, or promise fast solutions and quick cures. Safe groups will never pressure you to buy products or give out sensitive financial information—or even medical information you do not choose to share.

■ Diabetes support groups come in all shapes and sizes, including those for children, teens, adults, couples, families, and women. They are offered in many locations (and languages, too). Ask your doctor, local hospital, or diabetes educator for a referral to a group near you.

■ Online support groups can be an immediate help. Use good judgment when browsing online groups. To see what is out there, Google: "diabetes support groups online."

■ For the reasons we discussed yesterday, be especially on guard for depression. A study published in the *Journal of the American Medical Association* found that depressed people increase their risk of developing Type 2 diabetes and vice versa.[113] Depression often causes people to eat more and gain weight, putting them at risk for diabetes. If you have diabetes, you may feel discouraged about taking care of yourself, making it harder to manage your glucose levels, exercise, or make the necessary changes in your diet. You may even isolate yourself. But joining a diabetes support group could help you end that isolation and find new friends who are facing the same kinds of changes you are.

# Set Up a "Wisdom Council" on Your Own

Would you believe that your success in managing diabetes is directly linked to the level of support you get from your friends and family? Research proves it—as long as you can recognize which type of support works best for you.

Not everyone in your life can be supportive. But all you really need are just a couple of people you can always count on. It is important to know the difference between those who will support you from those who will make it easy for you to have some cake, drink a few beers, and go out of control. Here are some pointers on setting up your own support system:

- Like any healthy relationship, tell your friends what you need. Educate them about diabetes and the 30-day plan you are following. Let them know you are asking for their support and be specific about how they can help you.

- Talk to your friends and family honestly about your condition. Share your real feelings about the disease, and let them know how much you value their help and their support.

- Tell them up front that you are going to need their help eventually, and make sure it is okay to call them when you need to.

- Share your plans to take control of your health. Explain what you have learned about the foods that contribute to health and well being—and the ones that don't. Talk to them openly about what's working for you and what is not. This will help them support you when they see you are "slipping."

- Invite them over for a potluck of dishes containing your favorite diabetes-healing superfoods. Share your knowledge about how these foods heal diabetes.

- Confess how hard it is to ask for help sometimes. You will be breaking down barriers that keep you isolated, and you will be building the support you need just by letting them know that you do need them.

- You could be saving their life in the process. While none of your friends or family may have diabetes now, it is entirely possible they eventually may develop it. A 2007 study published in the *New England Journal of Medicine* found that a person's chance of becoming obese increased a whopping 57% when a friend became obese. (For *close* friends, the risk level was an astronomical 171%!)[114] Researchers also found that the effect was the same when friends *lost* weight. Imagine how powerful your recovery from diabetes could be for everyone's health! Get a friend to start eating better and walking with you. By sharing your healing experience with your friends, you could be saving lives.

## Consider Professional Counseling

Feeling like you hit a roadblock? Sitting with a counselor for a few therapy sessions can sharpen your awareness, rewire your old way of seeing life, and shift your thought and behavior patterns.

## Lean on Your Friends, Too

Kathy W. has eaten healthfully and maintained an ideal weight most of her life. Kathy's A1C was a mere 5.3 until 2007. One morning that November, Kathy skipped breakfast and found herself shaking at work. She visited her doctor and discovered she had Type 2 diabetes. Her A1C had shot up to 7.3 in one month.

Her doctor advised medication, but Kathy wanted to beat her diabetes with diet and exercise. She was an occupational therapist, helping people recover from diabetes-related surgeries. She'd seen how years on diabetes medication had ravaged her patients' health.

Kathy did well until both her parents became terminally ill. The stress returned her A1C to 7.3, and she gained weight. Her doctor put her on *metformin*. Even so, her A1C hovered around 6.4. "I felt terrible, too," she says. "Metformin gave me bowel problems."

Kathy read *The 30-Day Diabetes Cure* and realized that processed foods were ruining her health. She ate a lot of white flour. "I thought I was eating healthy," she says, "but the book helped me see that most of my diet was refined carbohydrates, which can raise your blood sugar just like sugar does."

Kathy replaced her favorite white-flour pizza with a veggie-laden, whole-grain one. A slice or two satisfies her. Social situations sometimes present challenges. "At parties, people offer me junky foods and say, 'It won't hurt you.' I tell them, 'Actually, it will kill me.'" Kathy says having a good support system has been crucial. Her friends help her stay motivated. "We all encourage each other to go to the gym," she says.

Kathy says *The 30-Day Diabetes Cure* is "not just about diabetes. It's about becoming your own health advocate." She tells everyone she meets, "I feel better than I have in years."

It is no secret that food represents much more than nutrition. It is tied up with emotional issues, habits, rules, memories, and what people around us eat. Making the adjustments outlined in our 30-day plan can trigger some surprising (and sometimes disturbing) emotional responses. Here is where a trained therapist can really help. He/she can help you uncover hidden associations with food so you can understand them and learn new responses. Together, you can define the problems, work together on solving them, set goals, and plan for continuing support.

Counseling can also propel you toward new ways of interacting with friends and family. It is true that family members do not always know how to accommodate a chronic illness. Even the person with diabetes may not realize the impact of the illness on the family. Professional guidance can open your eyes to the effect your condition and special needs are having on others. Here are some suggestions for locating a qualified counselor:

- Look for a therapist trained in cognitive behavioral therapy (CBT), which helps you identify negative thoughts and actions and replace them with constructive ones.[115] In a nutshell: You will learn how to retrain your mind so it sees the glass half-full, rather than half-empty. It is also a documented way of lowering stress hormones—and when they drop so does your blood glucose.[116]

- Start by asking your doctor or diabetes educator for a referral.

- Ask your support group for recommendations.

- Ask the therapist about his/her qualifications and experience in dealing with diabetes. Also make sure to ask how much they charge and whether they take your particular insurance plan.

## Today's Action Steps

•Assemble a support system tailored to provide you with encouragement and guidance.

•Choose an existing diabetes support group, a trusted friend, or a therapist. There is no need to carry this load alone (or overburden your spouse). The help you need is out there waiting for you.

•Use Smart Monitoring to test what type of support is best for your blood glucose levels.

**Extra credit:** The website *http://www.defeatdiabetes.org/* has a comprehensive list of diabetes support groups by state. Contact one, find out when they next meet, and put it on your calendar. Commit to one visit to see if more will be helpful to you.

# DAY 25

# REDUCE YOUR EXPOSURE TO ENVIRONMENTAL TOXINS

*"Food, one assumes, provides nourishment:*
*but Americans eat it fully aware that small amounts of poison have been added*
*to improve its appearance and delay its putrefaction."*

—JOHN CAGE, American composer, 1912–1992

**Tip of the Day:** Minimize your exposure to toxins and strengthen your liver to help heal your diabetes.

TOXINS ARE EVERYWHERE. Persistent organic pollutants (POPs) from the environment build up in body tissues, stressing the liver as it tries to eliminate them, causing cell mutations, disrupting the endocrine system, and depressing your immunity, which leaves you vulnerable to infections, disease, and cancer. POPs are in our water, air, and household cleaners. They are even in shampoo and lotion. As unbelievable as it sounds, they are in our food, too.

## What Exactly Are POPs?

The Environmental Protection Agency defines POPs as, "toxic chemicals that adversely affect human health and the global environment. Because they can be transported by wind and water, most POPs generated in one country can and do affect people and wildlife far from where they are used and released. They persist for long periods in the environment and can accumulate and pass from one species to the next through the food chain."[117] Here are some specific POPs and where they "pop up" in your daily life…

- Antibiotics and growth hormones. These are routinely added to the grains eaten by factory feedlot animals. They lodge in the animals' fat and in your body when you eat these meats. What your body is able to eliminate ends up in your neighborhood wastewater system (which is recycled in tap water). The balance is absorbed into your body's fatty tissue. Needless to say, the more body fat you have, the more accumulation you get.

- Pesticides and fungicides are routinely sprayed on non-organic crops and absorbed by the plants themselves.[118] These have been linked to serious health issues, including birth defects and cancer.[119]

- Genetically modified (GMO) crops, which have had their very DNA tinkered with.

■ Meats and vegetables packed in plastic and Styrofoam, two sources of PVC (polyvinyl chloride), BPA (bisphenol A), and styrene—all known human toxins. Also, BPA is linked to a higher incidence of diabetes![120] Most food cans are lined with BPA and hard plastic water bottles are also made of it.

■ Dioxins and furans are produced when bleaching wood pulp to make paper and from burning medical and municipal waste. They are also in wood preservatives and garden and agricultural herbicides. Nearly 90% of human exposure comes from eating animals (or dairy products) with these chemicals in their tissues and fats.

## In Your House—and Your Body

A tremendous amount of plastic is used in our food supply—and some of its residue ends up in our bodies. Think of all those plastic food containers you use everyday such as milk jugs, yogurt tubs and bags of peanuts. Now add plastic spatulas, rubber scrapers, plastic cups, and plates, which often come into contact with heat through cooking or in the dishwasher.

Cleaning products are another source of toxic exposure. They contain dangerous chemicals such as formaldehyde, trisodium phosphate, hydrofluoric acid, and others labeled as "irritants." Shampoos are made with *sodium laureth sulphate*, a suspected carcinogen linked to kidney and liver damage. Parabens are known hormone disrupters, yet they remain in deodorant, cosmetics, and hair dyes. Hormone disrupting *phthalates*—in hair spray, nail polish, and products containing "fragrance"—are banned in Europe because of their link to birth defects and cancer, but are largely unregulated in the US.[121] In 2008, Jane Houlihan, director of research for the Environmental Working Group, told a US House subcommittee that personal care products, including shampoo and cosmetics, are "the single largest source of risky chemicals that Americans are exposed to." Houlihan told the subcommittee, "Companies are free to use almost any ingredient they choose in personal care products, with no proof of safety required."[122]

## Research Links Toxins to Diabetes

How do these common (yet harmful) toxins affect diabetes? A 2012 study revealed that even exposure to trace amounts of synthesized substances can alter hormone signals.[123] If you have diabetes, BPA is a very real danger to you. Canned foods are considered the main cause of BPA exposure, because the chemical is known to transmigrate from the lining of cans into the liquids or foods they hold.

Researchers who looked at populations exposed to massive toxic disasters say these people show a significant increase in the risk of diabetes over time, particularly women. These studies focused on a Taiwanese manufacturing accident that caused rice bran oil to be contaminated with PCBs (*polychlorinated biphenyls*) and PCD FS (*polychlorinated dibenzofurans*) and an Italian pesticide factory explosion that exposed thousands of residents to toxic levels of dioxin.

Other studies show that BPA causes a variety of female reproductive organ disorders which women experience as ovarian cysts, fibroids, endometriosis, and several cancers. US soldiers who were part of the Vietnam Agent Orange campaign in the 1960s and 70s (which involved spraying a dioxin-based herbicide called *paraquat* over the jungles to kill foliage) experienced a 200% higher incidence of diabetes 20 years later than those who didn't participate. In fact, epidemiologists at the University of Texas Health Science Center actually found the diabetes risk correlated to the number of days the soldiers were exposed to spraying this deadly compound.

Even ordinary Americans who live far from factories, chemical waste sites, or large farming operations are at elevated risk. Toxic compounds are so pervasive throughout our culture that we all carry a toxic load. The Toxic-Free Legacy Coalition in 2005 tested hair, blood and urine samples from study participants for an array of chemicals present in ordinary household products, including nonstick cookware, cleaners, and plastics. The researchers found a minimum of 26 toxic chemicals present in every person—with the highest toxic load of 39 chemicals in a single human being!

## How to Protect Yourself

It is impossible to prevent your body from being contaminated by these environmental toxins. Even the Inuit Eskimos of Greenland, which generates no real pollution at all, have unacceptably high levels of man-made toxins that are produced in distant industrial countries.[124] It is astonishing how far these toxins can travel to end up in the fat of the whale, seal, and polar bear meat that make up the traditional Inuit diet.

You cannot escape today's toxic chemicals, but you can reduce your danger by changing the way you shop. More importantly, you can help the body's elimination system to rid your bloodstream and fat tissues of toxins that have built up over time. Happily, your liver is your body's "toxin filter," which disarms them and sends them over to the kidneys for further processing before they are excreted *via* urine. (Yet another reason to keep your kidney function healthy.) Your colon is involved in this detoxification process too. Its mucous membrane keeps bacteria and other toxins from entering your body, and beneficial bacteria in your large intestine remove toxic wastes from the food you eat.

Here's the best news of all: You've been detoxing your body since the first week of *The 30-Day Diabetes Cure!* Here's how:

- By eliminating processed foods and factory meats, you have been removing a major source of toxic chemicals from your life.

- Loading up on vegetables, fruits, and whole grains provides extraordinary support to your digestive system—including your liver—in clearing toxins from your body.

- And our focus on fiber works in your favor too, since fiber binds to wastes and moves them out of your system.

- Your daily exercise began stimulating your respiratory system—heart and lungs—all natural detoxifiers!

- As the weight comes off, you shed the fat that stores toxins.

- When you quit sugary drinks and replaced them with water, you began flushing your body with one of life's greatest detoxifiers. Water is the best choice for washing away impurities. Well, *pure* water is, anyway.

## How Pure Is Your Water Supply?

We couldn't survive very long without water, and yet our supply is swimming with toxins. Health officials stress that the toxin levels are extremely low, but do not believe it. A little later, I will explain why you should get a good-quality water filter right away. For now, consider these facts:

- In 2009, a comprehensive survey of US drinking water found widespread levels of pharmaceuticals and "hormonally active" chemicals all across America. The Southern Nevada Water authority tested tap water from 19 US locations and found the most common residues included *atenolol*, a beta-blocker used to treat heart disease, antidepressant drugs used by people with bipolar disorder, estrogen hormones, the tranquilizer *meprobamate*, an epilepsy anticonvulsant, plus numerous antibiotics.[125]

- A 2010 Chicago Tribune story looked at the gender-bending effects of atrazine, the most common chemical found in US streams and rivers.[126, 127] Researchers at Indiana University discovered an increase in nine different types of birth defects in infants whose mothers were pregnant during the spring planting season (April through July), when atrazine is sprayed on farmland. Farmers, as well as golf course owners and homeowners, use this weed killer, which is banned in Europe but not in the US. Atrazine is a *feminizing endocrine disruptor* (a chemical that disrupts human hormones)—and it's more dangerous at lower concentrations than once believed, according to this research.

Atrazine ultimately ends up in our drinking water. Even at concentrations that meet federal standards, atrazine is linked to low birth weight, birth defects and menstrual problems. Wildlife is severely damaged by the chemical as well: Male frogs reared in an atrazine environment turned into females and were able to breed with males.* *That's simply mind-bending!*

## Do You Need a Special Detox Diet?

People talk about detox diets so much that you might start to think you need one. The truth is, the steps you take in this book to kick diabetes out of your life are the same steps it takes to detoxify your body. Remember, you are eating fruits, vegetables, meat, and dairy that's raised without the use of antibiotics and pesticides. You are drinking fresh water and working up a sweat through exercise. You are already detoxifying your body as you

---

*http://www.biologicaldiversity.org/news/press_releases/2009/atrazine-08-27-2009.html

work through *The 30-Day Diabetes Cure*. I do not recommend fad detox "cleansing" diets and fasting because they can disturb your metabolism—and may even do long-term damage. People with diabetes need a steady source of food to support their blood glucose, so stay away from the fads. It's important for you to reject any diet that could overstress your body's metabolism.[128] But there are steps you can take to improve your environment...

# 11 Ways To Detox Your Environment

Believe us, we recognize that making big shifts in your lifestyle can be challenging and tough to implement all at once. That is why our 30-day plan gives you plenty of time to get used to new ideas, foods and habits. It is the same with detoxing your environment and your body. You will not do it in a single day, but you *can* start taking steps that will clear your kitchen, bathroom and cosmetics shelf of products that make it harder to heal your diabetes. Here are some pointers...

**Get a water filter.** Stop buying bottled water—it is bad for your budget and health, plus all those plastic bottles represent an environmental disaster. Instead, buy a high-quality water filter to remove pesticides, pharmaceuticals, and other impurities from your drinking water. You do not have to buy an expensive filter, but we actually recommend you make this investment if you can. You're now drinking 64 ounces of fresh water every day, so make your drinking supply as clean as possible. We recommend the Katadyn Combi Water Filter, with an attachment for your tap. Its ceramic element filters more than 13,000 gallons of drinking water before requiring replacement, removing bacteria and toxic chemicals. You pay a little more up front, but you get water filtered to .2 microns, and that is as safe as you can get. Use a glass bottle, glass-lined thermos or stainless steel bottle to carry your drinking water with you.

**Pitch the plastic.** Replace plastic wrap, bags, and storage containers with good old-fashioned wax paper and foil. Wax-paper sandwich bags are available in natural foods stores. Or just buy a roll of wax paper or foil. Wrap sandwiches with it and use it to cover glass bowls in the fridge. Then use it again.

**Go with glass.** Look for Pyrex storage containers with rubber lids, in a variety of sizes. They may seem heavy to carry to work, but they are far safer for your food, especially in the microwave (but no lids please!). Plastic containers and plastic wrap should never be heated in a microwave. Repurpose (or "upcycle") all your used plastic containers and yogurt tubs. Every workshop, mechanic, and gardener can use them for screws, nails and small tools. If they are overwhelming your kitchen, toss into the recycle bin. Avoid buying more in the future.

**Check your city's approved plastics for recycling.** If you must purchase plastic products, check your city's recycling program and learn which plastics they recycle; not every city recycles plastics. For example, your city might only recycle plastics with codes 2, 4, and 5.

**Avoid non-stick.** Replace non-stick cookware with steel baking sheets, glass pans, and casserole dishes, enamel cookware and cast iron or copper-clad skillets. Teflon and other non-stick coatings decompose at high heat—even if you don't cook at super-high temps.

Teflon releases toxic gasses, including carcinogens, global pollutants, and other dangerous compounds.

**No plastic utensils.** There is no need for plastic serving and cooking utensils now that you've ditched your non-stick pans. Your cast iron skillet goes well with wooden spoons and metal spatulas. Replace plastic cups and plates with lightweight reusable bamboo ones when packing your lunches, snacks, or picnics. If you can't eliminate plastics entirely, at the very least keep them away from the dishwasher and other heat. Consider using silicone utensils instead, as silicone is not known to interact with foods and drinks or release toxins. As there are no conclusive studies that speak to its use over heat, it would be prudent to avoid overheating it.

**Avoid canned food products, unless you're certain of their safety.** While canned food products have made solid safety strides in recent years with improved composition and lining and BPA leaching is not as prevalent as it was even five years ago, it still can potentially be an issue with products made by the major food manufacturers.[129] If you must purchase canned foods, do a bit of research beforehand about the safety record of a particular brand. Major manufacturers with brands that have good track records with eliminating BPA include Hain Celestial, ConAgra, and H.J. Heinz.

**Clean green.** Advertisers want you to believe you need a different product for every cleaning task but, of course, you don't. There's a host of toxic chemicals in most cleaning products; and manufacturing them generates huge amounts of environmental waste. Wean yourself off standard household cleaners with a trip to the natural foods store, where you'll find products made with naturally derived ingredients—and without phosphates and other environmental pollutants. Or go completely natural. Ask your grandma or cruise the Internet for easy, inexpensive, clean and green cleaners made from ingredients like baking soda, lemon juice and white vinegar. They will leave your home clean and fresh with no toxic residue. Congratulate yourself for taking this step by buying a few glass spray bottles!

**Avoid toxic body care products.** Using chemical-laden makeup and other body products can add an astonishing five pounds of toxic chemicals to your body each year. Look for skin products free of sodium laureth sulfate, parabens, and petroleum products. Parabens (para-hydroxybenzoic acids) are the most widely used preservatives in cosmetics. They're in everything from shampoo and soap to make-up, deodorant, and baby lotions. Parabens have even been detected in breast cancer tumors. Start reading the labels on your shampoo, body lotion, and cosmetics. Consider that some European countries and Japan have banned many of these chemicals in order to protect their consumers. Chemical-free products for your body will protect your system from these toxins. The Environmental Working Group maintains an excellent database of body care products at *http://www.ewg.org/skindeep/* (which can also be accessed via its Skin Deep mobile app), where you can find how safe and healthy a particular product is. You can also see the highest-rated products in a particular category (such as shampoo, lip balm, and toothpaste).

**Better body care.** Chemical-free products for your body are more expensive than others. But just like buying organic produce, wild salmon, and grass-fed beef, it is worth the extra money to protect your system from toxins. Plus, you can offset the cost of chemical-free body products by making at least one of your own: shampoo. Use baking soda-water solution (one tablespoon baking soda to one cup of water) to wash your hair and a vinegar-water solution (one tablespoon vinegar to one cup of water) to condition it. Just wet your hair and gently massage in baking soda, adding more water as needed. Rinse with the vinegar-water solution and then with plain water. There you go—simple, cheap shampoo. Now head back to your natural food store and look for skin products free of sodium laureth sulfate, parabens, and petroleum products. These safe, low-cost options will offset the extra you pay for chemical-free cosmetics. You will also discover that a lot of the products you thought you needed are actually unnecessary. Sticking to a few basic, natural products while eliminating the others will free up your budget as well as your toxic load.

**Forget the fragrances.** Remove all air fresheners and scented dryer sheets, lotions, and candles from your house today, including anything with a fake scent. The Natural Resources Defense Council released a study in 2007[130], which found most air fresheners and other scented products contain chemicals called phthalates—known hormone disruptors that affect reproductive development. Especially harmful to young children and babies, they affect testosterone levels and produce abnormal genitals and decreased sperm production. The state of California says no fewer than five kinds of phthalates are "known to cause birth defects or reproductive harm" and advises pregnant women to stay away. Get these scented products out of your house now! One last note: A study in the *American Journal of Respiratory and Critical Care Medicine* found that people using air fresheners and household cleaning sprays regularly have a stunning 30% to 50% higher incidence of asthma than people who didn't use them. At the University of Washington, professor Anne Steinemann, PhD, did an analysis of some widely used scented products and discovered a whopping 100 unique volatile organic compounds, some of which are linked to cancer and problems with neurological, reproductive, and respiratory systems.[131]

## Today's Action Steps

•Commit to clearing toxins from your body and environment.

•Toss toxin-laden cookware, cleaning supplies and body care products.

•Support your body's natural detox system by drinking lots of fresh water and kicking up your exercise until you sweat.

•Check that your body care products use safe ingredients and replace as necessary.

•Keep eating high-fiber foods to maintain good elimination.

**Extra credit:** Order a water filter today and install it on your kitchen tap.

# DAY 26

# ADD VITAMINS AND SUPPLEMENTS

*"Take care of your body. It's the only place you have to live."*

—JIM ROHN, American entrepreneur and author, 1930–2009

**Tip of the Day:** Vitamins—vitamin D in particular—and some supplements can help heal and even prevent diabetes.

WHY TAKE VITAMINS when you are already eating high-quality whole foods naturally loaded with nutrition? Simple. Because even when you are eating the best diet, having diabetes increases your need for certain nutrients—and getting the amount you need isn't always possible with food alone.

As you work through our 30-day plan it is essential you get maximum nutritional support. Supplementing your diet with a high-quality multivitamin is a simple and effective means of ensuring you do. Consider it a nutritional "insurance policy" that covers you with a regular supply of critical nutrients for extra demands that having diabetes places on your body. Consult a natural practitioner to determine the supplements and doses that are best for you.

## Why You Need Supplements

Even the most balanced of diets does not deliver all of the vitamins and minerals necessary for optimal health. This is because modern agricultural methods have leached the soil of many essential minerals and nutrients—and if the soil is lacking in vitamins and minerals, the food grown in it will be lacking too. Studies show that today's produce has significantly lower nutrient content than the crops grown just 50 years ago.[132] So, even if you consumed a "perfect" diet of fresh whole foods, it is no guarantee that your body would receive optimal levels of the vitamins and minerals necessary to support healthy blood glucose. The good news is that additional nutrients, taken in supplement form, can help heal your diabetes and support your general health.

## Go for a Good Multi

Starting today, we want you to begin taking a high-quality multivitamin that will boost your daily intake of essential nutrients.

We do not recommend the vast majority of one-a-day multivitamins you find in the drugstore because their nutrient levels are based on the Recommended Dietary Allowances (RDA), which are the official nutritional guidelines used by the USDA and FDA. These are *minimal* levels designed to prevent their nutritional deficiency diseases based upon the old Minimum Daily Requirement (MDR) thinking. This criterion is a bit ludicrous. For example, the RDA for vitamin C is a scant 75–90 mg—the dose required to prevent scurvy, a potentially fatal disease that afflicted British sailors in the 1700s.

Your chances of coming down with scurvy these days are about the same as being attacked by sharks in Indiana. But your prospects of coming down with heart disease are far greater, and numerous studies have shown that vitamin C doses higher than the RDA actually lower this risk. (The famous Harvard Nurses' Health Study involving more than 85,000 women over 16 years is just one of these studies.)[133]

Our point is that the RDA system is antiquated because it is based on nutrient doses that prevent deficiency diseases, not chronic diseases. Rather than basing your purchasing decisions on *minimal* levels, you should be looking for *optimal* amounts.

With literally dozens (if not hundreds) of individual vitamins, minerals and other nutrients to consider, there simply is not enough space here to list the optimal levels for each one. Besides, this would require a tedious label-reading undertaking on your part every time you shopped. So let us save you the time by listing a few general guidelines to follow when shopping for a multivitamin…

**Are the ingredients absorbable?** Just as important as the nutrient levels are the *form* the ingredients nutrients come in. For example, many companies boast high levels of magnesium, but use forms of magnesium your body can't absorb. It looks great on the label, but actually does you no good. Look for supplements—that are from natural, absorbable sources of vitamins and minerals.

**The one pill myth.** Natural, absorbable forms of vitamins and minerals take up a lot of space inside a pill. So do not be surprised when the label says, "Six capsules provide…" (The multivitamin Jim takes suggests this, so he simply takes three in the morning and three before bedtime.)

**Quality will cost.** To get a supplement made from top quality raw materials, that is highly absorbable and that will make positive improvements in your health—you are going to have to pay a premium price. But since your good health is your most prized possession, it is worth it, right?

**Get good advice.** Big Pharma is not the only industry capitalizing on consumer confusion about health. Many supplement companies make products that are highly questionable—and they invest plenty on "educating" the clerks in health food stores about the benefits of their products. Remember: Most of these clerks are there to sell you products (and often the ones with the biggest profit margins, which are not necessarily high quality). Your best defense is to educate yourself before you go shopping.

**Avoid supplement gimmicks.** Two of the most popular gimmicks today are liquid multivitamins and "fermented whole food" vitamins. Promoting higher-priced liquid vitamins as providing better absorption is a marketing ploy. The "fermented whole food vitamins" concept is also a scam. We are all in favor of fermented foods, but when it comes to total nutritional support, they are no substitute for a high-quality multivitamin.

**Physician-sold supplements.** Beware of nutritional products available only in a doctor's office. This strategy leverages the enormous influence doctors have over their patients—and their reward is usually a big mark-up. If your health care provider is selling you some product that is not available without a "prescription" or special professional advice—or it can't be found anywhere else—that's just hogwash. The same goes for multi-level marketing schemes. We have never found a single multivitamin product that was so special that it required a closed network of sellers. In fact, there are so many middlemen profiting at each one of these "multi-levels" that the price is jacked up sky-high (which usually means the actual cost of the product is dirt cheap). And what about the products bearing the name of "celebrity doctors?" In almost every case, the doctor merely licenses his name to a third-party formulator and has very little to say about the product or what it contains.

**Our favorite products.** Having said all that, here are some suggestions for multivitamin brands that we know and like, starting with the multivitamin made by Pure Encapsulations called Nutrient 950. (If you are over 50, we suggest you take their UltraNutrient.) Solgar is a manufacturer that's been around for a long time and we have come to trust their products. Another company that makes an excellent line of supplement products (including a good-quality multi) is Thorne. But do your own research by consulting with Consumer Reports and Consumer Labs. Make sure you shop around for the best prices.

## Why You Need Extra Vitamin D

One nutrient that all multivitamins score low on is vitamin D (known as the "sunshine vitamin" because our bodies manufacture it when solar rays hit our skin), so this is one individual nutrient we want you to take in addition to your multi. In our opinion, it is the most important, yet highly underrated, nutrient you can take today—especially if you have diabetes.

The epidemic of vitamin D deficiency in America and other Western cultures today is a major reason why we are experiencing such poor health. In fact, it is the leading nutritional deficiency in our nation: the majority of Americans are not getting enough vitamin D.[134] Numerous studies suggest this deficiency is directly linked to our soaring rates of diabetes, Types 1 and 2…

- Finnish men and women with higher blood levels of vitamin D had a 40% lower risk of developing Type 2 diabetes than those who had less vitamin D, according to a study published in the October 2007 issue of *Diabetes Care*.[135] This was the conclusion from researchers who spent 17 years following a population of 4,000 people in Finland.

- Vitamin D appears to prevent or delay the onset of diabetes.[136] And in people who already have diabetes, it reduces complications such as heart disease, according to research published in *Diabetes Educator* in 2009[137] by scientists at Loyola University.

•Women who took at least 800 IU (international units) of vitamin D and 1,200 milligrams of calcium each day had a 33% lower risk of developing Type 2 diabetes compared with those taking less. That is another conclusion from the Nurses' Health Study[138], which provided the most powerful evidence linking Type 2 and vitamin D.

There are a few reasons that so many of us are deficient in vitamin D. Most crucially, we are not spending enough time outdoors anymore. That is partly because doctors and health experts have turned us into "solar scaredy-cats," making us afraid of going out in the sun unless we slather ourselves with sunscreen and don ridiculously wide-brim hats. In addition, we're being discouraged from eating organ meats (such as calf's liver) and animal fats, dairy foods and eggs—foods all naturally high in vitamin D.

## Vitamin D Improves Insulin Sensitivity

A report appearing in the June 2009 issue of *Nutrition Research Review*,[139] involving several clinical studies, shows that vitamin D actually improves insulin sensitivity. In fact, *vitamin D might be all that some people with mild Type 2 need to improve their condition*. Here's more good news...

•Insulin-resistant women significantly decreased their risk of developing diabetes simply by taking more vitamin D. Research published in the *British Journal of Nutrition* in 2010[140] looked at a group of Asian women who had all been diagnosed with insulin resistance, a precursor to full-blown diabetes. The women were randomly assigned to take either 4,000 IU of vitamin D daily or a placebo. After six months, insulin resistance in the vitamin D group dramatically decreased, along with their fasting insulin levels.

•Researchers reported in the *American Journal of Clinical Nutrition* in May 2004[141] that vitamin D improves insulin sensitivity by up to 60%! Those are better results than *metformin* (Glucophage) achieves, and it's the leading diabetes drug prescribed today! A 1998 study published in the *New England Journal of Medicine*[142] showed that *metformin* lowers blood glucose by a meager 13%.

## Doctors Have Been Wrong About Skin Cancer

There's no getting around the fact that sunshine is our primary source of vitamin D. Staying out of the sun is bad advice for everyone, but especially for people with diabetes, for whom vitamin D has been proven to be beneficial. Your body produces it when the sun's ultraviolet (UV) rays penetrate the skin, with lighter skin producing more vitamin D than darker skin.

Vitamin D actually *protects* against many cancers, including skin cancer. Studies show that people with the lowest levels of vitamin D actually have *higher* rates of the skin cancer melanoma and other cancers. Plus, being deficient in vitamin D *increases* the risk of death from all causes. Sunscreen not only blocks the sun, it blocks your body from making health-giving D (and some of sunscreen's ingredients have been found to be carcinogenic).

## The Top 10 Vitamin D Foods

1. Liver and other organ meats

2. Wild salmon (not farm raised)

3. Shrimp

4. Cod

5. Anchovies

6. Fish oil

7. Eggs

8. Milk (fortified)

9. Red, yellow, and orange fruits and vegetables

10. Dark-green, leafy vegetables

## Become a Sun Worshiper

Sunbathing for 10 to 15 minutes a day in the summer is actually good medicine. Lying in the sun feels good because it *is* good for you. Solar rays nurture all of life, and we humans are no exception. We should, therefore, do as our ancestors did and expose our skin to the sun instead of hiding from it. Take care not to burn because sunburn generates free radicals and is linked to skin cancer. But don't wear sunscreen unless you know you'll have an extended stay in the sun—sunscreens block vitamin D production by 95%.

Minimize your exposure during peak midday hours when the sun is at its strongest (11 am to 3 pm). Take a short walk in the morning or late afternoon when the sun is less intense than midday, with arms and legs uncovered, to soak up as much sunshine as you can.

## Getting Enough Vitamin D with Supplements

Getting 100% of your vitamin D requirements from food sources is nearly impossible (though we recommend you eat generously of these foods for their other nutritional benefits). Additionally, sunbathing isn't always realistic—or practical—during cold winter months. To get enough vitamin D, you'll almost certainly need to rely on supplements. Here are a few tips to keep in mind when choosing the right ones for you:

**The ideal form.** Purchase only high-quality brands of vitamin D3 (*cholecalciferol*). This is the same form of D that our skin produces from sunlight. Good old cod liver oil works just as well as a source of Vitamin D. Avoid vitamin D2 (*ergocalciferol*), because it is inferior and potentially harmful.

**The right dose.** Take a minimum of 1,000 IU of vitamin D3 on days when you can't expose your body to sunshine (a maximum of 2,000 is usually sufficient). African-Americans, who have higher cancer rates and lower blood levels of vitamin D, should double this dose. The skin of African Americans does not seem to convert UV rays into vitamin D efficiently, which causes chronic deficiency, particularly among those living in Western countries. This may help explain why African-Americans generally have a higher incidence of many cancers and in more aggressive forms.

**Attention, seniors.** Your body's ability to produce vitamin D declines with age. A 70-year-old's skin makes about a quarter of the D that it manufactured from the sun's rays when in his 20s. Seniors should take 2,000 to 3,000 IU daily.

## Superstar Supplements

Beyond a good multivitamin and supplemental vitamin D, there are other key supplements that you should incorporate into your diet regularly. Chief among those that support healthy blood glucose are magnesium, L-arginine, coenzyme Q10, fish oil, and vitamin C. Let us take a look at how each of these nutrients helps to normalize blood glucose:

**Magnesium.** This essential mineral relaxes the tiny muscles in the walls of your arteries so blood can circulate with greater ease. We recommend at least 600 mg of magnesium daily. Magnesium is also found in spinach, almonds, cashews, soybeans, lentils, and whole grains.

**Coenzyme Q10 (CoQ10).** This humble enzyme acts as a spark plug for the mitochondria, the energy-producing "furnace" in your cells. It also is a powerful antioxidant that helps arteries manage blood flow. We recommend taking 100 mg of CoQ10 with breakfast and with lunch. Some people prefer *not* to take it in the evening because it can have an energizing effect.

**Fish oil.** Omega-3 fatty acids found in fish oil can expand blood vessels. Eicosapentaenoic (EPA) and docosahexaenoic acids (DHA) are found in fish. We recommend a daily dose of between 3 to 10 grams of high-quality fish oil daily. Note: People with diabetes should consult their physicians before taking this much fish oil because it can raise fasting blood glucose levels. Diabetics can safely consume 1 g (1,000 mg) of fish oil every day.

**Vitamin C.** An invaluable antioxidant, vitamin C fights and neutralizes free radicals, those rogue molecules that bind with oxygen and destroy cells. Up to 12 g (12,000 mg) of vitamin C can be consumed daily.

## Other Helpful Supplements

As with the other supplements mentioned above, consult your natural practitioner to determine if these should be included in your supplement regimen.

**Chlorella is a green algae powder that contains protein and vitamins C, K, B-12, beta-carotene, iron, and several amino acids.** This powerful superfood is a natural detoxifier.

**Coleus Forskohlii.** Used in the Ayurvedic tradition for thousands of years to treat heart-related illnesses, Coleus forskohlii has anti-inflammatory properties. A common supplement dosage includes 125 mg Coleus forskohlii standardized for 10% forskolin.

## Choosing the Right Vitamins and Supplements

Look for the GMP seal. This signifies that the company follows Good Manufacturing Practices (GMP). These voluntary standards describe exactly how supplement manufacturers should receive and handle raw materials, produce supplements, check for safety, and track problems and consumer complaints. Quality supplement manufacturers adhere to GMPs to distinguish themselves from disreputable companies. Compliance is monitored and graded by third-party audits to help ensure that the manufacturer is conforming to these guidelines. If you don't see this seal, don't buy the supplements.

**Don't cheat your health with cheap supplements.** Your health and diabetes healing are too important to scrimp on. No matter how inexpensive a brand, it is not a bargain if it does not help you. Does this mean you should buy the most expensive supplements? No way. A high price tag is not a reliable indicator of quality, although very low cost is a dead giveaway that a product is of inferior quality.

**Use caution with store brands.** While store brands of basic food staples is an acceptable way to stretch your dollar, when it comes to vitamins and supplements you almost always get what you pay for. Plus, paying half-price for a product that does your body no good not only wastes your money, it cheats your health. You're better off finding a brand you can trust. How? Two independent organizations regularly test nutritional supplements:

**Consumer Reports** (*www.consumerreports.org*) is a non-profit, independent organization that tests and evaluates a wide range of consumer products, including nutritional supplements. A few years ago, they tested 12 brands of joint supplements that supposedly improved arthritis symptoms. Three of them failed the exam, and *Consumer Reports* published the names of these inferior products. A one-year subscription to *Consumer Reports* gives you access to thousands of current and past evaluations. For just $29, it's a tremendous bargain—and a smart investment.

**Consumer Labs** (*www.consumerlab.com*) is another independent testing organization, though it is a for-profit corporation. A 12-month membership costs $36. They test and evaluate vitamins and supplements exclusively.

Testing in pairs will provide you with concrete measurements of a particular vitamin or supplement's impact on your blood glucose levels. Use Smart Monitoring to determine how different brands and dosages affect your blood glucose.

## Today's Action Steps

•Schedule an appointment with a natural practitioner who can advise you on a supplement regimen.

•Begin taking a high-quality multivitamin every day.

•Start taking a vitamin D supplement daily in the doses recommended above.

•Don't be afraid to let the sun shine on your bare skin every day for 10–15 minutes, if possible, so your body can naturally make its own vitamin D.

•Eat more vitamin D-rich foods.

•Use Smart Monitoring to discover which supplements have the biggest positive impact on your blood glucose.

# DAY 27

# BECOME A VOLUNTEER

*"What is important are family, friends,
giving back to your community, and finding meaning in life."*

—ADRIAN GRENIER, American actor

**Tip of the Day:** Volunteering will help you feel happy and connected.

## Volunteering Feels Good

HELPING OTHERS IMPROVES your own self-esteem. It can also help you beat loneliness, depression, and the negative emotions that can make diabetes worse. As a volunteer, you will gain a variety of benefits, including the pleasure of helping others, feeling connected, and developing enhanced people skills. There is so much need in today's world. Begin today to make a difference in your life and the lives of others.

The funny thing about volunteering is that you often benefit as much—or more—than those you help. Studies show that being a Good Samaritan lights up pleasure centers in the brain.[143] This warm, happy feeling decreases stress and elevates mood, which can help improve your blood glucose levels. *Helping others may be one of the best things you can do to help yourself.*

Scientists have long theorized that the antidepressant boost people get from volunteering is triggered by positive social interaction. People are always happy to see a volunteer, and this positive feedback stimulates good feelings for both parties involved. Volunteering increases your confidence, which makes it easier for you to accomplish goals in other areas of your life.

## Connect with Your Community

Volunteering connects you with your community, exposes you to new people and helps widen your circle of friends. Having a sense of connection to the world outside your door is a significant contributing factor to good mental, emotional, and physical health. Volunteering helps you see how important your time and energy can be in the lives of others or toward the advancement of a good cause.

In addition, volunteering keeps your mind sharp, because you are usually learning new skills in the process. These skills can then be used to enhance your career and enrich your personal life. Volunteering is an easy way to explore new interests and make your life more fulfilling.

## Clarify Your Goals and Interests

Before you begin, take time to clarify your goals and interests. Which causes are you passionate about? Where do you prefer to spend your time? Do you like to be outdoors or indoors? Do you prefer to work with children, teens, adults, animals, or plants? Do you prefer group activities or would you be happier in a one-on-one situation? Are you better behind the scenes in a support capacity, or are you comfortable in the spotlight? What skills and abilities do you bring to the table? How much time can you realistically commit to volunteering?

## Volunteering Opportunities

Volunteering opportunities are everywhere. Many local newspapers even have a section where organizations put out a call for volunteer help.

Pick an organization that is a good match for you. Start off slowly, enjoy yourself, and you can create a win-win situation for all involved. Imagine how your loving assistance and attention might change the lives of those in great need...

- Teach an adult to read.

- Visit a lonely, elderly person in a nursing home.

- Do something to help a veteran suffering from a shattered psyche or body.

- Help children by becoming a foster parent, tutoring, or donating goods during the holidays.

- Volunteer to help at a battered women's shelter.

- Walk dogs or play with cats at the animal shelter.

- Remember members of your own family who may feel forgotten and alone.

## Look How Far You Have Come

You are not the same person who began this journey 27 days ago. You are very different. You have developed a more mindful approach to life by paying attention, being calm, and choosing the path of healing. You are developing the wisdom and personal power to improve your life and our world. You are accomplishing something that very few people are able to: You are transforming your life. What a miracle!

But there is an even bigger miracle in store for you—it lies in helping others to transform their own lives. We urge you to step out into the world and lend a helping hand.

Be conservative and start small. Do not over-commit yourself, or you could lose the positive benefits of volunteering. Try spending just one hour a week or even one day a month—whatever you can fit in—to volunteer in your community. Visit the sick. Serve food to the hungry or homeless. Be a shoulder for someone's tears. Write a letter to a relative. Become a mentor in a support group. Share your wisdom and experience. Inspire someone who feels powerless. Join a movement. Register people to vote. Donate your old belongings. You get the idea; just look around—there are hundreds of ways you can be of service.

## Today's Action Steps

Which of the volunteer categories above appeal to you most? Do you have a particular new interest or skill you would like to develop? Is there a worthy cause you would like to support?

- Set aside some time today to investigate volunteer opportunities in your area and make an appointment to meet the people involved.

- Start small by volunteering a little of your time in the beginning and then take on only as much as you can without feeling stressed.

**Extra credit:** Invite a friend to come with you to your new volunteering program.

# DAY 28

# START BUILDING MORE MUSCLE

*"Energy and persistence conquer all things."*

—BENJAMIN FRANKLIN, American philosopher, inventor,
founding father, 1706–1790

**Tip of the Day:** Adding to your body's muscle mass will boost your insulin resistance.

THE MORE MUSCLES you have, the more calories your body burns in a day. A solid muscle foundation also increases your ability to participate in daily activities and strengthens your bones and joints against falls and breaks. As you work to build these muscles, you will improve your body's response to glucose *and* feel your mood brighten. Frankly, we couldn't think of more wonderful motivators to embrace a more active lifestyle!

Strength training, or progressive resistance training, is the most effective way for you to achieve these results. Resistance training is the use of weights, or another form of resistance, to build muscle and increase strength. You will be working your muscles to "failure," then increasing weight as your muscles strengthen.

If this description brings to mind images of gyms full of body builders and massive barbells, don't fret. You will start with small weights appropriate to your ability and work slowly toward strengthening your body in a healthful way. Remember to use Smart Monitoring to track your progress, as well as find the type of strength training that works the best for you.

## Reasons to Build More Muscle

Building more muscle can benefit you in so many ways. The benefits below attest to why a regular strength training program is one of the smartest—and healthiest—choices you can make for your diabetes and general well being.

**Improve insulin resistance.** Progressive strength training reduces blood glucose and insulin resistance about as much as adding a second diabetic medication would.[144]

**Burn more calories.** Muscles need up to nine times more calories than fat to simply maintain themselves. This means that your resting metabolic rate will increase as you increase your muscle mass. Ultimately, you will burn more calories throughout the day, even while sleeping, if your body is composed of a higher percentage of muscle.

**Elevate your mood.** As you exercise feel-good hormones are released in your body. This will improve your mood immediately, and these effects can last up to 12 hours after an intense workout.[145] Having a regular exercise routine can combat the depression so often associated with diabetics.

**Live longer and better.** Exercise improves the health of your body, which extends your lifespan. Regular exercise also increases brain function, so building muscle actually builds your brain! Strength training accomplishes this boost in brain function by increasing the body's production of the growth factors responsible for the growth, differentiation, and survival of neurons.

**Be more capable.** Resistance training increases your athletic ability in daily life. This will enable you to do chores and lifting around the house you might not have been able to do before. You will also have the energy to help those friends and family that might rely on you.

**Prevent injuries.** Building and strengthening your muscles, in turn, strengthens your bones and ligaments. This increased strength will improve your balance, which will help you avoid situations in which you could fall. If you do fall, having strong bones, ligaments, and muscles will help prevent injury.

## Strength Training Basics

The key to strength training, and what produces the most successful improvement in your glucose levels, is the progressive increase in your strength and the responding addition of weight and difficulty to your routine. If you always complete the same exercise routine your body will acclimate and stop giving you all the positive results it did when you first started the routine. Instead, you must respond to your body's increasing strength by challenging it just a little more. While a personal trainer can advise you on a strength training program that's best for you. it's helpful to keep these pointers in mind:

- The weights you use should be light enough for you to complete a 12 to 15 set of repetitions, but heavy enough that your muscles are being strengthened. You will know you have the right weight when you need to focus more on finishing the last couple of repetitions in your set.

- Keep your strength training routine simple. You want to establish a routine that is easy for you to maintain.

- Varying your routine periodically (every four to six weeks, for example) will help you increase your strength more quickly.

## Alternate with Aerobic Exercise

Combining strength training with aerobic exercise will increase your fitness most effectively. Try jumping rope in between weight repetitions in order to burn fat as well as build muscle. Or, try this Lateral Step exercise to add some cardio to your workout:

**Lateral Step exercise: This isn't your mama's step aerobics.** Get the heart pumping and quads firing with a lateral step over move. Start standing with a knee-high bench to the right.

## Strength Training Options

The best way to increase your fitness is to find an activity that you love and will stick with. There are numerous ways to effectively develop muscle strength. Here are a few options available to you:

- **Free weights**
- **Resistance bands**
- **Stacked weight machines**
- **Nautilus circuits**
- **Soloflex**
- **Bowflex**
- **Delta Trimax machine**
- **Pilates equipment**
- **Total Gym**

Lift the right leg, and place it on the other side of the bench without touching the foot to the top of the bench. Follow with the left leg, so the bench is to the left of both legs. Repeat going the opposite direction. Go as fast as you can for short intervals (one minute or less) while keeping form for a tougher challenge![146]

## Add Variety and Appeal

Building muscles throughout your body and strengthening yourself in a variety of ways will increase your overall fitness. Finding the motivation to stick with it can be challenging. Having a variety of exercises will also keep you interested and excited about getting active. Make these various exercises more appealing and enjoyable, and you will be much more likely to succeed in your fitness goals. Here are a few ways to change your routine or increase its intensity, as well as keep it fun and positive.

- Find an activity that gets your excited. If you agonize over going to a dance class or running on the treadmill, try something else. Dread is a motivation-killer.

- Try doing your workout routine in a place that has positive associations for you. Perhaps you find a particular park or nature trail uplifting and invigorating. Maybe you know of an upbeat gym with great music and a nonjudgmental atmosphere. It could even be as simple as working out in front of a window in your home that provides your favorite view.

- Try adding resistance bands. They are cost-effective, adaptable to many fitness levels and routines, can benefit the whole body, are portable and storable, and are easy to use on your own.

- Listen to your favorite upbeat music. Hearing a great song can encourage you to finish your routine or even lose track of time and do extra work!

- Celebrate your small successes instead of focusing on a long-term weight loss goal. Being proud of your daily, weekly, and monthly increases in strength will keep you confident and motivated.

## The Power of Exercise

When Doug N. was diagnosed with Type 2 diabetes at age 18, he didn't do much to help himself. For the following 30 years, Doug didn't notice any problems. But the effects of the disease eventually began showing up, one-by-one. He had 11 laser surgeries to correct his failing vision, he endured six aortic stents to unblock his blood vessels, and he suffered agonizing neuropathy in his legs and feet. At one point, he was on 20 different prescription medications.

Doug realized his life was in danger the night he had a sudden heart attack, which required open-heart surgery. "They split me open and replaced an artery," he says. "When I came to, I knew I needed to make some changes." But what to change—and how? Although he continued to follow his doctor's orders and faithfully took medicines for his heart, his eyes, and his blood sugar, he wasn't improving. That's when his brother presented him with a copy of *The 30-Day Diabetes Cure*. "I read the whole thing in two days," he says.

Doug says the best thing about *The 30-Day Diabetes Cure* is it educated him about the good foods he should be eating. "After the first 10 days, I realized that this was going to work because my blood sugar kept going down." As he progressed, he reintroduced exercise into his daily routine. He's now walking every day and lifts weights three times a week. Instead of finding that exercise tires him out, he says he feels rejuvenated. "I just stick with it one day at a time," Doug says. "I know that if I cheat I'm going to start making excuses. Every day gets easier. My only regret is that I didn't start the exercise much sooner."

Now, completely off of his cholesterol medication, he has also discontinued his insulin use. "I want to tell my story to help other people with diabetes avoid the pain and misery I've gone through," he says. "Don't stick your head in the sand and live in denial like I did. Your diabetes isn't going to go away unless you take action. Drugs and medications won't make you well. Only you can do that. And *The 30-Day Diabetes Cure* can show you how to help yourself."

# Workout Success Tips

**Plan ahead.** If you are going to be working out at your local gym, make sure you have a gym bag packed and in your car at all times. This will allow you to complete your exercise routine regularly as well as drop in for an impromptu session.

**Get enough sleep.** If you consistently miss out on sleep, or do not sleep soundly, your hormone levels might not be properly balanced. Poor sleeping habits particularly affect hormones related to stress, muscle recovery, and mood.

**Hire a trainer.** A trainer can help you develop a wonderful exercise routine that is tailored to your specific needs and desires. Make sure your trainer is fit, as that is an indicator of how effectively he or she will be able to motivate you and keep you accountable in and out of the gym.

**Challenge yourself without straining or overtraining.** Remember that the benefit of exercise comes when you are exerting your muscles and building more. Steadily push your limits. However, overtraining causes your body to go into shock and lock up fat cells. Or, you may have a significant increase in appetite. The way to test if you are challenging your muscles healthfully is to focus on those last couple of repetitions, while still being able to finish. Find the balance between too much work, which can cause injury or muscle damage, and too little, which will not improve your fitness level.

**Rest and recover.** The process of exerting your body and your body adapting to and recovering from that exertion creates the diabetes-healing results desired. After your exercise routine, aid the active recovery of your muscles with a low-intensity cool-down exercise. In the hours after exercise, make sure to eat and drink in order to restore your body's energy. This will help the short-term recovery period when your muscles, tendons, and ligaments are being repaired.

## Today's Action Steps

Purchase a set of light weights to begin your strength training today.

- Visit your local gym or its website to find out which strength training classes are available.

- Research fitness trainers in your area to benefit from their direction and support.

**Extra credit:** Write down a list of fitness goals for the upcoming week. What is the most personally meaningful motivator you have for sticking with it? Write that message to yourself and post it on your fridge, mirror or somewhere you will see and read it everyday.

# DAY 29

# ADD TRAVEL, RESTAURANTS, AND PARTIES

*"Certainly, travel is more than the seeing of sights;
it is a change that goes on, deep and permanent,
in the ideas of living."*

—MIRIAM BEARD, historian, 1876–1958

**Tip of the Day:** Using the knowledge you have already gained will help you tiptoe through the most dangerous dietary minefields out there.

YOU HAVE BEEN LEARNING and practicing for more than three weeks. Now it is time to spread your wings and fly off into the outside world and put your newfound skills and knowledge to the real test. It is out of the incubator for you! We want you to feel confident that you can have an active social life without constantly worrying about the temptations and pressures you are going to face—and the nagging doubt that you cannot succeed. You can!

Restaurants, parties, and travel represent the most challenging situations that a person with diabetes faces. Finding healthy, healing meals in these circumstances will test you to the limits. And facing down those ooey, gooey splurge foods you could not resist in the past might make you sweat a little. It is a lot like running into an old flame—you know, the one who trashed your heart so badly—and having him or her invite you over for a "friendly drink."

You may not succeed perfectly your first time out. In fact, it may prove more difficult than you imagined. But you are wiser now; there are ways to avoid the temptation—or else, just simply say no. We have every confidence that in having come this far, you have what it takes to go all the way.

## The Most Important Decision: *Where* to Eat

Planning is everything, right? You learned how important it is to have a shopping list at the supermarket…to pack your lunch whenever possible…and to never be without a baggie of safe snacks. Well, planning which restaurant you'll dine at is equally important. You never want to be hungry in a place that does not offer you healthy menu options.

**Fast food restaurants.** You already know about the unhealthful ingredients that they pack into the menu. You are not going to get a satisfying, healthful meal in these establishments. Even their "healthy" salads are bad for you. The salad dressings they serve are loaded with excess calories and unhealthy fats, as well as high fructose corn syrup, artificial flavors, and chemical preservatives. The point is that you are developing an appreciation of—and a hankering for—real foods that are artfully prepared. If the gang is headed off to the Golden Arches, excuse yourself—it's just not worth the stress and frustration.

**National chains.** The same is true for most of the big restaurant chains, but if you are disciplined, you can likely find something tasty and healthful. You may have to ask the waiter for substitutions (such as a side salad for the fries), but it is possible to get a good meal. A few chains offer humanely raised meats and organic produce (Chipotle Grill is one in particular). When ordering Chinese stir-fries, request minimum oil and no MSG. Do not be afraid to speak up for yourself. Most restaurants are happy to accommodate special needs and requests. After all, you are the one paying the bill. Here are some safe bets when deciding on a restaurant:

- **Seafood specialists.** It is hard to go wrong with a nice piece of fresh fish or a pile of seafood surrounded by fresh veggies. Just be sure not to order anything fried, no matter how much you crave the Coconut Shrimp.

- **Thai food.** Always a good choice because the cuisine is loaded with veggies, while featuring seafood, lean meat, and poultry. Stay away from the pad Thai (which is fried noodles), but the soups, curries, and stir-fries are healthful and low in calories. Most restaurants even offer brown rice.

- **Japanese.** This cuisine sits high on our list of diabetes-healing restaurants. There is always fish—raw and cooked—and there may be brown rice instead of white for sushi. Nibbling steamed edamame (soybeans) as an appetizer is a sure hit. You can usually get teriyaki wild salmon beautifully presented with a choice of vegetables. You cannot go wrong with soba noodles (made of buckwheat) in a veggie stir-fry. Avoid the white rice and anything "tempura" (deep-fried).

- **Other Asian cuisine.** Keep clear of the Chinese buffet please, with its chemically fluorescent sweet and sour sauces and oil-drenched veggies and meats. Stick with smaller Korean, Chinese, and Vietnamese restaurants offering home-style meals. Go for the brightly colored vegetable stir-fries on a bed of brown rice. Add some tofu or seafood for protein. Have the chef go easy on the oil and request no MSG.

- **Mediterranean.** Restaurants that feature fish, lean meat, lots of vegetables, and yummy salads are a great choice. Italian-themed restaurants are hit and miss because they tend to feature pizza and pasta, which contain a lot of refined carbs. Some pizzerias offer whole wheat or whole grain crust, however. While not ideal, such pizzas are not terrible alternatives. Jim usually requests half the normal amount of cheese, plus extra veggies and tomato sauce.

- **Diners.** Believe it or not, most diners offer a wide array of real foods, starting with the ubiquitous omelet. Eggs are your friend any time of day and can be accompanied by a number of diabetes-healing ingredients, including spinach, tomatoes, mushrooms, and green peppers. Diners usually have a decent selection of veggie side orders, too. Order green beans and a salad in place of toast and potatoes.

## Dining Out with Savvy

Restaurants are redolent with memories of the days when you ate whatever and as much as you desired. Those were the days before you knew there were consequences to such indulgence. Yet all those alluring triggers still linger. First comes the bread basket. Then the waiter asks if you want a cocktail or wine. The menu is filled with so many temptations: Fried this… double-stuffed that…and outrageous entrées that have not touched your lips for weeks. And— oh my God!—look at those desserts! Your friends are ordering to their heart's content. What will you do? What will you choose? How the heck will you ever manage not to give in?

**Awareness is your saving grace.** You have a powerful new force working for you now— your *awareness*. You have developed the skill to be mindful as all these temptations arise. You are no longer living unconsciously, reacting to every trigger compulsively. Instead, you are able to view these seductions objectively—the ones pestering you as if they were little children begging you to put every treat and goodie they see on the supermarket shelves in your shopping cart. Do you do it? Of course not: You know that junk is not good for them.

**Begin with Smart Monitoring.** Excuse yourself to the restroom while everyone is getting settled. Keeping yourself honest and accountable by obtaining the concrete proof of how your actions are affecting your blood glucose levels is a fine motivator.

**Navigate the menu.** By now you should be pretty adept at knowing what you should and should not eat. Skip the bread basket. If you are having wine, sip it with your meal instead of before. Start with soup to fill you up. Follow that with salad with extra virgin olive oil and balsamic vinegar on the side so you can control the amount. Then pick an entrée of fish, poultry or lean meat—surrounded by lots of veggies. If you must have a potato, request a small one without the sour cream and bacon bits, add a small pat of butter and eat it skin and all. If you are at a restaurant that serves exceptionally large portions, immediately divide your plate and ask your waiter to put half in a doggie bag so you will not be tempted to overeat.

**What about dessert?** You just ate a lot of food (volume-wise, but not in calories), so you should be stuffed. If you still have room for dessert, pick something sensible and split it with your dining companions. Sample it knowing that one or two spoonfuls will be enough. Studies show that after three bites, our taste buds do not register the sweetness anymore. So savor those first spoonfuls. Have a cup of herbal tea with dessert and alternate sips with bites.

Most of all, relax and enjoy yourself. Dining out should not be a science project. Nor should it be a self-indulgent reward for being "good" all week. The real treat is that you don't have to cook or clean up!

## How to Survive Parties and Holidays

You have been invited to a holiday party, a potluck dinner, or you are meeting up with friends to watch the big game. You know there will be bowls of chips and snack foods, a cooler with sodas, and a fridge full of beer. Unidentifiable potluck casseroles will line the kitchen counter.

No matter what the holiday, it seems there are always piles of cookies and bowls of candy. It is time to strategize…

**Eat before you go.** This may sound counterintuitive—after all, you are going to a party and there is going to be a lot of food there! That is exactly why you should eat a filling, balanced meal with plenty of protein and vegetables shortly before you leave the house. With a full stomach, you will be far less tempted by the snack table and dessert foods. When you arrive, find some club soda and sip a glass throughout the party.

**But I am going to a party right after work.** The secret of living a diabetes-healing life in the outside world is planning ahead. When you know there is going to be an after-work party, plan the night before to take some leftovers you can microwave and eat before you leave work. Or put together a heftier snack pack than usual, including protein (hard-boiled eggs, turkey slices with cheese), plus some nice slow carbs (raw vegetables and a half-cup of kidney bean salad, bean dip or hummus), and don't forget to take a small bag of nuts.

**Test in pairs.** Remember to use the tool of Smart Monitoring. Knowing that you will test your blood glucose level two hours after the party will motivate you to choose your party food wisely.

**Potluck jackpot.** Potlucks are always appealing propositions for those of us who enjoy eating well. Someone (maybe it is you) always brings a big salad. Someone (you again?) ensures that there is a colorful raw vegetable tray filled with freshly cut carrots and celery sticks, chopped broccoli, and cherry tomatoes. "Someone" (you, perhaps?) might include a tangy dip made with garlicky Greek yogurt and herbs. The possibilities are endless and healing. For instance: Cook up a pot of chili from grass-fed ground beef (or bison) with two or three varieties of beans. Make coleslaw with vinegar and oil dressing (instead of the traditional mayo), plus lots of freshly chopped herbs. The bottom-line? Bring diabetes-friendly dishes that you can enjoy—you can't guarantee anyone else will.

**Buffet survival skills.** Cruise the offerings for those with maximum protein. Choose meatballs over pasta salad. Skip the mac-and-cheese and choose the chili. Load up on salad and vegetables. Nibble from the cheese tray, but leave the crackers behind. If you are having a cocktail, go for a Bloody Mary (or a white wine spritzer) and nurse it to the max.

**Focus on friendship.** You are at the party to enjoy being with friends and meeting new people. If you do not make food your primary focus, you will have the time and energy for the people around you

## Tips for Travel

Travel presents an endless series of obstacles and hurdles to eating well. If you are on the road —in an airport, on a train, or driving—do not be tempted to mess up your progress by eating what is available. Airports and conference hotels are virtual dead zones when it comes to finding fresh, nutritious food and so is much of the US highway system. Along with an abundance of packaged processed food, greasy-spoon restaurants, and fast food chains, it is difficult to find truly healthy options. But it is not impossible. Here are some tips that can help…

**Pack your snacks.** Remember our advice to never leave home without a personal food supply? This is especially important when traveling long distances. You will never find a healthy meal or snack on an airplane (unless you are traveling First Class to Europe). Yes, you will have a little more pre-travel packing to do, but given flight delays and the absolutely dismal offerings in travel hubs, you will be very glad you took the time.

**Use a map.** If you arrive at an airport or a train station without food, check a map. Locate all nearby restaurants and, if possible, scan online menus to choose places that at least offer a salad and/or fresh fruit.

**A cooler for your car or train trip.** Long stretches of US highways are food wastelands, filled with convenience stores and fast food chains. When you travel with a cooler full of your own food, you can enjoy all your favorites. Pack veggies, dips, hard-boiled eggs, canned tuna and sardines, plus artisan cheeses. Be sure you include lean meats, lettuce and tomato, plus condiments for making sandwiches on whole-grain bread. By keeping your cooler chilled, you can have a meal whenever you are hungry. (Take a blanket so you can park at a rest stop, get out, and enjoy a mini-picnic.)

**Other food cultures.** Traveling is all about adventure, as we experience new vistas and other cultures with their own cuisines. Many other cultures take food far more seriously than we in the US do, meaning your food selections in other countries could actually be easier. Fast-food outlets are just about ubiquitous everywhere and they should be avoided at all costs. Small, family-run eateries often serve the most traditional fare: Grilled fish with beans and salad in Mexico; antipasti along the Mediterranean; a perfect omelet with herbs in France. Healthy dining outside the US can be much easier.

## At a Friend's Home

As a guest in someone's home for a meal, honor your hosts by enjoying what they have prepared. Be vigilant about portions, choosing mostly vegetables and lean protein. Of course, you should try at least a small spoonful of any special dishes the host slaved over, and you will relish every bite. If it is a close friend, be sure to confide in them about your condition, your food preferences and what is off-limits. They should be more than willing to accommodate you, and may become a valuable part of your support system.

## Today's Action Steps

- Go to lunch or dinner at a restaurant with a partner or friend and outline your intentions.

- As you order and eat, explain your reasons for your menu choices and how they are helping to improve your condition. This practice run will help you choose your restaurant meals wisely in the future.

- Remember to test in pairs, even when eating out.

**Extra credit:** Prepare for your next trip by making a list of the healthy foods you will take along. Keep the list handy in your travel bag.

# DAY 30

# CELEBRATE!

*"The more you praise and celebrate your life,
the more there is in life to celebrate."*

—OPRAH WINFREY, talk show host, producer and actor

**Tip of the Day:** If you have completed this plan, you are reversing your diabetes. Don't forget these 30 days and what you are capable of achieving!

YOU MADE IT! With your determination and willpower, you are saving yourself from diabetes and a lifetime of medicated misery. You looked diabetes square in the eye and decided to make your life an *exclamation*—instead of an excuse. In just 30 days, you turned your entire life around, transforming it from one of weakness, dependency, and sickness into one filled with personal power, wisdom, and new diabetes-healing skills. You are amazing!

## Welcome to the Diabetes-Healing Lifestyle!

We don't know you personally (although we hope one day our paths will cross), but we bet you are looking, thinking, acting, and feeling much better than you were 30 days ago. Are we right? So let us celebrate your liberation from diabetic captivity with a day of diabetes-healing meals and activities that you embraced throughout these last weeks. Below are several ideas for today—and beyond.

1. Wake up earlier than usual to give yourself extra time to appreciate this day and your accomplishments. Spend 20 to 30 minutes quietly contemplating or meditating.

2. Start your celebration with your favorite diabetes-healing breakfast. Enjoy creamy whole-milk yogurt with berries and walnuts…or a slice of whole-grain bread with almond butter…an omelet with sautéed broccoli, cheese, and tomatoes…or perhaps one suggested in Appendix C.

3. Listen to some peaceful music as you eat and dress. Notice the changes you have made in the past four weeks.

4. Do something special for yourself. Take yourself out to the movies…spend the afternoon in a museum surrounded by beauty and creativity…or buy yourself a new outfit. Think about buying yourself a big bouquet of flowers, some new music, a massage, or something else you especially enjoy.

5. Pick a new spot to walk, holding your head up proudly, and smile at every single person you see.

## Seven Steps for Cultivating Gratitude

Here is a small but enormously important exercise that Jim starts his day off with. It only takes about 10 or 15 minutes, but the results last for an entire day. He finds it especially helpful on days when nothing seems to go right.

1. Wake up a bit earlier than normal. Go to a quiet spot and sit comfortably with your eyes closed. Pay attention to your breath as it naturally flows in and out, and let your mind clear. Scan your body from the inside, beginning at the tips of your toes. Inhale and sense your attention flow all the way to the top of your head as you exhale. Doing this a few times will calm and center you.

2. Invite a feeling of gratitude to overtake you with each breath, gradually surrendering to it. Feel grateful for the moment. For being alive. For your physical body. For the health and vitality you have. For the loved ones in your life. For all the things you are able to enjoy. And everything else in your life that you appreciate.

3. Allow a smile to form—even if you have to force it at first. Keep it there as you breath in and take inventory of everything in your life you are grateful for. In a short time, you should feel your smile blossoming into a sensation of happiness that will spread throughout your body.

4. Filled with this joy, allow yourself to be thankful.

5. One by one, visualize the faces of people with whom you'd like to share this feeling. As each person comes into your awareness, radiate your wish for health and happiness to him or her.

6. Finally, send this joy outward to our entire world and to the universe itself. Let it pour from your heart like a beam of golden light as you repeat three times:
   "May all beings be Peaceful.
   May all beings be Well.
   May all beings Prosper.
   May all beings be Happy."

7. Gather yourself by taking a big breath. Now open your eyes. Notice your surroundings in detail. With another large inhalation and exhalation, stand up and step into your day, open-minded and ready to learn the lessons that life has in store for you.

6. Make a plan to share this special day with your friends and family members. Let them know what you have accomplished and show your appreciation for their support.

7. Remind yourself that you now have every tool you need to keep moving toward a full, happy, peaceful, and healthy life.

8. Feel confident that you are well equipped for the next phase of your life: Living free of disease, pharmaceuticals, and junk food.

**9.** Let yourself feel gratitude for having made this transformation. (See Cultivating Gratitude Exercise on page 359.)

## Get Even More Inspired

You have probably inspired friends and family who have watched your transformation. You are a hero to them and have set a wonderful example for them to follow. You have overcome diabetes! Plan a movie night with someone special and view the moving true story of another person's determination and passion.

The film we want you to rent is *A Man Named Pearl*, and it follows Pearl Fryar, son of a poor sharecropper, as he creates a stunning 3.5-acre topiary garden from plants other people have discarded. In the process, Fryar rises to international prominence as an acclaimed topiary artist and brings together one of the poorest communities in South Carolina. Pearl will make your heart sing as you set a course for your future.

## It's Time for Your Graduation

Congratulations for being so dedicated to healing yourself these past 30 days!

Remember, this is not the end—it is just the beginning. Stick to the path you are on and build on your success these past 30 days. Science is making new discoveries about diabetes every day. To stay in touch with new healing developments and to discover other diabetes-healing superfoods—plus delicious free recipes that incorporate them—we invite you to visit *www.bottomlineinc.com* to continue your "education."

## Today's Action Steps

- Take time to reflect on what you have accomplished.
- Reinforce your success by sharing it with others.
- Thank those who have helped you.
- Help—and inspire—others with your story.
- Look forward to living a life of vitality, adventure, and good health.

**Extra credit:** Prepare a special diabetes-healing recipe (or two) as part of your celebration. See pages 375 to 402 for ideas. And, enjoy!

# Endnotes—Part 2

## Day 1: Smart Monitoring

[1] http://diabetes.niddk.nih.gov/dm/pubs/A1CTest/

## Day 2: Sodas and Alcohol Swap

[2] Schulze MB, Manson JE, Ludwig DS, Colditz GA, Stampfer MJ, Willett WC, Hu FB. Sugar-sweetened beverages, weight gain, and incidence of Type 2 diabetes in young and middle-aged women. *Journal of the American Medical Association*. 2004;292:927-934.

[3] http://www.uthscsa.edu/hscnews/singleformat2.asp?newID=3861

[4] Nettleton, Jennifer A., PhD, et al, "Diet Soda Intake and Risk of Incident Metabolic Syndrome and Type 2 Diabetes in the Multi-Ethnic Study of Atherosclerosis," *Diabetes Care* (January 2009)

[5] http://download.cell.com/images/edimages/Trends/EndoMetabolism/tem_888.pdf

[6] http://www.tandfonline.com/doi/abs/10.1080/15287390802328630?url_ver=Z39.88-2003&rfr_id=ori:rid:crossref.org&rfr_dat=cr_pub%3dpubmed&#.UlmUbBZDEjE

[7] http://articles.mercola.com/sites/articles/archive/2005/09/29/liquid-candy-the-rise-of-soft-drinks-in-america.aspx

[8] Ibid

[9] *Journal of the American Medical Association*. July 2003

[10] Dehydration information: http://www.mayoclinic.com/health/dehydration/DS00561

[11] Diabetes Friends Action Network: http://www.dfandiabetes.com/

[12] http://pubs.acs.org/doi/abs/10.1021/jf048052l

[13] Tea research in the UK: http://news.bbc.co.uk/2/hi/5281046.stm

[14] Dulloo, A.G. et al, "Green tea and thermogenesis: interactions between catechin-polyphenols, caffeine and sympathetic activity," *International Journal of Obesity* (February 2000)

[15] Green tea information, University of Maryland Medical Center: http://www.umm.edu/altmed/articles/green-tea-000255.htm

[16] http://www.sciencedaily.com/releases/2008/04/080402212428.htm

[17] Huxley, Rachel, DPhil, et al, "Coffee, Decaffeinated Coffee, and Tea Consumption in Relation to Incident Type 2 Diabetes Mellitus," *Archives of Internal Medicine* (2009)
Kleemola, MSc, Paivi, "Coffee Consumption and the Risk of Coronary Heart Disease and Death," *Archives of Internal Medicine* (December 2000)

[18] http://www.mindbodygreen.com/0-5825/Why-Everyone-Should-Drink-Chai-Tea.html

## Day 3: Fruit Swap

[19] http://www.womenshealthmag.com/nutrition/why-eat-fruit-peels?page=4

[20] http://www.womenshealthmag.com/nutrition/why-eat-fruit-peels?page=4

[21] http://health.howstuffworks.com/wellness/food-nutrition/natural-foods/natural-weight-loss-food-grapefruit-ga.htm

[22] "Strawberries Reduce Inflammation in Blood Vessels," www.diabetesincontrol.com/index.php?option=com_content&view=article&id=5440&catid=53&Itemid=8

## Day 4: Take a Break from Sweets

[23] http://ezinearticles.com/?Not-So-Sweet...The-Average-American-Consumes-150-170-Pounds-of-Sugar-Each-Year&id=2252026

[24] Editors, "Does Sugar Feed Cancer?" ScienceDaily.com (August 2009).

[25] http://ajcn.nutrition.org/content/95/5/1182.abstract?etoc

26 (24 HR Pg. 92)

27 http://www.huffingtonpost.com/dr-mercola/americas-deadliest-sweete_b_630549.html

28 https://www.health.harvard.edu/healthbeat/HEALTHbeat_033005.htm#art1

## Day 5: Eat Breakfast Every Day

29 Vander Wal, J.S. et al, "Egg breakfast enhances weight loss," International Journal of Obesity (2008)

30 Katz DL, Evans MA, Nawaz H, et al. Egg consumption and endothelial function: a randomized controlled crossover trial. *International Journal of Cardiology* 2005; 99(1): 65-70.

31 Yogurt benefits: http://www.naturalnews.com/010204.html

32 Zemel, M.B. et al, "Dairy augmentation of total and central fat loss in obese subjects," *International Journal of Obesity* (2005)

## Day 7: Carbohydrate Swap

33 http://www.nejm.org/doi/full/10.1056/NEJMra010852

34 http://toxnet.nlm.nih.gov/cgi-bin/sis/search/a?dbs+hsdb:@term+@DOCNO+7493

35 *http://www.college.ucla.edu/news/03/barnard.html*

36 http://www.hsph.harvard.edu/nutritionsource/more/type-2-diabetes/

37 http://www.bu.edu/bwhs/

38 Riccardi, G. et al, "Effects of dietary fiber and carbohydrate on glucose and lipoprotein metabolism in diabetic patients," *Diabetes Care* (1991).

39 Cinnamon research: http://www.ars.usda.gov/(search "Cinnamon")

## Day 8: Add Diabetes-Healing Vegetables

40 http://diabetes.diabetesjournals.org/content/early/2008/08/04/db06-1003.abstract?maxtoshow=&HITS=10&hits=10&RESULTFORMAT=&fulltext=sulforaphane&searchid=1&FIRSTINDEX=0&sortspec=relevance&resourcetype=HWCIT

41 http://lpi.oregonstate.edu/infocenter/vitamins/vitaminC/

42 http://www.medicinenet.com/script/main/art.asp?articlekey=41765

43 Ma, Le et al, "Effects of lutein and zeaxanthin on aspects of eye health," *Journal of the Science of Food and Agriculture* (September 2009)

44 http://umm.edu/health/medical/altmed/supplement/manganese

45 Yoshida, Makiko et al, "Effect of Vitamin K Supplementation on Insulin Resistance in Older Men and Women," *Diabetes Care* (August 2008).

## Day 9: Smart Protein Swap

46 Omega-3 information: http://www.umm.edu/altmed/articles/omega-3-000316.htm

47 http://www.hsph.harvard.edu/nutritionsource/eggs/

## Day 11: Ease Stress

48 http://currents.plos.org/disasters/article/the-great-east-japan-earthquake-experiences-and-suggestions-for-survivors-with-diabetes-perspective-2/

49 http://www.prevention.com/health/healthy-living/workplace-hazard-diabetes

50 Ibid.

51 http://www.alternet.org/environment/studies-show-amazing-ways-nature-boon-your-health

52 http://care.diabetesjournals.org/content/28/9/2145.abstract

## Day 12: Smart Lunch Swap

[53] http://www.ncbi.nlm.nih.gov/pubmed/17597516

## Day 13: Snack Sensibly If You Must

[54] http://www.nytimes.com/2002/11/27/us/nuts-may-help-prevent-diabetes-study-of-83000-women-shows.html?n=Top%2fReference%2fTimes%20Topics%2fSubjects%2fF%2fFood

[55] http://www.sciencedirect.com/science/article/pii/S0308814604002948

[56] Jenkins, David et al, "Almonds Decrease Postprandial Glycemia, Insulinemia, and Oxidative Damage in Healthy Individual," *Journal of Nutrition* (December 2006)

[57] Josse, Andrea R. et al, "Almonds and postprandial glycemia—a dose-response study," *Metabolism* (March 2007)

[58] Lamarche, Benoit et al, "Combined effects of a dietary portfolio of plant sterols, vegetable protein, viscous fibre and almonds on LDL particle size," *British Journal of Nutrition* (2004)

[59] Tapsell, PhD, Linda C. et al, "Including Walnuts in a Low-Fat/Modified-Fat Diet Improves HDL Cholesterol-to-Total Cholesterol Ratios in Patients With Type 2 Diabetes," *Diabetes Care* (December 2004)

[60] http://www.ncbi.nlm.nih.gov/pubmed/17125534

[61] http://www.whfoods.com/genpage.php?tname=foodspice&dbid=98

[62] http://www.sciencedirect.com/science?_ob=ArticleURL&_udi=B6T6R-4CWBKYV-2&_user=10&_coverDate=05%2F31%2F2005&_rdoc=1&_fmt=high&_orig=search&_sort=d&_docanchor=&view=c&_searchStrId=1331517642&_rerunOrigin=google&_acct=C000050221&_version=1&_urlVersion=0&_userid=10&md5=ebbd6626cbee00d825c94ef44c6cdf92

[63] http://www.huffingtonpost.com/2012/04/30/dark-chocolate-health-cholesterol-blood-sugar_n_1452799.html

[64] http://www.huffingtonpost.com/dr-mercola/sugar-may-be-bad-but-this_b_463655.html

## Day 15: Step Up Your Activity Level

[65] http://walking.about.com/cs/poles/a/polestudy00_2.htm

[66] http://walking.about.com/cs/music/a/musicbrain.htm

[67] http://www.cbsnews.com/8301-204_162-57583903/american-heart-association-pets-especially-dogs-are-good-for-the-heart/

[68] http://aeawave.com/Portals/2/Research/AKWARESEARCHREVIEWS2012.pdf

## Day 16: Conquer Self-Sabotage

[69] http://www.dukemagazine.duke.edu/issues/030408/depgaz13.html

[70] Ibid

[71] AARP March-April 2010

[72] http://www.sciencedaily.com/releases/2009/09/090902112103.htm

[73] http://www.nature.com/ejcn/journal/v63/n9/abs/ejcn200937a.html

## Day 17: Eliminate Toxic Food Ingredients

[74] https://www.cspinet.org/new/201006291.html

[75] http://undergroundhealthreporter.com/the-10-worst-food-ingredients#ixzz2GOQByadQ

[76] http://www.holisticmed.com/aspartame/abuse/methanol.html and http://www.holisticmed.com/aspartame/abuse/

[77] http://undergroundhealthreporter.com/the-10-worst-food-ingredients

[78] http://www.collective-evolution.com/2012/04/10/you-have-the-right-to-know-17-chemicals-to-avoid-in-cosmetic-and-personal-care-products/

[79] http://ajpregu.physiology.org/content/295/5/R1370

[80] http://www.iatp.org/documents/table-a-total-mercury-detected-in-55-brand-name-foods-and-beverages-high-in-hfcs

[81] http://www.washingtonpost.com/wp-dyn/content/article/2009/01/26/AR2009012601831.html

[82] http://www.huffingtonpost.com/dr-mark-hyman/high-fructose-corn-syrup_b_4256220.html

[83] http://articles.mercola.com/sites/articles/archive/2009/09/05/another-poison-hiding-in-your-environment.aspx

[84] http://www.healthcentral.com/diet-exercise/c/299905/160111/leave-processed-meats/

## Day 18: Eat More Beans and Legumes

[85] http://www.nutritionandmetabolism.com/content/1/1/8

[86] http://digestivehealthinstitute.org/2013/05/10/resistant-starch-friend-or-foe/

[87] http://www.healthdoc.org/faq

[88] http://lpi.oregonstate.edu/ss01/anthocyanin.html

[89i] http://content.nejm.org/cgi/content/short/342/19/1392

[90] Ravussin E et al. "Effects of a traditional lifestyle on obesity in Pima Indians." *Diabetes Care* 1994 Sep;17(9):1067-74.

[91] http://consumer.healthday.com/encyclopedia/diabetes-13/diet-diabetes-news-178/fiber-an-all-natural-medicine-for-type-2-diabetes-644145.html

## Day 20: Consider a Detox Program

[92] http://www.webmd.com/balance/natural-liver-detox-diets-liver-cleansing?page=2

[93] http://www.wholehealthchicago.com/knowledge-base/m/milk-thistle/

[94] http://aje.oxfordjournals.org/cgi/content/short/164/9/898

[95] http://www.renegadeneurologist.com/turmeric-and-brain-health/

## Day 21: Sleep Longer and Better

[96] Gottlieb, MD, MPH, Daniel J. et al, "Association of Sleep Time With Diabetes Mellitus and Impaired Glucose Tolerance," *Archives of Internal Medicine* (April 2005).

[97] Vgontzas, Alexandros N. et al, "Chronic Insomnia Is Associated with Nyctohemeral Activation of the Hypothalamic-Pituitary-Adrenal Axis: Clinical Implications," *Journal of Clinical Endocrinology & Metabolism* (2001).

[98] http://www.uchospitals.edu/news/2004/20041206-sleep.html

[99] http://www.ncbi.nlm.nih.gov/pmc/articles/PMC535701/

## Day 22: Add Yoga

[100] http://www.ncbi.nlm.nih.gov/pubmed/18227915

[101] http://osuwmc.multimedianewsroom.tv/story.php?id=715&enter=

## Day 23: Reduce Depression and Boredom

[102] http://www.cdc.gov/diabetes/pubs/estimates11.htm

[103] http://bjp.rcpsych.org/cgi/content/full/184/5/404

[104] Akbaraly, PhD, Tasnime N., "Dietary pattern and depressive symptoms in middle age," *British Journal of Psychiatry* (2009)

[105] http://ajp.psychiatryonline.org/cgi/content/abstract/167/3/305

[106] http://ajp.psychiatryonline.org/cgi/content/abstract/167/3/305

[107] Sandyk, Reuven, "L-Tryptophan in Neuropsychiatry Disorders: A Review," *International Journal of Neuroscience* (1992)

[108] http://www.med.nyu.edu/content?ChunkIID=21399

[109] http://www.ncbi.nlm.nih.gov/pubmed/15671130

[110] http://lpi.oregonstate.edu/infocenter/othernuts/omega3fa/

[111] http://www.ncbi.nlm.nih.gov/pmc/articles/PMC2077351/

[112] http://www.huffingtonpost.com/2013/08/23/volunteering-happiness-depression-live-longer_n_3804274.html

## Day 24: Add a Support System

[113] http://jama.ama-assn.org/cgi/content/full/299/23/2751

[114] http://www.nytimes.com/2007/07/25/health/25iht-fat.4.6830240.html?pagewanted=all&_r=0

[115] http://www.diabetesselfmanagement.com/Articles/Diabetes-Definitions/cognitive-behavioral-therapy/

[116] http://www.dukehealth.org/health_library/health_articles/rxfordiabetes

## Day 25: Reduce Your Exposure to Environmental Toxins

[117] http://www.epa.gov/oia/toxics/pop.htm

[118] http://www.epa.gov/oia/toxics/pop.htm#table

[119] http://www.epa.gov/pesticides/food/risks.htm

[120] http://www.ncbi.nlm.nih.gov/pmc/articles/PMC1332699/

[121] http://www.ewg.org/research/down-drain

[122] http://www.ewg.org/skindeep/research

[123] http://www.huffingtonpost.com/2012/02/14/bpa-chemical-hormone-obesity-diabetes_n_1276996.html

[124] http://news.bbc.co.uk/2/hi/europe/2906357.stm

[125] *New Scientist*, 12 january 2009

[126] http://chicagoist.com/2010/04/18/trib_tackles_gender_bending_chemica.php

[127] http://www.treehugger.com/files/2009/08/todays-toxin-atrazine.php

[128] http://www.webmd.com/balance/natural-liver-detox-diets-liver-cleansing?page=2

[129] http://greencentury.com/wp-content/uploads/2013/05/bpareport2010.pdf

[130] http://www.nrdc.org/media/2007/070919.asp

[131] http://ajrccm.atsjournals.org/cgi/content/full/176/8/735

## Day 26: Add Vitamins and Supplements

[132] http://www.motherearthnews.com/homesteading-and-livestock/nutrient-value-of-food-zm0z11zphe.aspx

[133] http://www.hsph.harvard.edu/nutritionsource/diabetes-full-story/

[134] http://www.ncbi.nlm.nih.gov/pmc/articles/PMC2621390/

[135] Mattila, Catharina et al, "Serum 25-Hydroxyvitamin D Concentration and Subsequent Risk of Type 2 Diabetes," *Diabetes Care* (October 2007).

[136] http://www.sciencedaily.com/releases/2009/01/090112121821.htm

[137] Loyola University Health System (2009, January 14)

[138] The Nurses' Health Study: http://www.channing.harvard.edu/nhs/

[139] Teegarden, Dorothy et al, "Vitamin D: emerging new roles in insulin sensitivity," *Nutrition Research Reviews* (June 2009).

[140] von Hurst, Pamela R. et al, "Vitamin D supplementation reduces insulin resistance in South Asian women living in New Zealand who are insulin resistant and vitamin D deficient—a randomised, placebo-controlled trial," *British Journal of Nutrition* (2010).

[141] Chiu, Ken C. et al, "Hypovitaminosis D is associated with insulin resistance and ß cell dysfunction," *American Journal of Clinical Nutrition* (May 2004).

[142] Inzucchi, Silvio E., MD, et al, "Efficacy and Metabolic Effects of Metformin and Troglitazone in Type II Diabetes Mellitus," *New England Journal of Medicine* (March 1998).

## Day 27: Become a Volunteer

[143] http://opinionator.blogs.nytimes.com/2010/10/17/morals-without-god/

## Day 28: Start Building More Muscle

[144] https://www.logicalhealthalternatives.com/rhc.php?action=displayArticle&docs_id=928
[145] http://fitness.mercola.com/sites/fitness/archive/2013/09/20/exercise-health-benefits.aspx
[146] http://greatist.com/tips/cardio-workout-cardio-bodyweight-circuits

# APPENDIX A

# THE DIABETES-HEALING KITCHEN MAKEOVER

In order to heal your diabetes, your kitchen will need a makeover. All foods, beverages, and ingredients that spike your blood glucose must be removed. Only with these out of your life can you take the first steps toward reversing your diabetes.

Go through your kitchen today and remove all the foods and ingredients listed in the left columns below. Then replace them with the more healthful options on the right. When possible, always purchase organic. These are the foods and ingredients that you will come to rely on in The 30-Day Diabetes Cure Plan.

## REFRIGERATOR

| REMOVE THESE | ...AND REPLACE WITH THESE |
|---|---|
| Margarine | Dairy butter, coconut butter |
| Low fat and nonfat cheese | Full-fat cheese |
| Mayonnaise | Vegenaise, aioli made with extra virgin olive oil |
| Skim milk, coffee creamer | Whole milk, half and half, unsweetened soy milk |
| Sweetened yogurt | Plain Greek or homemade yogurt |
| Conventional produce | Organic produce |
| Factory-farm eggs | Omega-3 free-range eggs |
| Store-bought salad dressings | Homemade vinaigrette |
| Condiments containing HFCS | HFCS-free condiments |
| Unhealthful dips | Hummus and salsa |
| Soda | Sparkling water |
| Most juices | Fresh fruit or a splash of unsweetened pomegranate juice |
| Whole wheat or processed bread | 100% whole grain bread |
| Breakfast and lunch meats with nitrates/nitrites | Lunch meat without nitrates/nitrites |

# FREEZER

| REMOVE THESE | ...AND REPLACE WITH THESE |
| --- | --- |
| Artificially sweetened frozen desserts | Frozen fruit for yogurt smoothies |
| Ice cream (full fat, low fat, nonfat) | Frozen fruit for yogurt smoothies |
| Frozen juice concentrate | Seltzer or club soda with a splash of 100% unsweetened fruit juice |
| TV dinners and frozen packaged meals | Healthful leftovers in one portion servings |
| Frozen vegetables in cheese and other sauces | Plain frozen vegetables |
| Breaded/farmed fish | Wild-caught fish |
| Breaded/conventional chicken | Free-range local chicken |
| Factory farmed beef | Local grass-fed and finished beef |

# CUPBOARDS

| REMOVE THESE | ...AND REPLACE WITH THESE |
| --- | --- |
| Sweetened applesauce | Apples |
| Sweetened cocoa | Unsweetened cocoa |
| Flavored/canned coffee | Green teabags and whole coffee beans (store in freezer) |
| White flour pasta, macaroni and cheese | Whole grain pasta |
| White rice, Rice-a-Roni | Brown rice, wild rice, quinoa, amaranth, barley, and the other whole grains |
| Canned beans | Dry beans |
| BPA-containing canned goods | BPA-free canned goods |
| Canned soups | Homemade soup |
| Chips and crackers | Nuts and seeds |
| Instant oatmeal | Steel-cut oats |
| Cold cereal | Unsweetened whole grain hot cereal |
| White flour | Whole grain, high-fiber flour (such as oat) |
| White sugar | No sweeteners |

| | |
|---|---|
| Canola oil and standard vegetable oil, Crisco | Grape seed, coconut, sesame, peanut oil, lard (store in fridge) |
| Poor-quality olive oil | Fresh, reputable extra virgin olive oil |
| Sugary liqueurs and mixers | Red and white wines |
| Sugar-added tomato sauce | Unsweetened tomato sauce |

# APPENDIX B

# THE GLYCEMIC INDEX AND GLYCEMIC LOAD FOR 100+ FOODS

The glycemic index and glycemic load offer information about how foods affect blood sugar and insulin. The lower a food's glycemic index or glycemic load, the less it affects blood sugar and insulin levels. For a more complete explanation, see Chapter 10.

On the following pages a list of the glycemic index and glycemic load for more than 100 common foods created by Harvard Medical School's Harvard Health Publications. For additional details, please visit http://www.health.harvard.edu/newsweek/Glycemic_index_and_ glycemic_load_for_100_foods.htm.

| Food | Glycemic index (glucose-100) | Serving size grams | Glycemic load per serving |
|---|---|---|---|
| **Breads and Cakes** | | | |
| Banana cake, made with sugar | 47 | 60 | 14 |
| Banana cake, made without sugar | 55 | 60 | 12 |
| Sponge cake, plain | 46 | 63 | 17 |
| Vanilla cake made from packet mix with vanilla frosting (Betty Crocker) | 42 | 111 | 24 |
| Apple, made with sugar | 44 | 60 | 13 |
| Apple, made without sugar | 48 | 60 | 9 |
| Waffles, Aunt Jemima (Quaker Oats) | 76 | 35 | 10 |
| Bagel, white, frozen | 72 | 70 | 25 |
| Baguette, white, plain | 95 | 30 | 15 |
| Coarse barley bread, 75%–80% kernels, average | 34 | 30 | 7 |
| Hamburger bun | 61 | 30 | 9 |
| Kaiser roll | 73 | 30 | 12 |
| Pumpernickel bread | 56 | 30 | 7 |
| 50% cracked wheat kernel bread | 58 | 30 | 12 |

| | | | |
|---|---|---|---|
| White and wheat flour bread | 71 | 30 | 10 |
| Wonder bread, average | 73 | 30 | 10 |
| Whole wheat bread, average | 71 | 30 | 9 |
| 100% Whole Grain bread (Natural Ovens) | 51 | 30 | 7 |
| Pita bread, white | 68 | 30 | 10 |
| Corn tortilla | 52 | 50 | 12 |
| Wheat tortilla | 30 | 50 | 8 |
| **Beverages** | | | |
| Coca Cola, average | 63 | 250 mL | 16 |
| Fanta, orange soft drink | 68 | 250 mL | 23 |
| Lucozade, original (sparkling glucose drink) | 95±10 | 250 mL | 40 |
| Apple juice, unsweetened, average | 44 | 250 mL | 30 |
| Cranberry juice cocktail (Ocean Spray) | 68 | 250 mL | 24 |
| Gatorade | 78 | 250 mL | 12 |
| Orange juice, unsweetened | 50 | 250 mL | 12 |
| Tomato juice, canned | 38 | 250 mL | 4 |
| **Breakfast Cereals and Related Products** | | | |
| All-Bran, average | 55 | 30 | 12 |
| Coco Pops, average | 77 | 30 | 20 |
| Cornflakes, average | 93 | 30 | 23 |
| Cream of Wheat (Nabisco) | 66 | 250 | 17 |
| Cream of Wheat, Instant (Nabisco) | 74 | 250 | 22 |
| Grapenuts, average | 75 | 30 | 16 |
| Muesli, average | 66 | 30 | 16 |
| Oatmeal, average | 55 | 250 | 13 |
| Instant oatmeal, average | 83 | 250 | 30 |

| | | | |
|---|---|---|---|
| Puffed wheat, average | 80 | 30 | 17 |
| Raisin Bran (Kellogg's) | 61 | 30 | 12 |
| Special K (Kellogg's) | 69 | 30 | 14 |
| **Grains** | | | |
| Pearled barley, average | 28 | 150 | 12 |
| Sweet corn on the cob, average | 60 | 150 | 20 |
| Couscous, average | 65 | 150 | 9 |
| Quinoa | 53 | 150 | 13 |
| White rice, average | 89 | 150 | 43 |
| Quick cooking white basmati | 67 | 150 | 28 |
| Brown rice, average | 50 | 150 | 16 |
| Converted, white rice (Uncle Ben's) | 38 | 150 | 14 |
| Whole wheat kernels, average | 30 | 50 | 11 |
| Bulgur, average | 48 | 150 | 12 |
| **Cookies and Crackers** | | | |
| Graham crackers | 74 | 25 | 14 |
| Vanilla wafers | 77 | 25 | 14 |
| Shortbread | 64 | 25 | 10 |
| Rice cakes, average | 82 | 25 | 17 |
| Rye crisps, average | 64 | 25 | 11 |
| Soda crackers | 74 | 25 | 12 |
| **Dairy Products and Alternatives** | | | |
| Ice cream, regular | 57 | 50 | 6 |
| Ice cream, premium | 38 | 50 | 3 |
| Milk, full fat | 41 | 250 mL | 5 |
| Milk, skim | 32 | 250 mL | 4 |
| Reduced-fat yogurt with fruit, average | 33 | 200 | 11 |

| **Fruits** | | | |
|---|---|---|---|
| Apple, average | 39 | 120 | 6 |
| Banana, ripe | 62 | 120 | 16 |
| Dates, dried | 42 | 60 | 18 |
| Grapefruit | 25 | 120 | 3 |
| Grapes, average | 59 | 120 | 11 |
| Orange, average | 40 | 120 | 4 |
| Peach, average | 42 | 120 | 5 |
| Peach, canned in light syrup | 40 | 120 | 5 |
| Pear, average | 38 | 120 | 4 |
| Pear, canned in pear juice | 43 | 120 | 5 |
| Prunes, pitted | 29 | 60 | 10 |
| Raisins | 64 | 60 | 28 |
| Watermelon | 72 | 120 | 4 |
| **Beans and Nuts** | | | |
| Baked beans, average | 40 | 150 | 6 |
| Black-eyed peas, average | 33 | 150 | 10 |
| Black beans | 30 | 150 | 7 |
| Chickpeas, average | 10 | 150 | 3 |
| Chickpeas, canned in brine | 38 | 150 | 9 |
| Navy beans, average | 31 | 150 | 9 |
| Kidney beans, average | 29 | 150 | 7 |
| Lentils, average | 29 | 150 | 5 |
| Soy beans, average | 15 | 150 | 1 |
| Cashews, salted | 27 | 50 | 3 |
| Peanuts, average | 7 | 50 | 0 |
| **Pasta and Noodles** | | | |
| Fettucini, average | 32 | 180 | 15 |
| Macaroni, average | 47 | 180 | 23 |
| Macaroni and Cheese (Kraft) | 64 | 180 | 32 |

| | | | |
|---|---|---|---|
| Spaghetti, white, boiled, average | 46 | 180 | 22 |
| Spaghetti, white, boiled 20 min, average | 58 | 180 | 26 |
| Spaghetti, whole wheat, boiled, average | 42 | 180 | 17 |
| **Snack Foods** | | | |
| Corn chips, plain, salted, average | 42 | 50 | 11 |
| Fruit Roll-Ups | 99 | 30 | 24 |
| M&M's peanut | 33 | 30 | 6 |
| Microwave popcorn, plain, average | 55 | 20 | 6 |
| Potato chips, average | 51 | 50 | 12 |
| Pretzels, oven-baked | 83 | 30 | 16 |
| Snickers Bar | 51 | 60 | 18 |
| **Vegetables** | | | |
| Green peas, average | 51 | 80 | 4 |
| Carrots, average | 35 | 80 | 2 |
| Parsnips | 52 | 80 | 4 |
| Baked russet potato, average | 111 | 150 | 33 |
| Boiled white potato, average | 82 | 150 | 21 |
| Instant mashed potato, average | 87 | 150 | 17 |
| Sweet potato, average | 70 | 150 | 22 |
| Yam, average | 54 | 150 | 20 |
| **Miscellaneous** | | | |
| Hummus (chickpea salad dip) | 6 | 30 | 0 |
| Chicken nuggets, frozen, reheated in microwave oven 5 minutes | 46 | 100 | 7 |
| Pizza, plain baked dough, served with parmesan cheese and tomato sauce | 80 | 100 | 22 |
| Pizza, Super Supreme (Pizza Hut) | 36 | 100 | 9 |
| Honey, average | 61 | 25 | 12 |

# APPENDIX C

# DIABETES-HEALING BREAKFASTS

Breakfast is the most important meal of the day—especially if you suffer from prediabetes or diabetes. But how do most of us start our days?

A donut and candy-cane flavored coffee. A bowl of cold cereal and packaged orange juice. The remains of last night's take-out pizza. Something wrapped in paper that vaguely resembles an old-fashioned bacon and eggs sandwich obtained from a drive-thru window and eaten while also juggling a cell phone and a steering wheel. Sound familiar?

Breakfast has gone from being the most important meal of the day—the one that not only "breaks the fast" of the long night of sleep, but also sets up your energy level for the day to come—to something that offers convenience, as well as lots of sugar, refined carbohydrates, bad fats, and heaps of sodium that are devoid of nutritive benefit; a meal that inflames your arteries, causes your body to retain fluid, and drives up your blood sugar (as well as your weight).

Typical American breakfasts like the ones mentioned above need to be avoided at all costs. Most processed breakfast foods only add excess calories and excess pounds with little, if any, nutritional value; plus, they are a *major factor* contributing to your blood sugar problems and increasing your risk for other related conditions such as artery disease, stroke, heart attack, hypertension, poor circulation, and others.

If you truly want to take control of your blood sugar, the first place to start is with the first meal of the day. We urge you to commit yourself to start every day with a diabetes-healing breakfast.

## Basic Ingredients of a Diabetes-Healing Breakfast

In this appendix, you'll find 10 diabetes-healing breakfast recipes designed to satisfy you and energize you for the day ahead. These meals will lower your blood sugar, reduce inflammation, cut excess calories, increase your energy, help you shed fluid and excess weight, and lower your blood pressure.

The elements of the ideal breakfast are pretty simple. You want to build your meal around high-quality, "clean" protein. Then you want to add healthful fats. Finally, your breakfast will include complex carbohydrates (fruits and vegetables) that pack in as much fiber as possible. Let's look at each element individually…

**Protein.** Healthful sources of protein such as omega-3-rich eggs, cheese, yogurt, and non-processed meats represent the most important part of breakfast. They build muscle, promote tissue repair, and provide sustained energy throughout the morning. They also satiate your hunger longer than carbohydrate-based meals, which in turn helps to control your weight.

**Fats.** The key here is to select healthful fats that will not inflame your arteries or oxidize your bloodstream. Generally speaking, you want to choose fats that are either monounsaturated or saturated, as well as non-refined polyunsaturated fats (PUFAs). Omega-3 fats found in fish and pasture-raised meat and poultry represent healthful PUFAs. Meat, butter and other dairy products, and coconut oil are healthful sources of saturated fats. Avocado, nuts, and seeds are good sources of healthful monounsaturated fats. Avoid refined vegetable oils and all food products containing trans fats.

**Carbohydrates.** Vegetables, fruits, beans and legumes, nuts and seeds, plus whole grains in their natural state are good examples of complex carbohydrates. These also provide the greatest volume of fiber, which helps normalize blood pressure. Shoot for 50g of fiber per day—or more.

# 10 Diabetes-Healing Breakfasts

To help you get started, what follows are recipes for 10 delicious breakfasts that will satisfy your taste buds and help normalize your blood glucose levels.

### Poached Egg on Ezekiel Bread with Creamy Spinach and Roasted Red Pepper Sauce

**Serves:** 2

**Total Time:** 10 minutes

A plethora of powerhouse diabetes-healing ingredients combine in this quick and easy breakfast to make your morning healthy and hunger-free. Omega-3 eggs reduce inflammation, whole grains help stabilize blood sugar levels, and probiotics in the yogurt boost your immune system. Add the natural sweetness of roasted peppers and you have a true breakfast of champions.

**Ingredients:**

1 medium roasted bell pepper

1 tablespoon lemon or orange juice

1 teaspoon extra-virgin olive oil

1 cup fresh spinach

1 clove garlic, minced

2 omega-3 eggs

1 dash vinegar

2 tablespoons Greek yogurt

2 slices sprouted whole grain bread, toasted

**Instructions:**

Puree the roasted pepper in a blender with the citrus juice. Leave some chunks if you like or blend until smooth.

In a sauté pan, heat the olive oil and sauté the spinach for 2–3 minutes, stirring constantly. Add the garlic and cook for one minute more.

In another large sauté pan heat 2–3 inches of water. Just before it starts to boil, lower the heat and add a splash of vinegar (1 teaspoon per pint of water) to help the eggs hold their shape while poaching. Use ring molds if you have them or just gently break the eggs and drop them in the water. Cook for 3–5 minutes or until yolk is as hard as you like.

Stir the yogurt into the spinach, and put half the spinach on each slice of toast. Scoop the eggs out with a slotted spoon, slide them on top of the spinach, and top with the pepper sauce.

**Tips:**

Try this with sautéed mushroom or caramelized onions instead of spinach. You can also try yellow or orange pepper in the sauce.

**Nutrition Facts:**

| | |
|---|---|
| **Serving Size** 124g | **Sodium** 166mg |
| **Calories** 259 | **Carbs** 21g |
| **Total Fat** 14g | **Saturated Fat** 3g |
| **Cholesterol** 188mg | **Sugars** 3g |
| **Fiber** 4g | **Protein** 8g |

## BLT Breakfast Wrap with Avocado Spread

This is a quick on-the-go breakfast that will make you feel like you sat down to a full meal. Classic BLT flavors combine with creamy avocado, to give you an all-day energy boost in the palm of your hand. And, it is protein-rich for steady energy throughout your morning.

**Serves:** 2

**Total Time:** 15 minutes

**Ingredients:**

4 slices low-sodium, all-natural turkey bacon

2 teaspoons extra-virgin olive oil

2 omega-3 eggs, beaten

½ large tomato, diced

1 cup fresh spinach leaves

1 small avocado, pit and skin removed

2 Ezekiel sprouted whole grain tortillas

**Instructions:**

In a small bowl, mash the avocado and stir until creamy and smooth. In a medium sauté pan, cook the bacon until crispy. Drain the fat and rinse the pan. In the same pan, heat the olive oil and scramble the eggs to desired doneness. Heat the tortillas for a minute over a gas flame or in the oven and then spread with the avocado spread. Add the tomato, spinach, bacon, and eggs and wrap together.

**Tips:**

If you like a spicy breakfast, add some jalapenos or hot sauce to your wrap. Sliced black olives are also a nice addition.

**Nutrition Facts:**

| | |
|---|---|
| **Serving Size** 188g | **Sodium** 356mg |
| **Calories** 248 | **Carbohydrates** 15g |
| **Total Fat** 15g | **Fiber** 3g |
| **Saturated Fat** 5g | **Sugars** 3g |
| **Cholesterol** 192mg | **Protein** 11g |

## Cinnamon Rice Pudding with Currants and Nuts

**Serves:** 4

**Total Time:** 45 minutes

For breakfast—or even dessert—you'll love this diabetes-busting pudding. The warm, aromatic tones of cinnamon, creamy milk, and the satisfying crunch of nuts make this brown rice irresistible. The whole grains, cinnamon, butter, and nuts all help put the brakes on glucose. But nothing curbs the comfort, so dig in!

**Ingredients:**

1 cup brown rice

2 cups whole milk

1 cup water

1 tablespoon cinnamon

1 tablespoon butter

¼ cup currants

¼ cup nuts (cashews, almonds, walnuts, pecans), chopped

**Instructions:**

Combine the rice, milk, and water and simmer for 30–35 minutes or until rice is al dente.

Add the cinnamon and cook for 10–15 minutes more or until rice is tender and sauce is thick.

Stir in the butter, currants, and nuts and serve with extra milk on top.

**Nutrition Facts:**

**Serving Size** 105g  **Calories** 293

**Total Fat** 13g  **Saturated Fat** 6g

**Cholesterol** 20mg  **Sodium** 54mg

**Carbs** 37g  **Sugars** 6g

**Fiber** 3g  **Protein** 8g

## Wild Mushroom Frittata with Sage and Blue Cheese

No need for an omelet pan or any fancy flipping skills with this easy delicious frittata. Simply add veggies and protein-packed eggs to a pan and pop it in the oven. You'll have a savory herbal meal with the earthiness of mushroom and the tang of blue cheese. Serve this as breakfast, nibble a slice as a midmorning snack, or have it with a salad for a light lunch or dinner.

**Serves:** 4

**Total Time:** 30 minutes

**Ingredients:**

2 cups mushrooms (shitake, crimini, oyster, Portobello), sliced

1 tablespoon extra-virgin olive oil

1 tablespoon unsalted butter

6 omega-3 eggs, beaten

2 tablespoons whole fat milk

½ small onion, diced

¼ cup gorgonzola, crumbled

2 tablespoons fresh sage, minced

**Instructions:**

Preheat the oven to 375 degrees. Heat the oil in a large sauté pan and cook the mushrooms on medium high heat for 5–7 minutes or until they start to wilt and caramelize. Add the onion and cook for 3 minutes more, stirring often. Add the butter and let melt. In a bowl, stir together the milk, eggs, and sage and add the mixture to the pan. Stir quickly to mix in the mushrooms and onions. When the edges start to set up, sprinkle the cheese over the top and transfer to the oven for 7–10 minutes or until center is set.

**Tips:**

Try this with feta cheese and oregano, instead, for a Greek-flavored frittata, or add cooked turkey sausage for extra protein.

**Nutrition Facts:**

| | |
|---|---|
| **Serving Size** 134g | **Sodium** 217mg |
| **Calories** 197 | **Carbohydrates** 4g |
| **Total Fat** 11g | **Fiber** 5g |
| **Saturated Fat** 7g | **Sugars** 2g |
| **Cholesterol** 287mg | **Protein** 11g |

## Flax Yogurt Bread

**Serves:** 6–8

**Total Time:** 1 hour 15 minutes

I looked at the ingredients of this dense bread and thought it would never work. Boy, was I wrong! This hearty whole grain bread is packed with texture and flavor and digests slowly for balanced blood sugar. The sunflower seeds add texture and the yogurt provides probiotics and moisture. It's easy to make and tastes amazing topped with homemade jams or nut butters for a filling breakfast or snack.

**Ingredients:**

1½ cups whole wheat flour

1 cup spelt flour

1 cup brown rice flour

¼ cup flax seed meal

½ cup rolled oats

½ cup raw sunflower seeds

½ cup walnuts, chopped

1 teaspoon vanilla extract

1 teaspoon sea salt

1 teaspoon baking soda

½ cup whole milk

2–2¼ cups Greek yogurt

### Instructions:

Preheat oven to 350 degrees. Lightly oil sides and bottom of a large loaf pan. In large mixing bowl, mix all ingredients except flours. Add flour one cup at a time. As the last of the flours are added, begin using kneading motions. Shape into a loaf and put into bottom of greased loaf pan.

Bake for one hour. Remove the bread from the oven and move to a rack. Brush the top with butter or oil.

### Tips:

If you have nut allergies, substitute extra sunflower or other types of seeds for the walnuts.

### Nutrition Facts (based on 8 servings):

| | |
|---|---|
| **Serving Size** 81g | **Calories** 201 |
| **Total Fat** 17g | **Saturated Fat** 1g |
| **Cholesterol** 1mg | **Sodium** 149mg |
| **Carbs** 34g | **Sugars** 6g |
| **Fiber** 4g | **Protein** 9g |

## Green Curry Eggplant and Eggs

**Serves:** 10–12

**Total Time:** 25 minutes

This antioxidant and omega-3 super-meal reduces inflammation and insulin resistance as well as being incredibly tasty! Serve it for a unique breakfast, over brown rice for dinner or in a low-carb whole wheat tortilla for a lunch on the go. The spicy green curry is soothed by the creamy coconut eggs, and the vegetables add texture, flavor, and nutrients that will have your diabetes running for the hills.

### Ingredients:

*Eggplant:*

1 tablespoon pure olive oil

1 small eggplant, peeled and diced

1 small onion, diced

2 cloves garlic, minced

1 tablespoon ginger, minced

2 cups spinach, chopped

1 medium tomato, seeded and diced

½ cup low-sodium organic vegetable stock

2–4 tablespoons green curry paste

*Eggs:*

12 omega-3 eggs, beaten

½ cup coconut milk

1 tablespoon unsalted butter

## Instructions:

In a large pan, heat the olive oil on medium heat, Sauté the eggplant and onion for 5–7 minutes or until they start to soften. Add the garlic and ginger and cook for 2–3 minutes more. Add the curry paste and stir to coat the vegetables. Add the stock and bring to a simmer. Add the spinach and tomato and cook until sauce is reduced by half, about 3–4 minutes. Combine the eggs and coconut milk and in a separate pan heat the butter on medium high heat. Scramble the eggs for 3–4 minutes. Serve the eggs with the curry over the top.

## Tips and Notes:

For a different take on this dish try cutting the eggplant into thin slices and rolling the eggs inside, roulade-style. Add an extra cup of stock to the curry sauce and pour over the eggplant rolls in a baking dish. Bake for 20–25 minutes. Replace the eggs with ground lamb or turkey for a meatier dish.

## Nutrition Facts (based on 10 servings):

| | |
|---|---|
| **Serving Size** 124g | **Calories** 112 |
| **Total Fat** 8g | **Saturated Fat** 3g |
| **Cholesterol** 214mg | **Sodium** 99mg |
| **Carbs** 8g | **Sugars** 1g |
| **Fiber** 6g | **Protein** 9g |

## Crockpot Buffalo Carnitas

**Serves:** 12

**Prep Time:** Overnight (unattended)

This diabetes-friendly version of a classic slow-cooked Mexican dish is perfect to put in a crockpot, leave overnight and use the next day. Serve it with a poached egg for breakfast or wrap it in a tortilla for a hearty lunch on the go. Prepare a nice green salad and some black beans and you have an amazing dinner. The possibilities are endless.

**Ingredients:**

3 pound lean buffalo roast, cut into quarters

1–2 fresh poblano peppers, chopped

1–2 jalapeno peppers, chopped

1 large onion, chopped

4–6 cloves garlic, chopped

2 teaspoons ground coriander

½ teaspoon cinnamon

3 teaspoons ground cumin

2 teaspoons oregano

2 tablespoon extra-virgin olive oil

Juice of 2 limes

Juice of 2 oranges

3–4 cups low-sodium organic vegetable broth

2 omega-3 eggs

**Instructions:**

Combine the dried spices and the olive oil into a paste. Coat the meat with it. In a large crockpot combine all the ingredients and cook on low for 8–10 hours. In the morning shred the meat with a fork and poach the eggs. Serve with pico de gallo or salsa verde.

**Tips:**

Experiment with the amount of pepper you use so it's not too spicy for you. This can be frozen in batches and used as needed.

**Nutrition Facts:**

| | |
|---|---|
| **Serving Size** 218g | **Calories** 173 |
| **Total Fat** 6g | **Saturated Fat** 2g |
| **Cholesterol** 66mg | **Sodium** 203mg |
| **Carbs** 5g | **Sugars** 2g |
| **Fiber** 2g | **Protein** 22g |

## Romaine and Mushroom Frittata with Brie

**Serves:** 4–6

**Prep Time:** 20 minutes

A breakfast frittata is a beautiful thing, and this one has just about everything you could want. Romaine adds its fresh flavor and diabetes-fighting chromium while brie adds its creamy decadence and mushrooms offer earthy meaty flavor. All of these are a perfect complement to omega-3 rich eggs. You can also serve it with a simple side salad for a delicious light dinner.

### Ingredients:

2 cups romaine, chopped

½ cup crimini mushrooms, sliced

2 cloves garlic, minced

½ cup brie, rind removed

8 omega-3 eggs, scrambled

½ tablespoon extra-virgin olive oil

### Instructions:

Preheat the oven to 350 degrees. Heat the oil on medium heat in a sauté pan. Add the mushrooms and sauté for 2–3 minutes. Add the romaine and garlic and sauté for 2 minutes more. Pour the eggs over and stir gently. Dot the top with spoonfuls of brie. Bake for 7–10 minutes or until eggs are set.

### Tips:

Add a little bit of turkey sausage to this or extra veggies like peppers, onions or broccoli. You can also try different cheeses such as goat cheese or feta.

**Nutrition Facts** (based on 6 servings):

| | |
|---|---|
| **Serving Size** 106g | **Calories** 128 |
| **Total Fat** 9g | **Saturated Fat** 3g |
| **Cholesterol** 288mg | **Sodium** 133mg |
| **Carbs** 5g | **Sugars** 1g |
| **Fiber** 3g | **Protein** 10g |

# Pumpkin-Walnut Bread

**Serves:** 10–12

**Prep Time:** 45 minutes

I love waking up to this moist, flavorful crunchy breakfast bread, perfect all by itself or with a spread of sugar-free preserves or nut butter. Toast slices in the oven for a few minutes. Olive oil stabilizes blood sugar and nuts add the healthy fats and protein in this easy home-made bread.

## Ingredients:

1 ½ to 1 ¾ cups cooked pumpkin, mashed (15-ounce can organic pumpkin puree)

1 cup garbanzo flour

½ cup almond flour

½ teaspoon baking soda

2 large omega-3 eggs

½ cup pure olive oil

1 tablespoon vanilla extract

1 cup unsweetened applesauce

⅓ cup water

½ cup walnuts, chopped

½ cup pumpkin seeds

## Instructions:

Preheat oven to 375 degrees. Combine the pumpkin, applesauce, vanilla extract, olive oil, eggs and water and mix well. Mix the dry ingredients in a separate bowl and add to the wet ingredients. Gently stir in the walnuts and pumpkin seeds. Pour into a greased 9-inch loaf pan and bake for 35–45 minutes or until a toothpick comes out clean.

## Tips:

Add a bit more water if the mix is too lumpy. Try this bread with sweet potatoes or butter-nut squash instead of pumpkin. Use other nuts or seeds such as almonds, pecans, or sunflower seeds. For even more texture add raisins, currants, or dried blueberries.

**Nutrition Facts** (based on 10 servings):

| | |
|---|---|
| **Serving Size** 102g | **Calories** 201 |
| **Total Fat** 12g | **Saturated Fat** 2g |
| **Cholesterol** 35mg | **Sodium** 44mg |
| **Carbs** 19g | **Fiber** 3g |
| **Sugars** 8g | **Protein** 6g |

# High-Fiber Pear Mango Pecan Breakfast Bars

**Serves:** 16 bars

**Total Time:** 1 hour

Scrumptious, wholesome bars don't cost an arm and a leg and are full of healthful nuts, whole grains, and yogurt. This grab-n-go breakfast is full of the fiber and protein to keep you satisfied all morning.

**Ingredients:**

1¾ cup oat flour

¼ cup honey

½ cup unsweetened dried mango, chopped

¼ cup oat bran

1 teaspoon baking powder

½ teaspoon salt

2 tablespoons unsweetened coconut, shredded

¼ teaspoon baking soda

½ cup pecans, chopped

1 pear, grated

¾ cup Greek yogurt

¼ cup pure olive oil

2 omega-3 eggs

**Instructions:**

Preheat oven to 350 degrees. In a large bowl, mix flour, honey, mango, bran, baking powder, coconut, salt, baking soda, nuts, and pear. Whisk together yogurt, oil, and eggs. Stir into dry ingredients just until combined. Spread in a lightly oiled casserole dish. Bake for 35-40 minutes or until toothpick inserted in center comes out clean. Let cool, then cut into bars.

**Tips:**

Make these the evening before. Bars can be stored in an airtight container for up to three days, or individually wrapped and frozen for up to one month.

**Nutrition Facts:**

| | |
|---|---|
| **Serving Size** 61g | **Calories** 152 |
| **Total Fat** 8g | **Saturated Fat** 2g |
| **Cholesterol** 23mg | **Sodium** 74mg |
| **Carbs** 19g | **Fiber** 3g |
| **Sugars** 7g | **Protein** 4g |

# APPENDIX D

# DIABETES-HEALING LUNCHES

If you think you can do yourself a favor by skipping lunch and eating a bag of chips or pretzels and a soda from the vending machine, think again. You already know how little energy such a nutritionally empty "lunch" is going to provide for your afternoon's work. Snack food and fast food lunches can lead to increased snacking (and more calories) later in the afternoon, as well as a lack of energy and inability to concentrate. Without a substantial meal, your blood sugar levels plunge, only to spike when you eat a high-carb snack in search of energy. It's a deadly cycle.

But what if you could have an inexpensive lunch that filled you up, was low in calories and high in fiber, and actually helped balance your blood sugar and reverse your diabetes? The good news is that you can! But you won't find it at some newly opened restaurant. Instead, it's going to come from the same place all your other diabetes-healing superfoods come from: Your own kitchen.

As lunch is not always easy to plan and fit in to our hectic schedules, we have placed special importance on that meal in this section. Note, however, that all of these diabetes-healing lunches can be enjoyed equally for dinner.

## The Diabetes-Healing "Brown Bag Lunch"

If you are serious about healing your diabetes with every bite of food you eat, then you are going to want to pack a healthful lunch with you to take to work, or to know your options when you go out. You might also want to re-think the entire concept of lunch. Lunch should not be a sandwich and a salty, fatty side dish like chips or fries or a full entrée complete with bread-basket and a sugary drink. Your healing brown bag lunch might be a number of small containers offering a variety of tastes and textures. It might have some fruit, some vegetables, and a one-bowl entrée of rice, vegetables, and a bit of last night's grass-fed steak, grilled salmon, or chicken breast. You might have a jar of mixed nuts, an apple, and some slices of cheese, or a salad with cold chicken and sliced almonds.

Fresh vegetables, prepared raw or lightly steamed, are loaded with phytonutrients like antioxidants, vitamins, and minerals. They also are a centerpiece of the diabetes-healing diet and are easy to take to work. You can even buy carrots and other vegetables already peeled and sliced in small packages for those mornings when prep time is limited. Sliced carrots, sweet bell peppers (red, yellow, and green), and cucumbers are easy to prepare; just rinse, toss in a container, and go. Try a sprinkle of salt on peeled cucumber; add peanut or some kind of nut butter or cottage cheese to your celery sticks for a nutritious treat.

Chopped broccoli and cauliflower are abundant sources of antioxidants and the anti-inflammatory chemical sulforaphane. The night before, rinse and chop the vegetables, steam them, and then add to a container of cooked brown rice. Result: Perfectly steamed vegetables on rice ready for your lunch. Add a pat of butter or a drizzle of olive oil and you are good to go.

You know that wild Alaskan salmon is one of your best sources of omega-3 essential fatty acid, an important anti-inflammatory. But, you might not know that most canned salmon is wild Alaskan salmon, making it a convenient choice for a healthful lunch. Canned and left-over salmon can be made into a number of delicious dishes, including salmon patties or salmon loaf, all of which work perfectly well as lunchtime alternatives.

A small amount of fresh fruit eaten with protein (like cheese, yogurt, or peanut butter) is important for keeping your blood sugar in check, as well, and very easy to bring to work. Keep fresh berries on hand; store them in the refrigerator and fill up a container to take to work. Berries are rich sources of anthocyanins, which are powerful anti-inflammatory agents.

High-quality cheeses that are organic, grass-fed, and hormone-free give you a protein boost and make a great companion to sliced apples. Plain yogurt, with fruit and nuts stirred in, is a healthful treat that also soothes that sweet tooth. A small square of high-coca dark chocolate is all the dessert you need when you have a satisfying meal of diabetes-healing superfoods, even one you have brought to work in a brown bag.

## 10 Diabetes-Healing Lunch Tips

**1. Avoid microwaves and plastic containers.** The most important decision you can make about your lunch away from home is to avoid using any plastic containers, especially in the microwave (and that includes containers labeled "microwave-safe," a term that is unregulated and therefore meaningless). Plastic containers (and beverage bottles) can be made with bisphenol A (BPA); the National Institute of Health reports that BPA may lodge in tissue and affect the prostate, brain, and development of fetuses, infants, and children. Microwaved plastic also can release dioxins, which are known carcinogens, into your food under high heat.

You'll want to have a stash of small glass containers on hand for your lunches, and don't use the plastic lids or plastic wrap in the microwave (a piece of wax paper or a paper napkin on top of the food is sufficient). While microwaving makes brown-bagging more convenient, keeping a toaster-oven in the office lunchroom can go a long way toward reducing your risk while still allowing you to enjoy a hot meal in minutes.

**2. Skip the brown bag.** Instead, purchase a re-useable tote bag in which to carry your lunch to work. This signals your commitment to making your own diabetes-healing meals. Lunch bags today have a wide array of features, including insulated pouches, pockets for different sizes of containers, and matching thermoses. In addition to the kids' lunch box aisle, you can also try an outdoor supply shop for larger, more rugged lunch containers. Or, if you want to recycle, small gift bags are the perfect size for a light lunch.

**3. Assemble your meal at work.** Bring a bowl of rice, a container of veggies and another with cold meat. Take a few minutes in the lunchroom to mix them together and heat, then drizzle with olive oil and a shake of garlic powder, curry powder, or grated parmesan cheese. Giving yourself the extra time to slice tomatoes, add homemade dressing to salad, or sprinkle chopped nuts on your yogurt, can make the difference between feeling rushed and having a real lunch break.

**4. Be prepared.** Planning takes the guesswork and the frantic last-minute frenzy out of your morning routine. Slice or chop vegetables the night before. Put dinner leftovers in containers you can take for lunch. Put all your lunch components in one place in the fridge so you can find them easily in the morning, or pack your whole lunch and leave your lunch bag in the fridge overnight.

**5. Use leftovers.** Before making dinner, assess its lunch potential. If you are making a casserole or large meal for dinner, make an extra serving or two for tomorrow's lunch. Remember that almost anything you've had for dinner—grilled salmon, steamed broccoli, brown rice— can be mixed together for a one-bowl meal the next day. Grate some cheese on top, or sprinkle in some lightly roasted almonds or your favorite fresh herbs, like basil, dill, or cilantro, for a new twist to yesterday's meal.

**6. Soup is super.** Add a small thermos of soup to your brown bag lunch. Eat it before the rest of your meal. Studies show that when you have soup as a first course, it will fill you up and you'll actually eat 20% fewer calories. Beans are a superior diabetes-healing food and make for a hearty soup, along with plenty of vegetables. Soup can be made at night or on the weekend and divided into several containers for easy lunches later in the week. Freeze homemade soup in small containers, as well, so you have a backup supply.

**7. Find some allies.** Dine with coworkers who are committed to eating healthful lunches, too. Not only will you have support for bucking the fast food trend, you'll have someone with whom to share meal ideas. Research shows that lifestyle choices like exercise and weight loss, just like obesity and smoking, are all influenced by the people you interact with the most. You might even make some new friends at the office.

**8. Break your routine.** If you always eat at your desk, go outside to a local park and have a picnic on a bench, or take a brisk walk after you eat. If you have access to a bookstore or museum, hop inside for 15 minutes and nourish yourself with new ideas. You'll face your afternoon refreshed and energized in mind and body. The downside to eating at your desk is that you tend to eat without thinking—thus eating more and gaining weight. You also end up spending more sedentary time, which is bad for your circulation and your metabolism, and leads to a host of medical conditions from arthritis to heart disease. Physical activity is a necessity for healing your diabetes, so taking every chance you can to get out and walk around for a while is one of the most important things you can do for your health.

**9. Get help in the kitchen.** If you have a houseful of family members all getting ready in the morning, put everyone to work, so that making a healthful breakfast and lunch is easy. Your kids can assemble an appropriate lunch with just a few directions to make sure nothing gets missed. Teaching them responsibility early on not only prepares them for a life of healthier eating, it gives parents a big break in the caretaking department.

**10. Make lunch simple.** It's just lunch, after all. A jar of mixed nuts, an apple, and a slice of cheese or some leftover chicken and rice make a satisfying meal that can be thrown together in minutes. Don't stress—it's bad for your heart! Enjoy the many ways that the diabetes-healing superfoods can be mixed and matched to provide a super healthful brown bag lunch.

# Diabetes-Healing Lunch Recipes

## Mini Smoked Salmon Pizza with Capers, Red Onion, and Dill

**Serves:** 10–12

**Total Time:** 1.5 hours

Soft and chewy on the inside and crisp on the outside, this whole-wheat pizza crust is not only delicious, but also a great source of fiber and nutrients that help stabilize blood sugar and control your weight. The smoky and creamy toppings will remind you of a Sunday morning in New York. Sit down and enjoy the paper with this simple brunch, lunch, or light dinner.

**Ingredients:**

*Crust:*

½ cup warm water (110–115°)

½ teaspoon honey

1 tablespoon active dry yeast

1 ½ cups whole wheat flour, plus additional or kneading

½ teaspoon kosher salt

½ tablespoon extra-virgin olive oil

*Topping:*

½ cup nonfat cream cheese

½ cup Greek yogurt

½ cup cottage cheese

Juice of 1 lemon

Zest of 1 lemon

2 cloves garlic, minced

¼ cup capers

½ small red onion, minced

½ cup dill, chopped

12–14 oz smoked wild salmon, thinly sliced

*Garnish:*

10–12 dill sprigs

**Instructions:**

Combine the honey and warm water and whisk. Sprinkle the yeast over the top and let sit for 10 minutes or until foamy.

Stir the olive oil and salt into the yeast mixture and add the flour. Stir until a dough forms. Roll dough onto a floured surface and knead for about 5–7 minutes or until dough becomes smooth. Place in a lightly oiled bowl and cover with a towel. Let stand until doubled in size, about an hour.

While the dough is rising combine the cream cheese, yogurt, cottage cheese, lemon juice, lemon zest, and garlic in a food processor and blend until smooth. Stir in the red onion, capers, and dill. Refrigerate.

Preheat the oven to 475°. When the dough is doubled remove from the bowl and onto a floured surface. Roll the dough into a log about 2¼ inches in diameter and cut into ½–1 inch thick slices. Pat or roll the slices into discs and place slightly apart on a lightly oiled baking sheet. Bake for 5–8 minutes or until brown and crisp.

Spread about 2 tablespoons of the cream cheese onto each crust and top with slices of the smoked salmon. Garnish with dill sprigs.

**Tips:**

This versatile crust can be topped with anything. Try your favorite pizza toppings or be experimental and use them as an open faced sandwich with lean turkey and avocado or tuna or chicken salad. For a pleasing appetizer, top with fresh mozzarella, tomato, and basil and cut into bite-sized squares.

**Nutrition Facts** (based on 12 servings):

| | |
|---|---|
| **Serving Size** 80g | **Calories** 121 |
| **Total Fat** 4g | **Saturated Fat** 0g |
| **Cholesterol** 8mg | **Sodium** 698mg |
| **Carbs** 16g | **Fiber** 5g |
| **Sugars** 2g | **Protein** 11g |

## Turkey Burger Sliders with Sautéed Onions, Sharp Cheddar, and Horseradish

**Serves:** 4

**Total time:** 30 minutes

Forget McDonald's! These diabetes-healing burgers have mega-flavor packed into bite-sized snacks. Whole grains, garlic, onion, and grass-fed turkey help keep blood sugar stable while lively horseradish adds pure pizzazz.

### Ingredients:

1 tablespoon extra-virgin olive oil

1 small onion, sliced

1 pound grass-fed turkey, ground

2 cloves garlic, minced

2 slices sharp cheddar cheese, cut into quarters

¼ cup horseradish, prepared

2 whole grain buns, toasted and cut into quarters

1 medium tomato, seeded and diced

½ cup romaine lettuce, chopped

### Instructions:

Heat the olive oil and sauté the onions for 10–15 minutes or until soft and starting to caramelize.

Mix the ground turkey and garlic and form into 8 patties. Cook on medium heat for 3–5 minutes. Turn, top with the cheese and cook for 3–4 minutes more.

Spread horseradish on the buns, top with the burgers and onions, and serve open-faced.

### Tips:

Add jalapenos and roasted peppers to make these even heartier burgers.

### Nutrition Facts:

| | |
|---|---|
| **Serving Size** 154g | **Calories** 140 |
| **Total Fat** 7g | **Saturated Fat** 2g |
| **Cholesterol** 46mg | **Sodium** 139mg |
| **Carbs** 8g | **Fiber** 4g |
| **Sugars** 1g | **Protein** 13g |

## Chicken and White Bean Cassoulet

**Serves:** 8

**Total time:** 2 hours, 55 minutes

Protein-packed white beans, antioxidant-rich onion and garlic, and blood sugar-stabilizing olive oil combine with succulent chicken in this rich and tasty version of a French classic. We've made this infamous, time-consuming dish not only diabetes-healing but much simpler and quicker to prepare. You don't need Julia Child in the kitchen with you to wow your friends with this amazing one-pot meal.

**Ingredients:**

8 oz chicken breast, boneless

1 tablespoon extra-virgin olive oil (plus more to coat chicken)

8 oz chicken ground, white meat

2 sprigs thyme fresh, minced

1 bay leaf

6 cloves garlic, minced

4 oz all-natural turkey bacon, diced

1 large onion, diced

4 cups low-sodium chicken or bone broth

5 cups canned white beans, drained, and rinsed

**Instructions:**

Preheat the oven to 375°.

Drizzle a little olive oil on the chicken breast and bake for 20–30 minutes or until cooked through. Let cool.

In a medium sauté pan, heat the olive oil and sauté the ground chicken, thyme, bay leaf, and 3 cloves garlic for 5–7 minutes or until chicken is cooked through. Remove mixture from the pan and discard the bay leaf.

Add the bacon, remaining garlic, and onion to the pan and sauté for 5–7 minutes or until bacon is cooked through and onions are soft.

Puree the bacon-onion mixture in a blender with 1 cup of low-sodium chicken stock until smooth.

When the chicken breast is cool, shred with a fork or dice in small pieces.

In a deep casserole dish layer the ingredients. Start with a layer of beans, then chicken breast, then beans, then ground chicken, etc. Spread a spoonful of the onion mixture between each layer and finish with beans on the top.

Pour just enough chicken stock to cover the beans and bake in the oven for 2 ½–3 hours. If it starts to look dry add more chicken stock.

Broil for 7–10 minutes at the end for a nice crisp top.

**Tips:**

Try this dish with lamb or bison instead of chicken. You could even do a seafood version with shrimp, scallops, and salmon. Just dice the shrimp and scallops to replace the ground meat and flake the salmon to form the other "meat" layer.

**Nutrition Facts:**

| | |
|---|---|
| **Serving Size** 174g | **Calories** 351 |
| **Total Fat** 10g | **Saturated Fat** 2.6g |
| **Cholesterol** 50mg | **Sodium** 263mg |
| **Carbs** 39g | **Fiber** 8.3g |
| **Sugars** 1.4g | **Protein** 28g |

### Muffaletta Tuna Salad in Red Cabbage Pockets

A taste of New Orleans without all the regrets. You'll be able to tell everyone about this experience as you help your diabetes and bounce around the office. These crispy, tasty wraps take no time to make in the morning and will stay fresh-tasting and delicious until you gobble them up at lunchtime.

**Serves:** 4

**Total Time:** 15 minutes

**Ingredients:**

2 tablespoons pitted black olives, drained and chopped

2 tablespoons pitted green olives, drained and chopped

½ small red onion, chopped

2 tablespoons red wine vinegar

Juice of 1 lemon

2 tablespoons extra virgin olive oil

2 cloves garlic, minced

1 teaspoon dried oregano

1 teaspoon dried basil

¾ teaspoon black pepper

½ cup artichoke hearts, chopped

1 small tomato, seeded and diced

¼ cup turkey salami, diced

8 oz tuna, canned in water and drained

8 small red cabbage leaves, spine removed

4–6 tablespoons Dijon mustard

**Instructions:**

Combine all ingredients for the salad and mix gently. Spread each cabbage leaf with a spoonful of mustard and fill with about ¼ cup of filling. Roll into an eggroll shape.

**Tips:**

Try this salad with canned salmon or diced chicken instead. You can also use lettuce leaves or whole wheat tortillas instead of the cabbage.

**Nutrition Facts:**

| | |
|---|---|
| **Serving Size** 219g | **Sodium** 421mg |
| **Calories** 216g | **Carbohydrates** 14g |
| **Total Fat** 10g | **Fiber** 4g |
| **Saturated Fat** 2g | **Sugars** 7g |
| **Cholesterol** 27mg | **Protein** 18g |

## Avocado Beet Salad with Grapefruit and Thyme-Infused Olive Oil

**Serves:** 4

**Prep time:** 60 minutes

This beautifully colored composed salad has both a variety of textures and flavors. The creaminess of the avocado contrasts with the earthiness of the beets, brininess of the olives, and sharpness of the crumbled Mexican cheese. What brings it all together is the pungent aromatic infused olive oil. Two tablespoons a day provides wonderful heart protection.

**Ingredients:**

*Salad:*

3 large beets

2 avocados, sliced

3 cups arugula

½ cup Romano cheese, crumbled

½ cup olives, assorted

*Dressing:*

½ cup extra-virgin olive oil

2 sprigs thyme

1 grapefruit peel

Juice of 2 grapefruits

**Instructions:**

Preheat the oven to 400°. Roast the beets in a small casserole dish for 30-40 minutes or until fork tender. Cool.

Make an infused oil by gently heating the olive oil on the stovetop with sprigs of fresh thyme and the peel of one grapefruit. Make sure to heat only to warm not to cook. Let cool.

When the beets are cool, wrap each in a paper towel or clean kitchen towel and rub the skin off. Dice.

Whisk together the grapefruit juice and oil and toss the beets, avocado, and arugula separately in the dressing. Arrange on plates and sprinkle with the olives and cheese.

**Tips:**

You can make infused oils with any combination of flavorings. Try rosemary and lemon peel or chili flakes and basil. Store in an airtight container after it has cooled.

**Nutrition Facts:**

| | |
|---|---|
| **Serving Size** 146g | **Calories** 363 |
| **Total Fat** 32g | **Saturated Fat** 6g |
| **Cholesterol** 7mg | **Sodium** 318mg |
| **Carbs** 16g | **Fiber** 6g |
| **Sugars** 3g | **Protein** 6g |

## Cajun Red Beans with Chicken Sausage and Quinoa

**Serves:** 4

**Total Time:** 40 minutes

The number-one diabetes-healing superfood, beans, and high protein quinoa match up in this recipe to create a vitamin packed perfect substitute for the traditional New Orleans style beans and rice. Quinoa is a gluten-free grain with all eight essential amino acids and beans are the best antioxidant and blood sugar controller there is. Add some all-natural chicken sausage and you can feel like it's Mardi Gras any night of the week. You can make this healthy version of a New Orleans classic into a stew by adding a few extra cups of stock, or use leftovers in a healthy low-carb tortilla wrap the next day for lunch.

**Ingredients**

1 tablespoon extra-virgin olive oil

2 links chicken sausage all natural, cut into ½-inch slices

½ medium onion, diced

3 cloves garlic, minced

1 large carrot, chopped

1 can red beans, drained and rinsed

1 cup low-sodium chicken stock or bone broth

½ cup tomato, jarred, diced

½ teaspoon cayenne powder

1 tablespoon Cajun seasoning no-salt

1 cup quinoa raw

**Instructions:**

Heat the olive oil on medium high heat and sear the sausage for 2-3 minutes on each side or until dark brown and crispy. Remove the sausage and turn the heat down to medium.

Sauté the onions, garlic, and carrot for 5 minutes.

Puree ½ cup of beans, ½ cup of chicken stock and the tomatoes in a blender until smooth. Add the tomato-bean puree, spices, remaining stock, remaining beans, and sausage and cook for 20-25 minutes or until thick.

Rinse the quinoa and drain. In a separate pot, add two cups of water, bring to a boil and reduce heat to simmer for an additional 15–20 minutes or until water is absorbed.

Serve the red beans and sausage over the quinoa.

**Nutrition Facts:**

| | |
|---|---|
| **Serving Size** 201g | **Calories** 482 |
| **Total Fat** 9g | **Saturated Fat** 2g |
| **Cholesterol** 21mg | **Sodium** 315mg |
| **Carbs** 72g | **Fiber** 26g |
| **Sugars** 4g | **Protein** 32g |

## Creamy Yellow Split Pea Soup

**Serves:** 6

**Total time:** 60 minutes

In the fall, make a big batch of this diabetes-healing soup and stock it in the freezer. You'll love the deeply warming nature and hearty flavor of this soup. Split peas are experts at slowing digestion and switching off the glucose spike/crash cycle, leaving you with some solid energy for hours. Enjoy!

**Ingredients:**

1 tablespoon pure grapeseed oil

½ medium white or yellow onion, diced

1 medium carrot, diced

3 cloves garlic, minced

8 cups low-sodium vegetable broth or bone broth

1½ cups yellow split peas

Dash cayenne pepper and sea salt to taste

**Instructions:**

In a stockpot, sauté the onion, carrot, and garlic in the olive oil for 5–7 minutes or until soft.

Add the stock and split peas and bring to a simmer. Cook for 45 minutes or until peas are tender.

Add the cayenne and puree soup in a blender or food processor until smooth.

**Tips:**

Experiment with different spices such as curry powder or cumin. Garnish with fresh cilantro, a spoonful of yogurt or a squirt of hot sauce for some extra kick. Make a big batch of this hearty soup and freeze it in individual servings for a quick lunch.

**Nutrition Facts:**

| | |
|---|---|
| **Serving Size** 119g | **Calories** 247 |
| **Total Fat** 5g | **Saturated Fat** 1g |
| **Cholesterol** 0mg | **Sodium** 111mg |
| **Carbs** 34g | **Fiber** 13g |
| **Sugars** 5g | **Protein** 9g |

## Turkey Chili Mac Casserole

**Serves:** 8–10

**Total Time:** 45 minutes

A kid's favorite that you can enjoy and feel healthy, too! Whole grain pasta is great for weight control and stabilizing blood sugar levels. In this dish, it boosts a favorite comfort food to a whole new healthy level. The beans add protein and blood sugar regulation to make this not only a substantial and tasty meal but a diabetes-fighting superpower.

**Ingredients:**

1 lb lean ground turkey

8 oz whole wheat elbow macaroni

½ cup canned black beans, drained, and rinsed

½ cup canned kidney beans, drained, and rinsed

2 cups canned crushed tomatoes

1 cup canned diced tomatoes

3 cloves garlic

1 small onion, diced

1 small green bell pepper, diced

1 small red bell pepper, diced

1 jalapeno, seeded and diced

1–2 teaspoons cumin

1–2 teaspoons chili powder

¼ teaspoon cayenne

½ cup cheddar cheese

**Instructions:**

Cook the pasta in a large pot of boiling water until al dente. Drain and rinse. In another large pan cook the onion, garlic, peppers and turkey on medium heat or until turkey is cooked through. Add the spices and tomatoes and cook for 15 minutes.

Preheat the oven to 375°. Add the pasta to the sauce and stir. Pour into a casserole dish and top with the cheese. Bake for 10–15 minutes or until sauce is bubbly and cheese is melted.

**Nutrition Facts:**

**Serving Size** 201g　　**Calories** 248

**Total Fat** 8g　　**Saturated Fat** 3g

**Cholesterol** 45mg     **Sodium** 315mg

**Carbs** 29g          **Fiber** 8g

**Sugars** 2g          **Protein** 0g

## Romaine Salad with Curried Nuts and Sweet Potato

**Serves:** 4

**Total time:** 40 minutes

Romaine is a powerhouse of diabetes-healing nutrients, including chromium for insulin sensitivity, vitamins to fight free radical damage, and folates for your heart. The sweet potato satisfies your sweet tooth and the curried nuts add yet another superfood to your lunch or dinner salad. Add extra veggies such as carrot, bell pepper, or cucumber for a bundle of extra diabetes-friendly foods.

**Ingredients:**

1 large sweet potato, peeled and diced

½ cup almonds

1 tablespoon extra-virgin olive oil

1 tablespoon yellow madras curry powder

½ teaspoon onion powder

½ teaspoon garlic powder

2 tablespoons fresh ginger root, minced

2 cloves garlic, minced

¼ cup Greek yogurt

1 tablespoon coconut milk

2 tablespoons grapefruit juice

1 head romaine lettuce, cleaned and torn

3 green onions, chopped

**Instructions:**

Preheat the oven to 350º.

Spritz sweet potatoes with coconut oil spray and bake for 25–35 minutes or until fork tender.

Toss the nuts with the olive oil and bake for 5–7 minutes. Mix the curry powder, onion powder, and garlic powder in a bowl and toss with the hot nuts.

Combine the ginger, garlic, yogurt, coconut milk, and grapefruit juice and mix well.

To serve, place the romaine on the plate and top with the sweet potatoes, nuts, green onions, and dressing.

**Nutrition Facts:**

| | |
|---|---|
| **Serving Size** 142g | **Calories** 195 |
| **Total Fat** 11g | **Saturated Fat** 2g |
| **Cholesterol** 4mg | **Sodium** 47mg |
| **Carbs** 20g | **Fiber** 6g |
| **Sugars** 5g | **Protein** 7g |

## Eggplant Mushroom Melt with Marinara and Mozzarella

**Serves:** 4

**Total Time:** 45 minutes

This may not be the neatest sandwich to eat at your desk, but the flavor combinations will let you fly away to Italy for at least a half an hour. Bring a knife and fork and gobble into this succulent diabetes-friendly lunch that will have you licking your fingers and slurping up every drop of sauce.

**Ingredients:**

*Marinara:*

2 cups canned crushed tomatoes

3 cloves garlic, minced

1 teaspoon red chili flakes

¼ cup fresh basil, chopped

*Sandwich:*

1 tablespoon extra-virgin olive oil

1 small eggplant, peeled and diced

2 cups button mushrooms, sliced

½ small onion, chopped

¾ cup low-fat mozzarella, shredded

1 cup spinach

4 whole grain thin sandwich rolls

## Instructions:

In a small saucepan, combine the tomato, garlic and red chili flakes. Bring to a simmer and cook for 15–20 minutes or until slightly thickened. Stir in the basil.

In a sauté pan, heat the olive oil on medium heat and sauté the eggplant and mushrooms for 7–10 minutes or until soft. Add the onion and cook 3–5 minutes more. Add the marinara to the vegetables and stir to combine. Using a slotted spoon, ladle the vegetable mixture onto a toasted bun, draining off most of the sauce. Top with the mozzarella and broil for 3–4 minutes or until cheese is melted. Top with the spinach and the other half of the bun. Serve the remaining marinara on the side to dip.

## Tips:

This is a great dish to make the night before. Serve it over pasta or quinoa and then just pack it on a bun the next day. You can also just make a big batch of the super simple marinara and freeze it in individual portions. This way you can bring it for your lunch with any kind of sandwich or make it into an easy dinner or weekend lunch.

### Nutrition Facts

| | |
|---|---|
| **Serving Size** 317g | **Sodium** 4mg |
| **Calories** 222 | **Carbohydrates** 34g |
| **Total Fat** 5g | **Fiber** 9g |
| **Saturated Fat** 1g | **Sugars** 7g |
| **Cholesterol** 4mg | **Protein** 15g |

# INDEX

# AUTHORS' ACKNOWLEDGMENTS

## From Dr. Canfield:

- To my wife, Kate Canfield, MD, I love you and so appreciate all your support and encouragement over the last 20 years;
- To my children, Grace and Ian, thanks for putting up with all the interesting whole foods that end up in the grocery shopping cart;
- To my parents, Mary and Ernie, for encouraging me to follow my dreams even when my ideas were a bit different from the status quo;
- To my sisters, Tammy and Sarah, for enduring my brotherly teasing when we were growing up and still cheering me on;
- To Jim Healthy, thanks for your patience and kindness in our working together;
- To my departed Nana, Jeanne Chatigny, for your inspiration over the years and teaching me to be a creative problem-solver in this life;
- To my mentors with the American Holistic Medical Association, Institute for Functional Medicine and American Academy of Ozonotherapy for giving me permission to think differently and for the proven tools to offer truly healing therapies to our patients;
- To my patients at 360 Medicine in Santa Fe for allowing me the opportunity to practice medicine in a way that just feels right and has been so healing to me personally;
- To the native people I served for a time at the Acoma Laguna Canoncito PHS Hospital, I appreciate the gift that native peoples bring to the planet and thank you for trusting me and inviting me into your homes;
- To my high-performance team at 360 Medicine, for your dedication, service and expertise every day. I bow to you.

## From Jim Healthy:

- To my wife and best friend Martina, who inspires me daily to "keep getting better";
- To Steven Horak, for his excellent editing, management, and devotion to this project;
- To Daisy Brumby, for her incomparable professionalism, research, and editorial skills;
- To Kyky Knowles, for "taking care of business"; and for her tireless commitment to our mission of helping people achieve "awesome health and an awesome life!;"
- To Carlos Mendivil and Miguel Yi-Sandino for layout and cover design; and to Suzanne Herzstam for her eagle-eye proofreading;
- To Marjory Abrams, Michael Feldstein, Carmen Suarez, Adrienne Makowski, Rita Shankewitz, John Niccolls, Maureen Naccari, and the entire staff at Bottom Line Books: thanks for believing in and supporting this project;
- To Pat Corpora, with great appreciation for your invaluable help and guidance;
- To Anthony Lupo, for your astute legal counsel and amazing friendship;
- To Doug N. and the many other indefatigable Diabetes Rebels who have become "ex-diabetics"—and who now are inspiring their family, friends, and coworkers to do the same;

- To the dedicated, tireless, and courageous alternative-minded doctors, researchers, journalists, and entrepreneurs who are educating and encouraging people with Type 2 diabetes and other "lifestyle diseases" to take back their health, independence, and personal freedom from today's dysfunctional profit-crazy healthcare system; and
- To people with Type 2 diabetes and prediabetes all around the world: May this book inspire and motivate you to say "no more" to the habits that still your strength—and "hell, yes" to the people who love you and desire many more years in your presence!

# ABOUT THE AUTHORS

**Russ Canfield, MD**, is board-certified by the American Board of Family Medicine (1999-present). He has extensive experience in treating type 2 diabetes and has instituted diabetes prevention and treatment programs with the US Public Health Service. He has been trained as a Certified Diabetes Educator and is committed to patient education.

Dr. Canfield has been an assistant clinical professor at the University of New Mexico School of Medicine, teaching medical students and residents a holistic approach to primary care. Dr. Canfield is currently in private practice in Santa Fe, New Mexico. He directs the multidisciplinary 360 Medicine Health Center that specializes in care of the whole person which offers a number of healing modalities including medical consultations, IV nutrient therapies, detoxification programs and functional medicine lifestyle coaching.

**Jim Healthy**™ is a health coach and activist, medical reporter, publisher, and author. He is the author or coauthor of *The Healthy Body Book*, *Arthritis Interrupted*, *The 30-Day Diabetes Cure*, *The Diabetes Healing Cookbook*, and *Healing Heart Disease with Chelation Therapy*.